Unbundled Government

Public sector bureaucracies have been subjected to harsh criticism. One solution which has been widely adopted over the past two decades has been to 'unbundle government' – that is to break down monolithic departments and Ministries into smaller, semi-autonomous, 'agencies'. These are often governed by some type of performance contract, are at 'arm's length' or further from their 'parent' Ministry or Department and are freed from many of the normal rules governing civil service bodies.

This is the first book to survey the 'why' and the 'how' of this epidemic of 'agencification', with case studies from every continent. From Japan to America and from Sweden to Tanzania, these 14 case studies (some covering more than one country) critically examine how such agencies have been set up and managed. The introductory chapter distils the main elements of the agencification movement. An international panel of contributors then move on to explore how this relates to other similar, structural changes to government; agencies, quangos and contracts; autonomization in continental Europe and Japan and autonomization in developing and transitional countries. The concluding section locates this change to agencification in a theoretical context, looking at how it has been explained by both policy-makers and academics.

Unbundled Government will be essential reading for advanced students and researchers of public management.

Christopher Pollitt is currently Professor of Public Management at Erasmus University, Rotterdam. He has worked as a UK civil servant, as an academic and consultant. He has been President of the European Evaluation Society and has advised many public organisations and the European Commission.

Colin Talbot is currently Professor of Public Policy at the University of Nottingham. He has worked in the public sector, as an academic and consultant and founded the consulting group 'Public Futures'. He has been a Special Advisor to the UK Public Administration Select Committee and advised many public organisations, in the UK and internationally.

Routledge Studies in Public Management

Unbundled Government

A critical analysis of the global trend to agencies, quangos and contractualisation

Edited by Christopher Pollitt and Colin Talbot

Routledge
Taylor & Francis Group

LONDON AND NEW YORK

First published 2004
by Routledge
11 New Fetter Lane, London EC4P 4EE

Simultaneously published in the USA and Canada
by Routledge
29 West 35th Street, New York, NY 10001

Routledge is an imprint of the Taylor & Francis Group

Typeset in Baskerville by Wearset Ltd, Boldon, Tyne and Wear
Printed and bound in Great Britain by MPG Books Ltd, Bodmin

British Library Cataloguing in Publication Data
A catalogue record for this book is available from the British Library

Library of Congress Cataloging in Publication Data
A catalog record for this book has been requested

ISBN 0-415-31448-8

Contents

Figures

Tables

Contributors

Dr Bidhya Bowornwathana is an Associate Professor at the Public Administration Department, Chulalongkorn University, Bangkok, Thailand. He has published widely on administrative reform and governance with particular reference to Thailand. He is an editorial board member of *Public Administration and Development* and *Asian Journal of Public Administration*. He was chairman of the public administration department of Chulalongkorn University twice. He also served as the secretary and member of administrative reform commissions for various Thai governments.

Professor Geert Bouckaert is Professor of Public Management and Director of the Public Management Institute at the Katholieke Universiteit Leuven in Leuven, Belgium. His main research interests are in performance management, public sector productivity measurement, and financial management techniques in the public sector. He is a member of several editorial boards. His latest publication is an Oxford University Press book on Public Management Reforms (with Professor Christopher Pollitt).

Dr Janice Caulfield is Research Assistant Professor in the Department of Politics and Public Administration, University of Hong Kong, where she teaches public sector management and public policy analysis. Her current research interests include performance and accountability in the public sector, public sector reform and development administration. She is co-editor with Helge O. Larsen of *Local Government at the Millennium* published in 2002 by Leske and Budrich.

Dr Francesca Gains is the Research Co-ordinator for a five-year evaluation of new council constitutions in English local government for the Office of the Deputy Prime Minister. She formerly taught public policy in the Department of Government at the University of Manchester and has previous management experience in local government and the probation service. She has worked on a number of government-sponsored research projects and her most recent research was into the introduction of new political management arrangements in UK civil service through the establishment of executive agencies.

Andrew Graham is an Adjunct Professor in the School of Policy Studies, Queens University Kingston, Ontario, Canada. He teaches public management and public finance. He has recently retired from the federal public service, serving in a variety of operational, planning, policy advisory and corporate management roles. His last posting was as Assistant Deputy Minister, Corporate Service, Agriculture Canada. Mr Graham is also a research associate at the Conference Board of Canada involved in a variety of research projects for governments in Canada. Mr Graham has extensive experience in many aspects of government, including policy, field operations and corporate management. He is past President of APEX, the Canadian federal government's executive association.

Dr Oliver James, Senior Lecturer in Politics, University of Exeter, UK is a researcher of public organization and regulation, and co-ordinator of MA in Public Administration and Public Policy. Publications include: *The Executive Agency Revolution in Whitehall* Basingstoke (Palgrave/ Macmillan, 2003) (on which the chapter included in this collection draws); *Regulation Inside Government* (Oxford University Press, 1999) (with C.C. Hood and others); 'Business models and the transfer of business-like central government agencies' (2001) *Governance* 14, 2, 233–52; 'Regulation inside government: public interest justifications and regulatory failures' (2000) *Public Administration* 78, 2, 327–43. Webpage: http:/www.ex.ac.uk/shipss/politics/staff/james/index.htm.

Dr Jocelyn M. Johnston is Associate Professor of Public Administration at the University of Kansas, where she teaches state and local public finance, intergovernmental relations and research methods. She currently serves as chair of the national Association for Budgeting and Financial Management. Her research on intergovernmental policy has been published in several journals, and her current research focuses on state contracts for social services. She is co-recipient of the Kaufman Award for the best paper in Public Administration presented at the 2001 American Political Science Association national conference, with Barbara S. Romzek. Johnston has conducted applied research for governmental clients, and serves as a field research associate for the Rockefeller Institute's State Capacity Study. She received her PhD in public administration from the Maxwell School of Citizenship and Public Affairs at Syracuse University in 1994.

Linda McGuire is a lecture in the Department of Management at Monash University, Australia. She is the author of *Australian Services Marketing and Management* published by Macmillan in 1999. This chapter draws on her doctoral research into quality standards and indicators for professional public services. She once held a position as a research economist in the agency which is now responsible for the performance reporting examined in this study. A related study, Benchmarking Community Services: 'nailing Jell-O to a tree', has been published in *The Journal of Contemporary Issues in Business and Government* 9, 2, 63–74.

Professor Guy B. Peters is Maurice Falk Professor of American Government at the University of Pittsburgh, and Honorary Professor at the City University of Hong Kong. Among his recent publications are *Rewards for High Public Office in Asia*, *The Future of Governing* (2nd edition), and *The Handbook of Public Administration* (co-edited with Jon Pierre).

Professor Jon Pierre is a Professor of Political Science at the University of Gothenburg, Sweden and an adjunct professor at the University of Pittsburgh. He has published extensively on administrative reform, public administration, and governance. His latest publications include (co-edited with Guy Peters), *Handbook of Public Administration* (Sage, 2003), (ed.), *Debating Governance* (Oxford University Press, 2000), and (with Guy Peters), *Governance, Politics and the State* (Palgrave, 2000).

Professor Christopher Pollitt is Professor of Public Management at Erasmus University Rotterdam. Previously (1990–8), he was a Professor of Government at Brunel University, West London. Among his many publications the best-known are probably *The Essential Public Manager* (2003), *Public Management Reform: A Comparative Analysis* (with Geert Bouckaert, 2000) and *Managerialism and the Public Services* (2nd edition, 1993). Pollitt has also worked as a consultant and advisor to many governmental organizations, including the European Commission, the OECD, the World Bank and the UK government. He is a past editor of the journal *Public Administration* and past President of the European Evaluation Society.

Dr Alasdair Roberts is an associate professor in the Maxwell School of Citizenship and Public Affairs at Syracuse University and also Director of the Campbell Public Affairs Institute at Syracuse University. He received a JD from the University of Toronto Faculty of Law in 1984, a Master's degree in Public Policy from the Kennedy School of Government at Harvard University in 1986, and a PhD in Public Policy from Harvard University in 1994. He was a fellow at the Woodrow Wilson International Center for Scholars in Washington, DC in 1999–2000 and an Individual Program Fellow of the Open Society Institute in 2000–1. He received the Dimock Award for best lead article in Public Administration Review in 1995, and the Hodgetts Award for best English article in Canadian Public Administration in 2000.

Professor Barbara S. Romzek is Associate Dean for Social Sciences and Professor of Public Administration at the University of Kansas. Romzek's teaching and research focus on public management, emphasizing accountability, privatization and government reform. She has consulted on these topics with federal, state and local governments as well as national and international professional management associations. Romzek is a Fellow of the National Academy of Public Administration and is listed in *Who's Who of America* and *Who's Who of American Women*. She is a co-recipient of the Mosher Award from the American Society for Public Administration and the Kaufman Award from the American Political Science Association.

Amanda Smullen is a researcher in the Department of Public Administration, Erasmus University, the Netherlands. She is currently writing her Doctoral Dissertation about the rhetoric of agency reform. This is an international comparative research of agency reforms in Sweden, the Netherlands and Australia. Her academic interests include public management, discourse analysis and new institutionalism.

Professor Colin Talbot is Professor of Public Policy at the University of Nottingham and head of the Nottingham Policy Centre. He holds an MSc (Southbank) and a PhD (LSE). He has written widely on public management reform policies, especially agencies and performance. He has acted as advisor to the UK government, the National Audit Office, Parliamentary committees, and numerous public bodies, as well as several other governments. He has been an invited speaker at conferences in over two dozen countries. He is a member of the Editorial Boards of *Public Administration Review, Public Money and Management* and *International Journal of Public Sector Management.*

Dr Robert R. Taliercio Jr is a public finance economist in the World Bank's East Asia Poverty Reduction and Economic Management unit. His interests are primarily in the area of fiscal and public sector reform, and he has worked extensively in Latin America and Asia. Prior to joining the World Bank in 2000, he was a lecturer in the public finance group at the Harvard Institute for International Development (HIID). He holds a PhD in public policy from Harvard University, as well as degrees from Princeton and Stanford.

Dr Sandra van Thiel is assistant professor of Public Administration at Erasmus University Rotterdam, the Netherlands. Her main research activities deal with the increase in the number of quasi-autonomous bodies in many western states. Also, she is interested in the performance of public sector organizations. She has published both internationally (*Governance, Public Performance and Management Review*) and in the Netherlands. In 2000 she obtained her doctorate for her dissertation on *"Quangos: Trends, Causes and Consequences"* (published in 2001).

Sandra van Thiel is one of the founders of the international research network on quasi-autonomous government (www.shef.ac.uk/quangos).

Professor Kiyoshi Yamamoto is Professor of Financial Management at the Center for National University Finance in Japan. Dr Yamamoto served as Director in the Board of Audit before moving into academica. His main research includes public sector management and accounting, especially performance management in the public sector. He has published numerous articles and books on government accounting and auditing, performance evaluation, and governance. Now as an advisor, he has worked for the Japanese Ministry of Finance, Ministry of Public Management and other government organisations including local governments.

Part I

Setting the scene

1 The Agency idea

Sometimes old, sometimes new, sometimes borrowed, sometimes untrue

Colin Talbot

It is indisputable that the idea of creating 'agencies' has become something of a fashionable initiative in the realms of public management, and especially central government, reform. If there were any doubt about this, the chapters assembled in this volume attest to the fact that agency-creation or modification initiatives – many allegedly drawing at least partial inspiration from the UK 'Next Steps' programme – have proliferated on virtually every continent and in many different kinds of states.

This book is not 'for' or 'against' agencies – it seeks merely to try understanding them and to draw together, as far as possible, evidence about their successes and perils. Interestingly, the agency movement has taken place with few of the 'how to do it' recipe books which usually accompany management – public or private – reforms. To be sure, agencies are mentioned as a 'good thing' in various popular prescriptive public management reform texts (e.g. Osborne and Plastrik 1991). One of the current authors has even been responsible for a (somewhat more cautious and sceptical) 'handbook' on agencies for policy-makers and practitioners (Talbot 2002). But the latter was written (and commissioned) specifically because many policy-makers and practitioners were implementing 'agency-type' programmes (in this case via international aid programmes to developing countries) without any systematic guidance about what agencies were, are, or could be or about their strengths and weaknesses.

The World Bank has been especially active in promoting individual and programmatic agency creation initiatives, but when the authors asked the self styled 'knowledge bank' (Stiglitz 2000) for a list of such initiatives or any policy guidance on them, nothing was forthcoming because nothing existed. Into this vacuum have often stepped the big consultancies and we have come across numerous oversimplifications, misconceptions, half-truths and sometimes even downright fabrications about various 'agency' experiences (especially the UK's) in the many countries we have visited. This book is intended, in part, to address this lack of coordinated knowledge about 'agencies'.

In some cases, the idea of arms-length, 'executive-type', agencies is very old. Sweden and the federal government of the United States of America have long had these sorts of organisations. Even in 'Whitehall-style' states with traditional large-scale Ministries there have been quangos (in the developed world) and 'parastatals' (in the developing). Some types of functions have more often than others been organised along 'agency' lines – most frequently law enforcement bodies (usually to keep politicians out of operational policing matters) and taxation organisations (to keep politicians' hands out of the tills). The Central Intelligence Agency (CIA) is after all sometimes known colloquially as simply 'The Agency'. One of the most famous US books on bureaucracy is subtitled *'What Government Agencies Do and Why They Do It'* (Wilson 1989).

But even where 'agencies' is an old concept, new approaches have been developed – the 'performance-based organisations' at the federal level (see Graham and Roberts, Chapter 7, this volume) and 'charter agencies' at state level in the USA (Behn 2001) start from existing organisational 'independence' but go on to add new, genuinely novel, aspects to the mix. In other cases – including countries as diverse as the UK, Hong Kong, Latvia and New Zealand – have seen much more radical and all-encompassing changes.

So what exactly is the 'idea of agency', which appears, superficially at least, to have gripped so many governments around the world? How has it become so fashionable and why has the idea spread so widely? Is it, in fact, the same idea, or are there several versions all masquerading as 'agencification'? Or, are we converging only in the rhetoric, describing the changes, or in reality, or in both?

To a considerable extent the answers to these questions lie in the chapters assembled for this book. Authors have written from, or about, agency initiatives on every continent – from the North and South of the Americas, from Africa, Europe and Asia. These are not uniform case studies, but living and lively accounts and analyses of a wide variety – in location, content and style – of 'agency-type' initiatives and closely linked reforms. Some have come from practitioners closely engaged in the reform process but most from more detached observers of the agency movement. Some have touched on issues of theory and others have given more descriptive analyses. We make no apology for this – the book is an attempt to capture a very animated wave of reforms and like all 'waves' it is a messy, tumultuous, process prone to undertows and eddies as well as forward leaps. In this introductory essay and the final reflective and more theoretical chapter, we seek to put some greater form onto the various ebbs and flows recorded in the individual contributions.

Given the fluidity and fuzziness about what constitutes an agency initiative or an agency, we still have to attempt some definitional boundaries to our subject. We have therefore defined agency, in part, by exclusion. We exclude, for example, state-owned enterprises whose primary existence is within the market (albeit with subsidies) rather than in public services, and which are usually joint stock companies founded in private law.

Thus, we would not include state-owned companies such as the Finnish Post Office or Dutch railways or the French electricity companies. This also of course excludes privatised entities (e.g. electricity in the UK, the national airline in New Zealand, telecommunications in many countries).

Similarly, we exclude social, charitable and voluntary organisations even where their primary funding comes from the state. Some of these are referred to as agencies in, for example, the Netherlands or Sweden. But they are not staffed by public servants (under whatever conditions of service), do not appear on state budgets, are not directly accountable to executive politicians and are not usually founded in public law.

For the sake of sanity, we have mostly excluded sub-national agencies, simply because if we started looking at these types of bodies at state (in federal systems) or local government levels, the issue would become too complex to manage. This still leaves us with a lot of territory to explore and, as we shall see in the chapters that follow, it is certainly not true that there is only one species, or even breed, of 'agency' inhabiting this particular ecological niche.

Our criteria for examining this phenomenon specify that, to be an 'agency', an organisation should be:

- at arm's length (or further) from the main hierarchical 'spine' of central ministries/departments of state
- carrying out public tasks (service provision, regulation, adjudication, certification) at a national level
- staffed by public servants (not necessarily 'civil servants')
- financed (in principle) by the state budget (in practice some are financed up to 100 per cent from their own revenues, but even here the state remains liable for their financial condition)
- subject to at least some public/administrative law procedures (i.e. they are not predominantly or entirely private law bodies).

One further distinction that seems to recur within the agency 'family' is that between quasi-autonomous agencies within departments or the civil service (e.g. Next Steps agencies in the UK; many federal agencies in the USA) and those outside departments or the civil service (e.g. Independent Administrative Institutions (IAIs) in Japan; Non-Departmental Public Bodies (NDPBs) in the UK; Zelf-standige besturrsorganen (ZBOs) in the Netherlands). Often the second group are called 'quangos' rather than 'agencies' (van Thiel 2000).

Strictly speaking neither of these types of organisations are 'quangos'– i.e. quasi-autonomous non-governmental organisations – because they are very much 'governmental', just not 'departmental' or civil service staffed, bodies.

Nevertheless, the term 'quangos' has come to be applied to most of the second type (and even some of the first). For example the UK government's website for non-departmental public bodies is now called the 'The Quangos Site' (www.cabinet-office.gov.uk/quango). This is more than somewhat ironic as the title 'NDPB' was adopted precisely to emphasise that these were not 'non-governmental' bodies, just non-departmental (Pliatsky 1992).

The importance of this distinction can be exaggerated – as publicly funded, staffed and tasked organisations, largely directed by Ministerial decisions and accountable in similar ways, they are in practice very similar. The main differences are to do with the formal status of the bodies and their staff and have little effect outside of the organisations. The strong similarities between 'agencies' and most executive 'quangos' are sufficient for us to group them together into a single analytical category.

Three central elements to the idea of 'agency'

In our own research and thinking about the 'agency' movement we originally thought that it was possible to pin-point two central concepts which encapsulated the 'idea of agency' (Talbot *et al.* 2000). After much reflection and discussion we have come to the conclusion there are actually three central elements which make up the core of the 'agency' programme – two of which are often explicit (but not always) and one which is mostly implicit (but again, not always).

These three ideas are:

- Structural disaggregation and/or the creation of 'task specific' organisations.
- Performance 'contracting' – some form of performance target setting, monitoring and reporting.
- Deregulation (or more properly reregulation) of controls over personnel, finance and other management matters.

These three elements – structure, performance, reregulation – will be explored in more detail in a moment, but first a word about their interrelationship (or lack of it). We have singled out these three ideas because taken together they capture the essence of the 'agency' idea as it has circled the globe, but they do not always appear in the same intensity, or even at all, in all 'agency-type' initiatives in specific countries.

Sometimes this is due to 'path-dependency' – for example, it is not possible to structurally disaggregate something which is already organised along disaggregated agency structural lines, so any reforms will be limited to addressing the 'performance' and 'reregulation' components (e.g. with US PBO's – see Graham and Roberts, Chapter 7, this volume).

Nor do all initiatives necessarily embrace the whole agency package anyway – some have focussed on structure and/or reregulation but largely ignored performance, for instance (e.g. see the chapters on the Netherlands and Latvia in Chapters 8, 9 and 15 of this volume). Conversely, many countries adopted the idea of 'Management by Objectives' (Odiorne 1965) during the 1970s. It constituted a form of 'performance contracts' – agreeing objectives with individual managers and reviewing their achievements against these – and it was usually implemented without either structural or regulatory changes.

It is thus perfectly possible to have any of the three reforms – structural separation, performance contracting or reregulation of public services – independently of one another or in any combination. It is where these come together that the full force of the 'agency' concept becomes most apparent.

These are not the only ideas associated with the concept of agencies. Numerous other elements of public sector reform – efficiency, customer orientation, service standards, transparency and accountability, innovative management, revenue generation, resource (accruals) accounting, etc. – have been more or less associated with agency initiatives. Sometimes these have been present from the start, whilst sometimes they have appeared as 'add-ons' as the initiatives evolve.

These core notions appear relatively simple and are easily communicated – which has probably helped their acceptability and spread. As we 'unbundle' each of the three core notions we will find, however, that what appear initially as very simple ideas turn out to be far more complex in reality. Paradoxically this probably also helps to account for their transferability – their actual complexity makes them very adaptable to different circumstances and tastes.

Health warning – possible limits to explanation

Some years ago an intriguing idea emerged from social psychology, which may have much wider application in social sciences. This was that in attempting theoretical explanation or model construction it was possible to have simplicity, generalisability and accuracy, but not all three at once (Thorngate 1976). It is possible that the analysis that follows in this chapter has striven for 'simplicity' (only three core notions) and 'generalisability' (being at least partially applicable to all cases) at the expense of 'accuracy' for individual, concrete cases. Readers must judge for themselves. For those who prefer a more complex approach, the final chapter provides multiple theoretical perspectives to feast on.

Structure

By structural disaggregation we mean simply the splitting up of larger bodies into a 'parent' body and various subordinate 'agencies'. This has mostly been applied to splitting up 'Ministries' into a core central body and several agencies carrying out specific tasks.

Many of the countries that have pioneered the 'agency' movement – including especially the UK – have Whitehall or Whitehall-like systems of central government organisation, obviously from their colonial inheritance – e.g. Australia, Canada, Hong Kong, Jamaica, New Zealand and Tanzania. Some scholars have suggested that the 'Next Steps' agency programme in the UK constituted a key element in the end of the Whitehall model (Campbell and Wilson 1995). But it was not just 'Whitehall-style' central government institutions which succumbed to the (supposed) ills of 'Big Government' (Rose 1984) in the past 50 years. As the other countries represented in this volume attest, many other types of states have government organisations that have been deemed worthy of 'unbundling'.

In this general account the principle 'unbundling' into agencies has been focussed on Whitehall-style central Ministries: large, multi-functional, politically headed but professionally staffed, rule-bound, combined policy-making and implementation organisations. These bodies are commonly said to have expanded in size and functions in the post-World War II growth of the welfare state until they became dysfunctional. Structural disaggregation into their constituent parts, along the lines of a policy-execution or purchaser-provider split, is seen as the solution to 'diseconomies of scale'. It may also overcome some of the lack of transparency which affects multi-functional organisations, where it is difficult to discern what funding and actions contribute to which functions.

The elements of structural change have generally been:

- Creating an identifiable, separate, organisational structure with its own name.
- Usually the body is given a single, or small set, of functions.
- Usually these functions are primarily about 'delivery', 'execution' or 'provision' and not about policy-making.
- Giving the above body a clear 'constitution' – in the form of some sort of legislation, or at least a formal (if not statutory) 'framework document' – which sets out its purpose, powers and governance arrangements.
- Making a single, named individual – usually called a Chief Executive (CE) – responsible for managing and reporting on the new body. This person is usually appointed – actually or potentially – through an open process, separate from the normal civil service recruitment.
- Making the staff of the new body different in some way from mainstream civil servants, usually by changing their formal employment status.
- Putting in place formal reporting arrangements, including separate accounts, for the new body.

These are in essence management changes – creating a separately managed, quasi-independent, body. They need to be distinguished from issues of autonomy, or as we prefer to call it 'regulation'. Separation does not necessarily mean autonomy – many formally independent public organisations are tightly regulated in matters of personnel, finance, procurement, and a host of other issues, which severely limit managerial autonomy, as we will discuss below (see also Graham and Roberts, Chapter 7, this volume).

So far, so unproblematic – but this relatively simple list of easily understandable changes has been far more complex in reality. Let us examine each in turn.

First, structural separation. If we ask the question of what precisely is meant by structural separation we immediately enter a minefield of fuzzy definitions, complexly interrelating factors and problems about distinguishing between formality and reality. Public organisations – being public – always have a complex relationship with their superior public bodies (Ministries, Finance Ministries, central personnel functions, etc.). Their separation is usually one of degrees rather than absolutes, with some being clearly far more 'separate' but with none being entirely independent. Even 'public corporations' with a secure legal basis and seemingly unquestionable 'independence' have been shown to not always be quite as independent as the formalities might suggest. So most agency 'separations' are more often movements along a spectrum (or multiple spectra) rather than 'quantum leaps'.

In the UK, for example, 'agencies' are said to be separate but within the parent Ministry, and have no real legal 'personality' outside of their Ministry (or formal legal basis). Staff remain civil servants. A (highly questionable) analogy is often drawn with subsidiary companies within a conglomerate. In Japan and Tanzania, by contrast, the new agencies are established with a legislative basis, clearly outside of Ministries and staffs have ceased to be civil servants. These are qualitatively different degrees of separation. So the degree and types of organisational 'separation' need to be carefully specified in each case and superficial allusions to organisational change treated with caution.

Second, let us examine the idea of the 'single function', task-specific, agency. Generally, it is true that much 'unbundling' has tried to move to such a model. But there are also many examples where the new agencies have in fact been multi-functional. The revenue agencies in the UK, and elsewhere, are nearly all multi-functional in character dealing with a wide range of tax-collection, enforcement, and other duties (some even have their own intelligence and 'physical force' sections).

The focus of trying to create 'single function' agencies has also had unexpected consequences. The functions of governments are diverse, but they are not of equal sizes. Probably the largest and certainly the most 'symbolic' agency creation programme has been the 'Next Steps' programme in the UK. Whilst it has created around 140 agencies, only a handful of these account for most of the people working in agencies, whilst many of the rest are tiny (fewer than 100 staff). These structural imbalances have all sorts of consequential effects in relationships between agencies and 'their' Ministers and Ministries – in some cases making agencies less 'unbundled' and far more powerful than might have originally been intended and in others the reverse is true (Alexander and Agency Policy Review Team 2002; Talbot 2003).

A further complication has been the perennial focus-coordination dichotomy. As new bodies have been created with a greater focus on a single function, so the issue of better coordination across closely related functions has become a matter of concern. There is some evidence that public administration in general has periodically cycled between an emphasis on coordination and integration (through creating 'super-Ministries' for example) and focussing on task-specific organisation (breaking up Ministries, creating agencies and quangos, etc.) (Pollitt 1984; Hood and Jackson 1991). Similarly, as the agency movement has developed in various countries – especially those where it has had a significant impact (especially the UK) – issues of 'joined up government' have been raised. Agencification is probably not solely responsible for the new emphasis on coordination, but it has certainly contributed to it (Pollitt 2003a).

The division between 'policy and execution' or 'purchaser and provider' has been generally accepted as part of agency programmes, even though some who have been centrally involved have always denied this was the aim (Kemp 1993; Kemp 1996). In principle, the division seems straightforward, but practice has proved trickier. In the UK's larger agencies, for example, we have had cases where policy and execution have both been vested in the agency (Prisons), as well as being separated (Benefits) or shared (Employment).

The 'constitution' of agencies has also varied enormously from single agency legislation (USA, Australia) through generic agency legislation (Tanzania) to no legislation at all (UK). These variations often relate broadly to administrative traditions in the countries concerned, but not always (e.g. in the UK there is a long tradition of individual executing agencies being specifically legislatively based, in the 'Non-Departmental Public Bodies' category of organisations, but this was not applied to 'Next Steps').

The institution of a 'Chief Executive' figure apparently solely responsible for the new agency is very common, and has been the practice of many agency programmes. They have varied greatly in how openly competitive these have been, how many new agency heads have been drawn from outside traditional civil service ranks and just how genuinely individually accountable the new CE has been (see the controversy over the sacking of the Prisons Director General (DG) in the UK (Talbot 1996b).

Again, staffing changes have varied enormously – in some cases staffs have been removed from the civil service (Jamaica, Tanzania) and in others they have remained fully within the civil service (UK).

Finally, reporting arrangements for agencies have also varied – in most cases there has been a requirement for formal reporting of at least finance, and usually separate audit of accounts (although this has not always been carried out in practice – e.g. Tanzania). Performance reporting – as will be seen below – has been less universal.

So the idea of 'unbundling', in this less than complete survey, already throws up a host of questions about what exactly has been 'unbundled' in a structural sense. It may be useful to end this section with an example.

In 1964 the UK Prison Department (which organised prison establishments in England and Wales) was taken into the Home Office. It remained a single entity inside the larger Ministry, with the vast bulk of its staff on a separate pay and grading system, with its own 'Director General' who reported directly to both Ministers and the Permanent Secretary (with a somewhat fuzzy line of accountability). Culturally, the Prison Service remained very distinct from the 'parent' Ministry and interchange between the two was limited to a few senior civil servants (the DG was nearly always a career civil servant rather than a career prisons manager). It had many of its own internal management systems for finance, personnel, etc. Now, was the Prison Service inside or outside of the Home Office?

The position is even more confusing when the Prison Service became an 'agency' in 1993. It got a 'Framework Document', a Chief Executive (although still called the Director General), a set of targets and, over time, a set of managerial freedoms. The new agency was said – in common with all UK agencies – to be a separate body, but still part of its parent department (in distinction from so-called 'Non-Departmental Public Bodies', which belonged to a department but are more clearly 'outside' of it). Staff remained officially civil servants. The DG now reported formally, exclusively, to the Minister and was also now the 'accounting officer', but the Permanent Secretary remained the 'accounting officer' for the whole Home Office, which included the Prison Service.

(Incidentally the Immigration and Nationality Department (IND) remains a unit within the Home Office, which has many of the structural, performance and regulatory characteristics of an agency but is not designated as one.)

This example is instructive because it shows that even when an organisational unit may be formally 'bundled' within a Ministry, it may have many of the structural characteristics of a supposedly separate agency, and vice versa.

Reregulation

We deal with the issue of 'reregulation' next because it links so closely from the previous 'structure' section. Indeed, structural separation and reregulation have often been confused under the label 'decentralisation'.

Whilst structural and regulatory changes often do go together, they are not the same. It is perfectly possible to have structurally separated organisations which have equal, lesser or even greater levels of regulation than their 'parent' bodies.

By regulation we mean the 'standard operating procedures' and rules which are laid down within government for how public bodies must operate. The idea of 'deregulating government' (Osborne and Gaebler 1992; DiIulio 1994) has been a strong one – independently of the agency idea – but it has also come to be associated with the structural change represented by agency-type initiatives (Behn 2001, especially Chapter 10) as well as wider decentralisations and disaggregations (Hood, Scott *et al.* 1999).

The argument runs that public organisations have taken Weberian rule-based bureaucracy, which may have been ideal for creating fair and independent organisations in the past, too far (Barzelay 1992; Osborne and Gaebler 1992; Denhardt 1993). Public organisations have become weighed down with mountains of unnecessary 'red tape', which hampers their efficient management and puts enormous burdens on their functioning. Creating separate agencies can – indeed should – therefore be accompanied by a significant amount of deregulation, freeing up the new bodies from much of the superfluous accretions of decades of over-enthusiastic rule-makers.

This over-regulation argument clearly has some validity and it is undoubtedly the case that it has been a significant problem within many public administrations. Many examples can be found of overly complex, stultifying and sometimes gloriously stupid regulations (over, for example what size desk each grade of staff is allowed). Many of these regulations can, and probably should, be done away with.

In relation to agency programmes, regulatory change has taken several forms. These mostly relate to the different functions which deregulation addresses. These may include personnel, finance, purchasing, equality, probity and ethics, and so on. In some cases, it is freeing agencies from rules imposed by specific regulatory bodies (e.g. Public Service Commissions) and in others from central Ministries and in some cases both. They may include staff remaining under general civil services rules and conditions of employment (e.g. UK) or move to completely different terms and conditions (e.g. Jamaica).

There are several points about this 'regulatory' aspect of agencies which need to be carefully examined. First, it can be not so much deregulation as reregulation. Despite some of the rhetorical excesses (see especially Osborne and Plastrik 1991; Osborne and Gaebler 1992) regulation of public administration cannot easily be entirely abolished, or even slimmed down beyond a certain point, without creating problems of accountability, probity and ethics (Wilson 1994; Pollitt 2003b). In the USA Paul Light has shown that a recurring theme in reforms has been establishing proper standards for behaviour in public services – that is regulations (Light 1997).

Moreover, however hard governments might try to effectively abolish or strongly minimise regulation they have a habit of re-surfacing in other forms (Hood, James *et al.* 1999). Indeed, it can be the case that agency creation leads to effectively greater regulation, in some areas, than before. A small agency may have to conform to all sorts of regulatory and reporting arrangements which place a disproportionate burden upon their management (Talbot 1996a; Alexander and Agency Policy Review Team 2002), in much the same way as small businesses often complain that generic private sector regulations place disproportionate burdens on them. In the general context of the rising levels of audit and scrutiny of public bodies (Power 1997; Pollitt *et al.* 1999) the creation of many separate organisations may increase the audit burden – both for the organisations and for the auditors or inspectors (Hood, James *et al.* 1999).

Moreover, policy changes need to be viewed with due caution because they are not always what they appear – in some cases deregulation is less radical, or at any rate far more problematic, than it appears at first sight (Talbot 1997; Pollitt *et al.* 1998).

Finally, where there has been too much deregulation this has caused severe problems. Research on Latvia's agency programme shows this graphically (see Pollitt in Chapter 15 of this volume). On a lesser scale, in the UK several cases of highly questionable management decisions – mostly related to 'deregulated' parts of public service – came in for severe criticism from Parliamentarians (Public Accounts Committee 1994).

Having said all of the above, it is clear that the issue of regulation in an agency context is primarily addressed as a mechanism for liberating management and allowing greater freedom of action. This freedom is clearly for a purpose – improving performance. It is assumed that managerial freedoms will allow much greater prospects of improving performance, unfettered by cumbersome rules.

One strategy has simply been to give agencies an agreed level of autonomy and leave it at that. In other cases, the levels of autonomy have been gradually increased over time as central agencies, politicians and others have grown to trust that increased freedoms will not result in misbehaviour. A more recent conceptual development has been the notion of 'earned autonomy' (Behn 2001). This idea suggests that as agencies demonstrate good performance one of their rewards should be greater deregulation and autonomy.

The above discussion has focussed on 'external' regulation within government of one agency by another (Hood, James *et al.* 1999). However, another argument is that agencies may have the ability to deregulate themselves internally because they become to some degree self-regulating. There is certainly evidence of some agencies using their more relaxed external control regimes to implement internal deregulation (Fogden

1993). Some have argued this is leading to the creation of new, post-bureaucratic, public organisations (Barzelay 1992; Denhardt 1993).

But in an interesting analysis of generic organisational change, it has also been suggested that much deregulation has produced not 'post-bureaucratic' organisations but what the authors call a 'deceptive variant' – the 'cleaned bureaucracy' (Heckscher and Donnellon 1994). In other words the organisations have been 'reregulated' – in simpler, leaner, ways – rather than 'deregulated' in the sense of abandoning regulation altogether as some of the more extreme 'deregulators' seem to suggest. It is arguable that in terms of their internal systems, agencies may have become 'cleaned bureaucracies', rather than 'post-bureaucratic' organisations.

Performance

The third leg of the agency tripod is the idea of performance contracting. By 'performance' we mean any system of setting targets for, and reporting on (not necessarily publicly) the activities of an agency. As we shall see, definitions of what constitutes 'performance' vary enormously.

Let us also immediately say we use the term 'contracting' loosely – we do not necessarily mean a formal contract, but any self-generated, agreed or imposed set of performance targets for agencies, formulated into a specific agreement, contract, plan or statement of some sort. Research has shown that there are indeed many varieties of 'performance contract' in the public sector in general (Lidbury and Petrie 1999). The agreements may be very tightly worded and detailed agreements very close to a legal contract, at least in form if not substance. However, there are no examples, that we are aware of, of agencies actually being held to account through the courts. These also differ in a very important sense, 'contracts' in the legal sense – contracts in law are a two-way process in which both parties can default and be held to account for doing so. In the case of even the most legalistic agency performance agreements, it is pretty clear that these are mainly one-way 'contracts' – the purchaser (government) telling the provider (agencies) what they are expected to provide in performance terms. In no sense, and in none of the cases we are aware of, has it been that agencies have been able – or even tried – to use performance 'contracts' to hold government to account for changing the resources allocated, changing the rules within agencies work or varying the performance targets themselves.

On the other hand, there is also little evidence of contracts being operated in a legalistic way by governments. Agency failures – i.e. not meeting agreed targets – are most often the subject of discussion, negotiation and eventual consensus rather than punitive action. Where punitive steps have been taken over agency failures (for example in the cases of the UK Prison Service or the UK Child Support Agency) then it has usually been the agency Chief Executive who has been punished and not the agency itself. We are not aware of overt examples of agencies specifically having funds removed because of performance failures, as would usually be the case in the world of commercial contracting (through financial penalty clauses). In the government-agency relationship, performance contracting is clearly used more as a management tool between superiors and subordinates, rather than as a contract between independent bodies.

For agencies, some form of performance contract will usually form one basis of judgements about the agency's performance by its 'parent' department or Minister and other stakeholders.

Performance has nevertheless been seen as crucial to the agency project – whilst it has been related to the ideas of a purchaser-provider split, or principal-agent relationship it has in practice been a new way of managing. The new (or in some cases old) agency is subject to a new contractual or quasi-contractual arrangement in which resources are linked to results to be achieved. These results are usually specified in terms of service delivery, outputs or outcomes but may also include measures of processes and even of resource utilisation or inputs (see, for example, the analysis of UK agency targets in Talbot 1996a). In this sense it is seen as a 'performance contract'.

Who sets targets may also vary considerably. In the UK, the agency's key performance indicators are mostly the 'minister's' or 'Secretary of state's' targets – that is they are set, indeed sometimes unilaterally imposed, by the responsible politician. In the USA, by contrast, the Government Performance and Results Act (GPRA) mandates agencies to produce their own targets, but these are formally approved by both executive and legislative branches. In Sweden, agencies have broad areas for performance improvement set by their parent ministries, but specific measures and targets are entirely a matter for the agencies themselves.

Again, this raises problematic issues about the supposed 'principal-agent' nature of these 'contracts'. In most cases, there is no single 'principal' with whom to contract. In the United States the constitutional split between the Executive Office of the President and the Congress immediately means there are at least two principals. Even where there is supposedly only one executive authority, as in the case of the UK and most Westminster-style systems, in practice there are usually several principals – in the UK, case the parent Ministry, the Treasury and often the Cabinet Office. These examples only include the formal, managerial, authorities. Usually, there are also various other bodies charged with 'regulation inside government' (discussed above). They also effectively set performance targets or performance parameters for agencies (e.g. on equal treatment of personnel; proper handling of purchasing contracts; etc.).

So who exactly it is that is contracting with the agency for its performance is often not a single body. In reality, of course, whatever the formal process, nearly all agency target setting is a resultant of a 'zero sum' power game between these various actors – Ministers, 'parent' departments, the agencies themselves, legislatures, and in some cases regulators such as inspectorates and audit bodies. The balance between these various actors may vary markedly, even within the same formal institutional setting and of course over time.

Similarly, the balance of focus in what is meant by 'performance' and what targets are set may also vary enormously. Performance can be defined in narrow 'economic' senses – traditionally the three Es – economy, efficiency and effectiveness. Or it can address much wider concerns – some of the other Es such as equality, equity, evaluation, etc. In formal linear models of public sector production, the sequence is often defined as:

inputs > processes > outputs > outcomes

with many variations on, and additions to, this basic model. Performance can focus on any or all of these things.

For example, in an analysis of all 140 UK agencies conducted in 1997 we found that their targets broke down as: input targets – 8 per cent; efficiency targets – 20 per cent; process targets – 11 per cent; output targets – 61 per cent. (There were an insignificant 0.3 per cent outcome targets). So even in this case, where the official position was that performance contracts were supposed to be about specifying 'deliverables', only 61 per cent of targets actually set were about outputs. Generally, there has been a move from input and process targets towards service delivery and output targets, but this is not as complete as some of the official rhetoric would seem to suggest (Chancellor of the Duchy of Lancaster 1996; Talbot 1996a; Chancellor of the Duchy of Lancaster 1997; Talbot 2000; Alexander and Agency Policy Review Team 2002).

In the USA agencies performance plans have been of variable quality and focus (General Accounting Office (USA) 1997; 1999). They have also been the subject of much controversy. After the first set of performance plans had been delivered the GAO was asked, by Congressional leaders, to draw up a set of criteria with which various Congressional committees could approach their task of scrutinising the plans. The resulting set of

Table 1.1 Percentage performance indicator types for all UK agencies 1994–7

Year	Inputs	Efficiency	Process	Outputs	Outcomes	No. of Agencies
1994	11.2	20.9	12.2	55.4	0.3	103
1995	8.3	18.8	11.3	61.0	0.6	111
1996	7.7	20.6	13.2	58.1	0.5	131
1997	8.3	19.5	11.0	61.0	0.3	140

Source: analysis of Next Steps Review annual reports.

criteria was then turned into a crude 'score-card' and applied to Agency plans, the judgements being made by Congressional staffers. This was under a Republican dominated Congress and a Democrat White House – the resulting 'league table' of Agency plans/performance was naturally the subject of a great deal of heat and very little light was generated. This episode eclipsed the more serious evaluations conducted by the GAO itself (cited above) and illustrated the reality of having more than one principal (President and Congress) in a supposed 'principal-agent' relationship.

Interestingly, 'principle-agent' notions also seem to have informed a view that performance contracting is just about 'purchasing outputs' and this seems to have caused some governments to deliberately avoid setting outcome targets (e.g. UK, New Zealand). In other cases (e.g. Canada, USA) agencies have had outcome targets. An interesting comparative analysis of Australian and New Zealand experience suggests that the latter's focus almost exclusively on 'outputs' compares unfavourably with the former's use of a more balanced (or at any rate mixed) approach (Campbell 2001).

More recent developments – which relate to this notion of 'balanced' performance – has been the use of ideas imported from the private sector such as 'balanced score-cards' or other performance frameworks or assessment tools. In the UK and Denmark, the European Foundation for Quality Management's (EFQM) 'Excellence' model has been widely used for assessing agencies performance. More recently, the European Union has used something called the Common Assessment Framework, developed from both EFQM and the Speyer Institute's bi-annual Awards, as a similar tool for a European-wide competition in assessing public agencies performance. In the UK and USA the 'Balanced Score-card' (Kaplan and Norton 1996) has been widely adopted in the public agencies and in the USA many such agencies have also participated in the Baldrige Awards whilst the Canadians have their own version in their National Quality Awards. Such ideas have spread widely – in Tanzania the EFQM self-assessment framework was used to help proto-agencies get an idea of their own performance levels (see Caulfield, Chapter 12 of this volume).

There is, as yet, insufficient real evidence as to the realities (as opposed to formal set-up) of how performance information is used in managing the 'contract' between agency sponsors and agency managers or in other processes, such as making resource allocation decisions (as between different agencies and different programmes within or across agencies), public accountability and so on. We know that there are few, if any, examples of agencies themselves receiving more or less funding depending on their performance. We know that there are few, but not many, cases where agency managers have been castigated or sacked for performance failures. We know there are many cases where agency managers have been rewarded, through performance related pay, for organisational successes.

We know there have been many instances of agency failures and/or crises in which the formal performance arrangements seem to have been forgotten. Finally, we know that in some cases, at least, the use of formal performance contracting arrangements are more formal than real – instances of the formalities being preserved without any real content (see for example Alexander and Agency Policy Review Team 2002).

Final thoughts

It seems somehow inappropriate to have a 'conclusion' in an opening chapter of a collection of case studies. Our conclusions, in so far as we can draw them, are in the analytical framework offered in this chapter, in the individual chapters and, more generally, in the final chapter.

A word of warning should be given to readers embarking on the journey through individual chapters. Within the restrictions of space provided it is, of course, difficult to address all the administrative differences, large and small, in the countries covered. There are some excellent sources of general comparative public administration (e.g. Heady 1991; Bekke *et al.* 1996) and specifically on public management reform (Pollitt and Bouckaert 2000) which give much greater context for some of the specific case studies presented here.

To end this beginning, it would be good idea to leave the reader with some questions to keep in mind when examining the individual chapters, based on the analysis presented here. This list is not exhaustive, but it may help readers put some order on the myriad experiences which pop-up under the 'agency' umbrella from all corners of the globe.

To what degree do 'agencies' – whether new or old – constitute really separate entities within national public administrations? Are some of the new agencies really new organisations, or simply re-badging of existing structures with a few minor tweaks? To what degree do the formal arrangements and the informal correspond – where a change in status is taking place how far has there been a real, as opposed to merely formal, change in how things are done? Has the changed (or existing) semi-autonomous status of agencies really given managers of the agencies the 'freedom to manage'? (The latter is also linked to the question of reregulation as well as structural/managerial separation). What are the consequential effects on the structures of non-agency functions – especially (where relevant) on 'parent' departments and ministries? Have the latter become truly 'strategic' or do they still seek to 'micro-manage'? Do large agencies and small ministries, or conversely small agencies in large ministries, create substantial power and information asymmetries?

Does 'agency' status necessarily mean that these organisations escape from the clutches of system-wide 'regulation within government' and if they do, is it a good thing? Has the burden of auditing, inspecting and monitoring on organisations which are 'agencified' been eradicated, merely reduced, perhaps shifted into other forms or maybe even increased? Have the state organs charged with scrutinising agencies proved capable and willing to do so? Has the result been an increased transparency of agencified functions or a loss of traditional forms of public accountability?

What – if any – forms of 'performance contracting' have been introduced for agencies? Indeed, are agencies required to produce any performance information at all about their activities? If so, what does this information focus on: Inputs? Processes? Efficiency? Outcomes? Equity? Equality? Or some combination of these? Do agencies have targets for performance and, if so, who sets the targets? The agencies themselves? Their 'parent' bodies? A process of negotiation (and, if so, who is the dominant partner in the bargaining)? Who enforces any 'contract' or who is responsible for taking action if an agency is seen to be 'failing'? Similarly, what happens if an agency is 'successful', who decides, and what actions are taken? Is performance information publicly available and, if so, how accessible, understandable and credible is it? Is performance information audited? Do parliamentary or other democratic institutions take an active part in the 'performance regime' in setting targets, monitoring results and rewarding/punishing the poor/good performers?

These, we suggest, are the types of questions it will be useful to be asking yourselves as you peruse the studies collected in this volume. They may not be able to provide all the answers – indeed it is sometimes the silences on some of these issues which tell us interesting things about the focus and concerns of the various programmes which have appeared under the 'agency' banner.

Bibliography

Alexander, P. and Agency Policy Review Team (2002) Better Government Services – Executive Agencies in the 21st Century (The Agency Policy Review – report and recommendations). London, Cabinet Office.

Barzelay, M. (1992) *Breaking Through Bureaucracy – A New Vision for Managing in Government*, Berkley: University of California Press.

Behn, R. (2001) *Rethinking Democratic Accountability*, Washington: Brookings Institution.

Bekke, H.A.G.M. *et al.* (eds) (1996) *Civil Service Systems in Comparative Perspective*, Bloomington and Indianapolis: Indiana University Press.

Campbell, C. (2001) 'Juggling inputs, outputs, and outcomes in the search for policy competence: recent experience in Australia', *Governance* 14, 2, 253–82.

Campbell, C. and Wilson, G. (1995) *The End of Whitehall: Death of Paradigm?*, Oxford: Blackwell.

Chancellor of the Duchy of Lancaster (1996) Next Steps Agencies in Government – Review 1996 (Cm 3579), Cabinet Office.

Chancellor of the Duchy of Lancaster (1997) Next Steps Agencies in Government – Review 1997, Cabinet Office.

Denhardt, R.B. (1993) *The Pursuit of Significance – Strategies for Managerial Success in Public Organisations*, Fort Worth: Harcourt Brace College Publishers.

DiIulio, J.J. (ed.) (1994) *Deregulating the Public Service*, Washington DC: The Brookings Institute.

Fogden, M.E.G. (1993) 'Managing change in the employment service', *Public Money and Management* 13, 2.

General Accounting Office (USA) (1997) Agencies' Strategic Plans Under GPRA: Key Questions to Facilitate Congressional Review. Washington DC: General Accounting Office (USA).

General Accounting Office (USA) (1999) Managing for Results – Opportunities for Continued Improvements in Agencies' Performance Plans. Washington DC: General Accounting Office (USA).

Heady, F. (1991) *Public Administration – A Comparative Perspective*, New York: Marcel Dekker, Inc.

Heckscher, C. and Donnellon, A. (eds) (1994) *The Post-Bureaucratic Organization*, London: Sage.

Hood, C. and Jackson, M. (1991) *Administrative Argument*, Dartmouth: Aldershot.

Hood, C., James, O. *et al.* (1999) *Regulation Inside Government*, Oxford: Oxford University Press.

Hood, C., Scott, C. *et al.* (1999) *Regulation Inside Government*, Oxford: Oxford University Press.

Kaplan, R. and Norton, D. (1996) *The Balanced Scorecard*, Harvard: HBS Press.

Kemp, P. (1993) *Beyond Next Steps: A Civil Service for the 21st Century*, London: Social Market Foundation.

Kemp, P. (1996) Interview with author.

Lidbury, C. and Petrie, M. (1999) Lessons from Performance Contracting Case Studies and A Framework for Public Sector Performance Contracting. Paris: OECD.

Light, P.C. (1997) *The Tides of Reform – Making Government Work 1945–1995*, New Haven: Yale University Press.

Odiorne, G. (1965) *Management by Objectives*, New York: Pittman Publishing Corporation.

Osborne, D. and Gaebler, T. (1992) *Reinventing Government – How the Entrepreneurial Spirit is Transforming the Public Sector*, New York: Addison-Wesley Publishing Company.

Osborne, D. and Plastrik, P. (1991) *Banishing Bureaucracy*, New York: Addison-Wesley Publishing Company.

Pliatsky, L. (1992) 'Quangos and agencies', *Public Administration* 70, 4.

Pollitt, C. (1984) *Manipulating the Machine*, Hemel Hempstead: Allen & Unwin.

Pollitt, C. (2003a) 'Joined up government', *Political Studies Review* forthcoming.

Pollitt, C. (2003b) *The Essential Public Manager*, Buckingham: Open University Press.

Pollitt, C. *et al.* (1998) *Decentralising Public Service Management*, Basingstoke: Macmillan.

Pollitt, C. *et al.* (1999) *Performance or Conformance*, Oxford: Oxford University Press.

Pollitt, C. and Bouckaert, G. (2000) *Public Management Reform – A Comparative Analysis*, Oxford: Oxford University Press.

Power, M. (1997) *The Audit Society*, Oxford: Oxford University Press.

Public Accounts Committee (1994) *Eighth Report: The Proper Conduct of Public Business (154)*, HMSO.

Rose, R. (1984) *Understanding Big Government – The Programme Approach*, London: Sage.

Stiglitz, J. (2000) 'Scan globally, reinvent locally: knowledge infrastructure and the localisation of knowledge', in Stone, D. (ed.) *Banking on Knowledge – The Genesis of the Global Development Network*, London: Routledge.

Talbot, C. (1996a) *Ministers and Agencies: Control, Performance and Accountability*, London: CIPFA.

Talbot, C. (1996b) 'The prison service: a framework of irresponsibility?', *Public Money and Management* 16, 1.

Talbot, C. (1997) 'UK civil service personnel reforms: devolution, decentralisation and delusion', *Public Policy and Administration* 12, 4.

Talbot, C. (2000) 'Performing "performance" – a comedy in five acts', *Public Money and Management* 20, 4.

Talbot, C. (2002) *So Who Needs Agencies?*, Pontypridd: University of Glamorgan.

Talbot, C. (2003) 'Small step or giant leap? Evaluating ten years of the "next steps" agencies in the UK (1988–98)', *Public Money and Management (forthcoming)*.

Talbot, C. *et al.* (2000) *The Idea of Agency.* Paper presented at the APSA Conference, Washington.

Thorngate, W. (1976) 'Possible limits on a science of social behavior', in Strickland, L.H., Aboud, F.E. and Gergen, K.J. (eds) *Social Psychology in Transition*, New York: Plenum.

van Thiel, S. (2000) 'Quangocratization: trends, causes and consequences', *Interuniversity Center for Social Theory and Methodology*, Utrecht.

Wilson, J.Q. (1989) *Bureaucracy – What Government Agencies Do and Why They Do It*, New York: Basic Books.

Wilson, J.Q. (1994) 'Can the bureaucracy be deregulated? Lessons from government agencies', in DiIulio, J.J. (ed.) *Deregulating the Public Service – Can Government Be Improved?*, Washington: The Brookings Institution.

2 What is available and what is missing in the study of quangos?

Geert Bouckaert and Guy B. Peters

Numerous structural changes occurring in the public sector have increased the awareness of the existence and importance of autonomous and quasi-autonomous organizations. The role of these organizations first came to academic prominence during the 1970s when the term "quango" was introduced into the lexicon of political science and public administration (Hague, Mackenzie, and Barker 1975), at least in the Anglo-Saxon world. More recently, governments have created, or attempted to create, "agencies" or other forms of more or less autonomous organizations, to implement programs. In most instances these organizations remain responsible to the minister but yet have substantial autonomy from the ministries. These forms of organization have come to be used more commonly in a wide variety of countries around the world. In addition to the Anglo-Saxon countries, where these forms of organization have taken on a number of different names, other industrialized democracies and many less developed countries have copied these formats for their own governments with an even wider range of terminologies.

As well as the practical increases in the use of more autonomous and quasi-autonomous organizations, there has been a spate of research on the role of these organizations in governing. Although there has been substantial description, and some analysis, of this type of organization, there are a number of notable deficiencies in this body of research. Indeed, despite the investment of time and energy on this topic, there is still a great deal more to do to place these organizations in the broader theoretical and comparative literature on the public sector. We do know that there are (apparently) more of these organizations and that there are a number of managerial and accountability issues arising from their use. On the other hand, there have been relatively few testable propositions that have developed from the literature and seemingly little interest in moving beyond the descriptive. Arguably, we think we know much more about these organizations than we actually do, given the numerous assumptions that have been somehow elevated to the level of fact.

This chapter will examine what we consider to be major deficiencies in the existing literature that attempts to describe and explain this type of public organization. The purpose of this exercise is not simply to criticize other scholars and their (substantial) contributions, but rather to attempt to advance the study of these organizations and their role in governing. To that end, the critique will point to means through which this area of inquiry could, in fact, be advanced. These means of intellectual advancement will be related directly to the existing problems, and also can be seen as moving toward a more comprehensive theoretical perspective on the structure of government. Indeed, the principal problem that we can see in the literature is that first, there has been little theoretical development, second, an absence of comparable data, third, little comparative analysis, and fourth, few empirically tested hypotheses in this field.

Problems in studying quangos

As already noted, we will now proceed to discuss some of the major problems that we can identify in the existing literature on autonomous and quasi-autonomous organizations, always keeping in mind what should be done to remedy these perceived problems. The purpose throughout will be to construct more reliable and useful generalizations about this important type of public organization. Further, we need to remember that for all the generalizations being advanced about the deficiencies in the literature, there is at least one counter-example. Still, we do believe that the tendencies that will be identified here are rather clear and are representative of the literature.

Definitions

Perhaps the most fundamental problem in this literature is that the participants are often less than clear about what is meant by autonomy, and indeed what is meant by an organization.[1] And, therefore, some scholars are less than clear about what types of organizations are actually to be considered in the analysis. Autonomy is a relational term and, therefore, the first question that must be asked is autonomous relative to whom, or to what, and for what purpose. It is quite possible that an increased level of autonomy for an organization relative to one actor may result in reduced autonomy relative to other actors. For example, gaining greater autonomy from Parliament may result in the organization having to lose some autonomy to interest groups.[2] Also, it appears that increased autonomy for agencies from their sponsoring ministries may mean that they become more subject to control from central budgetary and policy control agencies (Peters and Savoie 2001).

As well as the need to define the relative nature of autonomy for organizations, there is a need to define autonomy along a number of different dimensions. Much of the discussion to date has been concerned with the managerial autonomy of these organizations, and to some extent with political autonomy, implying the freedom of managers in these organizations to make decisions without reference to Parliament or the minister. At the same time that this autonomy may be relaxed, the budgetary controls may be as powerful as ever, and perhaps even more controlling given that other forms of control are known to have been loosened or abandoned. Likewise, the focus on political and managerial autonomy often ignores the legal basis of public organization (see below) and the importance of the initial legal definitions of the organization in shaping its autonomy.

Once those dimensions of autonomy are clarified conceptually, a second stage of definition and analysis will be required. This stage would be to develop some objective indicators of those dimensions that can be applied across a range of political systems. We need to have measures that, like the concepts that they are meant to measure, can "travel" (Sartori 1971) across cultures, and that can avoid being too closely linked with a particular governmental or intellectual tradition. It appears that most of the limited range of concepts that have to date been applied to the study of autonomous organizations are linked to the Anglo-Saxon tradition of administration, and therefore have low levels of conceptualization of the legal dimension. Further, there does appear to be some tendency to accept the formal autonomy of organizations at face value, rather than to assess more fully the range of different autonomies that are relevant for that definition. The indicators needed to address these questions more systematically need not be interval, aggregate indicators but will more likely be judgmental, ordinal scales or even nominal. It is useful to distinguish between the legal or theoretical autonomy, the actual level of autonomy exercised, and the perceived level of autonomy. Even nominal scales and perceived degrees, however, may make it possible to advance the inquiry over where we are at present.

Limited sample

The first point that stands out in a reading of the literature on quangos, agencies, and similar bodies in the public sector is how limited is the discussion in geographic terms. We noted above that the term quango was developed in reference to organizations that had emerged, or at least had become more apparent, in the United Kingdom. More recently, the literature on agencies has been dominated by the shift from a ministerial model to a more devolved set of structures in the United Kingdom and in the Antipodes. The other Westminster systems that have been less active in adopting this form of governmental structure, most notably Canada, have come to be regarded as almost deviant in the discussion.[3]

In many ways, this location of the discussion of these organizational forms within this particular political and cultural setting is at the root of many of the analytical and theoretical problems we will be identifying. Not only does this constitute a limited sample of countries and the possible manners of organizing government, but it represents a tradition of governing that has placed greater emphasis in theory (if not always in practice) on the role of ministers and ministries in the government (Marshall 1999). In particular, the Westminster tradition emphasizes the role of Parliament in holding public organizations accountable so that any deviation from that practice is likely to produce political and academic reactions. In addition, the political style of these countries has been liberal rather than corporatist so that the closer state-society relationships that may emerge by using quasi-autonomous organizations may threaten established understandings.

Non-random sample

As implied above, the "sample" on which much of the literature on agencies and other quasi-autonomous organizations has been developed is quite distinctive, and hardly representative of the nature of public organization in most of the world. Public administration in the United Kingdom has a substantially lower level of concern with public law than do most other political systems (but see Woodhouse 1997). Even other Anglo-American systems such as the United States and Canada assign a much greater importance to public law in the definition and management of organizations than does the United Kingdom. When the deeply-entrenched legal basis of organizations in Continental Europe is considered, the nature of administration in the United Kingdom is even more distinctive. Thus, given that much of the discussion of agencies has been based on the experience of the United Kingdom there is perhaps inadequate attention to the role of law.

As well as there being a fundamental question of basing the principal thrust of the research on a country, or set of countries that has a very different perspective on public organization from most other industrialized democracies, the basis of much of this research in the experience of the United Kingdom also has a more subtle, but perhaps more pervasive, influence. There is a sociology of knowledge operating in this literature that has tended to produce a set of emphases that would be unlikely to occur elsewhere, including other Anglo-American systems. At the most basic level, there might not be the alarmed discovery that there were organizations in the public sector that were somewhat loosely connected to ministerial authority if the research were conducted in other settings.[4] Ministerial responsibility has been such a mantra for the British study of politics that any deviations from that linear connectedness in the system may appear deviant. Likewise, the rather extreme centralization of government in the contemporary United Kingdom, in contrast to most other political systems that have been adopting more decentralized conceptions of governing, means that the loss of direct control often associated with the adoption of agencies has been more traumatic.

The focus on the managerial and political dimensions of autonomy in the British discussion of agencies and quangos is accompanied by a distinct disregard for legal questions, as implied above. The role of public and private law in defining the nature of organization has been discussed very little in the analysis of agencies and other "new" types of organizations. As already implied, the Anglo-American tradition in public administration assumes a great deal about the basis of organizations that cannot be assumed in other systems. Even in the United States, in which there is more likely to be a legal basis for organizations than in Westminster systems, the overriding assumption is that public organizations will be defined by public law. On the other hand, in continental systems many organizations providing public services may be organized under public law, and many people in those organizations, who would be hired under public law in Anglo countries, are employed under private labor law. The lack of any real concern with legal formats for organization represents yet another blind spot resulting from the social and cultural basis of the research.

Coming late to the study

In many countries, organizations equivalent to contemporary agencies, and a whole host of quasi-autonomous organizations, have existed for decades, if not for centuries. The most obvious example of the long-term existence of these organizations is the existence of agencies with substantial constitutionally protected autonomy from their ministries in Sweden since the eighteenth century. The other Nordic countries also have had organizations using this basic format, albeit with differing levels of autonomy from their ministries. In some instances, countries, and even individual organizations, have moved away from this more decentralized format, but in some cases have also reverted to this format at a later date (Kararup 1999). Also, the basic organizational format in the United States has been to have agencies beneath the level of the cabinet department with those organizations having a substantial degree of political and policy autonomy. Further, virtually all of these organizations have a status in public law so that their existence can not be threatened without an action of Congress.[5] This pattern of organization is obviously in marked contrast to the pattern of organization in other Anglo-American political systems.

In addition to the long-standing pattern of semi-autonomous agencies in a number of countries, organizations such as quangos have existed in many countries for decades if not centuries. These organizations have been evident in Continental Europe for some time, perhaps especially in the pillarized Low Countries (Belgium and the Netherlands) where the quasi-public sector has been crucial in delivering services. This style of government organization has been important in the social services and became used commonly when governments also became important economic actors. Even in the United Kingdom, historically there have been a number of organizations that have had substantial autonomy from Parliament and from ministers. The strict notions of parliamentary authority that made quangos so much of an issue in some quarters appear to have been violated for some time in the past.

The amnesia that appears to exist surrounding the persistence of long-standing patterns of organization in the public sector highlights the static nature of this body of literature. The analysis of government organizations has not tended to look at the development of patterns across time, or to think much about changes across time, and the implications of those changes for governance (for exceptions see Pollitt 1984; Darbel and Schnapper 1978; Peters and Hogwood 1991). For example, if there were a categorization scheme for public organizations that was meaningful across time then we could determine if indeed there had been a shift in the nature of organization and just what the organizational life-cycle or demographic change had been.

The nature of the analytic scheme to be applied would be crucial here. As already noted, all the dimensions of autonomy for public organizations do not necessarily covary, so that an increase in autonomy along one dimension may not mean an increase along all dimensions. Thus, if we could code these dimensions of autonomy over time, then we would be able to assess the extent to which shifts have actually occurred and the extent to which they have indeed covaried. As we have surmised above, an increase in managerial autonomy may not mean an increase in budgetary autonomy. Further, there may be cycles of autonomy through which organizations transit, beginning by gaining one type of change and then moving on to other dimensions. Dynamics of change of autonomy (What is the triggering field. Is the shift to another field adding autonomy?) are hardly covered. Also, allocated autonomy is different from the degree to which this autonomy is used in practice. De facto autonomy could be below or above de jure autonomy as a function of agency circumstances (Verhoest 2001). The problem is that without an adequate time dimension to the research, there has been no investigation of the patterns of change.

In summary of this one point, the rather recent alarmed discovery that there were organizations that exist at the margin of the public sector and which have a good deal of autonomy from direct ministerial control should not have been quite as dramatic as it appeared to be. There have been a variety of forms of organization in the public sector that have existed for some time, and recognition of the existence of those multiple forms should be an advantage to scholars attempting to understand the more recent development of organizational formats. There have been efforts, e.g. Next Steps, to create more of these organizations, but they might have been considered as a continuation of a pattern rather than as a massive innovation. Those organizational formats could have been a baseline (intellectual as well as quantitative) against which to assess the contemporary world of the public sector.

Structuralist perspectives

The above discussion has implied that there is a need to be more attuned to the multiple dimensions of public organization. To state that point a bit more directly, it appears that the literature on agencies and quasi-public organizations has focussed on their structures and the formal patterns of organization, to the exclusion of other issues. Those structural arrangements are certainly important but tell only part of the story about what is happening. Even the structural analysis has tended to focus on a single dimension of the changes and not at more subtle shifts. For example, given that most devolved organizations began their lives as components of other organizations, do they tend to retain the structural features that they had inherited from their past, or do they create other formats? Likewise, is there a common structure toward which devolved organizations evolve when they are cut loose from their ministerial home?

The point here is that structure is important but that it is only one dimension. Further, given that the dimension of structure is important, it needs to be developed more fully in addition to being supplemented by other perspectives on the characteristics of autonomous and quasi-autonomous organizations in the public sector. For example, one issue that should be addressed from a structural perspective is the place of collective, as opposed to individual, leadership in these organizations. Likewise, the formal connections that exist with societal actors should be assessed and could well be quantified. This list could be extended, but the basic point is that the literature needs to provide more usable information for analysis.

Developing data

One way of summarizing the points that have already been made is to point to the need for greater and more exact measurement and more conscious conceptualization for the subject matter of this area of inquiry. The dimensions of autonomy we discussed above, the nature of the structures, the size and nature of the work force, and a host of other aspects of these organizations are amenable to further investigation through quantitative means. This is not just quantification for the sake of quantification and attempting to look like a "proper" social science. Rather, this is a way to classify and typologize organizations in an inductive manner. The measurements themselves may be more deductively grounded, but the quantitative information would enable us to locate organizations in some multi-dimensional space and to cluster them.

This more inductive approach would enable us to address several interesting and important issues. For example, it would be interesting to know if country makes much difference in explaining the types of organizations that have been created. One alternative explanation for clustering of organizations is that policy areas produce greater uniformity than does country (Freeman 1985). Alternatively, the organizations may cluster on the basis of their size, or the nature of their personnel, or a variety of other factors. The problem is that we do not know, and given the import- ance of this type of organization in contemporary governance, it is crucial to begin to clarify these points.

Preliminary results

The top-down politico-administrative embeddedness of agencies refers to ministerial portfolios and ministries as a layered context of these autonomous units. To the extent that the study of agencies includes the dynamics of the interactions with this institutional environment, these shifts are relevant.

Reformers have had several logics in operation when deciding to disag- gregate the public sector in what, in many cases such as the United Kingdom and New Zealand, is a rather extreme way. One of the motiva- tions for the change was to create something approaching a market struc- ture within the public sector, so that competition would force organizations to be more efficient (Peters 1996). In many instances, the competition was more assumed than real, but in the case of separation of purchasers and providers in health care and some other services (see Jerome-Forget, White and Wiener 1995) some market forces could be created. Even when there was no competition the disaggregation of government has tended to limit the number of programs for which any one organization is responsible, thereby making accountability for performance and efficiency easier.

Politically, an often unintended consequence of the separation of organizations from a larger ministerial structure has been to make them more vulnerable to pressures from clientele groups, and hence to make them less capable of pursuing pure efficiency goals.

We will be arguing that although there are numerous similarities among the organizations being created in public sectors around the world, there is also a great deal of variation among those organizations. That variation occurs along a number of dimensions. First, organizations differ in their governance structures and their relationships with minister- ial authority. Although nominally all "agencies," these organizations may be governed very differently and have differing degrees of autonomy. Further, they may have autonomy in different aspects of performing their roles. Some may have autonomy over financial matters, while others over personnel appointments, and others still over policy decisions. Thus, simply saying that an organization is autonomous may disguise substantial variation in their ability to act on their own and their capacity to influence public policy. Finally, these organizations are not all charged with imple- menting policies developed elsewhere. Rather, they perform a variety of tasks for government and must be structured differently, and have differing degrees of autonomy, in order to perform those tasks.

The first of the questions about ministerial structure is the basis of organization of the ministry, as well as of the components of the ministry. Organization theory in the public sector points to four fundamental bases for structuring ministries, and other public organizations: area, clientele, purpose, and activity (Gulick 1937). These bases of organization may be manifested in the designation of portfolios at the ministerial level as well as at the sub-ministerial level. We will be interested in the way in which the disaggregation of ministries conforms to their general purposes, and how the detailed structure of these organizations matches their more generalized structures.

There is a variation of numbers of ministers and of ministries. Their relationship could take the form of 1–1 (one minister has one ministry), 1–N (one minister could have several ministries), N–1 (several ministers control one ministry), or N–N (several ministers control several ministries simultaneously. The Netherlands and Germany are more on the 1–1 side, whereas Belgium is more on the N–N side. There seems to be a pressure to shift to the 1–1 model. Even if the number of ministries is sometimes unclear and influenced by domestic elements like coalitions, regional visibility, or socio-economic divisions, there is a tendency to reduce the number of ministries. Minimizing the apparent size of a government is one crucial element. Keeping policy control and avoiding some accountability mechanisms by devolving competencies to autonomous bodies is another one. The average number of ministries seems to have shrunk from 18.1 in 1988 to 15.5 in 1998 (Bouckaert, Ormond, and Peters 2000). This shift is combined with the creation of superministries, the strengthening of the Prime Minister, and an increasing number of quangos.

New or renewed topics like, for example, environment, food issues, agricultural aspects, consumer affairs, trade and competitiveness, research and development, social integration, and cultural identity affect the organization of ministries, sub-ministerial levels, and quangos (Bovens, 't Hart, Peters 2001). The basic organizational patterns appear outlined below.

Conventional hierarchical structure

In this structure there is a minister who heads an organizational pyramid composed of several strata of subdivisions within the ministry. This is the rather conventional pyramid one sees on organograms, with direct lines of political authority flowing down from the minister through the components of the ministry. In this model, the components of the ministry have little or no legal standing of their own but rather exist at the discretion of the minister or perhaps the cabinet. Thus, these organizations have little or no autonomy, although organizations that are completely hived-off from government may exist within countries using this approach to structure, with those autonomous organizations generally being responsible to one or another minister.

In one variant of this structural model (France) there are generally field staffs linked to the ministry, so that central government will deliver the service directly. This pattern is also characteristic of Westminster countries that have not adopted one of the agency models mentioned below. This style of administration is also typical of Japanese government. In another model (Germany) the pyramid is usually severely truncated, with implementation being carried out through the intermediate level of government (the Länder, in the case of Germany. In all of these cases, however, there is a general movement toward contracting out the delivery of the service.

"Product lines"

A slight variation on the conventional hierarchical structure has departments organized around "product lines," using an analog to the structure found in many private firms. In this model the responsibility for managing a product line tends to be vested in a senior public manager, rather than in an organization per se. The organizational structure beneath the ministerial level tends to be rather fluid in these cases, or to exist as a matrix, with product lines cutting across more conventional organizational structures. That is, the product line format may not be expressed as clearly as are some more conventional organizational formats, such as the hierarchical structure mentioned directly above.

The ministries within which this structure tends to function appear to be those with clearly defined programs (which can be therefore readily considered analogous to product lines) that do not involve high levels of discretion about individual recipients. This style of structuring is becoming more common in Canada (and is also found in departments such as Housing and Urban Development (HUD) in the United States). HUD has been organized in this manner in part because it operates almost entirely through other providers, rather than providing services itself.

Internal political structuring

In Spain, and to some extent in Italy, there are a relatively small number of ministries, but each ministry has within it a number of departments headed by political officials. Each of these components of a ministry enjoys substantial autonomy, and is in essence a ministry within a ministry. In Spain this autonomy is enhanced by the power of the *cuerpos* (administrative corps) within the civil service, and the concentration of certain *cuerpos* in different ministries (Alba 2001). In this structure, the ministries become virtual holding companies for the activities of their internal units, although the formal structure is not as decentralized as the next two models. Further, the capacity to manage with this structural format is in part a function of the composition of the government, with coalitions presenting particular difficulties. Ministers nominally under the supervision of another minister may find the arrangement difficult to abide by if they are members of different political parties.

This structure has some similarities with the agency-ministry model in the United States discussed below. In both cases, there are political appointees with significant managerial responsibilities functioning below the ministry (or its equivalent). The titles of the positions convey a very different status (minister in Spain, versus Director or Administrator or whatever in the United States) but functionally they may be equivalent. In addition, the second tier of officials in the United States is more numerous than in Spain, with some departments having 20 or 30 agencies below the cabinet level. This proliferation of agencies appears to reflect more the general structural differentiation of American government, but it also creates a more complex management environment for the cabinet secretary.

Ministry-agency structure I

This is the standard organizational format found in Sweden, and to some extent in the other Nordic countries. It is characterized by a small ministry responsible for policy formulation and planning, and a number of (often much larger in employment terms) boards or agencies responsible for implementation. These largely autonomous boards generally have some corporate body responsible for making policy for the organization. Also, the politics-administration dichotomy implied by this structure is decaying as the boards become increasingly active in making policy on their own. Although this structure is usually conceptualized as existing at two levels, there are some cases in the Scandinavian countries in which larger and more important boards have other boards that report to them.

Although this is often considered a general Scandinavian model, it is far from universal and even when it is adopted, the dynamics may be different in the different political systems. Denmark, for example, has used this model for some ministries but not for others, and some ministries have changed back and forth between the agency model and a more hierarchical model rather frequently. Finland has been moving away from this structure somewhat, although its historical legacy is within this framework. Likewise, Norway has much of the Swedish legacy, but also has more departments that have a more hierarchical internal structuring and fewer fully autonomous boards.

It should also be noted here that as governments in general change their involvement in society, there may be a shifting role for agencies, and a changing relationship between ministries and the boards in the Scandinavian model. Some observers have argued that as the political, ministerial level of government shifts toward "the enabling state" style of governing, they have lost interest in making policies. This is especially true if those policies involve rather intrusive measures that might invite political reactions. The agencies are left in the position of needing to have clear policies to administer if they are to do their jobs and, therefore, often decide to make those policies themselves. This is especially true for some of the larger and more politically powerful agencies such as the Labor Market Board.

Ministry-agency structure II

An alternative version of the ministry-agency structure has been developed in the United Kingdom, and to some extent in New Zealand. In this version there is an agency headed by a chief executive who is responsible to the Department, rather than to an independent board. That chief executive is hired on the basis of a contract and can be dismissed for failure to meet the conditions of the contract. There is also a continuing debate about the capacity of ministers to dismiss chief executives simply on the basis of his or her displeasure with the performance of the executive. Further, there is a good deal of evidence that chief executives can be used as scapegoats when there are policy failures for which ministers do not want to be accountable (Polidano 1997).

This model is, therefore, in practice not much different from the more conventional hierarchical model of ministries, except that there is an executive who may be held more personally accountable for the actions of the agency. The notion that the agency can be a truly autonomous actor, responsible only to its own collective leadership, is quite different from this essentially managerialist conception. This is true, despite the belief of the designers of the system that they were copying the Swedish model.

Ministry-agency structure III

The third version of the agency model can be found in the United States. Of course, the United States government does not have "ministries" per se, but the executive departments are in essence the same variety of organization. Within these cabinet departments there are a number of agencies, almost all of which have their own status in public law and each of which has some political status of its own, reflected in separate budget lines. The heads of the agencies also tend to be appointed independently by the President, albeit often with the advice of the relevant cabinet secretary, and hence these officials have their source of "clout" in the policy process. Thus, this model has some important similarities to the embedded ministries in Spain.

In addition to the agencies existing as components of departments, there are also a number of independent executive and regulatory agencies. In some ways, the regulatory agencies appear rather like the Swedish agency model in that they have a corporate structure with a number of commissioners, each appointed for long terms of office. These regulatory organizations were designed to remove the regulation of some significant aspects of economic and social life from direct political control. The desired autonomy, however, left them subject to capture by the very interests they were designed to regulate, so that this model has been brought into some disrepute. Also, it should be noted that for many "agencies" in the American system, the actual implementation is through sub-national government (as in the case of Germany), although there are some organizations (especially regulatory organizations) that have their own field staffs.

The extent of autonomy of these agencies varies. In some instances, e.g. the Federal Bureau of Investigation (FBI) within the Department of Justice, the agency may have more political power than its department, and hence have substantial autonomy. In other cases, e.g. the Occupational Safety and Health Administration within the Department of Labor, the agency may be scrutinized very closely – both by the cabinet secretary and by Congress – and have rather little autonomy. Most agencies fall between those two extremes, with the ability to act autonomously within a range of issues but also face substantial scrutiny from both the executive and the legislative branches of government, and to some extent also by the judiciary.

Although one of these patterns may be more or less typical of a country, there are also differences within countries, apparently based on the types of activities being performed and the structure of the policy problems being addressed. For example, even in the Scandinavian countries that tend to utilize a ministry-agency form of organization, foreign ministries tend to be structured more along hierarchical lines. Likewise, even when other forms of organizations tend to prevail, social programs often are organized more as agencies, or in some other autonomous format. It may be, therefore, that the differences among countries may not be as significant as differences among policy areas.

Autonomous and quasi-autonomous bodies (AQUAs)

In addition to the ministries and the organizations that are rather directly connected to them, there is a large, and indeed increasingly so, collection of other types of public bodies existing within the set of governments with which we are concerned. These organizations, as we have already demonstrated, may exist in a variety of relationships with the political authority manifested by ministers or their analogs. In addition, they have a variety of legal forms of organization. Those legal formats for public organizations can be classified in the following way, based on a descending order of proximity to the formal, legal authority of the State. Just as the previous classification of organizations addressed the relationship of component organizations to ministerial power, this classification is an additional means of understanding how the contemporary State is evolving in meeting political and administrative needs. For the sake of completeness, this classification begins with some elements included in the previous taxonomy, but will then proceed to discuss more autonomous formats. These variations in the status of organizations are outlined below.

Components of ministries

These organizations are hierarchically subordinate to the ministry and have no legal personality of their own. The government of the day can change these structures at will, and as the experiences of the United Kingdom demonstrate, often do (Pollitt 1984). These are organizations in the sense that they have a distribution of power and authority and also may enjoy some identification by their members, but certainly could not be considered institutionalized or in any way autonomous.

Independent, but within a ministry

These organizations may have a legal personality of their own, but yet are legally subordinated to a ministry and/or to its minister. An example would be the executive agency in the British use of that term, with the chief executive and the agency actually having rather little independence from the minister in policy and financial terms. Thus, as we have already noted, this format represents a misinterpretation of the Scandinavian model of agencies, albeit perhaps a necessary misinterpretation given some of the realities of British politics. That is, the Westminster model tends to emphasize the importance of ministerial responsibility even in the face of attempts to create autonomy and efficiency.

Legal entity, but within a ministry

The case of American agencies mentioned above is the archetype of this category. Many agencies have a status in public law so that they can not be dissolved at the whim of a cabinet secretary. At the same time, these entities are also subordinate for many purposes to the Department within which they are located and also are (relatively) easily moved from one Department to another. It should also be noted, however, that the American system is rather flexible and lacks internal uniformity so that there may be some entities called agencies that are indeed creatures of their Department rather than of Congressional action (see Peters and Hogwood 1991).

Legal entity, public law

This is an autonomous or semi-autonomous organization founded under public law. It may be in some way responsible to a ministry, or to the minister, but is not hierarchically subordinate and often will have its own governance structure. An example would be agencies in the Scandinavian meaning of the term. The agencies report to Parliament through the minister for some purposes but have their policy decisions determined largely by their own boards. Also, public corporations in some societies (especially the Anglo-American countries) are organized as public entities connected with a sponsoring ministry, through which the corporation must report to the Parliament. In addition, this organizational format has been employed for organizations that perform some public functions but for which governments do not want to be held directly responsible (see Seidman 1999). It may, however, not be as easy for governments to deny or ignore their responsibility, and the actions of nominally autonomous corporations have been great embarrassments to some governments.

Legal entity, private law

These entities are organized under private law yet perform public functions. These private-law organizations may exist in a variety of relationships of responsibility and control with their ministries, but in general each will also have their own, independent governance structures. Examples would be many public corporations organized outside the public law structure, not-for-profit organizations providing public services, and universities and many health care providers in a number of countries.

The logics for choosing this form of organization are not dissimilar to those for the previous category, but here the separation from government is even greater. That separation may, as in the case of the universities, be there to insure the freedom of these institutions to operate and to conduct unfettered research. Even when these organizations have been placed at a good arm's length from direct government control, responsibility may be difficult to avoid. For example, the privatization and breaking up of British Rail might have been thought to remove government involvement, but given that the railways are conceptualized as a public service, the government has had difficulty escaping some responsibility for the appalling safety record of railways. The French concept of *services publics* may indeed be important here as governments move functions out of their control (Cohen and Henry 1997). Governments may not be able to avoid ultimate responsibility for basic services that the public expects, regardless of how they are delivered (Christensen and Pallesen 2001). This is in part because here, as in so many cases in which government moves an organization or a function outside the public sector, it maintains some regulatory role and hence has some responsibility.

Sui generis organizations

The organizations already discussed generally exist within the executive branch. There are, however, organizations performing public functions that are meant to be almost entirely free from executive control (some central banks and regulatory organizations, for example), or are responsible to Parliament (audit organizations in many political systems), or which are quasi-judicial state entities responsible for regulating other structures within the public sector (example would be the *Conseil d'Etat* and analogous bodies in Spain, Italy, and Portugal). While many of the autonomous organizations to be included in this study are rather recent innovations, many of these *sui generis* organizations have been in (public) business for some time.

One of the most important variety of *sui generis* organizations is the "non-majoritarian" organization charged with major economic and regulatory activities (Majone 1996). These institutions are argued to be a viable mechanism for enhancing the governance capacity of contemporary states. That is, rather than enhancing political control, an alternative strategy has been to create organizations, e.g. the German Bundesbank, that gain their legitimacy from expertise and from their independence from political pressures, rather than from their connections to electoral political officials. In such an approach to governing, holding the organizations accountable must be weighed against their expertise and their capacity to act autonomously.

Additional dimensions of variation

The above classification of organizations is based on the legal basis of the their existence, but at least two other dimensions are relevant for understanding how these organizations fit into the overall structure of governing. These are the degree of managerial involvement of ministries and other political entities or officials, and the financial relationship of the organizations with government. The degree of managerial involvement is to some extent identified in the discussion above of the alternative patterns of structuring of ministries.

Clearly those organizations that remain as formal components of ministries are more likely to be influenced by the minister than are those organizations with a more autonomous connection to political authority. That simple classification constitutes a good beginning for examining the role of political authority in shaping policy decisions, but additional measures of the forms of direct intervention in the management of an organization by political authorities may be required. This may involve questions such as controls over personnel, purchasing, the opportunity to issue binding regulations, and a number of other issues of managerial autonomy that may influence the role of the "autonomous" organizations.

The financial dimension of control is also crucial for understanding how autonomous an organization may actually be in performing its activities. For example, some of the organizations we are examining are able to raise their own revenues through charging fees or even levying earmarked taxes. Those organizations are certainly much more autonomous than are those that must depend upon the sponsoring ministry for funds. Likewise, an agency that has its own budget is likely to be more autonomous than is one that depends upon the ministry for funds.

These three dimensions of autonomy (legal, managerial, and financial) do not necessarily covary so that an organization may, for example, be organized under private law yet be financially very dependent upon the public sector and also be subject to a good deal of managerial intervention by the ministry with which it works. Thus, we will need to be able to locate organizations in some three-dimensional autonomy space and discuss the implications of differing patterns of autonomy on their behavior, and on their success in reaching state policy and management objectives.

Activities

The autonomous and semi-autonomous organizations we have identified as existing in these democracies perform a variety of functions for those governments. The assumption has been that these organizations were almost exclusively implementation organizations, but in reality they perform a number of very different tasks. Certainly implementation organizations constitute a major portion of the organizations we can identify, but even within that category there are differences in the way in which implementation is to be achieved. We were able to identify seven major classes of activities, which are outlined below.

1. Implementation

The major activity of autonomous organizations in all the cases for which we have evidence is implementing public policy. The emphasis on implementation activities reflects the intentions of governments when creating agencies (in both the Swedish and British meanings of the term). Of course, in both cases (and certainly in the case of American agencies) there is also policy making that goes along with the implementation. That is, first implementation is itself often making policy de facto as decisions are made about which cases meet criteria and which do not. In addition, administrative agencies are often empowered to make policies that ramify the more broadly construed policies adopted by legislatures (Rosenbloom 2001; Page 2000). Even when the agencies are designed as implementation structures their close connection to the reality of service delivery means that they may well be involved in making secondary legislation.

Within this broad category of implementation there are, in turn, two major ways in which these organizations are used to put policy into effect.

A. DIRECT SERVICE DELIVERY

The first is direct service delivery, the usual understanding of implementation through agencies. Thus, the creation of Next Steps agencies in Britain was seen as a means of delivering the range of services that ministries had previously, but doing so with greater autonomy from political control. Likewise, the position of agencies in Scandinavia has been one of legal autonomy in making decisions about delivering the policies that are made by Parliament and the ministries. In some cases, such as the Netherlands, these implementing organizations were hived off almost entirely from government, requiring some subsequent reassertion of control.

This service-delivery role for agencies is especially evident for education, as the nominal independence of these organizations can be maintained even when they are funded by the State. Thus, universities, in particular, but also secondary schools in other countries such as Italy may be organized as autonomous organizations. Also, increasingly hospitals are being organized as quasi-autonomous organizations in part to impose some market discipline on their activities, but also to provide somewhat greater autonomy from direct control by government, and with that also some capacity of politicians to insulate themselves for too direct culpability when there are problems in the health care sector, as there almost invariably are in such a complex and expensive service.

B. TRANSFER OF FUNDS

The second approach to implementation using AQUA organization – the transfer of funds – can be observed frequently in implementing social policy and in intergovernmental relations. A separate entity may be created to make decisions about grants and contracts as a means of insulating these decisions from direct political control. For example, the rate support grant for local governments, and the support grants for universities, are managed through quasi-autonomous organizations in the United Kingdom. Again, this style of service delivery permits service providers to make many other decisions about the actual use of the funds, and also to match better services with local conditions. At the same time, this mode of implementation will only exacerbate problems of ministerial control (Kearns 1996).

2 Regulation

Autonomous organizations are also used to regulate the economy and society. In theory, these organization are particularly suitable for the regulatory function, given that they can be isolated from immediate, partisan political pressures, while simultaneously involving the interests affected by regulations in the process of making those regulations. This presumed strength may also be a weakness, given that the isolation from direct political control also isolates them from direct political support. On the one hand, this isolation presents the now familiar "capture" problem, in which the regulatory organizations become the servants of the very interests they were designed to regulate (Krause 1999).

This mode of autonomous organization for regulatory organizations also produces a problem of ensuring that the organization remains faithful to the original policy directives coming from the legislature. This is the equally familiar principal-agent problem, in which the legislature attempts to develop mechanisms for binding the agent (McCubbins, Noll, and Weingast 1987). In practice "regulatory creep" is often observed as the autonomous organizations begin to assert their own standards, rather than those adopted by the legislature. Therefore, the question for managing these organizations and indeed for managing any AQUA organization is to balance their autonomy with some faithfulness to the goals for which they were established.

In addition to the organizations regulating the economy and society, there is an increasing number of regulatory organizations that regulate within the public sector itself, e.g. inspectorates that monitor and control services such as education, prisons, and transportation (Hood *et al.* 1999). These organizations tend to be structured to control organizations that provide services to the public and which may themselves be tied directly to ministerial authority or perhaps to other more or less autonomous organizations. This is a very old activity of government, with independent auditors being present for centuries, and inspections in France going back at least to the Revolution. What is most important for these organizations is their increasing number and the extent to which they have become a central feature of public accountability in many governments.

3 Advice and policy development

Another of the principal purposes of semi-autonomous organizations is to offer advice to government, and to provide assistance in policy development. Organizations performing this function involve a variety of experts in society in making decisions, and exist in a variety of political relationships to the government of the day. These organizations are designed to help government pursue long-range goals for the society as a whole. Of course, there is a great deal of partisan policy advice being offered within ministries and to the government as a whole, but the idea of these more autonomous advisory organizations is to create more unbiased positions on major policy issues. These organizations must find some means of balancing conflicting policy advice.

One important example of an organization such as this is the Dutch Scientific Policy Council that provides the government with rather dispassionate advice about policy, and about the changing parameters of policies. Likewise, the Evaluation Council in France provides some more retrospective policy advice and evaluation for government from a (relatively) independent perspective. The list could be extended, but the most basic point is that organisations often attempt to assist government in making good policy.

4 Information

In addition to generation of policy advice, some autonomous and semi-autonomous organizations are also involved in the collection and dissemination of information. For example, a number of countries have moved their statistical services out of the mainline departments and moved them into this group of less directly politicized organizations. These organizations, to some extent, fall between the previous category (policy advice) and the following one of research. They are involved in doing research and in collecting research conducted by others. These organizations are also involved in advising government with the statistical information that they gather.

Part of the reason for moving these organizations out to their autonomous and quasi-autonomous status is that there is a desire to insulate the collection of these important data from direct political influences. Significant socio-economic data – unemployment, economic growth, poverty, criminality and the like – also have substantial political importance, so it may be crucial to maintain objectivity in its collection and dissemination. Also, governments increasingly are charging users outside the political system for these data, and those commercial activities are, everything else being equal, easier to manage in devolved organizations than in mainstream government organizations. The danger for this movement toward greater independence for statistical organizations, however, is that data become more private than public, and some crucial areas of concern for citizens and scholars become proprietary information.

5 Research

Governments also frequently attempt to place some distance between themselves and scientific research organizations, and to provide those organizations with as much latitude as possible to make autonomous decisions about what to research and how to do that research. This separation from control is considered desirable in order to ensure the independence and integrity of the findings, and to prevent the formation of some form of official science. Maintaining such separation is, of course, difficult given that governments ultimately control the money that will be spent through the organization and hence will influence, if not control, what sort of research will be done (even if they may not be able to control the outcomes).

The above having been said, governments do not always choose to hive off the research function as completely as they might be expected to do if the relative purity of the research process was to be maintained. One government (Denmark) has a ministry of research, and several other countries include the research function in a ministry of education or higher education. Further, most government departments are involved in funding substantial amounts of research, whether on contracts with a great deal of direct control or through grants with somewhat less control. It appears, however, that research may have become too central to economic and social development to allow it to be carried on without some involvement of political consideration.

6   Tribunals and public enquiries

There are also a number of public organizations serving in a quasi-judicial function, assessing the legality of actions within specific policy areas or investigating major policy questions. In almost all countries, the level of adjudication required for a modern welfare state to deal fairly with its citizens is of such a magnitude that it could never be carried on in the regular court system. Therefore, an array of quasi-judicial organizations are created to cope with the problem of deciding about the appropriate application of laws concerning social benefits, taxes, labor markets, and the rest of the array of government programs.

A special case of autonomous organizations performing quasi-judicial functions are the French *Conseil d'Etat* and its analogs in other countries (Massot and Girardot 1999). These organizations are in some ways regulatory, and perform some of the functions of internal regulation of government described above in relation to the United Kingdom. They also are, however, very much involved in legal activities of a wider sort, providing advice to other government organizations and checking on the legality of actions taken by public administration. These organizations sit at the cusp of regulatory and quasi-judicial organizations and are crucial elements of the legalistic style of administration in the "Napoleonic" countries.

Most of the quasi-judicial organizations described above are permanent, and handle thousands of cases on an annual basis, like, e.g. the U.S. Department of Veterans' Affairs (Mashaw 1985) There are also a number of temporary organizations established to manage shorter-term issues. For example, public enquiries in the United Kingdom are established to deal with events and issues that are difficult to manage through conventional political means. The detachment of those organizations from politics means that their decisions are likely to be considered more legitimate than if they were made through the conventional mechanisms. This is especially true when these enquiries consider major disasters or policy failures that a government might like to cover up. A political process absolving the government of blame might not be accepted, but the independent enquiry might.

7 Representation

Finally, autonomous and semi-autonomous organizations are employed as a means of providing representational and participatory opportunities for segments of the civil society. These organizations supplement the representation provided through conventional political institutions and tend to focus on particular segments of society. As an extreme example, the Sami Parliament is described as an affiliated organization of the Department of Local Government and Regional Development in Norway. These autonomous organizations may be utilized to provide broad public participation around specific policy questions, e.g. facility siting or to involve more fully various social groups, especially groups usually excluded from active involvement, in the public sector. Economic and social councils in France, Belgium, the Netherlands, and Norway, are examples of particularly well-institutionalized representative organizations. More recently, organizations attempting to include the homeless, refugees, or ethnic minorities more directly in making decisions that concern them demonstrate the possible range of representative organizations in the public sector.

While these representative organizations are generally well-intentioned, they also may be seen as, or indeed may become, cooptive or, even worse, may create inauthentic forms of participation that alienate rather than involve citizens. So, for example, representative organizations were created as components of urban renewal programs and Model Cities programs in the United States in the 1960s. The idea motivating these organizations was to involve poor minority group members in government and to provide an alternative means of participation in policies that influenced their lives. The organizations did provide means of access for some period of time, but eventually became means for social mobility for the leadership, leaving the neighborhoods from which they came in many ways worse off, and less represented, than before they were formed (see Moynihan 1969).

Intended and unintended consequences

As intimated above, the creation of more autonomous organizations within the public sector is expected to have political as well as managerial consequences for governments. The creation of both area and clientele based organizations, in the context of declining capacities for control over these organizations from their supervising ministries, may enhance their capacity to manage government programs, and may have the possibility of increasing the efficiency of the public sector. This mode of organization may, however, also open those organizations to greater political influence, with less capacity to resist interest groups or local communities. In many cases, the ministerial level of control will have been downgraded to an extent that it may not be able to protect the organization from the particularistic pressures. Thus, responsiveness may be substituted for accountability in the control of the disaggregated public organizations (Mulgan 2000; Peters 2000). We would hypothesize, however, that when the subministerial structure conforms more closely to the overall ministerial structures the capacity for control, and with it the capacity for resistance to clientele pressures, will be higher.

Another unintended consequence of the creation of these more autonomous organizations, especially those organized on the basis of purpose, is to require further organization from above to ensure their coordination and coherence. This coordination function was performed through the minister and cabinet in a more unified version of governing, but with the disaggregation of these systems, there is the need for creating additional structures and processes to ensure that (as much as possible) these organizations all pull in the same direction. Thus, somewhat paradoxically, the disaggregation of the public sector has tended to push power back into the hands of central agencies and chief executives who are the only possible loci of such control (Peters and Savoie 2001). Also, the more proliferated organizations are, the more coordination is required. More existing and new coordination instruments require also more coordination, which may strengthen central agencies (Bouckaert, Verhoest, and Wauters 2000).

The above is a rather extensive catalog of nominal variables and the possible codings of those variables. Having those several dimensions is (at least to us) interesting and important in itself, but becomes all the more so when these dimensions of autonomy and structural characteristics are combined to create a multi-dimensional matrix that can be used to characterize types of organizations. For example, we may find that agencies in the British sense of that term are characterized by apparent autonomy from ministerial control but little financial or legal autonomy, and hence are less likely to be effective in achieving some of the efficiency goals set out for them than other organizational formats. On the other hand, true quangos, again in the British sense, may have sufficient autonomy to achieve their operational goals but may pose other problems of governance, namely accountability and greater politicization.

Not only can we develop some multi-dimensional classifications of these organizations, but also we can gain some sense of the degree of autonomy of different organizations. Clearly, organizations that have higher degrees of autonomy on all the relevant dimensions we have discussed are likely to be more fully autonomous than are those that are lower on all dimensions. What we can not yet know, however, is if there are relative weights for the different dimensions, so that (as we might surmise) those organization that are legally more autonomous can *ceteris paribus* also find ways to be more autonomous in their general transactions with government. On the other hand, those organizations that are financially more independent may in effect be able to go into business for themselves and largely ignore what appear to be important legal constraints on their actions. These are, therefore, empirical questions that deserve to be investigated.

In addition, the type of activity being undertaken by an AQUA organization may also influence its autonomy and the type of relationship that it has with ministries. On the one hand, an organization charged with implementing a program for a ministry may have nominal autonomy but may find it difficult to gain such autonomy in practice. On the other hand, a quasi-judicial organization is likely to be granted a great deal of autonomy, simply because of its tasks (and the composition of its personnel). Thus, all the dimensions which we have discussed should be considered when attempting to profile these organizations.

Next steps

To fully answer the question of how the trend toward agentification and quangocratization fits into the larger pattern of structural change in the public sector, organizations require enlarged and internationally comparative datasets over time according to the above suggested formats. One best practice single case is Norway, with a data set from 1947 till present and descriptions of organizational events per unit. Additional data on dimensions of autonomy, on managerial capacity, and on performance and results would allow for further causal modelling. This would allow a static, comparative static and dynamic analysis of embedded structures and their (coordinated) functioning in policy fields.

Conclusion

To this point, we have begged perhaps the crucial question in the entire research project. Why does a government, or why should a government, adopt the AQUA style of delivering a service to the public, rather than more conventional means through ministerial hierarchies? The autonomous and quasi-autonomous organizations we have been discussing may perform functions that in other settings are performed by ministries. For example, economic regulation may be performed by ministries (Competition Division, Industry Canada) or it may be performed by autonomous organization (Monopolies and Mergers Commission). On what bases can such choices be reasonably made?

One basis for this institutional choice may be the search for efficiency, with the assumption that moving government functions away from the typical "bureaucratic" form of administration and service provision will make these operations more effective and more efficient. As already noted, the ideology of many advocates of New Public Management, and therefore of many advocates of the movement toward the agency model for structure, is that removing implementation of programs from more directly political organizations will permit them to make decisions based on economy and efficiency criteria, rather than political criteria. Any efficiency improvements that are made may be purchased at the cost of some substantial loss of accountability and the use of scapegoats in the place of more genuine accountability mechanisms (Polidano 1997), but from a strictly managerial viewpoint this may be a good trade-off.

There may also be strictly political reasons to transfer functions away from the conventional ministerial hierarchies in government. In particular, organizations and activities that are difficult to manage, and therefore are potentially embarrassing to the governments, can be moved into quasi-autonomous status to create "plausible deniability" for the government if anything should go amiss in a program. Also, somewhat paradoxically, moving a program into a quasi-autonomous status may in some cases enable government to impose even more direct political control over that program, given the capacity to appoint the leadership of the organization (Skelcher 1997).

It is obvious that governments around the world have been adopting the more devolved framework for governing with great alacrity, but is this more than fad and fashion? Are there sufficient advantages of efficiency and effectiveness that can justify some of the problems of accountability and excessive discretion and loss of policy focus that may plague these groups? This is a difficult question, given that there may be as many answers as there are governments, or perhaps as many answers as there are autonomous organizations, but there is a need for governments (and more detached analysts) to consider the contributions that this organizational format may make to achieving the multiple and often competing goals of public management.

This chapter has been quite consciously and deliberately a preliminary exploration of a complex but yet crucial area of analysis for public management. As we noted at the beginning of the chapter, the study of these organizations is filled with a number of assumptions, most of which appear to be incorrect, or at best partial truths. Further, to the extent there is a single "dependent variable" it is the degree of autonomy, and the source of autonomy, for these organizations. Then, once we know the extent to which organizations are able to act autonomously we can begin to look at the question of what difference it makes for them, for the management of the public sector as a whole, and for citizens who are the ultimate recipients of their programs.

Notes

1 Although seemingly clear, many structures in the public sector may not have the characteristics that may be thought to be necessary for the existence of a formal organization. For example, some may have no permanent staff. See Peters and Hogwood (1991).
2 This argument would not be dissimilar to the capture argument familiar in the study of public organizations in the United States, especially the independent regulatory agencies that have little connection to political institutions and, therefore, are often excessively cozy with the very interest groups they are designed to regulate.
3 In fairness, Canada had for some time an organizational form, the Crown Corporation, that had many of the same properties of the organizations that have become the central focus of this literature and, interestingly, the Canadian government has been tending to reduce rather than to increase their number and importance.
4 Again, this would be true in other systems having some of the same intellectual tradition in public administration. See Seidman (1999).
5 Some organizations have been created through executive order of the President, and a few through orders of a Cabinet Secretary. Even in those cases, some formal action in law would be required to alter their existence and standing.

Bibliography

Alba, C. (2001) "Ministers and politicians in Spain," in Peters, B.G. and Pierre, J. (eds) *Politicians and Administrators in the Process of Administrative Reform*, London: Routledge.
Bouckaert, G., Verhoest, K. and Wauters, A. (2000) *Van Effectiviteit van Coördinatie naar Coördinatie van Effectiviteit* (From Effectiveness of Co-ordination to Co-ordination of Effectiveness), Brugge: Die Keure.
Bouckaert, G., Ormond, D. and Peters, B.G. (2000) *A Governance Agenda for Finland*, Helsinki: Ministry of Finance.
Bovens, M.A.P., 't Hart, P. and Peters, B.G. (2001) *Success and Failure in Public Governance*, Cheltenham: Edward Elgar.
Christensen, J.G. and Pallesen, T. (2001) "Providing public services: alternatives to public employment," Paper delivered at Conference of Comparative Public Service Project, Glasgow, Scotland, March 8–11.
Cohen, E. and Henry, C. (1997) *Service public, secteur public*, Paris: Documentation Française.
Darbel, A. and Schnapper, D. (1978) *Le système administratif*, Paris: Mouton.
Freeman, G. (1985) "National styles and policy sectors: explaining structured variation," *Journal of Public Policy* 5, 467–96.
Gulick, L. (1937) "Notes on the theory of organization," in Gulick, L. and Urwick, L.F. (eds) *Papers on the Science of Administration*, New York: Institute of Public Administration.

Hague, D.C., McKenzie, W.J.M. and Barker, A.P. (1975) *Public Policy and Private Interests: The Institutions of Compromise*, New York: Holmes and Meier.

Hood, C., Scott, C., James, O., Jones, G. and Travers, T. (1999) *Regulating Inside Government*, Oxford: Oxford University Press.

Jerome-Forget, M., White, J. and Wiener, J.M. (1995) *Health Care Reform Through Internal Markets*, Montreal: Institute for Research on Public Policy.

Kararup, A.S. (1999) "The agency model in the Danish Ministry of Education," Seminar Paper, Institute of Political Science, University of Aarhus.

Kearns, K. (1996) *Accountability in Non-Profit Organizations*, San Francisco: Jossey-Bass.

Krause, G.A. (1999) *A Two-Way Street: The Institutional Dynamics of the Modern Administrative State*, Pittsburgh: University of Pittsburgh Press.

Majone, G. (1996) *Temporal Consistency and Policy Credibility: Why Democracies Need Non-Majoritarian Institutions*, Florence: Robert Schuman Centre, European University Institute.

Marshall, G. (1999) *Ministerial Responsibility*, Oxford: Oxford University Press.

Mashaw, J.L (1985) *Due Process in the Administrative State*, New Haven, CT: Yale University Press.

Massot, J. and Girardot, T. (1999) *Le Conseil d'Etat*, Paris: Documentation française.

McCubbins, M., Noll, R. and Weingast, B.R. (1987) "Structure and process politics and policy: administrative arrangements and the political control of agencies," *Virginia Law Review* 75, 431–99.

Moynihan, D.P. (1969) *Maximum Feasible Misunderstanding: Community Action in the War on Poverty*, New York: Free Press.

Mulgan, R. (2000) "Accountability: an ever-expanding concept?," *Public Administration* 78, 555–73.

Page, E.C. (2000) *Government by the Numbers*, Oxford: Hart.

Peters, B.G. (1996) *The Future of Governing: Four Emerging Models*, Lawrence: University of Kansas Press.

Peters, B.G. (2000) "Is democracy a substitute for ethics?," in Chapman, R.A. (ed.) *Ethics for the Public Service in a New Millennium*, Aldershot: Ashgate.

Peters, B.G. and Hogwood, B.W. (1991) "Births, deaths and marriages: population ecology models of public organizations," in Perry, J. (ed.) *Research in Public Administration*, Greenwich, CT: JAI Press.

Peters, B.G. and Savoie, D.J. (2001) "Central agencies: the buckle of government," unpublished manuscript, Department of Political Science, University of Pittsburgh.

Polidano, C. (1997) "The bureaucrat who fell under a bus: ministerial responsibility, executive agencies and the Derek Lewis affair in Britain," *Governance* 12, 201–31.

Pollitt, C. (1984) *Changes in the Machinery of Government*, London: George Allen & Unwin.

Rosenbloom, D. (2001) *Building a Legislative-Centered Public Administration*, Chicago: University of Chicago Press.

Sartori, G. (1971) "Concept Misformation in Comparative Politics," *American Political Science Review* 64, 1033–53.

Seidman, H. (1999) *Politics, Power and Position*, 5th edn. New York: Oxford University Press.

Skelcher, C. (1997) *The Appointed State: Quasi-Governmental Organizations and Democracy*, Buckingham: Open University Press.

Verhoest, K. (2001) "Control by inputs, results or markets?," Paper presented at the Netherlands Institute of Government Conference, Twente, The Netherlands.

Woodhouse, D. (1997) *In Pursuit of Good Administration: Ministers, Civil Servants and Judges*, Oxford: Clarendon Press.

Part II

Agencies, quangos and contracts in the heartlands of the New Public Management

3 Adapting the agency concept
Variations within 'Next Steps'

Francesca Gains

Introduction

As chapter one outlines, the establishment of 'Next Steps' agencies is an idea that has been widely diffused and some form of the agency concept operates in many anglophone and non-anglophone countries. Yet, despite the popularity and simplicity of the agency idea, the implementation and operation of the agency concept appears to differ markedly both within and across countries. This raises theoretical questions about how new governance arrangements are transmitted and introduced. It is also of empirical interest for those in the public sector charged with understanding and implementing changes of this nature.

The development of agencies in the UK is often described as representing a move from traditional constitutional arrangements to a quasi-contractual or marketized arrangement (Harden 1992; Greer 1994; Lewis 1993). But these portrayals of the agency concept as representing 'New Public Management' (NPM) displacing traditional constitutional arrangements fail to capture diversity in the operation of the agency concept across government. Instead, this chapter suggests insights from the literature on historical institutionalism and particularly the concept of path dependency can be used to explore how the idea of agencification and, consequently, implementation varies greatly even within one country.

Historical institutionalists point to the way in which pre-existing institutional arrangements in a state or policy sector can constrain the introduction of policy change. Institutional arrangements stem from the formal constitution and organization of governance and also from the 'world view' or informal understandings of state actors. Thus theorists like Hall (1993) see the path dependency of institutional arrangements as explaining why the same forces for change impact differentially. Hall suggests institutions are "one of the control factors pushing historical development along a set of paths" (1996: 941). This tendency for policy change to be path dependent does not deny the possibility for exogenous or endogenous pressure for change to result in a new path. However, a change to a new path is difficult because of the costs of change (Pierson 2000) and because "institutions are resistant to redesign ultimately because they structure the very choices about reform that an individual is likely to make" (Hall 1996: 940). Pierson warns of the danger of using the concept of path dependence loosely and advocates that researchers must be clear and consistent in their usage of the concept (2000: 252).

This chapter looks at the introduction of the agency concept in the UK and the development of operating arrangements in the Department of Trade and Industry (DTI), Department of Social Security (DSS) and the Home Office. Here it is argued there was path dependency in the adaptation of the agency concept in the UK as change was mediated through the existing constitutional and organizational arrangements and the policy preferences of actors involved. Across government, the set of ideas, which came to be associated with the UK's agency policy, involved a marrying of new principal-agent and traditional constitutional concepts. Agencification led to the introduction of new rules and norms of behaviour developing alongside existing formal and informal rules. At departmental level, path dependency in decision making about what was appropriate and possible to move to agency status and how each agency should operate led to further adaptation of the agency concept. Thus, ultimately the extent to which each department agency relationship reflected a 'marketized' or a 'constitutional' relationship and ultimately the extent of tension caused by operation of the new rules of the game varied widely within Government. Although this empirical work solely examines the UK experience, it is suggested that an understanding of the operation of path dependency in the interpretation and introduction of the idea of agencification is illuminating in explaining the diffusion of new governance arrangements whatever the institutional starting point or exogenous and endogenous pressures for change. The analysis here offers insights of relevance to policy makers and implementers seeking to design, implement or operate in changing governance frameworks.

Background to UK agencification

The suggestion to introduce agencies into the UK Government came in a report to the Prime Minister from the Efficiency Unit reporting on the 'Next Steps' in improving management in government (known as the 'Ibbs Report') (Efficiency Unit 1988). It recommended that "agencies should be established to carry out the executive functions of Government within a policy and resources framework set by a Department" (Efficiency Unit 1988: 2) and this was accepted by the Prime Minister when presenting the report to Parliament (Hennessy 1989: 621). Under the new arrangements, ministers (guided by their permanent secretaries) would be responsible for making and setting the policy framework and would remain accountable to Parliament. Departments, in addition to their traditional policy role, would gain new responsibilities in setting and overseeing the policy and resource framework. Agencies would be headed by chief executives on a fixed-term contract, possibly recruited from outside the civil service, with a higher profile and personal responsibility for achieving results within the framework set (Goldsworthy 1991; Greer 1994). Famously, Sir Peter Kemp, the first head of the central 'Next Steps' Unit described the new arrangements as representing a "move from management by command to one of management by contract" (Kemp 1990: 28). The development of agencies in the UK civil service is extensive. Within ten years over three quarters of civil servants worked in agencies (Hansard, Written Parliamentary Answer, 18 June 1997, col 161). Agencification has undoubtedly led to a transformation in the operation of central government; however, the scale of the overall picture conceals a very differentiated picture of change in the way in which the new governance arrangements, and therefore the relationships they establish, operate (Gains 2000). This diversity is not clearly acknowledged in most of the literature on the UK experience of agencification.

Much of the literature draws on descriptive and prescriptive models of how agencification should work. These are then used to provide normative standards against which to judge the changes which agencies have made or are thought to have made. Thus, the politics and public administration literature assessed the change by how far it deviated from traditional constitutional practices (Davis and Wilman 1991; Plowden 1994; Giddings 1995; O'Toole and Jordan 1995; Pyper 1995; Wilson and Barker 1995; Theakston 1995). The more managerialist literature looked at the deviation of the agency concept from the kind of private sector models which influenced it (Efficiency Unit 1991; Brooks and Bate 1994; Horton and Jones 1996; Davis 1994; Public Service Committee 1996: 124, 130).

There are a few studies that seek to account for and typologize the differences between agencies (Efficiency Unit 1991; Trosa 1994; Greer 1994; James 1995; Massey 1995; Talbot 1995). These accounts highlight functional differences that clearly have a big impact on, for example, the degree of financial delegation. However, there are big differences in the way agencies with similar functions were established in different departments, which suggests that a functional typology does not tell the whole story. This chapter also suggests that a differentiated picture exists across government (Gains 1999; Gains 2000). The extent to which 'constitutional' or a 'marketized' arrangements and relationships are found varies. This variation stems, in part, from differing perceptions of the agency concept from the outset. The next section of the chapter will explore how the idea of path dependency in the adaptation of the agency idea contributes to an understanding of the differential implementation of the agency concept.

New institutionalism, historical institutionalism and path dependency

March and Olsen, in first articulating the need for new institutionalist analyses in political theory, sought to draw attention to a more state centric understanding and awareness that "the organisation of political life makes a difference" (March and Olsen 1984). 'New institutionalist' approaches are said to be differentiated from older variants by being less descriptive, having a concern to theorize and by looking beyond the formal, legal and constitutional rules to an acceptance of the importance of informal arrangements (March and Olsen 1984; Rhodes 1995; Lowndes 1996; Peters 1999). Discernible variants of 'new institutionalism' are identifiable and this chapter draws on Hall and Taylor's explanation of 'historical institutionalism' operating with a cultural approach to agency (Hall and Taylor 1996: 939). This encompasses Peter's normative and historical variants, acknowledging the alignment between the two (Peters 1999: 145).

Historical institutionalists emphasize the institutional influences on political and policy phenomena (Peters 1999). Institutional arrangements arise both from the formal constitutional and organizational set-up, which determines roles, rules and the allocation of institutional resources, and from informal understandings that structure, influence and guide behaviour and policy outcomes. The existing formal and informal institutional arrangements provide opportunities to facilitate change, and form constraints on change, in response to exogenous and endogenous factors. (Hall and Taylor 1996; Evans, Rueschemeyer and Skocpol 1985; March and Olsen 1984). 'Path dependency' is discernible in the nature and degree of change for two reasons. First, as change is mediated through the existing constitutional and organizational arrangements or 'state capacity', the existing decision-making procedures and organization of resources acts to militate against or facilitate new procedures or the reorganization of resources (Cortell and Peterson 1999). Second, as the introduction or response to change may reflect policy legacies, or the operation of policy paradigms, within which policy makers operate (Weir and Skocpol 1985; Hall 1993). Change often follows a 'critical juncture' but can involve incremental change (Hall 1993; Cortell and Peterson 1999). Recent studies of change in central government have drawn on this body of work (Richards and Smith 1997; Bulmer and Burch 1998; Newman *et al.* 1998).

Taking a historical institutionalist perspective suggests the following analysis. The institutional arrangements pre-agency, often described as 'management by command', led to close informal networks such as identified by Heclo and Wildavsky's famous study of the Whitehall Village (Heclo and Wildavsky 1981). The community of political administrators operated under the 'Whitehall model' with the attendant formal and informal rules and beliefs, which structured their actions and decisions. These included acknowledgement of parliamentary sovereignty, most particularly exercised through the doctrine of ministerial responsibility, an organizational culture based around the Haldane principles and uniformity across the service, and (in some cases) an organizational structure based around hierarchical, pyramidal departments. The roles of politicians and administrators, the institutional rules and appropriate behaviour was understood and shared by all parties (Judge 1993; Wilson and Barker 1995; Theakston 1995; Barberis 1995; Dowding 1995; Smith 1999).

Change to these institutional arrangements came in response to both exogenous and endogenous factors, including economic and ideological pressures for change and from political and managerial critiques of the 'Whitehall model' (Cmnd 3638 1968; Cmnd 8616 1982; Greer 1994; Pollitt *et al.* 2001). The agency concept introduced a policy operational split, which was formalized organizationally and supported by changed accountability, financial and personal arrangements. There has clearly been a change in the formal and informal institutional governance arrangements. Crucially, however, these arrangements reflect path dependency in their development. The next section of the chapter will examine how path dependency is seen in the introduction of the agency concept across government and then move on to look at dissemination at department level.

Path dependency in the development of the 'Next Steps' concept

The original Ibbs Report, completed in March 1987, was said to have proposed a more extensive devolution of finance and personnel functions and a change in constitutional practice to move away from the doctrine of ministerial responsibility (Hennessy 1989). These recommendations led to resistance from the ministers, the Treasury, and departments. The final report was not presented to Parliament until nearly a year later – in the interim the recommendations of the original report had been subject to delay, intense negotiation and change.

Burch and Holliday argue that the 'Next Steps' policy was driven by a small number of officials at the centre, backed by the endorsement of the Prime Minister (1996: 230). However, ministers, including the Prime Minister, were unhappy at the accountability changes (Hennessy 1989: 621; Zifcak 1994: 72). These concerns led to protracted and difficult negotiation leading Zifcak to suggest the policy process was politically driven (Zifcak 1994: 72). At a press conference after the presentation of the Ibbs Report to Parliament, it was made clear that the idea of setting up 'Next Steps' agencies to operate at arm's length would not alter the doctrine of ministerial responsibility (Hennessy 1989: 621). Accountability through ministerial responsibility would remain unchanged, but would be buttressed through a 'conventional understanding' that chief executives would have delegated authority from their ministers for agency operations (Efficiency Unit 1988: Annex A). The decision to go for an administrative and not a legal basis for the establishment of agencies reflected the UK's history of a non-statutory basis for Whitehall organizations (Harden 1992).

The Treasury and departments also had a strong influence in the details of the arrangements for financing and accountability. The Treasury were alarmed at the potential impact of devolution on public finances and negotiated the right to scrutinize candidates and be involved in establishing the policy and resources framework (Zifcak 1994: 82; Metcalf and Richards 1990; Chapman 1997). Departments perceiving the 'Next Steps' agenda to be tied up with cutting the size of the civil service pushed for the 'Next Steps' project to be about management improvement and not fundamental structural change to the shape of the civil service (Zifcak 1994: 71).

The multiple parentage of the policy as it developed reflects the complex bargaining which took place. The collection of ideas that came to be presented as the 'Next Steps' concept can be seen to reflect the debates and compromises during this gestation period. These ideas were sometimes contradictory. They included the appointment of a chief executive figurehead having clear oversight over an area of work, but with limited financial delegation, the proposal that departments were to maintain their role in advising ministers, yet were to develop new roles in managing operations at arm's length, and also the requirement of a policy operations split and yet the continuation of ministerial responsibility. New formal and informal institutional arrangements were grafted on to existing formal and informal practices. The 'idea' of the 'Next Steps' agencies reflected path dependency in its development partly arising from the existing state capacity. The role of departments and the Treasury in implementing the centre's policy led to negotiation and compromise. Path dependency was also reflected in the maintenance of policy preferences, firstly in the decision to take a non-legal path for establishing agencies, and secondly in the informal understandings about the nature of accountability held by ministers and officials. The Government's 'Next Steps' policy was ambiguous and permitted vastly different interpretations of the extent of managerial freedom and the meaning of accountability to flourish. Ambiguity, dynamism and compromise continued as agencies were established in departments. The next section of the chapter turns to examining how the 'Next Steps' idea was rolled out to departments.

Disseminating the 'Next Steps' concept to departments

The agency concept was not enshrined in legislation or placed on any statutory footing. The 'idea' of 'Next Steps' was not a shared vocabulary or creed and represented a compromise which 'papered over' substantially different approaches in the 'mind-set' of actors in different structural positions. This ambiguity was essential, allowing institutional actors to seek to fulfil their own wishes through its framework. To some extent, this ambiguity was deliberate. One official involved with negotiations at the start suggested, "either agencies could have been simply within the public sector, doing it better, which is what we said with one side of our mouth you might say. The other side of the mouth said 'there it is – packaging it for privatization'" (interview with former member of the 'Next Steps' team). One official involved in the early days reflected, "one of the great things going for 'Next Steps' was there wasn't much written down about it. There was just the original report and the PM's statement . . . thank goodness we didn't have to do any legal stuff really because we'd never have made it" (interview with former 'Next Steps' Team official).

The force for change was encouraged by the commitment of the Prime Minister and Head of the Civil Service to 'Next Steps', which provided strong incentives for co-operation. The appointment of Peter Kemp to oversee the project and drive it forward under the authority of the Prime Minister and the Head of the Civil Service was a deliberate attempt to provide the project with coherence and momentum. Kemp headed a small 'Next Steps' team whose role was to liaise with departments to assist with the establishment of agencies and drawing up of framework documents (Treasury and Civil Service Committee (TCSC) 1990). The 'Next Steps' team held a far more devolutionary approach towards the establishment of agencies than either the Treasury or most departments. They were concerned with wrenching control over routine management tasks, like pay and personnel, away from the centre and passing it to operational units, "to some extent, with the people who were keen to become agencies, we were sort of like liberators" (member of the 'Next Steps' Team). Their task involved battling with departments that were reluctant to engage with the idea of 'Next Steps'; "you had to identify friends . . . you identified friends, people on your side and you spent an awful lot of time going to meetings with permanent secretaries and things like that to push it along, trying to cash in on the strength which was at the back of you all which was Mrs Thatcher" (Interview with Kemp 1997).

To help with implementation, several project groups were established "to foster support for and a sense of purpose about 'Next Steps' at senior level" (Goldsworthy 1991: 22). However, one participant recalled the meetings as "dreadful, absolutely unspeakable, nightmarish . . . to some extent we swapped ideas on where we were at, but each agency at that stage was pretty much *sui generis* and there was a limit for which exchanged information was useful, they were totally formless and they really added no value at all". This really reflects the great antipathy towards the agency concept held by departments. An official in the 'Next Steps' team involved in the early days said, "departments were fairly

hostile to the whole concept, a lot of them thought 'this'll go away'".
There were several problems for departments in adopting a 'Next Steps'
approach, the fundamental change of role expected at the centre of
department, the focus on management skills with an expectation that
high fliers would have to do a spell in agencies and the idea that departments would have to 'stand back' from the operational details and leave
'managers free to manage'. This was problematic for civil servants who
were used to smoothing policy problems and who would have to continue
to operate under the system of ministerial responsibility. One deputy
secretary explained "departments can never resist meddling, partly
because ministers can't keep their hands out of it when things go pear-
shaped politically" (interview with former Deputy Secretary). For departments, the delegation involved in establishing agencies was very
threatening in terms of the control they exerted over resources: "it took a
certain amount of power away from the central departments which they
didn't welcome because a large part of their budgets were no longer
under their control" (interview with agency chief executive).

A key imperative in the implementation of agencies in departments was
momentum and this lent an urgency to negotiations. "The opposition we
had from permanent secretaries, from some ministers, from people down
in the machine was fantastic and the only way to do it was to crash at it
very very hard" (Interview with Kemp 1997). Another 'Next Steps' Team
member explained, "it wasn't a project for faint hearts ... there weren't
many prisoners taken in a sort of Whitehall way in the early meetings –
trying to persuade people to do things".

Acting against the unifying, though ambiguous, vision of the 'Next
Steps' idea was a pressure for results which led to considerable flexibility
in the arrangements – or 'rules of the game' – made for different agencies. Some of these differences are reflected in the formal arrangements
set out in the framework documents. Table 3.1 provides a summary of the
key features of selected agencies in the three departments. The agreements had a superficial similarity in covering the same areas working from
a central template (Greer 1992). They also contained, however, differing
governance arrangements. Further differences were apparent in more
informal 'standard operating arrangements'. There was room for considerable compromise and customization, "depending upon the personalities
in the 'Next Steps' team and the desk officer in charge, some of this
would have been resisted more fiercely ... and it's probably true to say
there wasn't a unified approach" (interview with former 'Next Steps' team
official). Consequently, there were enormous differences in the way
departments responded. The introduction of the agency concept into
departments was also path dependent upon the existing institutional
arrangements – the existing state capacities, in part, reflecting functional
differences (Hogwood 1993) – and the perceptions and policy preferences
of those involved. The next section of the chapter examines the adaptation

Table 3.1 Roles, responsibilities and governance arrangements in framework documents in selected DTI, DSS and Home Office agencies

Agency start date and dept.	Role of ministers	Role of chief executive	Role of departmental officials	Agency involvement in policy
Companies House (October 1988) DTI	Determine policy framework – not involved in day-to-day management.	Accountable to and reports to line manager and Steering Board, asked from time to time to report to ministers.	Link with Department via responsible line manager who will monitor and report to Ministers on performance of agency. Permanent Secretary is Accounting Officer.	Expected to contribute to development of departmental policy on subjects relevant to the activities of Companies House and on operational and management activities.
LGC (October 1989) DTI	Determine Policy – not normally involved in day-to-day activities.	Accountable to Ministers, asked to report regularly to Ministers, designated Agency Accounting Officer, reports to Chief Engineer and Scientist.	Link with Department via Chief Engineer and Scientist assisted by steering board, will advise Ministers on performance. Permanent Secretary is Accounting Officer.	ACE to report on Agency's place within departmental policy.
Insolvency Service (April 1990) DTI	Answer to Parliament on policy governing IS – not normally involved in day-to-day management.	Accountable to and reports to DTI Ministers, and to Steering Board, designated Agency Accounting Officer.	Permanent Secretary is Accounting Officer, link with DTI through Deputy Secretary who is assisted by Steering Board.	By introducing and developing a more pro-active approach to policy, to provide advice to Ministers on policy issues reflecting the changing economic needs of society.
Forensic Science Service (April 1991)	Secretary of State answers to Parliament for FSS. Not normally involved in day-to-day management. Advised	Director General of FSS is Chief Executive with delegated personal responsibility for managing	Deputy Secretary for Police advises Ministers assisted by an Advisory Board which Director General will attend.	Advice will be provided from the Agency as part of the Department in the usual way.

Table 3.1 continued

Agency start date and dept.	Role of ministers	Role of chief executive	Role of departmental officials	Agency involvement in policy
Home Office	by Home Office Deputy Secretary for Police on overall matters affecting policy for FSS and the performance of the Director General.	FSS effectively and efficiently and to meet targets. Director General is Agency Accounting Officer. Accountable to the Secretary of State.	Permanent Secretary is Accounting Officer.	
Prison Service (April 1993) Home Office	Home Secretary is accountable to Parliament for PS and allocates resources. Will not normally become involved in the day-to-day management of the PS, will expect to be consulted and receive reports from the Director General on handling of operational matters which could give rise to grave public or parliamentary concern.	Responsible for day-to-day management and is also the Home Secretary's principal policy adviser on matters relating to the Prison Service. The Director General is directly accountable to the Home Secretary for the Prison Service performance and operations. The DG is additional Accounting Officer.	Permanent Secretary is the principal adviser to the Home Secretary on matters affecting the Home Office as a whole and advising on the Prison Service's plans, targets and performance. Permanent Secretary is Principal Accounting Officer.	DG is Home Secretary's principal policy adviser on matters relating to the Prison Service.
Benefits Agency (April 1991) DSS	Secretary of State defines scope of Agency's activities, sets targets, resources, agrees its strategies, objectives and annual business plan.	Chief Executive has full authority delegated from Secretary of State for managing Agency in its day-to-day operations, is Secretary of State's principal	Permanent Secretary is principal adviser to the Secretary of State on matters affecting the management of the Department as a whole, also	ACE has personal access to the Secretary of State following consultation with the Permanent Secretary on issues affecting his responsibilities, will

		adviser on operational functions, provides reports for the Permanent Secretary, is Agency Accounting Officer.	responsible for advising Secretary of State about Agency and monitoring on his behalf.	participate in any discussions including policy proposals and is consulted by the Permanent Secretary before any proposals bearing on work of Agency put to Secretary of State. Contributes to Department's policy development providing operational info can make policy proposals designed to improve effectiveness with which Agency meets its objectives, after consulting with Permanent Secretary.
Child Support Agency (April 1993) DSS	Secretary of State defines scope of Agency's activities, agrees strategies, objectives and business plan and sets targets and resources.	Delegated authority from Secretary of State for managing operations, principal adviser on these matters, responsible for meeting targets, standards and objectives within resources. Agency Accounting Officer. Provides regular reports for the Permanent Secretary and information for Secretary of State.	Principal Adviser to the Secretary of State on DSS as a whole, responsible as Principal Accounting Officer, monitors and advises Secretary of State on performance of Chief Executive and Agency.	Chief Executive provides information required by the Secretary of State or Permanent Secretary for policy development and evaluation and for other purposes.

and customization of the already ambiguous agency concept in three departments.

Department of Trade and Industry

The DTI was established in a merger between the former separate Trade and Industry Departments and is perceived as being the department closest to the business world. Despite the initial reluctance of its Permanent Secretary, the DTI was keen to develop agencification in the Department. The DTI's response was coordinated though the Department's Finance and Personnel Section in February 1988. One official involved in preparing for the response explained:

> I hadn't particularly heard of this until suddenly, I think in February it became obvious that Government, driven from No 10, were going to activate it. So we very rapidly got to work on it ... and we went through the DTI functional directory and said that's a potential agency, that isn't, one afternoon, wrote them out on the back of the envelope if you like. And we presented the list to Ministers within a day or so and they said "Yes we're happy to go along with that" and I believe that every single one of those, either became an agency or was something similar.

Companies House was top of the DTI's list and became the second agency to be launched. It had clear executive responsibilities and a geographical base outside London, making it very suitable for agency status. The other activities identified were also those with a low policy content. The Department felt it was able to move quickly because it could benefit from previous hard work on the Financial Management Initiative (FMI). They had "the systems in place and had got clearly and quite well-defined objectives for most of the operations, and targets, and so it wasn't a huge step, it was literally a 'Next Steps' to turn them into agencies and give them more executive responsibility and public targets and the like" (senior official in DTI).

By 1991/92 the DTI had ten agencies with over 50 per cent of the Department's staff working in agencies. These included laboratories, regulatory agencies and one providing internal services. Despite this apparently early readiness to move down the 'Next Steps' path, there were differences of approach between the DTI and the 'Next Steps' Unit, reflecting the ambivalence outlined earlier. The DTI wanted more control over its agencies than the 'Next Steps' Unit thought appropriate.

In particular, the DTI had a house style for the governance arrangements of its agencies set out in the framework documents (see Table 3.1) each of which had a steering board chaired by the line manager in the department, usually the Deputy Secretary of the appropriate Division. The

Steering Boards also had one or two representatives of the finance division and one or two people with a policy interest in the relevant operational area from the DTI and one or two outsiders. This arrangement permitted a degree of close control and supervision. One official explained:

> We felt . . . that we had to have control, we had to decide what targets to set and we had to know enough about it, et cetera and . . . although we could have an arms-length relationship, it was not – we weren't going to put a blind screen down between us and it. And I don't think that any private sector company will do the same with a subsidiary. I mean we were following a model of parent company subsidiary although I don't think we ever expressed it in those terms but I think that was what we've set up (senior official in DTI).

This very direct and controlling role for the department led a former official in the 'Next Steps' team to express the feeling that "some of us here never found the DTI to be a particularly 'Next Steps' friendly department. It has always been a very centralist department . . . I think the chief executives, although they would tell you otherwise, have always had less latitude to do what they want than they might have had in some other departments".

The DTI's adaptation of the 'Next Steps' idea reflects path dependency arising from the existing state capacity, both in the fact that the Department could move quickly due to its experience in operating the FMI and because of the nature of the functions under its remit, which lent themselves to 'arms-length' management. Path dependency is also reflected in the policy preferences or cultural norms of officials in the Department. When established, from the historically distinct cultures of the former separate Trade and Industry Departments, it was said to have combined both a strong free trade and an interventionist ethos respectively (Richards and Smith 1997: 8; interviews with officials). Both of these aspects are apparent in its response to the agency concept and ultimately in its agency dealings and give the DTI's relationships with its agencies a distinct set of formal and informal rules. Its interventionist ethos led it to have a centralizing tendency towards its agencies. At the same time its close contact with the private sector meant the DTI was more familiar with private sector management models than most other departments.

Department of Social Security

The DSS (formerly Department of Health and Social Security – DHSS) is one of the largest departments in Whitehall in terms of budget and size of operation (Hennessy 1989). Unlike most other Whitehall departments it primarily delivers its own 'product'. As a department, it has always had a reputation for producing home-grown talent with many policy officials beginning their career in the local offices, delivering benefits and interviewing the public talent (Interviews with officials, Greer 1994: 43). There has always been a close relationship between policy and operations in the Department of Social Security and an awareness of the complexity and huge responsibility of delivering social security policies.

The 'Next Steps' idea became linked with long-term debates in the DSS about how social security operations should be conducted (Flynn *et al.* 1990; Greer 1994). The Department's response was guided by the 'Moodie Report' on the delivery of social security, which was published shortly after the Ibbs Report and drew on the 'Next Steps' idea (DHSS 1988). The DHSS, like the DTI, quickly offered up a candidate (the Resettlement Agency) in response to the call for candidates before the launch of 'Next Steps' in Parliament. (Unpublished memorandum to TCSC 1988). As one official involved in the response explained, "there was the usual Whitehall question of do you want to respond in token fashion to get the centre off your back or with something very big?" (senior official in DHSS 1987). This provided the possibility for a controlled response, whilst the Department contemplated the far bigger change suggested by the Moodie Report.

Michael Partridge, (who took over as Permanent Secretary of the social security side of the DHSS when the department split in July 1988) was keen on the idea of agencies, although concerned to avoid fragmentation (interviews with officials). The idea of a policy operational split reflected his experiences in the Home Office and the health side of the DHSS, where several service-delivery functions were provided at arm's length (policing, fire, probation and social services) and offered the opportunity to cut out a regional tier of management. Resistance to the idea largely stemmed from the finance and personnel division concerned with loss of control and power the centre could exert over finance, pay and personnel policies (Greer 1994: 51; interviews with senior Department of Social Security official).

A further study ('Hickey Report') commissioned in July 1988 examined whether social security operations could operate along agency lines, given the politically sensitive and unified nature of social security. Like the Moodie Report it reflected long-standing concerns in the Department and saw that a move to agency status would provide stimulus to achieve internally desired reforms (DSS 1989). There was pressure from the centre for the DSS to develop agencies along regional lines. Hickey specifically considered and rejected various options; regionalism due to loss of economies of scale; a functional split (with the exception of a separate contributions agency) as it would undermine managerial coherence and a 'benefit' split as it would cut across the whole person approach. The report recommended an early appointment of the chief executive and the development of a shadow agency structure prior to launch. It outlined a need for staff mobility and close working relationships between the policy and operational arms. A number of formal mechanisms for supporting informal close working were suggested: policy branches having clearly defined opposite numbers in the agency; 'benefit boards' could provide forums for debate about policy areas; and the establishment of a departmental management board to assist the permanent secretary in advising the minister. A further report examined the role of HQ in the light of agencification also stressing mechanisms for cross-collaboration, communication and coordination (DSS 1991).

Although the permanent secretary wanted to move to a more federal style department, ministers were less keen to relinquish control:

> Ministers were always twitchy and it remains the difficulty to this day that executive agencies are about handing over to somebody who's more at arm's length than a policy official or an official under their direct control ... decisions and actions which would be of extreme sensitivity and interest to members of Parliament. So ministers didn't awfully like it (Interview with DSS Official).

The risks of moving to agency status, however, were less than that of displeasing the Prime Minister (interview with officials). So in the spring of 1989, the Secretary of State announced that the Department of Social Security would have, in addition to a Resettlement Agency (due to launch the following week), an IT agency from April 1990, a Benefits Agency representing the whole of the department's former operations arm from 1991 and possibility of the development of a Contributions Agency. This would place the vast majority, approximately 98 per cent of the department into agencies, leaving a small policy orientated HQ. The first four were subsequently joined by two other agencies, the Child Support Agency (CSA) set up to administer new child support arrangements in 1993 and the War Pensions Agency in 1994.

The DSS agencification was the clearest shift to a new federal way of organizing and reflected a corporate approach to considering whether to have agencies, how to divide them and how they would work with the policy arm in HQ. This was seen in the framework documents and in informal understandings between the Benefits Agency and the DSS. Shared informal understandings of how to operate were more difficult between the CSA and the DSS as this agency was established from scratch. The coherence and continuity of departmental control was maintained, not through individual Steering Boards but through active staff mobility, historic links and departmental governance through a management board. These governance arrangements were in addition to the 'Next Steps' arrangements and supplemented central formal and informal rules governing the relationship between the Department and its agencies. The corporate nature of this approach disguised some major and fundamental disagreements between parts of the DSS, the 'Next Steps' team and the emerging agencies. The 'Next Steps' team felt that the Department had taken a too cautious approach and stifled the degree of delegation which was desirable (interview with officials at centre). The DSS's approach was markedly different to other departments not only in the scale of the shift to agencies, but also in the way in which relationships with the agencies were organized.

The adaptation of the agency concept in the DSS illustrates path dependency arising from existing state capacity. In many ways, the split replicated pre-existing organizational structures in the sense that the operational arm of the department (which became the Benefits Agency), the regional organization, always had a separate management and reporting structure. It reflects the unified and technical nature of the social security operations, which makes it impossible to plan to change a social security policy without considering how this could be administered. It also reflected the size of the operational or service-delivery arm of the department. It had the largest executive operation and therefore, logically, the largest percentage of work potentially suitable for agencies. Customization of the agency idea also reflected policy preferences of departmental officials, who shared an appreciation arising from the relatively contained staff culture of the DSS, of the need for close co-operation and a predisposition towards agencies as a solution to existing departmentally identified issues.

Home Office

The Home Office is traditionally described as 'conservative' in constitutional orientation whilst liberal in policy outlook (Dowding 1995; Hennessy 1989; Lewis 1997: 25; interviews with officials). Until re-organization in the mid-1990s, the Department was organized into separate divisions, which operated autonomously and decision making was vertically segmented. These features are evident when examining the way in which the Home Office responded to the agency concept.

The Home Office response was coordinated by a grade five official who headed a small unit (Home Affairs Select Committee, HC 177 1991). The Passport Office was put forward as a candidate for the publication of the *Ibbs Report* but in other respects the Home Office took a cautious approach (Treasury and Civil Service Committee, Unpublished memorandum 1988). A second candidate, the Forensic Science Service was announced in 1990, but neither were launched until April 1991, over three years after the publication of the *Ibbs Report* (Cm 1509 1991: 5). The Home Office was criticized for being slow to respond (Treasury and Civil Service Committee 1989) and Kemp, questioned about their progress, responded "we keep after them" (Treasury and Civil Service Committee 1990). The main pressure from the centre of government was on the Home Office to consider agency status for the prison service (interviews with officials).

The prison service had been a separate department until 1962 when it moved into the Home Office, becoming its biggest division. It was headed by a Director General, the equivalent of a Deputy Permanent Secretary, or grade two, and represented three quarters of central government expenditure by the Home Office and therefore presented, like the Benefits Agency in the DSS, a potentially huge transfer (Cm 611 1989). The possibility of the prison service becoming an agency was addressed by several reports from 1989 to 1992. A consultancy report in 1989, examining the location of the Prison Service HQ, was cautious about how the agency idea could be adapted to the prison service and led the then Director General of the Prison Service and senior Home Office officials to be 'nervous' about separating policy and operations (PA Consulting 1989; interviews with senior Home Office Officials). Subsequently the *Woolf Report*, commissioned to report after the Strangeways riot, was very critical of the management of the Service and neglect of these issues by successive ministers and recommended the separation of policy and operations (Cm 1456 1991; Cm 1647 1991; Lewis 1997).

A third report (the Lygo Report) commissioned specifically to look at the question of moving the Prison Service to agency status was also positive about agency status whilst recommending that it needed to be adapted to fit the needs of the Prison Service (Home Office 1991). It suggested the creation of a supervisory board to give the Home Secretary sufficient confidence in the management of the service to stand back (Home Office 1991, letter placed with report). The publication of this report coincided with the appointment of a Director General who was keener on the agency model. The Strangeways riot also persuaded the new Home Secretary, Kenneth Baker, that he would be better protected from political damage through agency status and, therefore, the Permanent Secretary changed his position (interview with senior official in the Home Office).

Another change of Home Secretary led to Kenneth Clarke taking forward agencification of the prison service. He held a far more bullish attitude towards agency status, privatization and contracting out initiatives (Lewis 1997: 5). He took an active part in the appointment of the new Director General, rejecting the existing civil servant in the role and appointing Derek Lewis from the private sector (Lewis 1997: 11). Two critical institutional decisions were taken during this period in the run-up to the launch of the agency. The first was that policy should stay with operations and become part of the new agency, reflecting the Home Office's historical concern that, without close ties, policy decisions were made that were un-implementable. The Permanent Secretary at the time who chaired the working party which prepared the framework document, explained the reasoning:

> I insisted that the Chief Executive of the Agency should be responsible not only for the operation of the Service but also for prisons

policy. I was quite clear, and I still am, that if I had set up a unit of bright young civil servants at the centre of the Home Office and outside the Prison Service and made them responsible for the development of prisons policy and confined the prison service to the operation of the prison system, we would have seen policy gradually becoming more unrealistic and less soundly based as it ceased to be informed by the hard facts of operational experience.

(Whitmore 1994: 10–11)

The Agency framework document describes the role of the chief executive (still called a Director General) as being "the Home Secretary's principal policy adviser" (unlike the Benefits Agency, which described the chief executive's role as being the minister's principal adviser on operational functions). Although the permanent secretary, according to the 'Next Steps' principles retained his overall role as the minister's principal adviser, this was not supported by any policy capacity in the department.

The second key decision was Clarke's refusal to establish a Ministerial Advisory Board to buttress the degree of direct oversight provided by the Minister and as advised in the Lygo Report. Clarke did not want to introduce any new arrangements: "Ken Clarke was the sort of person who said 'well I don't care what the norm is – is it going to be useful and in this case, if not then I'm not going to have it' " (interview with former Prison Service official). The 'Next Steps' team was unable to exert pressure for the establishment of an Advisory Board against Clarke's wishes and risk jeopardizing the move to agency status, "it would have damaged the credibility of 'Next Steps' . . . it would be seen as the prison service rejects 'Next Steps', or the Home Office rejects the 'Next Steps' approach. And so, the reality of the negotiation, is there is a balance, there are other issues which come into play" (interview with former 'Next Steps' team officials). After the Prison Service became an agency in April 1993, the Home Office 'caught up' with other departments, with over 78 per cent of its civil servants working in agencies (Cm 2508 1994).

The Home Office's response to the agency concept reflected path dependency arising from the existing state capacity. The compartmentalized structure of the Home Office meant there was no overall coordination of their response. This is reflected in the very different framework agreements that emerged between the Home Office and its agencies. In the case of the Prison Service, its previously separate status led to arguments that it could operate as an agency. Officials' policy preferences were also apparent generally in the conservative and cautious approach it took towards agencification. As one official put it, "it was a slow, thorough, precedent-driven culture, just about as antipathetic to the sort of new management as you could find in any government department" (interview with former senior Home Office official). The policy preferences of officials and the Minister were also apparent in consideration of the Prison Service Agency's governance structures. First, in the decision taken to keep policy capacity with the Agency and not in the Department, and secondly in the decision not to establish a Ministerial Advisory Board. Both decisions would subsequently become critical when the new arrangements came under strain.

Conclusion

The 'Next Steps' concept and the institutional arrangements surrounding its introduction were the product of compromise and accommodation to satisfy different actors across Whitehall. The institutional arrangements that developed illustrate the path dependency of policy change. Both the agency concept, and how this concept was adopted in departments, depended upon the existing formal and informal institutional arrangements. The agency policy carried a mix of old and new 'rules of the game', the introduction of arms-length control alongside a maintenance of the doctrine of ministerial responsibility. These ambiguous rules of the game became more customized when agencies were established in departments.

Departmental contexts – the existing structures of decision making, organizational histories, attitudes and beliefs about the policy area and roles led to differential formal and informal 'rules of the game'. Here again new formal and informal rules and roles developed and co-existed alongside the maintenance of existing cultures and beliefs. This highlights the ambiguous, dynamic and often departmentally specific interpretation. Path dependency at departmental level influenced decision making about what was appropriate and possible to move to agency status and how each agency should operate. This, in turn, affected what resources were transferred, what were the 'rules of the game' in department – agency networks and the role expectation of those involved. Ultimately the extent to which each department agency relationship reflected a 'marketized' or a 'constitutional' relationship varied widely within Government and directly informed how well key actors managed the tension inherent in the 'Next Steps' concept between ministerial responsibility and an arms-length approach (Gains 2000). At core, the 'Next Steps' orthodoxy was, and still is, a dynamic concept, reflexive and responsive to external events, institutional learning and political imperatives.

There are implications of this analysis of how the agency concept was adapted and customized for adoption in different UK departments, for those in other countries charged with importing, introducing or operating with the agency model. There will be path dependency in the process of change. The degree and direction of change will be mediated by the existing state capacity – the current constitutional and organizational operating practices – and by the policy preferences of those involved in implementing the change. The UK model does not provide a 'blueprint' which will lead to uniform change. As one former member of the 'Next Steps' Team pointed out about the reality and variety of agency arrangements operating in the UK: "I think it's whatever people can make work".

Acknowledgements

The author would like to thank officials for generously giving their time in providing information. Interviews were conducted between 1996 and 1999 and were associated with ESRC grant no. L124251023 'The Changing Role of Central Government Departments'.

References

Barberis, P. (1995) *The Elite of the Elite: Permanent Secretaries in the British Higher Civil Service*, Dartmouth: Aldershot.

Brooks, I. and Bate, P. (1994) 'The problems affecting change within the British Civil Service: a cultural perspective', *British Journal of Management* 5, 3, 177–90.

Bulmer, S. and Burch, M. (1998) 'Organizing for Europe: Whitehall, the British State and European Union', *Public Administration* 76, 4, 601–28.

Burch, M. and Holliday, I. (1996) *The British Cabinet System*, Hemel Hempstead: Prentice Hall.

Chapman, R. (1997) *The Treasury and Public Policy Making*, London: Routledge.

Cm 611 (1989) *Home Office Annual Report*, London: HMSO.

Cm 1456 (1991) *Prison Disturbances April 1990 (The Woolf Report)*, London: HMSO.

Cm 1509 (1991) *Home Office Annual Report*, London: HMSO.

Cm 1647 (1991) *Custody, Care and Justice: The Way Ahead for the Prison Service in England and Wales*, London: HMSO.

Cmnd 3638 (1968) *The Civil Service (Fulton Report)*, London: HMSO.

Cmnd 8616 (1982) *Efficiency and Effectiveness in the Civil Service*, London: HMSO.

Cortell, A. and Peterson, S. (1999) 'Altered states: explaining domestic institutional change', *British Journal of Political Science* 29, 177–203.

Davis, A. and Wilman, J. (1991) *What Next? Agencies, Departments and the Civil Service*, London: IPPR.

Davis, D. (1994) 'Management change in the Civil Service', *Public Money and Management* 14, 1, 4–6.

Department of Health and Social Security (1988) *The Business of Service: The Report of the Regional Organisation Scrutiny (Moodie Report)*, London: DSS.

Department of Social Security (1989) *Social Security Agency Study Report (Hickey Report)*, London: DSS.

Department of Social Security (1991) *Review of DSS HQ Role, Functions and Organisation*, London: DSS.

Dowding, K. (1995) *The Civil Service*, London: Routledge.

Evans, P., Rueschemeyer, D. and Skocpol, T. (eds) (1985) *Bringing the State Back In*, Cambridge: Cambridge University Press.

Efficiency Unit (1988) *Improving Management in Government: The Next Steps (Ibbs Report)*, London: HMSO.

Efficiency Unit (1991) *Making the Most of Next Steps: The Management of Ministers' Departments and their Executive Agencies (Fraser Report)*, London: HMSO.

Flynn, A., Gray, A. and Jenkins, W. (1990) 'Taking the Next Steps: the changing management of government', *Parliamentary Affairs* 43, 2, 159–78.

Gains, F. (1999) 'Implementing privatisation policies in Next Steps agencies', *Public Administration* 77, 4.

Gains, F. (2000) *Understanding Department Agency Relationships*, PhD thesis, Department of Politics, University of Sheffield.

Gidding, P. (1995) *Parliamentary Accountability: A Study of Parliament and Executive Agencies*, London: Macmillan Press.

Goldsworthy, D. (1991) *Setting up Next Steps*, London: HMSO.

Greer, P. (1992) 'The Next Steps initiative: an examination of agency framework documents', *Public Administration* 70, 1, 89–98.

Greer, P. (1994) *Transforming Central Government: The Next Steps Initiative*, Buckingham: Open University Press.

Hall, P.A. (1993) 'Policy paradigms, social learning and the state', *Comparative Politics* 25, 3, 175–96.

Hall, P.A. and Taylor, R.C.R. (1996) 'Political science and the three new institutionalisms', *Political Studies* 44, 4, 936–57.

Harden, I. (1992) *The Contracting State*, Buckingham: Open University Press.

Heclo, H. and Wildavsky, A. (1981) *The Private Government of Public Money*, London: Macmillan Press.

Hennessy, P. (1989) *Whitehall*, London: Secker and Warburg.

Hogwood, B. (1993) *The Uneven Staircase: Measuring Up to Next Steps*, Strathclyde Papers on Government and Politics No 92.

Home Affairs Select Committee (1991) *HC 177, Third Report: Next Steps Agencies, Session 1990–91*, London: HMSO.

Home Office (1991) *Management of the Prison Service: Report by Admiral Sir Raymond Lygo KCB (Lygo Report)*, Home Office.

Horton, S. and Jones, J. (1996) 'Who are the new public managers? An initial analysis of Next Steps Chief Executives and their management role', *Public Policy and Administration*, 11, 4, 18.

James, O. (1995) 'Explaining the Next Steps in the Department of Social Security: the bureau-shaping model of central state re-organization', *Political Studies* 43, 4, 614–29.

Judge, D. (1993) *The Parliamentary State*, London: Sage.

Kemp, P. (1990) 'Can the Civil Service adapt to managing by contract', *Public Money and Management* 10, 3 25–31.

Lewis, D. (1997) *Hidden Agendas*, England: Hamish Hamilton Ltd.

Lewis, N. (1993) 'The Citizen's Charter and Next Steps – a new way of governing'. *Political Quarterly* 64, 3, 316–26.

Lowndes, V. (1996) 'Varieties of new institutionalism: a critical appraisal', *Public Administration* 74, 181–97.

March, J.G. and Olsen, J.P. (1984) 'The new institutionalism: organisational factors in political life', *American Political Science Review* 78, 734–49.

Massey, A. (1995) 'Ministers, the agency model and policy ownership', *Public Policy and Administration* 10, 2, 71–87.

Metcalfe, L. and Richards, S. (1990) *Improving Public Management*, London: Sage.

Newman, J., Richards, S. and Smith, P. (1998) 'Market testing and institutional change in the UK civil service: compliance, non compliance and engagement', *Public Policy and Administration* 13, 4, 96–110.

O'Toole, B. and Jordan, G. (1995) *Next Steps: Improving Management in Government*, Dartmouth: Aldershot.

PA Consulting (1989) *The Organisation and Location of the Prison Service HQ*, PA Consulting.

Pierson, P. (2000) 'Increasing returns, Path dependence and the study of politics', in *American Political Science Review* 94, 2, 251–67.

Peters, G.P. (1999) *Institutional Theory in Political Science*, London: Pinter.

Plowden, W. (1994) *Ministers and Mandarins*, London: IPPR.

Pollitt, C. (1993) *Managerialism and the Public Services*, Oxford: Blackwell.

Pollitt, C., Bathgate, K., Caulfield, J., Smullen, A. and Talbot, C. (2001) 'Agency fever? Analysis of an international policy fashion', *Journal of Comparative Policy Analysis* 3, 3, 271–90.

Public Service Committee (1996) *HC 313, Second Report, Ministerial Responsibility and Accountability, Session 1995–96*, London: HMSO.

Pyper, R. (1995) *The British Civil Service*, London: Prentice.

Rhodes, R.A.W. (1995) 'The institutional approach', in Marsh, D. and Stoker, G. (eds) *Theory and Methods in Political Science*, Houndmills: Macmillan Press Ltd.

Richards, D. and Smith, M.J. (1997) 'How departments change: windows of opportunity and critical junctures in three departments', *Public Policy and Administration* 12, 2, 62–79.

Smith, M.J. (1999) 'The institutions of central government', in Holliday, I., Gamble, A. and. Parry, G. (eds) *Fundamentals in British Politics*, London: Macmillan.

Smullen, A. (2001) '*Lost in Translation? Shifting Interpretations of the concept of 'Agency': The Dutch Case'*, IRSPM5 Conference Paper, Barcelona.

Talbot, C. (1995) 'Central government reforms', in Jackson, P. and Lavender, M. (eds) *The Public Services Yearbook 1995/6*, London: Chapman and Hall.

Theakston, K. (1995) *The British Civil Service since 1945*, Oxford: Blackwell.

Treasury and Civil Service Committee (1988) *HC 494, Session 1987–88, Eighth Report: Civil Service Management Reforms – The Next Steps*, London: HMSO.

Treasury and Civil Service Committee. (1989) *HC 348, 5th Report Development in the Next Steps Programme, Session 1988–89*, London: HMSO.

Treasury and Civil Service Committee (1990) *HC 481, Eighth Report: Progress in the Next Steps Initiative, Session 1989–90*, London: HMSO.

Trosa, S. (1994) *Next Steps: Moving On*, London: Office of Public Service and Science.

Weir, M. and Skocpol, T. (1985) 'State structures and the possibilities for "Keynesian" responses to the great depression in Sweden, Britain and the United States', in Evans, P. *et al.* (eds) *Bringing the State Back In*, Cambridge: Cambridge University Press.

Whitmore, C. (1994) *A Civil Service for the Year 2000*, Leicester Business School: Occasional Paper 16.

Wilson, G.K. and Barker, A. (1995) 'The end of the Whitehall model', *West European Politics* 18, 4, 130–49.

Zifcak, S. (1994) *New Managerialism: Administrative Reform in Whitehall and Canberra*, Buckingham: Open University Press.

4 Executive agencies and joined-up government in the UK

Oliver James

The 'Next Steps' agency creation process was launched in 1988. At the beginning of the twenty-first century, over three quarters of all UK civil servants worked in 138 agencies or bodies working on agency lines (James 2003). The reform has been emulated in some aspect by several other countries, and issues surrounding the performance of agencies in the UK are of broad interest (Pollitt *et al.* 2000; James 2001b; James 2003; Talbot 2002). Individual agencies set up under the reform in the UK differ in many respects. However, they share two core features of the executive agency model, defined as the structures suggested in the report by the Prime Minister's Efficiency Unit (1988) that initiated the reform and early government guidance on setting up agencies (James 2003).

First, organisational separation on a 'vertical' dimension between the department, primarily responsible for strategic issues including policy, and the agency, responsible for specific tasks and with some autonomy in use of its resources and on a 'horizontal' dimension between agencies responsible for different tasks. The autonomy for each agency entails, to varying degrees, creating separate agency specific systems for personnel, recruitment, careers, resource use and patterns of working focused on the task at hand. About 10 per cent of agencies have further freedoms as 'trading funds' to develop and sell services direct to consumers.

Second, the model entails a performance-contracting system with a department exerting arms-length control, predominantly using a regime of performance targets, with a chief executive having overall responsibility for the agency. These characteristics make executive agencies 'semi-autonomous', without the independence afforded to the range of bodies often called 'quangos' (Greve, Flinders and van Thiel 1999). However, agencies have more delegated freedoms and more codified relationships with centres of departments than normally found for sections within departments.

In contrast to this model, contemporary UK policymakers' emphasise the need for 'joined-up' government – a key theme of the *Modernising Government* White Paper (Cabinet Office 1999), the *Wiring it Up* report by the Cabinet Office Performance and Innovation Unit (PIU 2000), the

Treasury Comprehensive Spending Review of 1998 and Treasury Spending Review of 2000 (Chief Secretary to the Treasury 2000). In its broadest sense, joined-up government is a vague set of aspirations for performance and organisational prescriptions, suggesting that outcomes citizens and their representatives value should be delivered in a way that is not dictated by organisational boundaries. However, more specifically, joined-up government, whilst acknowledging boundaries between sections within agencies and departments, focuses on the structures and performance consequences of boundaries between different departments, agencies, quangos, local government bodies and other units.

The joined-up government agenda suggests the desirability of certain organisational structures, including more collaborative and co-ordinated working, 'horizontal joining-up' between departments and agencies and vertical 'joining-up' of levels of government, especially between policy makers at one level and the full range of people involved in delivering services, including local bodies and other delivery units (PIU 2000: paras 3.1 and 3.2). The breadth of span for integrated organisational structures and depth of integration depends on how broadly the system is defined, with the potential for public service provision to be considered a single, giant, system with a comprehensive, integrated structure. More modest prescriptions include better links between separate organisations including more information exchange, joint planning, staff transfer and improved co-ordinating structures (Cabinet Office 1999; PIU 2000).

Proponents of joined-up government suggest that an absence of these structures creates performance problems from a systemic perspective, particularly in relation to certain types of activities. The main activities vulnerable to poor performance suggested in the reports (Cabinet Office 1999; PIU 2000) are of four main types:

- Similar policies and/or services operating separately in multiple organisations.
- Policies and/or services benefiting from consolidated provision to multiple organisations.
- Shared policies and/or services requiring several organisations to contribute to their achievement including the need for ranking priorities, making trade-offs between delivery options across multiple organisations and providing one stop shop services to potential users of public services supplied by several organisations.
- Spill-over effects where organisations' activities have effects on other organisations' activities without directly being part of shared policies or services.

The joined-up government agenda is very broad and not particularly novel in the problems it identifies or the solutions it suggests. A concern with systemic planning and co-ordination issues was, in part, behind attempts to create large integrated 'super departments' in the early 1970s in the UK (Kavanagh and Richards 2001). The organisational prescriptions and concerns about performance and analysis of performance problems resemble a range of organisational perspectives in public administration, economics, sociology, law and other disciplines (Pollitt 2001). The issue of co-operation between organisations is, in part, the latest manifestation of the long recognised trade-off between the need for a division of labour between organisations and the problem of co-ordination between parts of government (Gulick 1937). The movement towards a broader array of actors and proliferation of levels of government involved in public services has made these concerns more pressing in recent decades (Bardach 1998; Wollmann 2002; Balloch and Taylor 2001). One focus of interest has been the problem of public sector externalities, where control and perform-ance appraisal systems fail to reflect the wider effects of an organisation's activities on the goals of other organisations (James 2000b: 331). An example is found when schools exclude disruptive students to improve exam performance with undesirable social consequences that are the responsibility of other organisations, including the police and local authorities. These concerns are not limited to the public sector. Externali-ties are more conventionally discussed in the context of private markets and a variety of inter-organisational arrangements to pursue shared opportunities have been suggested, including strategic alliances, co-operative networks, joint working, partnerships (Gray 1989) and collabo-rative advantage (Huxham 1996).

The organisational prescriptions and concerns about performance in the current joined-up government agenda are more distinctive as a set of concerns and prescriptions in the contemporary post UK public sector. Joined-up government is a critique of the parts of New Public Manage-ment (NPM) (Hood 1991), or managerialist (Pollitt 1993) structures that were introduced into many English-speaking countries' public sectors in the 1980s and 1990s. NPM structures fragmented the public sector, pro-vided incentive systems for individual organisations to focus on their own missions, partially to the exclusion of systemic effects, and created pres-sures for competition rather than collaboration. In contrast, the parts of NPM involving a weakening of the boundary between public and private sector by involving private providers in delivering services would seem to be consistent with joining-up organisations to deliver services. However, the executive agency model appears to be a part of NPM that is inconsis-tent with joined-up government. The 'Modernising Government' White Paper suggested that 'Great gains in public sector management have come from definition of task and delegation of management and the Government is determined that these are not lost. However, this concentration on specific tasks has sometimes distracted attention from the wider general objectives of government and people. The Govern-ment wants to give more attention to the coherence of policy across institutional boundaries ... to operate in a joined up way.' (Cabinet Office 1999: 1).

In evaluating the performance of agencies, the joined-up government perspective suggests that as well as the costs and benefits of agency structures from a narrow perspective of the single organisation, there is a need to consider whether the benefits of agency structures outweigh the costs on the performance of other organisations and systemic performance. In particular, it suggests several problems of agency structures for broadly conceived performance. The 'horizontal' and 'vertical' organisational fragmentation of the executive agency model creates organisations focused on their individual tasks at hand, with distinctive ways of working. These features potentially make joint working to deliver services more difficult by limiting exchange of staff, or hampering the development of common conceptions of policy or delivery issues. The structures often involve fragmentation of strategy and policy, mainly handled by the department, and operations handled by the agency. The performance contracting aspect of the model focuses agencies' attention on narrow organisational performance, rather than the effect on other bodies or systemic effects (except to the extent these are written in to the agency's own aims). The target regimes and chief executive responsibility for the agency's own performance reinforce this narrowness of perspective, creating public sector externalities. Agencies report to individual departments, which, in turn, are separate from other departments' created performance systems organised as separate silos for each department.

Experience with the effects of executive agency structures on performance has been mixed and the evidence is limited (Talbot 1996; Pollitt and Bouckaert 2000; James 2001a). The following section in this chapter uses a case study of the largest agency, the Benefits Agency, to provide an indication of the significance of joined-up government performance problems in the UK. This chapter then advances an analytical framework to locate the different ways of dealing with the performance problems, drawing on the literatures on public sector co-ordination and control and situating current developments in this framework. Finally, some conclusions are drawn.

The Benefits Agency and systemic performance

The approach taken here is to examine the efficiency and effectiveness of the Agency's performance, a broad set of stakeholders consisting of those affected by the Agency's action. The Benefits Agency (BA) was established in 1991 to 'support the Government in establishing a modern welfare state ... by helping to create and deliver an active and modern social security service. The service will encourage independence and pay the right money to the right person at the right time, all the time' (Benefits Agency 1999: 5). The bulk of resources were devoted to achieving these goals within the organisation with direct benefits for stakeholders. Evidence from a variety of sources including National Audit Office reports, a survey of budget/output changes and measures of satisfaction with the agency suggests mixed performance in these narrow terms. There were improvements against key objectives, combined with substantial problems of fraud and error on payments and rising costs of administration at the same time as conflicting evidence about the changes to quality of service (James 2001a, 2003). However, this section assesses performance for a broader set of stakeholders in the social security system to explore issues of joined-up government performance. The Agency was involved in substantial joint working with other bodies. These organisations principally included the Department of Social Security, for delivering the Department's main programmes, the Employment Service Agency to deliver Jobseeker's Allowance benefit, War Pensions Agency for veterans welfare, Information Technology Services Agency for IT systems and the Contributions Agency in running the National Insurance system. More broadly, other bodies relied on the Agency to do their job properly, especially local authorities in delivering Housing Benefit. Each of these organisations had their own associated stakeholders in addition to general taxpayers' interest in the system as a whole. Beyond these groups could be posited counterfactually a set of potential stakeholders for the social security system. These would include the beneficiaries of services that could have been provided if the Agency had not existed, but instead some form of 'joined-up' organisation in the field of social welfare had been in its place. However, the nature of these groups and benefits is too speculative to assess and so they are excluded from this analysis.

Organisational separation

The Agency was separated 'vertically' from the Department of Social Security, solidifying a long-standing divide between policy making and operational parts of the social security system. The Agency had a seat on the Departmental Policy Board and was usually represented by the head of the Benefit Management Branch. However, the first Chief Executive commented that the views of people delivering services were still not taken sufficiently into account by those in policy making organisations (Bichard 1999: 7–8). The second Chief Executive, Peter Mathison, in response to criticism from the Social Security Committee about the level of performance, suggested the department should shoulder some of the responsibility. He said 'We have identified where there are weaknesses in the system, which may essentially be down to some detail of the policy design and we have identified some also where there are weaknesses around some of the rules and regulations' (Public Accounts Committee 1999: Q165).

The 'vertical' separation contributed to problems of communicating information between the Department and the Agency. Whilst this problem was general, it also led to specific failures, the largest of which was the State Earnings Related Pension debacle, involving a failure to make people claiming pensions aware of changes to policy on eligibility. Whilst the mistake was originally made in 1986, before the Agency's creation, the organisational structure imposed by the Agency seemed to have worsened the problem. The handling of state pensions required co-ordinating Benefits Agency staff in Leeds, Newcastle and in local offices responsible for various parts of delivery, and staff in the departmental headquarters in London responsible for supporting ministers in the development, maintenance and evaluation of pensions policy. Once the Department was made aware of the error in 1995, the information was not passed to the Benefits Agency and not incorporated in the information they gave to clients. Benefits Agency leaflets and staff continued to give wrong information until 1999. In the end, Age Concern, a charity representing users of the services, rather than the Agency or DSS staff, brought the full implications of the error to the attention of ministers (National Audit Office 2000c: 28). The absence of end-to-end responsibility and good communication, coupled with lack of communication inside the Agency, were major factors in the failure according to NAO (2000c: 10; 26).

'Horizontal' separation distinguished the Agency from other bodies in the Department for Social Security and the rest of government, although some common grading systems were maintained, and the previous systems before the agency had in any case not been fully unified. An important area of 'horizontal' co-working was with the Employment Service in delivering Jobseeker's Allowance from 1996. This benefit was delivered from Jobcentres run by the Employment Service, which paid the benefit as an agent of the Benefits Agency, although much of the administrative work behind payments remained with the Benefits Agency. Organisational separation contributed to performance problems. There was a lack of sharing of information resulting in the same information being requested twice, draining resources and inconveniencing claimants (Benefit Fraud Inspectorate 1999b; Appendix B). Differences between conditions of service in the two agencies contributed to these problems. Staff in the Benefits Agency worked behind screens to protect them from clients, whereas the Employment Service had a more open work environment. Under the so-called 'Bichard Agreement', named after the first head of the Benefits Agency, staff in the Benefits Agency were given the right not to be transferred to different working conditions when undertaking Jobseeker's Allowance related work. This restriction limited flexibility in the use of staff, contributing to lack of effective communication (Social Security Committee 1998: 176).

The agency model had a logic of separate organisational operations and separate accounting for performance for each agency. One senior official commented: 'both agencies would have preferred Jobseeker's

Allowance to go to one or another, rather than having to share it' (Interview with Senior Official, Benefits Agency). However, several structures were instituted in an *ad hoc* manner, which went against the grain of the agency model but facilitated more effective delivery. These systems included joint meetings to address problems at different management levels. The Benefits Agency Chief Executive, Peter Mathison and the Chief Executive of the Employment Service, Leigh Lewis, met with other members of their boards in a joint board on a quarterly basis and prepared action plans. There was a Joint Operations Team with members from both bodies to facilitate joint working and local level meetings (Social Security Committee 1998: Q163). The delivery was further smoothed by staff transfers between the organisations so that staff were doing very similar work as previously but in a different organisation. Such transfers ran against the grain of the agency model, which suggests different terms and conditions in different agencies focused on different organisational missions, making these sorts of transfers more difficult to achieve (James 2003).

There were significant problems in dealing with local government, a cross between 'horizontal' and 'vertical' problems if local government is considered to be, in some respects, a lower tier of government to the Agency. The Benefits Agency administered two benefits, Income Support and Jobseeker's Allowance, which had implications for a third benefit, Housing Benefit, mainly administered by local authorities. This was a sizeable programme costing about £11,100m per year in 1996–7 or 12 per cent of the total £90,000m spend on social security. The Agency passed information to local authorities about claimants to assist them in the administration of Housing Benefit. Because about 66 per cent of people claiming Housing Benefit were also on Income Support or Jobseeker's Allowance, there was substantial joint working (NAO 1997: 18). If a claimant was awarded Income Support or Jobseeker's Allowance by the Agency then the local authority had to assume that they had no income or capital, which affected the award of Housing Benefit (Benefit Fraud Inspectorate 1999d: Sec. 8.1). The Agency's problems with fraud and error on these benefits had a further externality effect in terms of fraud and error on Housing Benefit. In the mid-1990s, about 74 per cent of fraudulent claims on Housing Benefit were also fraudulent claims for Income Support (NAO 1997: 21). Overall, about 7 per cent of the Housing Benefit budget was paid out in fraud and error in the mid-1990s (NAO 1997: 1).

Performance contracting

There was a performance target system for the Agency, for example in 1997–8 the Agency's management team monitored performance against 124 Secretary of State's and related internal management targets (NAO

1998). The Department of Social Security kept some input controls, the Agency operating within a gross running cost system of control rather than being a trading fund. A proportion of the pay for people in the organisation, including the Chief Executive, was linked to achieving targets (Interview: Senior Official, Benefits Agency). The focus on targets for benefits hindered attempts to redesign systems. The targets were separately related to different benefits, so that each benefit was still treated largely as a separate activity within the organisation. The potential advantages from collaborating with voluntary groups and charities in disseminating information about benefits and developing innovative ways of dealing with clients were not facilitated by a regime which focused attention narrowly on hitting targets for specific aspects of specific benefits. However, the benefits forgone by this lack of co-operation are difficult to calculate.

More concrete issues of performance were apparent in difficulties in setting and using performance targets to control the Agency. The department was able to partially 'fine tune' the performance system to improve control, and the appointment of the second Chief Executive was used as a further means to exercise control over the Agency. One of the informal criteria used in the appointment of the second Chief Executive was that the appointee should be 'managerial' and follow the spirit of the framework and targets set down by the Department (Interview: Senior Official, Benefits Agency). However, ministers and civil servants in the Department became concerned about the divide emerging in the 'vertical' relationship and the Department's inability to act as an 'intelligent customer' for the Agency's services (Interview: Senior Official, Department of Social Security).

The problems of controlling the Agency became more acute after 1997 when a Labour administration came into office. Their agenda involved a change in emphasis towards encouraging employability and a social security system more 'responsive to, and providing a more direct service for the public' (Chancellor of the Duchy of Lancaster 1997: 192). The agenda required a more system-wide approach to social security and employment. The system was inappropriate for a client focus to welfare, because the targets were oriented towards performance in terms of separate benefits (Interview: Senior Official, Department of Social Security; Interview: Senior Official, Department of Social Security). The problem of a system that did not have end-to-end responsibility for the design and implementation of policy became even more acute.

The performance target regime encouraged the Agency to concentrate its efforts on its own activities, regardless of the 'public sector externality' effects on other bodies, exacerbating the problems of 'horizontal' working. The Agency's own targets did not include the effects of the high level of fraud and error and incorrect information being passed to local authorities. Whilst the Benefits Agency had service level agreements with local authorities since 1992, setting out the Agency's aims in co-operating with these organisations, an NAO study found that a majority of local authorities felt that these agreements were not working (NAO 1997). The Benefit Fraud Inspectorate (BFI) found that in 57 per cent of their inspections, liaison needed to be improved between the Benefits Agency and local authorities. The required improvements included better exchange of information, more cross-agency working and better feedback on fraud cases (Benefit Fraud Inspectorate 1999d: Sec. 1). Whilst local authorities were inefficient in their administration of benefits because of problems in the authorities, the Benefit Fraud Inspectorate found that the Agency made a substantial contribution to the difficulties (Benefit Fraud Inspectorate 1999d).

The Agency target system included targets for reducing fraud, which placed the body in competition with local authorities and placed emphasis on trying to raise levels of fraud detection rather than prevention. The schemes used the principle of 'finders-keepers' for bodies detecting fraud, which discouraged information sharing with local authorities, with Agency officials wanting to keep the savings to help achieve their own fraud targets (NAO 1997: 62–3). The Benefit Agency's 'Spotlight' anti-fraud initiatives did not involve local authorities as much as they could have, in part because of a concern to pursue its own targets (NAO 1997: 71). In some cases there was an atmosphere of mutual suspicion between the Agency and local authorities, although the relationship varied around the country (NAO 1997: 66).

The performance target system led to co-ordination problems with other agencies. In some senses the joint delivery of Jobseeker's Allowance with the Employment Service was a success, in that most of the targets relating to the benefit were met. However, the agency was always under pressure to use resources to promote the achievement of its own targets. The Jobseeker's Allowance working arrangements in part reflected non-agency structures established between the Benefits Agency and the Employment Service, including joint management boards. More severe problems caused by targets were reflected in working with the Contributions Agency, which was responsible for protecting the rights of contributors and interests of taxpayers through efficient payment and recording of National Insurance contributions, partly relying on forms processed by the Benefits Agency. There were no high level Benefits Agency targets for passing forms from the Agency to the Contributions Agency. Fifty-four per cent of forms took more than 16 days, resulting in out-of-date information being used to create National Insurance accounts, damaging the collection of contributions (Benefit Fraud Inspectorate 1999c: Secs 3.11–13).

Joining-up Executive Agency working

Several ways to mitigate the problems with agency working are suggested by the literatures in public administration, sociology, economics and law.

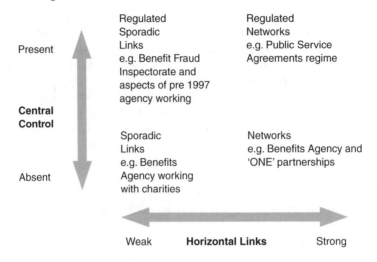

Figure 4.1 Structures for joining-up Executive Agency working.

One potential way of attempting to mitigate the problems is to reverse the agency reform. Such a solution internalises public sector externalities between the department and the agency and is a return to more traditional public sector structures. However, Figure 4.1 provides a framework for these perspectives and gives some examples of systems that have been used in the case of the Benefits Agency. The vertical dimension is the degree of central steering of the system by high level bodies, ranging from strong steering by a central source of authority to weak central steering, leaving individual organisations to their own devices. The horizontal dimension is how individual organisations at the lower level relate to each other, ranging from strong and enduring links in a network to weaker and more sporadic relationships. The four options are combinations of positions at opposite ends of the two dimensions: sporadic links, networks, regulated sporadic links and regulated networks.

Sporadic links

In this arrangement, co-ordination and co-operation between organisations is a matter for voluntary agreement between the parties involved in relation to particular opportunities rather than longer-term links. The links rest on mutually beneficial exchange and there is no intervention from higher-level bodies. The situation resembles the Benefits Agency occasional working with charities. Some local offices had relationships with these bodies to publicise the availability of benefits and there was some national co-operation with charities, for example, Age Concern, in publicising benefits available to pensioners. The Benefits Agency's relationship with local authorities appeared to be of this type. The relationships, whilst having formal Service Level Agreements, varied by local area and did not follow a set pattern.

However, new measures were instituted to 'join-up' government by voluntary action through the Treasury, creating budgetary incentives for organisations to work co-operatively. Two central funds were established to provide finance for projects involving joint working. The £230m per year Invest to Save budget funded innovative projects involving two or more departments, and the £2,500m Capital Modernisation Fund was awarded in part to encourage joint projects (PIU 2000: Box 9.1). One Invest to Save project developed electronic kiosks to present information about a range of services including benefits to users in a variety of locations outside of the Agency's premises (Segal Qunice Wicksteed Ltd 2000: 18).

Other possible ways for facilitating voluntary co-ordination have not yet been tried. Public sector externality compensation suggests that public sector bodies could bribe the producers of externalities to stop producing negative externalities or to start producing positive externalities (James 2000b: 341). The solution is analogous to the general solution to problems of externalities when bargaining is costless and there are clearly defined property rights. In this general case, those suffering the effects of an externality could, in theory, band together to try and bribe the people causing the externality to change their behaviour. For example, people living near a factory which pollutes their air could offer to pay the factory to use an alternative non-polluting production technique. The allocation of the property rights determines who compensates whom, in this case local residents do not have the right to clean air and must pay the factory.

The Benefits Agency, in working towards its own targets, pushed up fraud for local authorities by issuing faulty information for them to use in Housing Benefit case processing, a negative public sector externality. In this case, a hypothetical compensation solution would be the following. The department could decide whether local authorities have the right to accurate information, or whether they must pay the Benefits Agency to get it. The drawing up of contracts involving exchanges of budget for information could then be left to the local Benefits Agency offices and local authorities on the ground. These bodies are likely to be in a better position to know the value of the accurate information to their work with, for example, the value being different depending on levels of attempted fraud in the locality. Provided the transaction costs of arranging these contracts are not too great, they could be used to deal with the externality in a potentially less costly way than a higher-level body having constantly to intervene, for example, using regulation.

Networks

Networks are an alternative to sporadic links that, whilst having no higher-level central control, consist of more enduring, partnership, relationships between organisations. Links include professional ties between individuals in different organisations, staff exchange or arrangements for managing common interests. There are a variety of perspectives on how networks operate in the public sector and how partnerships can be encouraged (Kickert, Klijn and Koppenjan 1997; Bardach 1998). However, the Trosa Report found that, in general, arrangements for staff to move between departments and agencies had not been thought out and that moving to an agency was not thought to be advantageous to civil servants' careers (Trosa 1994: 48–9). To strengthen a common career structure and to encourage a corporate identity for the service, a Civil Service Management Committee, later renamed the Management Board, was set up in February 1999. The top 600 postings were more actively managed by the Board as part of this process (PIU 2000: 4.11).

However, the Performance and Innovation Unit found that it was still hard to get people to move across departments. The percentage of staff moving on loan outside their own department was just under 5 per cent in 1995/6, and had risen to only just under 7 per cent by 1997/8 (PIU 2000: Figure 8.2). The report suggested trying to get a 'critical mass' of civil servants with experience of working in other organisations in the civil service and beyond as soon as possible. The Unit also stressed the importance of career progression involving experience in a variety of settings (PIU 2000: Sec. 1.5). This principle was reiterated by Sir Richard Wilson in his report to the Prime Minister on Civil Service reform. He said that, in order to reach the Senior Civil Service, people should have experience in working in front-line delivery or operational management and of working in more than one culture. In the Benefits Agency, it was hoped that this change might improve movement of staff between the departmental sections and the Agency.

A more radical network-based solution for social security was the Single Work Focused Gateway, announced in September 1998, and later renamed ONE, which was piloted in several areas. There were two variants of ONE, the first using call centres and the second using partnerships between public and private sector bodies for the provision of services (Social Security Committee 1999: para. 10). The projects brought together the Benefits Agency, Employment Service, Child Support Agency, local authorities and other welfare providers, including charities, to provide a more coherent service for claimants. The idea was to give a claimant a personal adviser to take their details and assess employment, benefit and training options from an initial 'start-up meeting'. The personal adviser could call on a team of experts to provide advice to claimants and brought these organisations' services together to focus on the needs of the claimant.

The ONE projects were cited as examples of joined-up government in action in the 1999 *Modernising Government* White Paper. The pilots were co-ordinated by a partnership of departments with a Project Board answerable to a joint ministerial group. Management of the field was by traditional lines within the Benefits Agency through a series of district, area and regional offices. Relations between organisations were generally semi-contractual at the top, and by liaison at the delivery level, with stronger links between the Benefits Agency and Employment Service in the area of Jobseeker's Allowance. The pilots were managed through Project Management Groups at regional level bringing the Benefits Agency, Employment Service and local authorities together to manage pilots in their area. Each individual pilot was headed by a single manager who was drawn from one of the partner organisations and who oversaw a mixed team of Benefits Agency, Employment Service and local authority staff (PIU 2000: 10.11).

However, this style of working initially covered only a small part of the Benefits Agency's work. There were 12 ONE pilots from June 1999. In funding these pilots, £79.5m came from the Treasury 'Invest to Save' budget out of the total of £112m for all 12 pilots (Social Security Committee 1999: para. 1). There were several difficulties of joint working that emerged during the projects. The different target regimes set for the agencies meant that it was difficult to set targets for the pilots. No new targets were formally set, which made evaluation difficult. The Social Security Committee expressed concern that the job placement target would be too crude to measure the outcomes and that clearer assessment of the quality of advice about benefits be undertaken (Social Security Committee 1999: paras 68 and 70). The different target regimes affected the styles of working, which often clashed. Local authorities were felt to be more 'can do' and focused on solving clients' problems, whereas the Agency style was more 'hierarchical' (Social Security Committee 1999: para. 41). The hierarchical approach was partly because of a concern to meet management targets linked to the external accountability structures of the agency.

Differences in personnel systems between the Benefits Agency and other bodies caused co-ordination problems. Each agency involved in the joint working had its own pay banding and promotion structure (Social Security Committee 1999: paras 34 and 35). A further barrier was variety in IT systems. These systems, particularly web-based systems, are sometimes seen as a way of integrating different organisations to allow them to provide joint services (Dunleavy and Margetts 2000). However, in this case, the organisational boundaries affected how IT was designed and used. The main operational support was provided by the existing Labour Market System used by the Employment Service, OpStrat used in the Benefits Agency combined with a new Gateway Enquiry System. DfEE and DSS were exploring the possibilities of using small scale developmental IT prototypes, for example in Lewisham, to make better use of integrated IT

(Social Security Committee 1999: para. 44), but these were at an early stage in 2000.

Regulated sporadic links and regulated networks

In its very broadest definition, regulation is often used as a synonym for control. However, in this context, regulation is used to refer to 'oversight' involving a superior level of public authority exercising some form of control over lower levels (in contrast to systems having themselves under control, for example, through the voluntary adjustments in sporadic links) (Hood, Scott, James, Jones and Travers 1998, 1999; Hood, James and Scott 2000). Regulation is one way of addressing a key concern of the literature on 'governance' about how to co-ordinate and steer networks and decentralised systems (Rhodes 1994; Kickert, Klijn and Koppenjan 1997). Regulation of sporadic links involves control of organisations that co-operate spasmodically (and may even be in competition with each other in some areas), and contrasts with regulation of networks, where there are more extensive and enduring links between the lower level organisations.

An increasingly important form of regulation of government has been the use of standards or rule-based control by arms-length bodies with some form of official mandate to set standards, monitor and take enforcement action against public bodies (Hood, Scott, James, Jones and Travers 1999). Executive agencies incorporate a regulatory method of control in the department's relationship with the agency, with a performance contract. However, the Benefits Agency was subject to more extensive regulation with the launch of the Benefit Fraud Inspectorate in November 1997 to provide independent assurance about social security systems in central and local government. The BFI cost £6.5m to run in 1998/99 and employed 133 staff, a substantial investment in regulation of these bodies (Benefit Fraud Inspectorate 1999b). The Inspectorate was set up amid widespread concern about the high levels of fraud in the social security system (Secretary of State for Social Security and Chief Secretary to the Treasury 1999: 22). Establishing the BFI seemed to reflect a view that the Agency was not able to deal with the problem of fraud by itself and because it monitored the Agency and other bodies in the benefits system, with a mandate to take a more systemic perspective, it was a contribution to joined-up monitoring of the system.

An even more systematic approach to regulating public services as a network is emerging with the attempt to situate individual agency objectives and targets within broader objectives and targets for central government departments under the Public Service Agreements (PSAs) regime. PSAs arose from the Comprehensive Spending Review of 1998, conducted for different sectors of central government, and were intended to integrate target setting in different areas under an overall umbrella, setting out some departmental outputs and the funding allocated to them to improve the treatment of policies and services straddling organisational boundaries (Chief Secretary to the Treasury 1998: 1–3). PSAs were set up as public documents, like the agency performance targets, and departments had to report progress to the Ministerial Committee on Public Services and Public Expenditure (PSX) (PIU 2000: 7.18). But the first batch of PSAs was modest in joining up performance systems. There were 28 PSAs based on departmental boundaries with only three cross-cutting PSAs in criminal justice, drugs and help for young families with 50 targets, which are held jointly by two or more departments out of several hundred (PIU 2000: Box 9.1). The PSAs were predominantly process oriented in 1998, which tended to reflect separate departmental processes with more effort made to specify outputs and outcomes, which were sometimes the result of several departments' activities in the PSA set issued in 2000 (National Audit Office 2001: 21).

The PSA regime better integrated the Benefits Agency's performance plans with the broader system of plans for central government as a whole. The Benefits Agency's targets were incorporated in a Department of Social Security PSA and an Output and Performance Analysis statement based on the PSA and published in March 1999 (PAC 2000: Sec. 5). The BA instituted a new Performance Management Regime from April 2000 to take account of this development. This change reduced the tendency of the BA systems to focus attention on an overly narrow conception of the organisation's activities (Interview Senior Official, Department of Social Security). The PSA system resembled the arrangements already in place between the Benefits Agency and the Employment Service for delivering Jobseeker's Allowance. But there was a limit to how far targets could capture all the elements of working with other bodies which, combined with multiple and conflicting targets, limited the extent to which this approach could facilitate joined-up government.

Conclusion

Agency structures had a mixed effect on the performance of the Benefits Agency's own core business. However, agency structures created substantial undesirable systemic effects including a lack of coherence in policy making and set up public sector externalities, especially inaccurate information passed to local authorities and other bodies. Concern with these sizeable undesirable side effects was apparent early on in the Agency's life. However, the salience of systemic performance problems was increased by an emphasis on employability in social security policy under the Labour Government since 1997. This change in goals increased the need for the Agency to work with other bodies. The balance of these effects was a contributory factor in policy makers' decisions to embark on major reforms. In the ONE pilot project areas, the social security system resembled a move towards regulated networks as a way of joining-up systems. However, the difficulty of getting different partners to co-ordinate their separate systems and ensuring clear lines of accountability for performance created pressure for a recent more radical reform.

The recent reform has created a more integrated structure for social security, moving beyond the forms outlined in the second section of this chapter. These primarily constitute two bodies focused on different client groups, including an 'agency' of working age and a pensioners organisation as replacements for the Benefits Agency (Benefits Agency 2000). Whilst called an 'agency', the 'working age' organisation is intended to incorporate 'seamless' team working, with those developing policy in the Department (since 2001 the Department for Work and Pensions) also involved in specifying implementation systems and monitoring performance on the ground in the 'agency' (Interview Senior Official, Department of Social Security). The change can be seen as an attempt to remove the 'vertical' organisational barrier between Department and agency. The working age 'agency' combines Benefits Agency and Employment Service staff and resources to create a single new organisation, removing this 'horizontal' boundary. However, local authorities continue to be a separate set of organisations and the working age 'agency' has boundaries set by social security client groups, restricting the potential for organisation on other lines, for example according to purpose, process or place.

The significance of joined-up government performance problems created by agencies elsewhere in UK central government is a matter for empirical investigation. Whilst all agencies share core features of the model, most have more clearly distinct roles than the Benefits Agency (James 2003). However, the return of the Civil Service College to the Cabinet Office in the Autumn of 1999 and the strengthening of ministerial responsibility for the Prison Service in 1997 reflect similar issues. The UK experience presents a cautionary tale for other countries seeking to use the executive agency model. It suggests the need to consider the degree of inter-relation between activities when assessing an activity as a candidate for agency status and potential problems that would be created by having personnel and working practices specific to each agency. When establishing performance regimes, systems that provide strong incentives to focus on the agency's narrow mission can have undesirable effects beyond the organisation in the broader system. However, where the need for joint provision of services does not require integration into a single organisation, the arrangements outlined in this chapter offer a number of ways to link agencies to the broader public service systems in which they operate.

Bibliography

Balloch, S. and Taylor, M. (eds) (2001) *Partnership Working*, Bristol: Polity Press.

Bardach, E. (1998) *Getting Agencies to Work Together: The Practice and Theory of Managerial Craftsmanship*, Washington DC: Brookings Institution Press.

Benefits Agency (1999) *Annual Report and Accounts 1998–99 HC 580*, London: The Stationary Office.

Benefits Agency (2000) *Annual Report and Accounts 1999–2000*, London: The Stationary Office.

Benefit Fraud Inspectorate (1999a) *Report on London South Directorate (AD3) Benefits Agency* http://www.dss.gov.uk/hq/pubs/bfi/londons/.

Benefit Fraud Inspectorate (1999b) *Annual Report: Securing the System* http://www.dss.gov.uk/hq/pubs/bfi/bfiar/.

Benefit Fraud Inspectorate (1999c) *Report on the Social Security Contributions Agency* http://www.dss.gov.uk/hq/pubs/bfi/devon/.

Benefit Fraud Inspectorate (1999d) *Annual Report: Securing the System* http://www.dss.gov.uk/hq/pubs/bfi/bfiar/.

Bichard, M. (1999) *Modernising the Policy Process*, London: Public Management and Policy Association.

Cabinet Office (1999) *Modernising Government*, London: HMSO.

Chancellor of the Duchy of Lancaster (1997) *Next Steps Agencies in Government Review 1996 Cm 3579*, London: The Stationary Office.

Chief Secretary to the Treasury (1998) *Public Services for the Future: Modernisation, Reform, Accountability Cm 4181*, London: The Stationary Office.

Chief Secretary to the Treasury (1999) *Public Services for the Future: Modernisation, Reform, Accountability: March 1999 Supplement Cm 4315*, London: The Stationary Office.

Chief Secretary to the Treasury (2000) *2000 Spending Review: Public Service Agreements Cm 4808*, London: The Stationary Office.

Dunleavy, P. and Margetts, H. (2000) 'The advent of digital government: public bureaucracies in the internet age', Paper presented to the *American Political Science Association Annual Conference*, Washington DC, August 31–1 September.

Efficiency Unit (1988) *Improving Management in Government: The Next Steps*, London: HMSO.

Gray, B. (1989) *Collaborating: Finding Common Ground for Multi-party Problems*, San Francisco: Jossey Bass.

Greve, C., Flinders, M.V. and Thiel, S. van (1999) 'Quangos: what's in a name? Defining quangos from a comparative perspective', *Governance* 12, 1, 129–46.

Gulick, L. (1937) 'Notes on the Theory of Organisation', in Gulick, L. and Urwick, L. (eds) *Papers on the Science of Administration*, New York: Institute of Public Administration, pp. 3–45.

HM Treasury (1999) *The Government's Measures of Success: Output and Performance Analyses*, London: HM Treasury.

HM Treasury (2000a) *The Government's Expenditure Plans 2000–2001 to 2001–2002: Chancellor of the Exchequer's Department Part of Cm 4601–4621*, London: The Stationary Office.

Hoggett, P. (1991) 'A new management in the public sector?', *Policy and Politics* 19, 4.

Hogwood, B. (1997) 'The machinery of government 1979–97', *Political Studies* 45, 4, 704–15.

Hood, C. (1991) 'A public management for all seasons?', *Public Administration* 69, 3–19.

Hood, C., James, O., Jones, G.W., Scott, C. and Travers, T. (1998) 'Regulation inside government: where the new public management meets the audit explosion', *Public Money and Management* 18, 2, 61–8.

Hood, C., Scott, C., James, O., Jones, G.W. and Travers, T. (1999) *Regulation Inside Government: Waste Watchers, Quality Police and Sleazebusters*, Oxford: Oxford University Press.

Hood, C., James, O. and Scott, C. (2000) 'Regulation in government; has it increased, is it increasing, should it be diminished?', *Public Administration* 78, 2, 283–304.

Huxham, C. (ed.) (1996) Creating Collaborative Advantage, London: Sage.

James, O. (1995) 'Explaining the Next Steps in the Department of Social Security: the bureau-shaping model of central state reorganisation', *Political Studies* 43, 4.

James, O. (2000a) 'The Study of regulation: entering a mid-life crisis?', *Public Administration* 78, 1, 241–4.

James, O. (2000b) 'Regulation inside government: public interest justifications and regulatory failures', *Public Administration* 78, 2, 327–43.

James, O. (2001a) 'Beyond the "New Public Management": regulated partnerships in the UK', in Byong-Man, A., Halligan, J. and Wilks, S. (eds) *Reforming Public and Corporate Governance: Management and the Market in Australia, Britain and Korea*, London: Edward Elgar.

James, O. (2001b) 'Business models and the transfer of business-like central government agencies', *Governance* 14, 2, 233–52.

James, O. (2003) *The Executive Agency Revolution in Whitehall*, Basingstoke: Palgrave.

Kavanagh, D. and Richards, D. (2001) 'Departmentalism and joined-up government: back to the future?', *Parliamentary Affairs* 54, 1, 1–18.

Kickert, W., Klijn, E.-H. and Koppenjan, J. (eds) (1997) *Managing Complex Networks: Strategies for the Public Sector*, London: Sage.

Lan, Z. and Rosenbloom, D. (1992) 'Editorial', *Public Administration Review* 52, 535–7.

National Audit Office (1996) *Management of Telephones in the Benefits Agency HC 126 Session 1995–96*, London: HMSO.

National Audit Office (1997) *Financial Auditing and Reporting 1995–96 General Report of the Comptroller and Auditor General 11–XII*, London: The Stationary Office.

National Audit Office (1998) *Benefits Agency: Performance Measurement HC 952, Session 1997–98*, London: The Stationary Office.

National Audit Office (2000a) *Modernising Government: How the NAO is Responding: A Progress Report*, London: National Audit Office.

National Audit Office (2000b) *Good Practice in Performance Measurement and Reporting in Executive Agencies and Non-Departmental Public Bodies*, London: National Audit Office.

National Audit Office (2000c) *State Earnings-related Pension Scheme: The Failure to Inform the Public of Reduced Pension Rights for Widows and Widowers HC 320, Session 1999–2000*, London: The Stationary Office.

National Audit Office (2001) *Measuring the Performance of Government Departments*, London: National Audit Office.

Morgan, K., Rees, G. and Garmise, S. (1999) 'Networking for local economic development', in Stoker, G. (ed.) *The New Management of British Local Governance*, London: Macmillan, pp. 181–96.

Osborne, D. and Gaebler, T. (1992) *Reinventing Government*, Reading, MA: Addison-Wesley.

Performance and Innovation Unit (2000) *Wiring It Up: Whitehall's Management of Cross-cutting Policies and Services*, London: The Stationary Office.

Pollitt, C. (1993) *Managerialism and the Public Services*, 2nd edn, Oxford: Blackwell.

Pollitt, C., Birchall, J. and Putman, K. (1998) *Decentralising Public Service Management*, London: Macmillan.

Pollitt, C., Bathgate, K., Smullen, A. and Talbot, C. (2000) 'Agencies: a test case for convergence?', Paper presented to the *Fourth International Symposium on Public Management*, Erasmus University Rotterdam.

Pollitt, C. (2001) *Joined-up Government: A Short Review*, Erasmus University, Rotterdam.

Public Accounts Committee (1999) *Minutes of Evidence Wednesday 28th April 1999 HC 419 I, Session 1998–99*, London: The Stationary Office.

Ranson, S., Martin, J., McKeown, P. and Nixon, J. (1999) 'The new management and governance of education', in Stoker, G. (ed.) *The New Management of British Local Governance*, London: Macmillan, pp. 97–112.

Rhodes, R.A.W. (1994) 'The hollowing out of the state', *Political Quarterly* 65, 138–51.

Saward, M. (1997) 'In search of the hollow crown', in Weller, P. *et al.* (eds) *The Hollow Crown*, London: Macmillan.

Segal Quince Wicksteed Ltd (2000) Evaluation of the Invest to Save Budget: Final Report to HM Treasury and the Cabinet Office London, Segal Quince Wicksteed Ltd.

Social Security Committee (1998) *Social Security Committee: Minutes of Evidence: Thursday 21st May 1998 HC 587iii, Session 1997–98*, London: The Stationary Office.

Social Security Committee (1999) *Social Security Committee Seventh Report: The One Service Pilots HC 412, Session 1998–9*, London: The Stationary Office.

Talbot, C. (1996). *Ministers and Agencies*, London: The Chartered Institute of Public Finance and Accountability.

Talbot, C. (2002) *So Who Needs Agencies: A Handbook Exploring the Issues of Using 'Agencies' as a Reform Device in Central Government*, Glamorgan.

Trosa, S. (1994) *Next Steps: Moving On*, London: Cabinet Office (OPSS).

Wollmann, H. (2002) 'Co-ordination in the intergovernmental setting', in Peters, G. and Pierre, J. (eds) *Handbook of Public Administration*, London: Sage.

5 Contracting and accountability

A model of effective contracting drawn from the U.S. experience[1]

Jocelyn M. Johnston and Barbara S. Romzek

Introduction

Contracting for government services has become increasingly popular in the U.S., both across levels of government and policy arenas. Recent "devolution" of selected program responsibilities from the federal to state governments has accelerated this trend – especially for social services. This chapter offers a comparative case study of five social service contracts in the State of Kansas with a focus on how those contracts are designed to address issues of accountability. Kansas – a low-population state in the central U.S. – has been fairly aggressive in this area, and its experience is illustrative of the challenges facing governments that seek to use non-governmental and nonprofit organizations to provide social services.

Accountability and contracting are popular government themes, both aimed at reforming the delivery of government services and at alleviating longstanding concerns about government performance. Yet how does the state know when its contractor-vendors have met performance objectives and contractual obligations? Observers note that government agencies do not always hold contractors accountable when they fail to meet their contractual obligations (Fossett *et al.* 2000). This research examines whether such accountability tendencies are related to contract design issues. We present a model of accountability effectiveness which identifies key contract design variables that influence the effectiveness of contractor accountability.

The context for contracting

Privatization, globalization, and devolution have blurred the traditional roles of governments, private companies, and nonprofit organizations around the world and have spurred governments to craft new strategies aimed at delivering high quality public services. The use of the term privatization entails a wide range of activities, encompassing denationalization, load shedding, privatization of production, deregulation, and privatization of finance (Hodge 2000). The initiatives of interest to this discussion

are a type of privatization of production functions: contracting for services. Contracting seeks to introduce market relationships into the
bureaucratic production of public services, with the expectation that the
public sector can reap the advantages of the market and improve service
quality (Sclar 2000).

In the U.S., the past decade of devolution and government reform has
prompted an explosion of government contracting and shifts in the locus
of control for program delivery (Frederickson 1997; O'Toole 2000;
Milward and Provan 2000; Kettl 2000; Smith and Lipsky 1993). While contracting can increase service range, depth, and efficiency, it may dilute
government control and accountability. Governments using contracting
face new accountability challenges as services are contracted to networks
of multiple nongovernmental partners. Today's administrators must function in a "hollow state" with a core of public management surrounded by
an array of cross-institutional, primarily extra-governmental ties (Milward
and Provan 2000; O'Toole and Meier 1999; O'Toole 2000). Governments
at all levels – federal, state, and local – have expanded the range of contracted services from the traditional "make-buy" decisions such as defense
weaponry, highway construction, and fleet purchases, to contracting for
on-going provision of specialized social services, including welfare (Hodge
2000; Salamon 1999; Savas 2000; Sclar 2000).

Increasingly, government workers find themselves managing contractors instead of delivering services (Kettl 2000), often in the context of
diverse expectations such as reducing the size and cost of government,
improving service delivery, and increasing accountability. To do this,
public managers must strive to be "smart buyers" (Kettl 1993) or "prudent
purchasers" of contracted services (Fossett *et al.* 2000) by structuring
effective accountability mechanisms.

Contracting for complex social services, such as welfare or foster care
services, generally involves elaborate and unpredictable relationships
between purchasers and vendors. These services are substantially more
complex to provide and monitor than services provided under what Sclar
(2000) calls a "classical" or complete contract. Many of these contracting
initiatives are undertaken without much attention to accountability issues
(Light 2000; Frederickson 1997; Garvey 1995; Moe 1984), often because of
inherent assumptions that competition among potential providers will
ensure effective contractor performance (Sclar 2000).

Effective accountability under contracting

Not surprisingly, the widespread use of contracting manifests itself in a
broad range of approaches. The logic of contracting varies depending
upon whether one assumes the presence of market discipline among
prospective contracting agents as opposed to what Sclar (2000) refers to as
incomplete or *relational* contracts. Traditional market models of contracting

assume that contractors will be disciplined by market forces such as competition, ease of seller access to the contract market, and ready and inexpensive availability of relevant contract information and alternative providers. Accountability under such conditions relies on the market to ensure desirable behavior. A more common situation occurs under imperfect market conditions, or Sclar's incomplete contract scenario, characterized by frequent transactions among contractual parties and high levels of uncertainty about future situations covered by the contract and about product and/or process. Accountability in this setting tends to generate contracts that grow exponentially in detail, a "contract fattening" process.

Sclar's third type of contract is the relational model, which appears to be the prevailing model in the Kansas social service contracts. Relational contracting is based upon trust between purchaser-principals and vendor-agents in recognition of the absence of market competition and impossibly high information costs. Accountability under this type of contract tends to emphasize articulation and adjustment of performance expectations based upon negotiation and mutual experience – what Sclar refers to as "muddling through" (Sclar 2000; see also Lindblom 1959).

Starting with the fundamental notion of accountability as responsibility for performance, we suggest that effective accountability exists when the relevant government agency has met the minimum conditions of "prudent purchasing" (Fossett *et al.* 2000), i.e. the ability to assess contractor performance and the potential to hold the contractor responsible for that performance. This includes the ability of the state to obtain timely and accurate reporting from the contractor and to use that reported information to evaluate performance and correct shortcomings.

A model of accountability effectiveness

Studies of social service contracting in the U.S. context have found that state agencies often have difficulty holding contractors accountable for their performance (Johnston and Romzek 1999; Fossett *et al.* 2000). Our earlier research on social service contracting in Kansas led us to similar conclusions; that research focused on the contracting decision process and the subsequent contract management and implementation process (Johnston and Romzek 1999, 2000, 2001; Romzek and Johnston 1999, 2000, 2001, forthcoming). Our objective here is to explain variations in the effectiveness of contract accountability.

To explore this dynamic, we examine the nature of the contracts and the factors that we hypothesize to be important for effective accountability. We analyze the features of contracts to determine whether they are designed with accountability in mind. We consider whether the type of accountability strategies embedded in the contracts are congruent with the state's interests and the contractor's tasks and capacities. And we identify contract features that may enable governments to know whether contractors have met performance expectations. The data are drawn from five social service contracting cases in the State of Kansas. These cases deal with welfare clients in the areas of health care for the poor (Medicaid Managed Care, or MMC) and employment preparation services (EPS). The other two cases include services for other vulnerable populations: in-home care for the frail elderly (Home and Community Based Services, or HCBS), and foster care and adoption services (FCA) for children.

A summation of our model of accountability effectiveness is presented in Table 5.1. The dependent variable – "accountability effectiveness" – reflects the capacity of the state to design, implement, and manage accountability of these contracts for social services. We independently rated accountability effectiveness for each of the cases, using possible ratings of low (1), moderate (2), or high (3) in a comparative sense – that is, a high rating would indicate high relative to the other cases included in the analysis. These ratings were based on assessments of effectiveness derived from extensive interviewing of contracting and state agency officials, as well as document reviews The bottom row of Table 5.1 displays these ratings. We rated two cases as "high" and three cases as "moderate" in effectiveness.

Based on our earlier research and the literature on accountability and contracting, we identified a series of variables likely to affect accountability in a contracting environment. These variables were grouped into three categories: contract specifications, contract design issues, and accountability design issues. For each contracting case, we rated each of the independent variables, using a rating scale of low (1), moderate (2), or high (3). We summed the ratings of independent variables and compared these sums to our previously determined rating of overall contract management effectiveness. In the following sections we describe ratings for the independent variables as they emerged in these cases. In the interest of brevity we present only the broadest generalizations regarding the data.

Adequate contract specifications

An important aspect of any contract is a set of clear and mutual understandings about each party's contract obligations. Two aspects that are most central to contract specifications are clarity in roles and responsibilities and agreement about performance measurement criteria.

Clarity regarding accountability relationships

The logic of accountability under contracting includes advance specification of mutual expectations, responsibilities, and obligations of the contracting parties. We expect that contracts with clearly articulated responsibilities and reporting relationships are likely to enhance accountability effectiveness, while contracts that lack clarity or that involve

Table 5.1 A model of accountability effectiveness: contract features affecting accountability in social services contracts

Contract features	Home and Community Based Services (HCBS)	Medicaid Managed Care (MMC)	Foster Care and Adoption Services (FCA)	Employment Preparation Services – Comp (EPS-COMP)	Employment Preparation Services – Provider Agreements (EPS-PA)
Adequate contract specifications					
Initial clarity of accountability relationships	2*	2	3	3	3
Suitability of performance measures, obligations, and deliverables	2	3	2	3	3
Contract design issues					
Ease of performance data collection	2	1	2	3	3
Autonomy of contractor	2	2	1	3	3
State retention of risk	2	1	1	2	3
Ease of introduction of new technologies	1	2	2	3	3
Accountability design issues					
Appropriate accountability alignment	2	3	3	3	2
Column scores	13	14	14	20	20
Contractor accountability effectiveness**	M	M	M	H	H

Notes

* Scores are assigned as follows: 1 = low, 2 = moderate, 3 = high.

** Effectiveness ratings (bottom row) are derived from independent assessments of effectiveness, based on interviews and document review.

multiple stakeholders can complicate the accountability situation. While this may seem straightforward, one challenge of accountability for managers in complex western democracies, such as the U.S. and Westminster models of governance, is the presence of multiple, conflicting and shifting expectations for government performance held by the diverse, legitimate sources of expectations (Campbell and Wilson 1995; Khademian 2000; Romzek and Dubnick 1994; Wilson 1989). Nonprofits and other non-governmental organizations face similar tradeoffs in their own domains as they try to accommodate diverse expectations from state purchasers, clientele, governing boards, grant funders, and communities (Frumkin 2001; Herman and Heimovics 1991; Hayes 1996; Kearns 1996; Kettl 1993; Smith and Lipsky 1993).

THE FINDINGS

The Kansas contracts reflect high-to-moderate levels of initial clarity regarding accountability responsibilities. While all contractors reported early difficulties associated with lines of responsibility and the consistency between the state's expectations and contract provisions, three programs had relatively high levels of clarity, two were rated as moderate, and none fell to the level of "low" clarity.

Suitability of performance measures, obligations, and deliverables

Government's need for accountability and transparency in contracting leads to the establishment and communication of expectations about both program design and performance (Frumkin 2001). Yet the area of social services often lacks clear agreement regarding outcomes and performance measures. Traditionally, grants and contracts to nonprofits have relied on inputs, process, and output indicators, emphasizing staffing loads, funding compliance, and caseload headcounts respectively. So outcome-based performance measures present formidable new challenges, including the need for political agreement on performance standards. Other problems regarding performance measures include the time lag between the program intervention and the desired outcomes, the fact that contractors are rarely in total control of outcomes, and methodological problems associated with developing outcome measures (Romzek 2000; Johnston and Romzek 1999; Behn and Kant 1999).

THE FINDINGS

The five cases were assigned high to moderate ratings on appropriate performance measures, obligations, and deliverables. The two cases with "moderate" ratings were those that had unsettled performance designs at the start of the program and complex reporting obligations.

Contract design issues

Several different facets of contract design can have significant impacts on accountability effectiveness. These include the ease of collecting performance data, autonomy of contractors (or conversely, the extent to which contractors are dependent on other organizations as they deliver services), the extent to which risk has been retained by the state, and the introduction of new technologies associated with the service delivery and performance measurement.

Ease of performance data collection

Accountability presumes the availability of performance data, whether qualitative or quantitative. Occasionally the state-purchaser expects performance data to be more readily available than it is in reality. Of course, it goes without saying that difficulties in collecting performance data will hinder governments seeking to judge the performance of their contractors.

THE FINDINGS

The ability of the state to obtain timely and accurate performance data varied. In some cases, both parties to the contracts were satisfied with the data collection process, and with the quality and accuracy of the data. The state encountered the greatest difficulty regarding performance data collection in the poverty health care case (Johnston 2000); despite the relatively well-developed performance measures available in the field of health care, states are frequently stymied in their attempts to secure good performance data from their contractual health care providers (Landon *et al.* 1998).

Autonomy of contractor

Social service contracting in the U.S. may include two to three levels of government as well as the contracting organizations themselves, which often subcontract with other organizations for some aspects of their contractual obligation. These networks of contractors and subcontractors add to the layers and relationships that affect implementation and accountability (Milward and Provan 2000; Van Meter and Van Horn 1975; Moe 1984; Kettl 2000; Milward and Provan 2000; Agranoff and McGuire 1998). We expect that contractor accountability will be enhanced when contractors have relative autonomy regarding their contractual obligations because a contractor may find it difficult to meet its performance expectations if another player in the system has failed to do its part. When contractor autonomy is reduced through complex relationships with other contractors and sub-contractors, the state will have less clarity with regard to which members of the "network" are performing well and which are not.

THE FINDINGS

These cases exhibited a wide range of contractor autonomy. The foster care and adoption case was rated as low because of the complexity and size of the delivery network in which the contractors operated.

Risk retention by the state

Risk shifting is an increasingly popular component of government contracts. When governments shift risk to contractors, they do so under the assumption that risk provides incentives for efficient performance. Yet our previous research suggests that risk shifting may reduce the capacity of the contractor to meet performance standards. In such situations, the contractor is exposed to loss if the conditions it anticipated during contract negotiations with the state fail to materialize, leading to reductions in service quality, financial instability, and/or losses. Under risk-shifting conditions, the contractor may face incentives to "game" the system and subvert accountability accordingly. We expect that accountability effectiveness will be enhanced when government retains higher levels of risk.

THE FINDINGS

Risk-shifting varied considerably across the cases. The state retained the least risk for two of the most complex services: foster care and adoption, and health care for the poor. For these two cases, the state used a managed care approach, paying the contractor a pre-set amount per client. Under this system, all client health care costs, as determined by the service package included in the contract (i.e., preventive care, hospital in-patient care, etc.), must then be borne by the contractor. For example, the mental health costs for children in the foster care and adoption case greatly exceeded expectations, and many contractors experienced significant financial problems as a result (Klingner, Nalbandian, and Romzek, forthcoming). At least one threatened bankruptcy, and several of the sub-contractors still have not been fully reimbursed.

Ease of introduction of new technologies

As nongovernmental agencies take on new and broader social service programs under contracts, they often introduce new technologies to handle the breadth and complexity of service delivery and reporting requirements (Alexander 2000; Plantz, Greenway, and Hendricks 1997). Governments see information technology as facilitating accountability by increasing and standardizing both fiscal and programmatic reporting. Yet our previous research suggests that the introduction of new technology often hinders the state's capacity to hold contractors accountable (Johnston and Romzek 1999; 2000). This is especially true if the contractors have limited experience with complex information systems or with data-driven performance evaluation. Because of this, we expect complex new technologies to work against accountability effectiveness, compared to simpler technologies, which should reduce accountability complications.

THE FINDINGS

Some contractors experienced relatively few technological adjustments, and others were relatively well equipped to assume the data and reporting requirements associated with the new systems. Complex new technologies were incorporated into cases for poverty health care and in-home care for the elderly, and all parties in these programs reported difficulties associated with gearing up to become system "compatible" with one another. One of these contractors had to devote substantial resources – financial, staff, and time – to upgrading their computer and communications systems.

Accountability design issues

Accountability strategies can also play a significant role in informing the contracting authority about contractors' performance. The pattern in western democracies is to employ multiple accountability strategies that can overlap and operate simultaneously (Bovens 1988; Kearns 1996; Light 1993; Romzek 2000; Rosen 1989), resulting in a layering of accountability relationships within which public officials and their non-governmental contractors operate. The analysis which follows relies on a four-fold typology that reflects the different types of accountability: hierarchical, legal, professional, and political (Romzek and Dubnick 1987; Romzek 2000). While hierarchical accountability is likely to be operative within a contracting agency and can be affected by the presence of a contract, it is not typically part of a contractual relationship. Indeed, the complexity of contract management stems, in part, from the fact that the network systems increasingly used to deliver social services lack the stability offered by traditional hierarchical models of governance (Lynn, Heinrich, and Hill 2000; Milward and Provan 2000; O'Toole and Meier 1999). On the other hand, legal, professional, and political accountability are critically important to the contracting milieu; each can inform government agencies about contractor activities and thus enhance contract accountability.

To determine whether accountability strategies are appropriate for the

Table 5.2 Use of range of accountability strategies in contracting cases

Accountability strategies	HCBS	MMC	FCA	EPS-COMP	EPS-PA
Legal accountability (compliance)	2	3	3	2	1
Professional accountability (deference)	1	3	3	3	3
Political accountability (responsiveness)	2	2	2	2	3
Score of accountability use	5	8	8	7	7

contract as designed, one must understand the underlying components of this variable. Table 5.2 provides information about the extent to which each of the various accountability strategies are used in the different contracting cases. (The numbers are helpful to our analysis of the alignment and are included for readers' review.)

Legal accountability

This involves detailed external monitoring of performance for compliance with established standards and mandates; oversight and auditing procedures are typically used (Romzek 2000; Light 1993; Bardach and Lesser 1996). External auditing of case management, client eligibility, access to services, and program management also reflect this type of accountability.

THE FINDINGS

Some contracts are highly reliant on auditing and external monitoring based on explicit standards – many due to stringent federal regulations – which are often specified in the contract. In the foster care and adoption case, additional scrutiny results from court rulings on child custody issues, periodic monitoring by the state's performance audit office, and license reviews for foster care group homes. In the other cases, we observed detailed tracking of client services and outcomes, requirements for prior approval for all client plans of care, and detailed monitoring through audits reviewing 100 percent of case management records over the course of a year.

Professional accountability

Professional accountability relationships are based on high degrees of auto-nomy for individuals or agencies, deference to expertise, on-going consulta-tion, and emphases on performance that support professional judgments about best practices for achieving outcomes. A typical example of profes-sional accountability in social service contracting is specifying desired con-tract outcomes, such as reduced rates of infectious disease or successful integration of former welfare recipients into sustained employment, and leaving the contractor to determine how best to achieve the result. Contract-ing lends itself readily to professional accountability when state agencies see themselves as off-loading programs and tapping the capacity of the contrac-tor to address some of the more intractable service delivery problems.

THE FINDINGS

Professional accountability, with its emphasis contractor expertise, is heavily used in four of these five contracts. Contractors had a great deal of latitude regarding how to accomplish their tasks, and accountability focused on benchmarks and outcomes. In the case of in-home care for the elderly, the state initially had some concerns about the administrative capacity of the nonprofit contractors and designed training, financial, and technical assistance programs to reflect this.

Political accountability

Political accountability relationships emphasize discretion in pursuit of responsiveness to key stakeholders, such as the state-purchaser, legislators, peer service provider networks, and clientele. The historic dependence of nongovernmental and nonprofit organizations on donors and govern-ment grants and contracts for financing has led to the development of finely honed skills of responsiveness and network management (Herman and Heimovics 1991; Smith and Lipsky 1993; Milward and Provan 2000). In contracting, this type of accountability relies on external stakeholders' judgments that the contractor is doing a good job delivering the con-tracted service. Stakeholders can use a variety of indicators of perform-ance such as program products, donor and client satisfaction, and caseload ratios (Behn and Kant 1999; Light 1993, 2000).

THE FINDINGS

Strategies that emphasize responsiveness to the contract principal and clientele using predetermined outputs and benchmarks were most evident when contractor performance was based on caseloads, client participation, and feedback from clients.

Alignment of accountability relationships

The intensity of each accountability type may be dictated by the individual contracting context. Thus the alignment of the accountability mechanisms must be appropriate for each contract situation. The presence of a wide range of accountability strategies points to a critical issue in contracting: the determination of which of the potential accountability strategies are best suited to the contract. One type of accountability is not necessarily appropriate for each and every circumstance; some strategies are suited for different program emphases and tasks. Because of the multi-method approach to accountability that is typical in the U.S. – especially in a contracting environment – the presence of several simultaneous accountability relationships is commonplace, as are the less-than-ideal blended configurations of accountability. We expect accountability effectiveness to be enhanced when the configuration of accountability types reflects an alignment appropriate for the contracting regime.

Decisions as to which accountability relationships are appropriate are a function of the organization's managerial strategy and contracting tasks. While the conditions of accountability are rarely ideal, it is useful to discuss accountability configurations that reflect an appropriate alignment of managerial strategy and core task. Managerial strategies tend to reflect different emphases, including inputs, processes, outputs, and or outcomes. The nature of the core contract tasks can range from routine to complex, the former lending themselves to standardization and rules, the middle ground often involving a mix of routinization and discretion, the most complex tasks requiring nonroutine responses based upon individual discretion and expertise. The shaded cells in the figure below show ideal accountability alignments when managerial strategies and core tasks are appropriately aligned (Romzek 2000; Romzek and Dubnick 1994). When performance expectations are cast in terms of inputs and tasks are routine, hierarchical accountability, with its emphasis on limited discretion and close supervision is most appropriate. When performance standards emphasize processes and the tasks are relatively routine, legal accountability relationships can be the most effective alignment. If managerial strategies emphasize performance in terms of outputs and agency tasks are less routine, political accountability relationships, with emphases on responsiveness to key stakeholders (including clientele) may be most

		CORE TASKS			
		Routine			*Nonroutine*
	Inputs	HIERARCHICAL			
MANAGERIAL	*Process*		LEGAL		
STRATEGY	*Outputs*			POLITICAL	
	Outcomes				PROFESSIONAL

Figure 5.1 "Ideal" accountability alignments: managerial strategy and core task.

appropriate. Finally, contract performance specified in terms of outcomes, combined with complex agency tasks, tends to require professional accountability relationships.

Our analysis indicates that the administrative tasks, and managerial strategies in these cases lend themselves to blends of multiple accountability strategies. For the most part, these contracts encompass appropriate alignments of accountability. Three of the five cases operate under blends of accountability using highly appropriate alignments well suited to the managerial emphases and contract tasks. The remaining two cases exhibit moderately appropriate alignments.

The comprehensive employment preparation service case was rated as high in terms of alignment. The managerial strategy for the contract emphasizes outcomes, with performance payments explicitly tied to successful placements and additional bonuses for sustained employment. The task is fairly complex – to provide welfare clients with job skills necessary to successful transition to sustained workforce participation. We place this task three-quarters of the way toward the nonroutine end of the task complexity continuum. Initially, the contract used a blend of legal, political and professional accountability, involving close monitoring, explicit benchmarks, adaptability to individual client needs, and reimbursements based on results. After six months, the growing reliance on outputs and outcomes supported political and professional types of accountability strategies.

For the poverty health care case, the contract reflects multiple managerial emphases: processes (treatment of clients, intake procedures, etc.), outputs (reimbursement based on client enrollment), and outcomes (a goal of improved access and health status for welfare clients). The core task is highly complex and involves substantial professional judgment. Given these facets of the program, the accountability alignment should be a blend of legal, political, and professional strategies; in fact, all three types are in evidence.

The foster care and adoption contracts embody several managerial emphases: processes (timeliness of activating the case, a policy of treating all eligible clients), outputs (benchmarks regarding length of time in the state foster care system), and outcomes (reimbursement schedule based on client movement through the system). The nature of the contract management task reflects a range of complexity. Some tasks require compliance with legal mandates; others represent complex professional judgments of highly individualized cases; and somewhere in the middle of the range of complexity is the challenge of case management, mental health counseling, and long-term placement of children from abusive homes. The mix of tasks and managerial emphases indicates that a blend of accountability types would be well suited to these contracts. We find an appropriate blend of legal (in the sustained role of courts and audits), political (extensive periodic outside evaluations of contractor performance), and professional (contractors are reimbursed based on permanent child placements).

In the employment provider agreements, the tasks tend to involve discrete activities (resume preparation, job search) and the managerial strategy for such contracts tends to emphasize outputs, such as the numbers of clients who attend job training sessions, etc. The core task for such a program is about mid-way on the routine-nonroutine continuum; its emphasis on outputs, combined with this location, suggests that political accountability would be best. Yet the presence of professional accountability, as reflected in deference to contractors to decide how best to improve client job readiness, is an example of a complementary accountability strategy that is less than ideal in its alignment. It is complementary because professional strategy affords discretion needed for the task. It is less than ideal because the performance indicators do not emphasize or measure employment outcomes. As a result we rate this case moderate on accountability alignment.

In the contract for in-home care for the elderly, managerial emphases reflect a combination of inputs, process, and outputs. Multi-faceted tasks under the contract reflect some routine tasks, like forms and documentation, and there are other fairly complex tasks requiring professional judgments, such as developing plans of care to increase the likelihood that the frail elderly can continue independent living. As a result of the range of tasks, a blend of accountability types is appropriate: legal for the process items like eligibility, professional for the complex judgments about mental acuity and physical independence, and political accountability emphasizing an output orientation in billing by client caseload. In practice, the contract relies mostly on legal and political, with very little professional deference; we rate it moderate on accountability alignment.

Results

Table 5.1 indicates that when the case ratings for each of the independent variables were summed, the results were consistent with our expectations and with our ratings of effective contractor accountability (the dependent variable). The ratings assigned to the independent variables generated high accountability effectiveness scores for the two employment preparation service cases, in keeping with our original observations that for these two cases, the state was most successful in assessing contractor performance. The remaining three cases exhibited moderate effectiveness, and our results suggest that this is related partly to the influence of the independent variables. In short, we found notable variation in terms of contract specification, design issues, and accountability strategies. Our results indicate that those variations had systematic impacts on contract accountability effectiveness and that those impacts supported our original hypotheses.

Conclusion

Like any government reform, contracting for social services has its advocates and critics. Advocates see benefits such as increased efficiency, reduced size of government, greater program flexibility, and more transparent accountability. Critics often bemoan contracting reforms as misguided – either as prone to abuse by contractors, or thinly veiled excuses to reduce government and diminish the capacity of government. Not surprisingly, in a pluralistic setting such as the United States, there is ample empirical evidence to support the veracity of both perspectives. Looking at five cases of contracting for social services in the state of Kansas, we conclude that state administrators have done a good job designing contracts for effective accountability. While none of the cases we examined were problem-free regarding accountability, our data led us to conclude that for two of the five cases, accountability effectiveness was relatively high, with the other three cases exhibiting moderate effectiveness. Apparently these public managers know what contract design features to include in contracts, and the contract features contributed to the state's ability to discern whether contractors were meeting their contractual obligations.

These contracts included clear and objective contract specifications and used a range of accountability strategies appropriate to the contract tasks, managerial emphases and institutional environments. All in all, these five social service cases, while Herculean in their attempt to change the landscape of social service delivery in the state of Kansas, represent good efforts at designing effective accountability strategies into the contracts. The state had less success with other elements of contract design. State contract administrators encountered difficulties collecting performance data, found challenges inherent in contractor interdependencies that affected performance, and experienced the greatest complications when contracts involved risk shifting to contractors. New information technologies, intended to enhance accountability, actually served as a drag on accountability effectiveness because of the difficulties associated with contractor adaptation and coordination with the state.

The reality of the contracting milieu for these cases was such that, regardless of whatever early clarity existed about contract obligations, the terms and expectations of the contract were often renegotiated when experience suggested such adjustments were needed. In essence, parties to the contract adjusted contractual expectations through a process that Sclar (2000) and Lindblom (1959) characterize as "muddling through." The state readily admits that many of its initial benchmarks regarding caseloads, service levels, and compensation for these contracts were at best "guesstimates." The state's willingness to adjust benchmarks and compensation levels reflected their recognition that these early estimates were inaccurate and that it was important for the state to retain some of the financial risk associated with these service delivery contracts. These adjustments reflected the learning curve from both state agency and contractors as they gained experience with these contracting regimes.

We conclude that the difficulties encountered by the state with these contracts have more to do with the challenges of implementation than with design flaws. States need to carefully consider the political and economic contexts of contracting. We observed that factors external to the contract management context – factors related to the market environment and the level of political support for the state and the contractors – were often very important determinants of effective contract accountability. More specifically, the contracts typically contained consequences for inadequate performance – sanctions, penalties, termination clauses, etc. – thereby satisfying the "prudent purchasing" standard of incorporating consequences for inadequate contractor performance. But we observed that the state rarely invoked these consequences because of the absence of alternative providers or political suppression of sanctions. As Sclar (2000) and others have noted, the capacity of government to hold contractors accountable is substantially influenced by the type of contracting environment.

Accountability looks very different in a system highly dependent on collaboration and cooperation than it does in a more market-like system where multiple providers and competition facilitate accountability. The task for public managers is to prepare for the appropriate context, and to be ready for the unforeseen developments that typify social service contracts.

Note

1 This research has been funded by the PricewaterhouseCoopers Endowment for the Business of Government, the Kellogg Foundation through the Rockefeller Institute of Government, and the University of Kansas. For those wishing a fuller elaboration of the data detail and findings, see Barbara S. Romzek and Jocelyn M. Johnston, 2001, "Social Contracting, Social Service Networks, and Effective Accountability: An Explanatory Model," Proceedings of the 2001 annual meeting of the American Political Science Association, available online in the conference proceedings at: http://pro.harvard.edu.

Bibliography

Agranoff, R. and McGuire, M. (1988) "Multinetwork management: collaboration and the hollow state in local economic policy," *Journal of Public Administration Research and Theory* 8, 1 (January), 67–91.
Alexander, J. (2000) "Adaptive strategies of nonprofit human service organizations

in an era of devolution and new public management," *Nonprofit Management and Leadership* 10, 3 (Spring), 287–303.

Bardach, E. and Lesser, C. (1996) "Accountability in human services collaboratives: For what? And to whom?," *Journal of Public Administration Research and Theory* 6, 2, 197–224.

Behn, R. and Kant, P.A. (1999) "Strategies for avoiding the pitfalls of performance contracting," *Public Productivity and Management Review* 22, 4 (June), 470–89.

Bovens, M. (1988) *The Quest for Responsibility: Accountability and Citizenship in Complex Organisations*, New York: Cambridge University Press.

Campbell, C. and Wilson, G. (1995) *The End of Whitehall: A Comparative Perspective*, Cambridge, MA: Blackwell.

Fossett, J.W., Goggin, M., Hall, J.S., Johnston, J.M., Roper, R., Plein, L.C. and Weissert, C. (2000) "Managing Medicaid managed care: are states becoming prudent purchasers?," *Health Affairs* (July/August), 39–49.

Frederickson, H.G. (1997) *The Spirit of Public Administration*, San Francisco: Jossey-Bass.

Frumkin, P. (2001) *Managing for Outcomes: Milestone Contracting in Oklahoma*, The PricewaterhouseCoopers Endowment for The Business of Government, Arlington, VA.

Garvey, G. (1995) "False promises: the NPR in historical perspective," in Kettl, D.F. and DiIulio, J. Jr. (eds) *Inside the Reinvention Machine: Appraising Government Reform*, Washington DC: Brookings Institution.

Hayes, T. (1996) *Management, Control and Accountability in Nonprofit/Voluntary Organizations*, Ipswich, Suffolk: Ipswich Book Co.

Herman, R.D. and Heimovics, R.D. (1991) *Executive Leadership in Nonprofit Organizations*, San Francisco: Jossey-Bass.

Hodge, G.A. (2000) *Privatization: An International Review of Performance*, Boulder, CO: Westview Press.

Johnston, J.M. (2000) "Implementing Medicaid managed care in Kansas: politics, economics and contracting," Case Studies in Medicaid Managed Care Services, Albany, NY: The Rockefeller Institute of Government.

Johnston, J.M. and Romzek, B.S. (2001) "Examining the stability hypothesis: comparing stable and dynamic networks in social service contracting," paper presented at 6th National Public Management Research Conference, Indiana University, Bloomington Indiana, October 18–20.

Johnston, J.M. and Romzek, B.S. (2000) *Implementing State Contracts for Social Services: An Assessment of the Kansas Experience*. Grant report, The PriceWaterhouseCoopers Endowment for the Business of Government, May.

Johnston, J.M. and Romzek, B.S. (1999) "Contracting and accountability in state Medicaid reform: rhetoric, theories, and reality," *Public Administration Review* (September/October), 59, 5, 383–99.

Kaufman, H. (1977) *Red Tape: Its Origins, Uses and Abuses*, Washington DC: The Brookings Institution.

Kearns, K. (1996) *Managing for Accountability*, San Francisco: Jossey-Bass.

Khademian, A.M. (2000) "Is silly putty manageable? Looking for the links between culture, management, and context," in O'Toole, L. and Brudney, J.L. Jr. (eds) *Advancing Public Management: New Development Sin Theory, Methods, and Practice*, Washington DC: Georgetown University Press, pp. 33–48.

Kettl, D.F. (2000) Discussion paper prepared for Spring meeting of "The transformation of governance: globalization, devolution, and the role of government," Discussion paper prepared for Spring meeting presented at the National Academy of Public Administration, Albuquerque, NM, June 1–3.

Kettl, D.F. (1993) *Sharing Power: Public Governance and Private Markets*, Washington DC: The Brookings Institution.

Klingner, D., Nalbandian, J. and Romzek, B.S. (forthcoming) "Politics, administration and markets: conflicting expectations and accountability," *American Review of Public Administration*.

Landon, B., Tobias, C. and Epstein, A. (1998) "Quality management by state Medicaid agencies converting to managed care," *JAMA* 279, 3 (January 21), 211–15.

Light, P. (2000) *Making Nonprofits Work: A Report on the Tides of Nonprofit Management Reform*, Washington DC: Brookings Institution.

Light, P. (1993) *Monitoring Government: Federal Inspectors General and the Search for Accountability*, Washington DC: Brookings Institution.

Lindblom, C. (1959) "The science of 'muddling through,'" *Public Administration Review* 19, 79–88.

Lynn, L., Heinrich, C. and Hill, C. (2000) "Studying governance and public management: challenges and prospects," *Journal of Public Administration Research and Theory* 10, 2, 233–62.

Milward, H.B. and Provan, K.G. (2000) "Governing the hollow state," *Journal of Public Administration Research and Theory* 10, 2, 359–79.

Moe, T.M. (1984) "The new economics of organization," *American Journal of Political Science* 28, 739–77.

O'Toole, L.J. Jr. (2000) "Research on policy implementation: assessment and prospects," *Journal of Public Administration Research and Theory* 10, 2 (April), 233–62.

O'Toole, L.J. Jr. and Meier, K.J. (1999) "Modeling the impact of public management: implications of structural context," *Journal of Public Administration Research and Theory* 9, 4, 505–26.

Plantz, M.C., Greenway, M.T. and Hendricks, M. (1997) "Outcome measurement: showing results in the nonprofit sector," in Newcomer, K.E. (ed.) *Using Performance Measurement to Improve Public and Nonprofit Programs*, San Francisco: Jossey-Bass Publishers.

Romzek, B.S. (2000) "Dynamics of public sector accountability in an era of reform," *International Review of Administrative Sciences*, 66, 21–44.

Romzek, B.S. and Dubnick, M.J. (1994) "Issues of accountability in flexible personnel systems," in Ingraham, P.W. and Romzek, B.S. (eds) *New Paradigms for Government: Issues for the Changing Public Service*, San Francisco: Jossey-Bass Publishers, Inc.

Romzek, B.S. and Dubnick, M.J. (1987) "Accountability in the public sector: lessons from the Challenger tragedy," *Public Administration Review*, 47, 227–38.

Romzek, B.S. and Johnston, J.M. (1999) "Reforming Medicaid through contracting: the nexus of implementation and organizational culture," *Journal of Public Administration Theory and Research* 9, 1, 107–40.

Romzek, B.S. and Johnston, J.M. (2000) "Reforming state social services through contracting: linking implementation and organizational culture," in Brudney, J., O'Toole L. Jr. and Rainey, H.B. (eds) *Public Management: New Developments in Theory, Methods, and Practice*, Washington: Georgetown University Press.

Romzek, B.S. and Johnston, J.M. (2001) "Contracting, social service networks, and effective accountability: an explanatory model," paper presented at the annual meeting of the American Political Science Association, San Francisco, August, 2001.

Romzek, B.S. and Johnston, J.M. (forthcoming) "Contract implementation and management effectiveness: a preliminary model," *Journal of Public Management Research and Theory.*

Rosen, B. (1989) *Holding Government Bureaucracies Accountable,* 2nd edn, New York: Praeger.

Salamon, L.M. (1999) *America's Nonprofit Sector: A Primer,* revised edn, New York: Foundation Center.

Savas, E.S. (2000) *Privatization and Public-Private Partnerships,* New York: Chatham House Publishers.

Sclar, E.D. (2000) *You Don't Always Get What You Pay For: The Economics of Privatization,* Ithaca, NY: Cornell University Press.

Smith, S.R. and Lipsky, M. (1993) *Nonprofits for Hire: The Welfare State in the Age of Contracting,* Cambridge, MA: Harvard University Press.

Van Meter, D. and Van Horn, C. (1975) "The policy implementation process: a conceptual framework," *Administration and Society* 6, 4, 445–88.

Wilson, J.Q. (1989) *Bureaucracy: What Government Agencies Do and Why They Do It,* New York: Basic Books.

6 Contractualism and performance measurement in Australia

Linda McGuire

Introduction

Robust indicators and measures are the holy grail of performance management. The quest is central to the shift to performance measurement reflecting broader change in public management in 'NPM heartland' of the United Kingdom (UK), New Zealand (NZ) and Australia. NPM is shorthand for the trend to reform public services to make them more performance oriented and customer-focused (PUMA 1996). In practice, comparative studies reveal considerable diversity between and within countries (PUMA 1997a; Pollitt and Bouckaert 2000). Diversity is evident even within NPM heartland between the UK, NZ and Australia. Variation is partly explained by country specific institutional constraints. In Australia these are a Westminster system of responsible parliamentary government, the distribution of power in a federal system, and the Australian tradition of public provision of social services (Davis 1997).

Structural disaggregation and performance measurement have been identified as two key variables explaining diversity in agency relationships (Pollitt *et al.* 2001). The level of both structural disaggregation and performance measurement is high in Australia. A federal system that divides responsibility for public services between three levels of government, rather than a systematic agency structure such as Next Steps in the UK or Crown Agencies in NZ, explains structural disaggregation. Contracting and competitive tendering for social welfare services, the official policy of the Commonwealth Government, further fragments service delivery. High performance measurement is explained by NPM reform in the Australian Public Service (APS). Performance reporting is central to accountability and financial management, and agencies responsible for funding and delivering public services in Australia are subjected to systematic performance measurement. Indeed, Australia is considered a leader in developing performance indicators (PUMA 1997b).

This chapter examines a national system of performance measurement for social welfare services. The Review of Commonwealth/State Government Service Provision (the Review) is a cooperative development between the Commonwealth, State and Territory governments (the states) for 'whole-of-government' performance reporting. Efficiency and effectiveness indicators have been developed to benchmark the performance of what are described as 'social infrastructure services'. Transparent performance reporting against nationally agreed objectives is a means to improving accountability, policy coordination and service delivery. The Review compares service efficiency and effectiveness between the states in six areas – education, health, justice, housing, emergency and community services.

The first section of the chapter explains the historical and institutional context in which the Review developed. Social policy in a federal system of parliamentary responsibility and the shift to contractualism explain the growth of performance measurement in Australia. The Commonwealth Government dominates funding for social services, but responsibility for delivery is fragmented in highly complex federal systems. The philosophical stance of the Productivity Commission (PC) explains the approach to performance measurement in the Review. The head of the PC chairs the Steering Committee that manages the Review and the secretariat, responsible for performance reporting, is located in the Commission.

The second section examines performance measurement and reporting by the Review. This is directed at external accountability and central control rather than internal agency management. Key features of the approach are transparency, and independent performance measurement against agreed performance indicators. The Review is a work in progress guided by three broad principles – a focus on measuring outcomes, a balanced set of indicators and comparable measures for all governments. Effectiveness indicators and nationally comparable data both represent substantial progress in performance measurement. However, gaps in indicators and measures suggest balanced performance reporting is still elusive.

The third section considers the approach to performance measurement. Benchmarking results is a production process model and applying this to social welfare services raises two issues. The first is transferring performance measured from manufactured goods to professional services. Production and consumption are not separate for services and this requires a different approach to measuring efficiency and effectiveness. The second issue is transferring performance measures from private to public services. Performance is complex and contested for public services with multiple stakeholders and this also requires a different approach to measuring efficiency and effectiveness.

The chapter concludes by considering performance measurement as a mechanism for policy coordination in fragmented systems. This is an issue for agency reforms in general. Purchaser-provider arrangements are one manifestation of an international trend to decentralisation and automisation (Pollitt *et al.* 2001). Purchaser-provider arrangements are a variant of the principal-agent model of rational choice that separates policy agencies from service delivery contractors (Walsh 1995). Compressed by Osborne and Gaebler into a powerful slogan that 'governments should steer and not row' (Davis and Wood 1998), performance indicators are the steering mechanism in this model. The selection of indicators has consequences for policy coordination.

Performance monitoring is a strategy to reduce the gap between policy objectives and results achieved by autonomous agencies and contracted service providers. In theory, agreed objectives and transparent reporting against a balanced set of performance indicators overcome the problem of incomplete information in contractual relationships (PUMA 1994; IC 1996). In practice, suitable effectiveness indicators and outcome measures have inhibited balanced performance reporting for public services (Smith 1993; Carter 1998). Performance indicators developed by the Review are intended to fill this gap for social welfare services. The next section examines the contextual variables that explain the shift to performance measurement and the approach of the Review.

Contracting in a federal system

Australia is organised constitutionally as a federation of six states and two territories. Local government is a third tier not formally recognised in the constitution. Federalism in Australia has always been characterised by complex patterns of cooperation between two levels of government – the Commonwealth, and the states (Davis and Rhodes 2000). Local governments are mainly funded by states. Financial relations between the Commonwealth and states have always reflected a broad purchaser-provider type model (Keating 1996). A challenge in this system is horizontal policy coordination between programs and vertical coordination between different levels of government and agencies that deliver public services (Davis and Rhodes 2000).

Social welfare policy

Public services are funded by Commonwealth, state and local governments, and provided or delivered by a complex mix of public, community and private sector agencies. The Commonwealth Government has the major responsibility for taxation and therefore controls funding of public services through general revenue and specific purpose payments (SPPs) to the states. Responsibility for delivery rests primarily with state and local governments and increasingly private agencies. The Commonwealth Government influences policy through its control of SPPs and program grants direct to public and private agencies (IC 1996; Simms 1999).

Funding models and responsibilities vary between programs and services (Lyons 2001). SPPs to fund health, education and housing are formally negotiated Commonwealth-State agreements and are usually subject to conditions. Increasingly, SPPs are linked to specific outputs or outcomes and performance is audited based on agreed indicators (Duckett and Swerrissen 1996). Community services tend to be funded by grants paid directly to providers (Lyons 2001). Increasingly service agreements with private and community agencies are contracts for specific units of service for designated client groups, and performance reporting is a condition of funding.

Two decades of financial management reform at the Commonwealth level has changed the basis of purchaser-provider arrangements by shifting funding from historical costs to results. Under successive Labour Governments from 1983 to 1996, change was incremental rather than dramatic as social policy shifted from universal rights to a performance culture. This was reflected in greater targeting of expenditure on groups with clearly specified eligibility criteria and growth in performance reporting (Lyons 1998). The application of competition policy to public services and the election of the Howard Government in 1996 accelerated the shift to performance measurement as formal contract models have increasingly been applied to social welfare services.

NPM and microeconomic reform

As in the UK, the path to NPM in Australia has been characterised by evolutionary or incremental change (Talbot 2001; Wanna *et al.* 2000). Core objectives of efficiency and effectiveness have provided a degree of continuity and coherence to continuous reform (Davis and Rhodes 2000). A consistent theme has been changing accountability from inputs to results by developing output and outcome standards and indicators (MAB-MIAC 1992 and MAB 1997). Davis (1997) identified managerialism and contractualism as two distinct phases.

In the first phase from 1984, the language of management displaced administration in central agency policy and implementation guidelines, reflecting the application of business techniques to public services. Under the Financial Management Improvement Program (FMIP) there was a fundamental shift from traditional financial accountability for budget expenditure to results, defined as service outputs and program outcomes (MAB/MIAC 1992). Strategies included portfolio budgeting, strategic planning and program evaluation techniques. Performance reporting was a counterbalance to devolution of responsibility for resource management from central agencies to departments and service delivery agencies (Keating 1990; Wanna *et al.* 2000). However parliamentary and internal reviews expressed concerns about the slow pace of development of performance monitoring and the inadequacy of performance indicators (HRCSFPA 1990; MAB-MIAC 1992).

In the second phase of reform, the language of contractualism displaced management as the emphasis shifted from corporate planning and portfolio budgeting to contracts and contestable service delivery (Davis and Rhodes 2000). A substantive policy shift occurred in 1993 when the Commonwealth government decided to apply competition policy to the public sector and public services. Initially, reform concentrated on government business enterprises, but gradually the principles of contracting and contestability extended to social welfare services (IC 1996; Davis 1997). In 1995 the state and territory governments through the Council of Australian Governments (COAG) signed the National Competition Policy agreements. This was a catalyst for broad application of a contract model of service delivery that included social welfare services (Davis and Wood 1998).

NCP linked microeconomic, social welfare policy and financial management reform in the APS. The election of the Howard conservative government in 1996 accelerated the shift to contestable service delivery and Competitive Tendering and Contracting (CTC) became official policy in the first term of the Government (MAB 1997; Davis and Rhodes 2000). CTC exacerbates fragmentation with a service delivery model that favours competition between agencies. At the same time, the Howard Government has replaced program budgeting with a new resource management framework based on accrual accounting and outcomes and outputs budgeting (Wanna *et al.* 2000). Together these reforms compel agencies to specify outcomes, outputs and performance indicators.

In the language of contractualism, funds are appropriated to deliver specified services to achieve defined outcomes (IC 1996). Funding has changed from historical costs to defined outputs and outcomes, and there is greater emphasis on identifying the full cost of services (Lyons 2001). The shift from corporate planning and program budgeting to CTC and outcomes and output budgeting has changed the balance in performance reporting from internal evaluation to external audit. This has been reflected in the growth of performance reporting against quantitative indicators.

Whilst purchaser-provider arrangements for welfare services are not new in Australia's federal system, CTC further fragments service delivery, adding another layer of complexity to policy coordination (Davis and Rhodes 2000). Contracting has become an organising principle (Davis 1997) and great faith is placed in performance monitoring as a mechanism for improving accountability, policy coordination and responsiveness of service providers to clients. The contract state is a more evaluative state (Walsh 1995). Performance monitoring requires a robust framework of performance indicators and measures for reporting. The key institution influencing the method of performance measurement in the Review is the Productivity Commission (PC).

Productivity commission

Australia has a long tradition of influential autonomous policy advisory agencies (Davis and Rhodes 2000). As an independent statutory authority and the government's principal advisory agency on microeconomic reform, the PC is a powerful advocate for the primacy of the productivity imperative. Created in 1996 by the Howard Government, the PC carried forward the philosophical approach of the Industry Commission that supported the microeconomic reform agenda of successive governments from the 1970s (Quiggin 1996). The PC's first report recommended the broad application of CTC in the public sector and directly linked social welfare reform to improving productivity and competitiveness (PC 1996). The Commission has applied an economics framework, developed for evaluating industry assistance, to social infrastructure services and the social dimensions of public policy. Its recommendations have been instrumental in extending the microeconomic reform agenda to social welfare services (PC 1998a).

As Chair of the Steering Committee and Secretariat for the Review, the Commission has a major influence on performance measurement and reporting. Independent, transparent analysis, open consultative processes and intellectual rigour, hallmarks of PC inquiries, have been applied to the Review. In an earlier project for COAG the PC was responsible for comparative performance reporting on 'economic infrastructure services'. A general framework of efficiency and effectiveness indicators was developed to monitor electricity, gas, water, urban transport, railways and ports and government trading enterprises (PC 1998b). This performance indicator framework has been applied to what the PC describes as 'social infrastructure services' in the Review, and to local government services (IC 1997). The next section examines this framework and performance reporting on 'social infrastructure services' in the Review.

The Review of Commonwealth/State Service Provision (the Review)

Initiated by the Prime Minister, State Premiers and Chief Ministers of the Territories at a Special Premiers Conference in 1993, the Review is the first systematic attempt to develop objective and consistent data to compare the performance of social welfare services between governments. Performance is defined as "how well a service meets its objectives", and the emphasis is on comparing results defined as "outcomes against agreed national objectives". The primary purpose is to develop reliable efficiency and effectiveness indicators to compare the costs of services and results "to assist government decision making" (SCRCSSP 2001: 1). A second agenda is to examine ways of improving performance by changing to market-based approaches for service provision (PC 1999). To this end, the Review has published case studies of service delivery reforms (SCRCSSP 1998c).

An annual publication, known as the 'Blue Book', reports on performance in six key areas – education, health, justice, emergency services, community services and housing. These services accounted for $64 billion in 1999–2000, representing 27 per cent of government expenditure and 10 per cent of GDP (SCRCSSP 2001: 6). Comparative information on efficiency and effectiveness is presented for six state and two territory governments. The reports are intended for use in strategic budget, policy planning and evaluation.

The structure for implementing the Review, shown in Figure 6.1, is a cooperative approach based on participation of all governments. A Committee with the cumbersome title, the Steering Committee for the Review of Commonwealth/State Service Provision (SCRCSSP), comprising senior officials from central agencies of the Commonwealth and state governments, manages the Review. The Head of the PC is the independent Chair ensuring the cooperation of all governments (PC 1998a). An independent secretariat in the PC has responsibility for reporting against agreed indicators, which enhances the reliability of measurement (Pollitt 2000). The PC generally relies on data collected by external agencies, but has commissioned surveys of client views. Responsibility for establishing national objectives and developing performance indicators is delegated to expert Working Groups. Each group includes senior staff of relevant line agencies from the Commonwealth and states who take advice from specialist research groups, such as the Australian Bureau of Statistics and the Australian Institute of Health and Welfare.

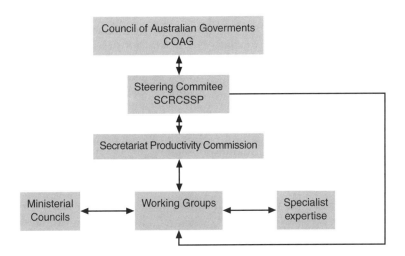

Source: Figure 2.1 SCRCSSP 1995, 40.

Figure 6.1 Review of Commonwealth/state services.

'Yardstick' competition

Benchmarking results by comparing 'cost-effectiveness', not best practice, is the basis of performance reporting in the Review. 'Value for taxpayer funds' is established by comparing the efficiency and effectiveness of service provision between the states. The language and logic reflects the philosophical stance of the PC. In the absence of market competition, 'yardstick' competition is a second best solution to improve productivity efficiency and responsiveness to users. Comparison based on efficiency and effectiveness criteria is a substitute for market competition. Perform-ance indicators and measures substitute for market price signals (SCRCSSP 1995; PC 1999).

The arguments for performance measurement are quite explicit. First, transparency improves accountability to users and lead to better policy outcomes. Second, outcome indicators focus debate on objectives rather than processes. Third, a suite of efficiency and effectiveness indicators captures all areas of performance. To this end the Review has concen-trated on developing a balanced set of indicators and nationally compara-ble measures for performance reporting.

The 'efficiency and *effectiveness' indicator framework*

Performance indicators in the Review provide quantitative information used to determine how successful governments are in achieving agreed objectives (IC 1996). A general framework of performance indicators, shown in Figure 6.2, is based on 'three Es' model of economy, efficiency and effectiveness' (SCRCSSP 1997: 10). Efficiency is defined as how well organisations use resources to produce units of service and the general indicator is inputs per unit of output. Outputs are defined as the services delivered to clients by or on behalf of government. Effectiveness is defined as how well the service outputs achieve the agreed objectives. The general framework has four effectiveness indicators. 'Overall outcomes' measures the impact or consequence of a service in relation to policy objectives. Short-term (or intermediate) output and longer-term (or final) outcome indicators are used. Access and equity indicators measure timeliness, affordability and services to designated groups. In response to a COAG request, the review is concentrating on developing access and equity indic-ators for indigenous Australians and people living in rural and remote loca-tions. Appropriateness indicators measure how well service delivery meets clients' needs. Quality indicators measure 'conformance to standards' and/or 'fitness for intended purpose'. These indicators are the basis for comparing performance between the states and making judgements about the efficiency and effectiveness of different approaches to service delivery.

Twelve Working Groups have adapted this general framework to develop a 'suite of performance indicators' for 22 different services.

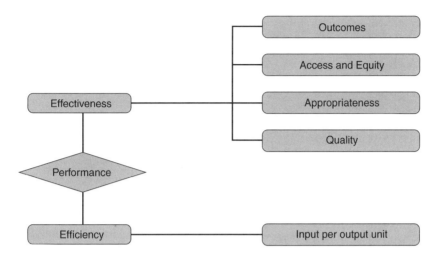

Figure 6.2 General performance indicators framework.

Health, housing and emergency management services each have a single Working Group. In contrast, education, justice, and community services have separate Working Groups for each service framework. Each Working Group is responsible for agreeing national objectives and selecting performance indicators and there is considerable variation between different services. Objectives may be specified in legislation, as for aged care; or in formal Commonwealth-State agreements, as for housing; decided by Ministerial Councils, as for school education; or, agreed by the Working Party, as for the health and police services. According to the Review, specific indicators 'take into account the characteristics of the service, its clients and providers' (SCRCSSP 1998a: xxiv).

Table 6.1 provides a comparative analysis of efficiency and effectiveness indicators for each service. The balance between effectiveness and efficiency is striking, as effectiveness accounts for 75 per cent of the total indicators. The number and ratio of efficiency and effectiveness indicators varies between services. Housing, police and corrective services have a relatively high ratio of efficiency to effectiveness indicators. Community services generally have the lowest ratio of efficiency to effectiveness indicators. There is also some variation in the type of efficiency indicators selected. All frameworks include a measure of cost per service unit. Schools, public hospitals, corrective services, SAAP, public and community housing use physical and financial measures of efficiency. For example, efficiency measures for government schools are expenditure per student and staff per student. Efficiency measures for corrective services are cost per prisoner and prison utilisation rate.

Table 6.1 Performance indicators and nationally comparable reporting 2001

Service framework	Efficiency		Effectiveness		Total	
	Indicators	Reporting	Indicators	Reporting	Indicators	Reporting
Education						
Schools	4	4	10	2	14	6
VET	4	4	12	8	16	12
Health						
Public acute care hospitals	5	4	14	5	19	9
General practice	1	1	18	13	19	14
Breast cancer	2	nil	11	3	13	3
Mental health	2	1	10	2	12	3
Justice						
Police services	14	nil	18	14	32	14
Courts administration	1	1	7	4	8	5
Corrective services	9	4	12	8	21	12
Emergency services						
Fire	1	nil	12	3	13	3
Ambulance	3	nil	8	2	11	2
Community Services						
Aged care	2	1	17	10	19	11
Disability services	3	nil	13	8	16	8
Child care	2	nil	9	1	11	1
Child protection and out-of home care	2	nil	18	4	20	4
SAAP	7	nil	8	5	15	5
Housing						
Public housing	5	5	7	6	12	11
Community housing	4	nil	7	nil	11	nil

Commonwealth rent assistance	2	2	10	10	12	12
Total indicators	73	27	221	108	294	135
Percentage	25%		75%		100%	
Reporting as percentage of total indicators		20%		80%		45%
Percentage of total reporting					100%	100%
Reporting on efficiency	100%	36%				
Reporting on effectiveness			100%	49%		

Source: SCRCSSP 2001: Volumes 1 and 2.

Notes

Indicator refers to specific performance measures against efficiency and effectiveness criteria. Reporting refers to data provided on a nationally comparable basis.

Police services aggregates indicators and reporting in four frameworks. All four frameworks have nationally comparable data on some effectiveness indicators but no nationally comparable data on efficiency indicators.

Children's services include day care and preschool services to children aged under 12 years.

Child protection and out-of-home placements is combined in one framework, but there are separate indicators for 'Child protection services' and 'Out-of-home care'. There are no nationally comparable data for child protection services.

SAAP is the Supported Accommodation and Assistance Program that funds services for individuals and families who are homeless or at risk of becoming homeless.

As shown in Table 6.2, there is considerably more variation in effectiveness indicators, both between and within service areas. Only general practice and mental health have selected indicators for all four effectiveness criteria in the general framework. Fire and ambulance services have specified output and outcome indicators. Public hospitals, aged care and housing have selected quality, appropriateness and access and equity indicators, but outcomes have not been developed. School education, Vocational Education and Training (VET) and the four police service frameworks have selected access and equity as well as outcomes indicators. Childcare has specified outcomes, access and equity, and quality indicators. However, a closer inspection of the designated indicators suggests there is considerable overlap between the criteria in different frameworks. For example, 'client satisfaction with appropriateness' is an access and equity indicator for disability services and 'satisfaction with hours of provision' is an outcome indicator for childcare services.

The balance between purchaser-provider and consumer interests also varies between services. School education has no client satisfaction or quality indicators, while VET has satisfaction indicators for both students and employers. There are separate indicators for clients' and carers' satisfaction with disability services. However, many of the service frameworks do not include client views. Complaints and redress are important alternatives to 'satisfaction' surveys to monitor effectiveness from a client perspective, but are not generally included as indicators. Only two frameworks, aged and child care, include complaints as a quality indicator. Rent assistance is the only framework that includes 'review of decisions', which is an indicator of appropriateness.

Variation in effectiveness indicators is to be expected, given a range of services with different objectives. There is no obvious systematic pattern in the variation. Funding arrangements do not appear to be a factor. For example, program funding for childcare and aged care is tied to accreditation systems. Compliance with service standards is a quality indicator for aged care but not childcare. Outcomes are specified for childcare but not aged care. Police services and emergency management, both funded primarily by the states, have quite different effectiveness indicators. Different Working Groups may explain some of the variation in effectiveness indicators. Housing and emergency management each has a single Working Group, and use consistent indicators. However, four health service frameworks developed by the same Working Group, use different indicators. Variation in effectiveness indicators may also reflect overlap and confusion between outcomes, access and equity, appropriateness and quality criteria in the general framework. Outcome indicators vary from intermediate short-term outputs, for example immunisation coverage and cancer screening rates in the general practice framework, to long-term outcomes, such as employment for people with disabilities. Ten frameworks do not have designated appropriateness and quality indicators.

Table 6.2 Performance indicators 2001

Service	Designated performance indicator					
	Efficiency	*Outcomes*	*Access and equity*	*Approp-riateness*	*Quality*	*Client views*
Education						
School education	✓	✓	✓	✗	✗	✗
VET	✓	✓	✓	✗	✗	✓
Health						
Public acute care hospitals	✓	✗	✓	✓	✓.	✓
General Practice	✓	✓	✓	✓	✓	✓
Breast cancer	✓	✓	✓	✗	✗	✗
Mental health	✓	✓	✓	✓	✓	✓
Justice						
Police						
Community safety	✓	✓	✓	✗	✗	✓
Crime investigation	✓	✓	✓	✗	✗	✗
Road safety and traffic	✓	✓	✓	✗	✗	✓
Judicial services	✓	✓	✓	✗	✗	✗
Court administration	✓	✗	✓	✗	✓	✓
Corrective services	✓	✓	✗	✓	✗	✗
Emergency management						
Fire	✓	✓	✗	✗	✗	✗
Ambulance	✓	✓	✗	✗	✗	✗
Community services						
Aged care	✓	✗	✓	✓	✓	✓
Disability services	✓	✓	✓	✗	✓	✓
Child care	✓	✓	✓	✗	✓	✗
Child protection and	✓	✓	✗	✗	✗	✗
out-of-home care	✓	✓	✗	✗	✗	✗
SAAP	✓	✗	✓	✓	✗	✓
Housing						
Public housing	✓	✗	✓	✓	✓	✓
Community housing	✓	✗	✓	✓	✓	✓
Commonwealth rent assistance	✓	✗	✓	✓	✓	✓

Source: SCRCSSP 2001: 20 Table 2.1.

Note
The report is available at http://www.pc.gov.au/gsp/2001/index.html.

Comparable performance reporting

Performance information is evidence about performance that is collected and used systematically to enable judgements (Barrett 1997: 10). The purpose of reporting in the Review is to enable policy makers to compare efficiency and effectiveness in the six states and two territories. National averages are the benchmark. There are no league tables of data for individual agencies. Performance reporting is independent and the main objective is to provide 'sound, reliable data' (PC 1999). The PC coordinates the publication of performance measures by presenting data from a range of sources in a consistent framework. Wherever possible, existing measures are used. Not all of the data published in the Reports is strictly nationally comparable. However, the PC argues it is better to publish imperfect data that enables some comparison and acknowledge its limitations.

This is a serious project backed by substantial resources and the political authority of COAG. The scale and scope of performance information is unprecedented in Australia. Published in December 1995, the first report was 681 pages and included more than 100 indicators for ten different services. Eight of the ten frameworks were designated preliminary, and the report revealed many gaps in available measures and data inconsistencies between the states (SCRCSSP 1995). By 2001 the report had expanded to 1,514 pages with 294 indicators for 22 different services. Since 1997 the 'Blue Book' has been published annually. Services are grouped into the six service areas (education, health, justice, emergency management, community services and housing), to monitor outcomes at a system level. Reporting consists of two parts – a qualitative profile of the service and policy developments, and quantitative results against agreed indicators. Comments from each government are included for each service. Definitions of performance measures and tables of all available data are published for each of the 22 service frameworks (SCRCSSP 2001).

Reporting on nationally comparable performance measures also varies considerably between services. The status of reporting in 2001 is shown in Table 6.1. Nationally comparable performance data is reported for 45 per cent of all indicators. Overall reporting is balanced with comparable measures for 36 per cent of efficiency and 49 per cent of effectiveness indicators. Whilst, reporting on efficiency indicators increased significantly in the 2000 and 2001, there is considerable variation between services. School education, VET, general practice, public housing and CRA have comparable data for all efficiency indicators, and public hospitals on four out of five efficiency indicators. In contrast, police, emergency services and four of the five community services frameworks have no comparable reporting on any efficiency indicators. The Review is working to develop nationally comparable efficiency measures that reflect the full cost to government (SCRCSSP 2001: 20).

From the first report in 1995, the need for better indicators of effectiveness has been explicitly recognised and comparable measures are not always available. Reporting is concentrated on outputs that are intermediate measures of outcomes. Rent assistance has nationally comparable reporting on all effectiveness indicators, making this the only framework with complete reporting. Public housing is almost complete with comparable data on six out of seven effectiveness indicators. At the other end of the spectrum, child protection services has no nationally comparable performance reporting on any effectiveness or efficiency indicators. State responsibility for service delivery and professionals resisting measurement may explain gaps in performance reporting. Police services, where the states are primarily responsible for funding and delivery, have comparable data on 14/18 effectiveness but no efficiency measures. Public hospitals, the largest item of health expenditure and funded primarily by the Commonwealth, have comparable reporting on 4/5 efficiency but only 9/19 effectiveness indicators.

Clients' views and access and equity measures are not widely available. Client and community perceptions have been identified as "a crucial missing ingredient in ensuring a 'client outcome focus' " (SCRCSSP 1997: v). A national client satisfaction survey was commissioned by the Review to fill this gap for disability services (SCRCSP 2001). Two target groups, indigenous Australians and rural and remote communities, have been designated by COAG for special attention. Some progress has been made on measures for indigenous Australians, but data for people in rural and remote locations is not yet available (see SCRCSSP 2001, Table 2.3).

Not withstanding the gaps, the Review represents substantial progress in performance reporting on effectiveness. Prior to this the only nationally comparable performance information for the states was Commonwealth Grants Commission (CGC) data comparing costs and expenditure per capita used to decide the allocation of general revenue grants by the Commonwealth to the states. In contrast, the data published by the Review enables some comparison between the states of the efficiency and effectiveness of services.

Impact of performance reporting

Assessing the impact of the 'Blue Books' is difficult. Performance reporting is a mechanism for external accountability, policy coordination and internal management improvement. The purpose of reporting in the Review is: 'to inform parliaments, governments, government service agencies, and the clients of these agencies – the wider community – about their overall performance, based primarily on results rather than inputs' (SCRCSSP 1995: iii).

Accountability, policy coordination and responsive service delivery are different ends. Parliament, policy makers, service providers, clients and the community have different interests and want different performance information. Monitoring results, against agreed national social policy objectives is the primary purpose of performance measurement in the Review. The target audience is central and line agency managers responsible for budget preparation, strategic planning and policy evaluation (SCRSSP 1998b).

A survey of users revealed a high level of awareness and use of the reports by government and non-government agencies. (SRCSSP 1998b). Users considered the Reports 'important or very important' for strategic and policy planning and evaluation (80 per cent), assessing resource needs (63 per cent), assessing performance (76 per cent) and benchmarking (65 per cent). Information was generally regarded as highly credible, relevant and timely. Central agency users considered the Reports more important for strategic or policy planning and evaluation than line agency users. In contrast, line agency users considered the Reports more important for assessing resource needs (SCRCSSP 1998b). Parliament and the wider community were not included in the survey.

COAG is committed to performance measurement for social welfare services, and the Review has facilitated agreement on national objectives and collection of comparable measures for performance reporting (SCRCSSP 1997). On the question of a balanced set of indicators, performance measurement attracts criticism on essentially two fronts. One argument is that measurement is not objective and value free but selective (Zifcak 1994). The counter argument, articulated by the PC, is that quantitative measures are only one input into policy evaluation and are transparent. A different but related criticism is that performance measurement is incomplete because indicators do not capture all the important dimensions. This is reflected in criticism of methodologies and debates about the merits of particular indicators and measures selected.

The next section examines the consequences for performance reporting of transferring a production process model to professional public services. Two issues are considered (Walsh 1995; Carter 1998; Pollitt 1998, 2000). First, there is the conceptual and technical complexity of measuring performance for professional services. The second issue is transferring performance indicators and measures from private to public services.

Selecting performance measures for professional public services

Service has a diversity of meanings that leads to ambiguity about performance measurement and confusion in selecting indicators (Johns 1999). What is described as a 'service process model', shown in Figure 6.3, is the basis for selecting indicators and measures in the Review. In the words of the PC (SCRCSSP 2001: 10):

> Governments have a number of objectives/desired outcomes for the community. To achieve these objectives or desired outcomes, governments fund service providers and products and/or services. Service providers transform these funds/resources (inputs) into services

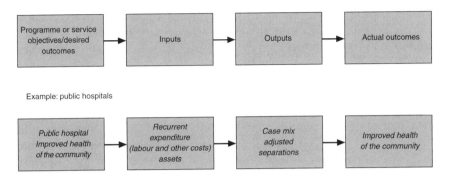

Figure 6.3 Inputs, outputs and outcomes model.

(outputs) and the outputs contribute to the achievement of a government's actual outcomes.

Inputs, outputs and outcomes are the currency of performance measurement in this model (Carter, Klein and Day 1992). Standardised service outputs and quantitative outcome measures enable comparison of the 'cost effectiveness' of service outputs that contribute to policy outcomes (Carter, Klein and Day 1992; Smith 1996; Talbot 1999). Separating and standardising inputs, outputs and outcomes is a production orientation based on manufacturing concepts (Grönroos 2001). However, manufacturing and services are different paradigms within management (Grönroos 1994). Services management starts from a fundamentally different perspective on process and this requires a different approach to measuring efficiency and effectiveness (see McGuire 1999 Chapters 3 and 13 and Grönroos 2000 Chapters 9 and 10).

The distinction between processes and outputs in manufacturing does not apply to services. Outputs from manufacturing processes are tangible products that lead to outcomes for consumers and providers. Service outputs are processes and intangibility creates uncertainty about outputs and quality that creates specification problems. A service process model overcomes the problem by monitoring the value of outcomes. Services vary on intangibility. Economic infrastructure services such as electricity, rail and postal services are processes, but the outputs are more tangible than human services such as education, health and justice. Specification and measurement of quality and outputs is more difficult as services' intangibility increases. A reliable electricity, rail or postal service is more easily specified and measured than a reliable school, hospital or court.

Production and consumption are not entirely separate in time, for services and consumers participate to some extent as producers in delivery. This 'coproduction' increases the complexity of service delivery and is the main difference between manufacturing and service processes. A production process model that separates inputs/processes and outputs/outcomes ignores coproduction. Separating and measuring processes (outputs) and outcomes is more difficult as service complexity increases. A service process model monitors inputs, outputs (processes) and outcomes (results).

Services cannot be separated from the providers and consumers. Direct provider-consumer encounters increase the variability of service processes (outputs) and outcomes. Consequently services are harder to standardise than manufactured goods. A production process model measures efficiency by the ratio of inputs to outputs, assuming standard units of service and constant quality. However, as direct encounters in service delivery increase, standardising processes (outputs) and quality is difficult. A service process model overcomes the problem by monitoring the cost of inputs and the value of outcomes using sales revenue as a proxy (Smith 1993; Talbot 1999).

Intangible outcomes, coproduction and provider–client encounters in delivery leads to ambiguity in transferring the 'input-ouput-outcomes' model from manufacturing to services. Furthermore, there is considerable variability between services on these three dimensions. Different types of services processes require different performance measures (Silvestro *et al.* 1992). With the exception of housing, the services in the Review are 'professional' signalling that delivery is process rather than product-oriented, customised rather than standardised and high on provider-client contact (Silvestro *et al.* 1992). Housing would be classified as a 'mass' service, where delivery is product–orientated, standardised and low contact. Performance measurement is more difficult for professional than mass services. Therefore, it is not surprising that housing has a more complete framework of indicators and measures than case-managed community services.

Professional services processes

Professional services offer care and advice and are delivered by service workers with specialist knowledge and usually technical qualifications (IC 1995; Harvey 1996). Intangibility of service outcomes leads to asymmetry or divergence between providers and consumers on 'appropriateness' and 'quality' (Walsh 1991). Service quality has technical and process features that require different measures (Grönroos 2000). Technical quality or 'reliability' relates to what is delivered and is usually measured by conformance to standards. Process quality relates to how the service is delivered and is usually measured by 'satisfaction' based on clients' subjective evaluation of encounters with providers. Professional services are high on 'credence attributes', which means providers have information about technical quality that clients cannot evaluate. Clients have more information about process quality or 'customer service'. For example, hospitals' patients cannot judge the technical expertise of medical professionals and focus more on what Talbot (1999) refers to as the 'hotel aspects of service' – courteous staff, palatable meals and clean wards.

The power of professional service providers derives from their specialist knowledge and control of technical quality standards, which critics argue has little regard for client perceptions (Pollitt 1988; Harvey 1996). Appropriateness indicators in the Review generally reflect a purchaser or provider perspective on client needs. External accreditation is one strategy to overcome provider capture and increase responsiveness to users, balancing reporting by monitoring client views is another (IC 1996). Four service frameworks in the Review include accreditation indicators. However, gaps in effectiveness indicators mean that client-user views are generally under-reported.

Coproduction increases the complexity of professional service delivery (Silvestro *et al.* 1992). Separating inputs and standardising outputs (processes) is difficult because of the active role of consumers in delivery and discretionary judgement on the part of providers (Harvey 1996). Applying a production process model focuses on technical outputs at the expense of client outcomes. Service providers get around the problem by monitoring the value of outcomes (Smith 1993; Talbot 1999).

Professional services are high contact and direct provider-client encounters increase the variability of service outputs and client outcomes (Silvestro *et al.* 1992). Standardising outputs and quality to measure efficiency is difficult (Walsh 1995). Physical and financial measures are used in practice (Grönroos 2000, Chapter 9). Resource efficiency and capacity utilisation are physical measures, but these do not measure cost or revenue effects. The problem is specifying standard units of outputs for services, as quality varies with direct consumer involvement. Costs per unit and revenue generating efficiency are financial measures. Cost per unit measures internal efficiency but ignores the quality of outputs. Revenue generating efficiency measures the value of outcomes to providers using sales revenue or profitability.

Difficulty in specifying indicators and availability of measures for professional services is one explanation of gaps in performance reporting. Rent assistance is the only framework with nationally comparable performance reporting on all efficiency and effectiveness indicators. Public housing has nationally comparable performance reporting on all efficiency indicators, six out of seven effectiveness indicators. Rent assistance and public housing are not professional services. VET and general practice are the only other services with nationally comparable performance reporting on more than 50 per cent of indicators. At the lowest end of reporting is child protection with no nationally comparable measures. The language of 'social infrastructure services', used by the PC, disguises not only the interpersonal, but also the public nature of these services. Measuring costs and quality is not easy for professional services, but is more difficult for public services (Walsh 1991; Smith 1993; Carter 1998; Pollitt 2000).

From private to public services

Confusion in the inputs-ouputs-outcomes model for public services is reflected in the many variations in practice (Carter, Klein and Day 1992; Smith 1996; Talbot 1999). The nexus between outputs and outcomes is more complex for public than private services and this requires a different approach to performance measurement (Smith 1996). Three 'public' characteristics of services add to the ambiguity in a production process model for professional services (McGuire 1997).

Public services have welfare objectives and value is measured using social indicators. Service outputs (processes) are intermediate measures of overall social outcomes against policy objectives. Gaps in indicators and measures in the Review also reflect the difficulty of specifying the link between outputs for clients and social outcomes for the community. Sales revenue and profitability are 'bottom line' measures of economic value for private services. Social impact and equity are 'bottom line' measures of social value for public services (Carter, Klein and Day 1992). Economic value and social value measure different outcomes. Social value is by nature more qualitative than quantitative and, consequently, indicators and measures are underdeveloped. 'Access and equity' indicators in the Review measure participation by different groups. However, access and equity is under-reported for many services because of gaps in indicators and measures.

'Cost effectiveness' or 'value for money' rhetoric disguises the complex and contested nature of performance for public services (Walsh 1991; Smith 1993; Carter 1998). 'Social protection', the welfare lobby label, has a different connotation to 'social infrastructure'. Value becomes values and is contested for socially controversial programs such as prisons and child protection (Walsh 1995; Pollitt 2000). Public services have multiple stakeholders with divergent views on 'outcomes' and 'appropriateness'. Balance reporting requires indicators and measures of different stakeholders. Performance reporting on users and community interests in the Review varies between services. Corrective services, for example, has containment and repatriation indicators and measures. VET has indicators and measures for employer and student.

Collective consumption distinguishes private and public services. A mix of satisfaction for 'client', 'customer' and 'community' as indicators of quality, outputs and outcomes suggests confusion about what is being measured, and why, in the Review. Customer is a slippery concept for public services, with a complex set of stakeholders to be 'satisfied'. The primary source of revenue for welfare service providers is not customers who pay, but budget-funded agencies or 'purchasers'. Access to services is decided by providers based on eligibility or assessed needs, not consumer choice. Giving voice to client views in performance measurement is important for professional public services, given information asymmetry between providers and clients and their non-traded status. However, clients' views are under-reported because of gaps in indicators and measures.

Public accountability is a fundamental distinction between public and private services. Rights are central to public accountability and performance has compliance dimensions (Barrett 1997). Clients are citizens rather than 'customers' and political processes decide access to services. Public accountability for social welfare services is a voice, rather than choice option based on public rather than private law (Walsh 1995). 'Output' quality resides in delivery processes for services. Transparent eligibility and access decisions are an indicator of process quality for public services. Complaints and redress are measures (Pollitt 1988; Walsh 1991; IC 1996).

Ombudsman's offices, administrative appeal and judicial review processes, dating from legislative reform in Australia in the 1970s, provide citizens with avenues of complaint and redress, and already collect data. Given this history, complaints and redress are a surprising omission in the Review. Only two services, aged and child care, measure complaints. Rent assistance is the only service that measures review of decisions. 'Prison offender complaints' and 'complaints' were deleted as effectiveness indicators for corrective services and police in the 2001 Report, without any comment or explanation for the change.

The benefits of performance monitoring are greater transparency of objectives and accountability for results (Barrett 1997). Agreed objectives and transparent, independent reporting by the PC are clearly the strengths of the Review. Effectiveness indicators change the focus of performance reporting from inputs to results and from internal management to external audiences (Pollitt 2000). However, gaps in indicators and comparable measures limit accountability for results. Indicators and measures depend on the purpose of performance measurement (Carter 1998). In the Review, this is comparing efficiency and effectiveness of services between governments. Technical measurement is one issue. The priority of the Review is filling the gaps in comparable measures to improve reporting. Conceptual ambiguity in efficiency and effectiveness indicators is another issue. Changes to performance indicator frameworks between reports are evidence of this problem. As the preceding discussion demonstrates, a production process model of efficiency and effectiveness is profoundly ambiguous for professional public services. The analysis does, however, provide some suggestions for improving performance measurement and reporting in the Review.

Towards balance in efficiency and effectiveness measures

Developing 'a balance suite of efficiency and effectiveness indicators', and comparable measures is a 'work in progress'. Selection of indicators and measures needs to start with a process model that recognises that the nexus of inputs-outputs-outcomes is different for professional services, and that public services require different performance indicators.

On the efficiency side, there is no equivalent to sales or customer profitability to measure 'revenue generating efficiency' for public services. The services included in the Review generally operate with fixed budgets and have excess demand. The power of the purse is in the hands of government purchasers not consumers' willingness to pay. Financial indicators measure costs but ignore the quality of outputs and value of outcomes (Carter, Klein and Day 1992; Talbot 1999). In practical terms, interdependency means that efficiency and effectiveness are two sides of the same coin for public services. Service failure is an efficiency as well as effectiveness indicator. For example, 'hospital misadventures' included as indicator of quality for public hospitals, increase costs to the health system. The cost of waste and inefficiency from service failures is measured at best indirectly. Physical indicators that measure waste and service failures should be included in the general framework that is considered for each service.

On the effectiveness side, equity indicators and measures, not an issue for private services, are underdeveloped. Service processes (outputs) are intermediate outcome measures. Social policy outcomes achieved by joint programme effort increases the complexity of service delivery so outcomes need to be monitored at different levels. Social indicator measures to monitor outcomes are underdeveloped and relying on existing measures will not close the gaps in performance reporting. Customer satisfaction is profoundly ambiguous for public services and client views are generally under-reported. Rather than 'customers', public services have multiple stakeholders with divergent and sometimes conflicting interests. Complaints and redress may be better indicators of responsiveness to users than 'customer service' indices, and should be included in the general framework that is considered for each service. Complaints and redress measures should be a norm rather than the exception.

Performance is always contentious for budget constrained public services. Conceptual and technical difficulties in measuring the performance of professional services add to the problem of the contested nature of performance for public services. Gaps in performance reporting in the Review reflect the limits of a production process model for professional public services.

Steering with performance measures

The general issue for agency reforms, raised in the introduction to this chapter, is the role of performance measurement in policy coordination. Performance measures have become an essential tool in central control of fragmented delivery systems (Carter, Klein and Day 1992). In theory, agreed objectives and transparent reporting on a balanced set of indicators overcomes the problem of incomplete information in contractual relationships. However, the language of 'purchasers and providers', 'outputs and outcomes' and 'customers' suggests a clarity for professional public services that does not exist in practice. Information asymmetry is more complex than suggested by the principle-agent model. Divergent interests of purchasers and providers, professional and clients, and multiple stakeholders all contribute to apparent policy failure. Incomplete efficiency and effectiveness indicators and measures in practice may increase rather than reduce the gap between policy intentions and service delivery results. Imprecise allocation of costs distorts efficiency judgements. Gaps in effectiveness indicators distort value judgements.

Performance monitoring changes the basis of policy evaluation from qualitative judgement to enumerative assessment (Pollitt 1990; Zifcak 1994). Supporters argue transparent indicators and performance reporting improve policy decisions (PUMA 1997b; MAB 1997; Barrett 1997; DoFA 2000). Critics argue limiting policy evaluation to what can be specified and measured leads to tunnel vision (Smith 1993; Walsh 1995). The question for policy coordination as Rhodes (2000) suggests, is whether monitoring enables more control over less. Quantitative objectives and measurable outcomes limit what gets counted as performance. Control based only on quantitative measures is limited control.

Performance information is fundamental to policy evaluation to steer fragmented service delivery systems. Monitoring using quantitative measures is one form of information. Qualitative evaluation is another. A fundamental issue for agency reforms in general is the extent to which auditing and quantitative measurement is displacing qualitative policy evaluation. Performance measurement to monitor results is necessary but not sufficient for public policy decisions (Pollitt 2000).

The PC's argument that the Review does not involve evaluations, but simply reports comparisons within the 'existing policy framework of governments', is disingenuous (IC 1997: 88). The inference that performance reporting is managerial and technical ignores the political dimensions of specifying social outcomes that are the goals of policy (Duckett and Swerrissen 1996). This also ignores the political dimensions of selecting indicators and measures that determine whose interests are taken into account.

Professional public services pose the biggest challenge for performance measurement. The Review does represent progress in shifting the balance in performance monitoring from efficiency to effectiveness, but it has met predictable hurdles. Effectiveness and equity are harder to measure. Linking outputs to social outcomes is difficult in complex delivery systems for public services. Costs are easier to quantify than quality. Monitoring outputs and outcomes does not resolve the tension between efficient use of scarce budget resources and responsiveness to individual client needs. The client imperative is weaker than the productivity imperative for public services. The risk of elevating costs over quality is dissatisfied citizens and declining trust in public services.

Accepting the role of measurement also means accepting the limitations of quantitative measures. Performance measurement, as Pollitt (2000) argues, cannot solve value differences but can help resolve policy debates by making differences more transparent. The paradox of performance measurement is that transparent indicators and comparable measures will increase rather than resolve political conflict over the funding and distributional consequences of social policy decisions.

Bibliography

Barrett, P. (1997) 'Performance standards and evaluation', *Australian Journal of Public Administration* 56, 33, 96–105.

Carter, N., Klein, R. and Day, P. (1992) *How Organisations Measure Success*, London: Routledge.

Carter, N. (1998) 'On the performance of performance indicators', *Evaluation des politiques publiques*, Paris: L'hartmattan.

Davis, G. (1997) 'Towards a hollow state? Managerialism and its critics, Chapter 11,' in Considine, M. and Painter, M. (eds) *Managerialism the Great Debate*, Melbourne: Melbourne University Press.

Davis, G. and Rhodes, R.A.W. (2000) 'From hierarchy to contracts and back again: reforming the Australian public service, Chapter 3', in Keating, M., Wanna, J. and Weller, P. (eds) *Institutions on the Edge?* Capacity and Governance, St Leonards: Allen & Unwin.

Davis, G. and Wood, T. (1998) 'Outsourcing', *Australian Journal of Public Administration* 57, 4, 75–88.

DoFA Department of Finance and Administration (2000) *The Outputs and Outcomes Framework: Guidance Document, Performance Improvement Cycle Guidance for Managers*, November.

Duckett, S. and Swerrissen, H. (1996) 'Specific purpose programs in human services and health: moving from an input to output and outcomes focus', *Australian Journal of Public Administration* 55, 3, 34–8.

Grönroos, C. (1994) 'From scientific management to service management. A management perspective for the age of service competition', *International Journal of Service Industry Management* 5, 1, 5–20.

Grönroos, C. (2000) 'Chapter 5 quality management in services and Chapter 9 managing service productivity', in *Services Management and Marketing: A Customer Relationship Management Approach, Second Edition*, Chichester: John Wiley & Sons.

Grönroos, C. (2001) 'The perceived service quality concept – a mistake?', *Managing Service Quality* 11, 3, 150–2.

Harvey, J. (1996) 'Productivity in professional services: to measure or not to measure Chapter 9', in Halachmi, A. and Bouckaert, G. (eds) *Organisational Performance and Measurement in the Public Sector. Towards Service, Effort and Accomplishment Reporting,* London: Quorum Books.

HRSCFPA (House of Representatives Standing Committee on Finance and Public Administration) (1990) *Not Dollars Alone: Review of Financial Management Improvement Program,* Canberra: AGPS.

IC (Industry Commission) (1995) *Charitable Organisations in Australia,* Report No. 45, 16 June, Canberra: AGPS.

IC (Industry Commission) (1996) *Competitive Tendering and Contracting by Public Sector Agencies,* Report No. 48, 24 January, Canberra: AGPS.

IC (Industry Commission) (1997) *Performance Measures for Councils Improving Local Government Performance Indicators,* Research Report, October, Melbourne: Industry Commission.

Johns, N. (1999) 'What is this thing called service?', *European Journal of Marketing* 33, 9/10, 958–73.

Keating, M. (1990) 'Managing for results in the public interest, C.G. Lewis memorial lecture to South Australian Regional Group IPAA', *Australian Journal of Public Administration* 49, 4 (June), 387–98.

Keating, M. (1996) 'Past and present directions of the APS: some personal reflections', *Australian Journal of Public Administration* 55, 4, 3–9.

Lyons, M. (1998) 'The impact of managerialism on social policy. The case of social services', *Productivity Management Review* 21, 4 (June), 419–32.

Lyons, M. (2001) *Third Sector: The Contribution of the nonprofit and cooperative enterprises in Australia,* Crows Nest: Allen & Unwin.

MAB (Management Advisory Board) (1997) *Beyond Bean Counting: Effective Financial Management in the APS – 1988 and beyond,* Public Service Merit and Protection Commission, Canberra, December.

MAB-MIAC (Management Advisory Board-Management Improvement Advisory Committee), Task Force on Management Improvement (1992) *The Australian Public Service Reformed. An Evaluation of Management Reform,* Canberra: AGPS.

McGuire, L. (1997) 'Service delivery contracts: quality for customers, clients and citizens, Chapter 8 in Davis', in Sullivan, G.B. and Yeatman, A. (eds) *New Contractualism?* South Melbourne: Macmillan.

McGuire, L. (1999) *Australian Services Marketing and Management,* South Yarra: Macmillan.

PC Productivity Commission (1996) *Stocktake of progress in microeconomic reform,* Canberra: AGPS.

PC Productivity Commission (1998a) *Annual Report 1997–98,* Canberra: AusInfo.

PC Productivity Commission (1998b) *Performance of Government Trading Enterprises, 1991–92 to 1996–97,* Research Report, October, Canberra: AusInfo.

PC Productivity Commission (1999) *Annual Report 1998–99,* Chapter 2 Improving Australia's social infrastructure services, Canberra: AusInfo.

Pollitt, C. (1988) 'Bringing consumers into performance management: concepts, consequences and constraints', *Policy and Politics* 16, 77–87.

Pollitt, C. (1990) 'Doing business in the temple? Managers and quality assurance in the public services', *Public Administration* 68 (Winter), 435–52.

Pollitt, C. (1998) 'Managerialism revisited', in Peters, B.G. and Savoie, D.J. (eds) *Taking Stock of Public Sector Reforms,* Montreal: McGill-Queens University Press.

Pollitt, C. (1999) 'Integrating financial management and performance management', PUMA/SBO(99)4/FINAL, Paris: OECD.

Pollitt, C. (2000) 'How do we know how good public services are?', in Peters, G.B. and Savoie, D.J. (eds) *Governance in the Twenty-first Century: Revitalizing the Public Service*, Montreal and Kingston: Canadian Centre for Management Development and McGill-Queen's Open University Press.

Pollitt, C., Bathgate, K., Caulfield, J. Smullen, A. and Talbot, C. (2001) 'Agency fever? An analysis of an international policy fashion', *Journal of Comparative Policy Analysis* 3, 3, 271–90.

Pollitt, C. and Bouckaert, G. (2000) *Public Management Reform – A Comparative Analysis*, Oxford: Oxford University Press.

PUMA Public Management Service Public Management Committee (1994) 'Performance management in government: performance measurement and results management', *Public Management Occasional Papers* No. 3, Paris: OECD.

PUMA (1996) 'Performance management in government: contemporary illustrations', *Public Management Occasional Papers* No. 9, Paris: OECD.

PUMA (1997a) *Managing Across Government – Country Case Studies*, Paris: OECD.

PUMA (1997b) *In Search of Results: Performance Management Practices*, Paris: OECD.

Quiggin, J. (1996) 'Great expectations, microeconomic reform in Australia', St Leonard's: Allen & Unwin.

Rhodes, R. (2000) 'The governance narrative – key findings and lessons from the ERSC's Whitehall programme,' *Public Administration* 78, 2, 345–63.

SCRCSSP Steering Committee for the Review of Commonwealth/State Service Provision (1995) *Report on Government Service Provision*, Secretariat, Melbourne: Industry Commission.

SCRCSSP (1997) *Report on Government Service Provision 1997*, Canberra: AGPS.

SCRCSSP (1998a) *Report on Government Services 1998*, Canberra: AGPS.

SCRCSSP (1998b), *Feedback on the Report of Commonwealth/State Service Provision*, Canberra: AGPS.

SCRCSSP (1998c) *Implementing Reforms in Government Services 1998*, Melbourne: Industry Commission, September.

SCRCSSP (1999) *Report on Government Services 1999*, Canberra: AusInfo.

SCRCSSP (2000) *Report on Government Services 2000*, Canberra: AusInfo.

SCRCSSP (2001) *Report on Government Services 2001*, Canberra: AusInfo.

Silvestro, R., Fitzgerald, L., Johnston, R. and Voss, C. (1992) 'Towards a classification of service processes', *International Journal of Service Industry Management* 3, 3, 62–75.

Simms, M. (1999) 'Models of political accountability and concepts of Australian government', *Australian Journal of Public Administration* 58, 1, 34–8.

Smith, P. (1993) 'Outcome-related performance indicators and organizational control in the public sector', *British Journal of Management* 4, 1, 135–51.

Smith, P. (1996) 'A framework for analyzing the measurement of outcome, Chapter 1', in Smith, P. (ed.) *Measuring Outcome in the Public Sector*, London: Taylor & Francis.

Stretton, H. and Orchard, L. (1994) *Public Goods, Public Enterprise, Public Choice*, New York: St Martins Press.

Talbot, C. (1999) 'Public performance – towards a new model?', *Public Policy and Administration* 14, 3, 15–34.

Talbot, C. (2001) 'UK public services and management (1979–2000) evolution or revolution?', *International Journal of Public Sector Management* 14, 4, 281–303.

Walsh, K. (1991) 'Quality and public services', *Public Administration* 6 (Winter), 503–14.

Walsh, K. (1995) *Public Services and Market Mechanisms: Competition, Contracting and the New Public Management*, Macmillan: London.

Wanna, J., Kelley, J. and Forster J. (2000) *Managing Public Expenditure in Australia*, St Leonards: Allen & Unwin.

Zifcak, S. (1994) *New Managerialism: Administrative Reform in Whitehall and Canberra*, Buckingham: Open University Press.

7 The Agency concept in North America

Failure, adaptation, and incremental change

Andrew Graham and Alasdair Roberts

Introduction

The "new paradigm" that was said to characterize reform in many of the advanced democracies over the last two decades (Organization for Economic Cooperation and Development 1995) contained three major themes. The first was a desire to release public servants from a welter of rules that were thought to make public organizations inflexible and inefficient. The second was a renewed emphasis on the reporting of results achieved by public organizations, and the use of this data to levy rewards or penalties. A final theme was said to be a new pragmatism about the choice of institutional structures used to deliver public services.

The "agency concept"[1] became popular among reform-minded policymakers because it combined all of these themes. In jurisdictions where the concept was applied most rigorously – such as New Zealand (Boston 1996) or the United Kingdom (O'Toole and Jordan 1995) – large government departments were divided into smaller units with more homogeneous cultures and clearer missions. These new single-purpose agencies were to be freed from central controls on human and material resources, but held responsible for performance targets set by political overseers. The relationship between agency heads and policymakers was to be detailed in a contract that tied tenure and compensation to success in attaining the agency's substantive goals.

The agency concept was not wholly alien to the United States and Canada. In the United States, there is a long tradition of relying on independent agencies to undertake regulatory functions (Eisner 1994) or major national projects, such as space exploration (through the National Air and Space Administration) or development of the Tennessee Valley (through the Tennessee Valley Authority). Similarly, Canada has a long history of pragmatism in creating distinct organizational forms to deliver public services. These "structural heretics" (Hodgetts 1973: 153) include boards, tribunals, commissions, and economic development agencies, in addition to a wide range of Crown – that is, government-owned – corporations. The new emphasis on the agency concept was distinctive because proponents expected that it could be applied widely within core government departments, and because of its reliance on quasi-contractual, performance-oriented governance mechanisms.

Reformers in the United States and Canada were also impressed by the British effort at agency-building. By the mid-1990s, attempts to replicate its Next Steps Initiative had been begun in both countries. But the agency concept was not easily transplanted. As we shall show in this chapter, an array of pressures – bureaucratic, fiscal and constitutional – shaped and sometimes stunted efforts at reform in each country.

In the United States, efforts to apply the agency concept began in earnest in 1995, when the Clinton administration unveiled a reform plan based closely on the Next Steps Initiative. Reformers within the Clinton administration hoped that the plan would generate large savings, and relieve pressure to balance the budget by eliminating programs. However, the Clinton plan was undermined when elements within the executive branch and Congress refused to provide agencies with significant new flexibilities. The distinctive features of the American system of government – notably a strong separation of powers and rules on appointment of senior officials – also made the plan unworkable. Dozens of American agencies were planned; by 2001, only three were created. The new Bush administration turned away from the agency concept, and focussed instead on broad reform of government-wide management laws.

An early Canadian effort at replicating Next Steps – the Special Operating Agency plan – also foundered because of bureaucratic resistance and the preoccupation of political executives with other issues, such as constitutional reform. In 1996, the government revived the agency concept by creating three substantial new Legislated Service Agencies (LSAs). The Liberal government anticipated that these new LSAs would produce substantial new savings, and facilitate cooperation with provinces in service delivery. These goals proved elusive. However, LSAs served as proving grounds for modest innovations in human resource and financial management. By the end of the decade, the Canadian government had also begun to emphasize reform of government-wide law, rather than agency-by-agency improvement.

In both countries, the agency concept played a minor role in the decade-long effort to reinvent federal bureaucracies. Efforts at agencification did not produce dramatic efficiency improvements and did little to ease overall fiscal pressures. On the other hand, concerns about the erosion of accountability that were sometimes made against the American and Canadian plans were equally overstated. Time also undermined the appeal of the agency concept. A reform which seemed radical in 1988 now seems modest when compared to efforts at privatization and public-private partnership – exercises that seem more likely to generate significant savings, and which at the same time raise sharper issues about accountability.

The agency concept in the United States

The agency concept attracted the attention of reformers within the United States government early in the 1990s. Staff within the U.S. General Accounting Office visited New Zealand and the United Kingdom in 1991–2 and reported favorably on the implementation on the agency concept in those countries (General Accounting Office 1995). However, policymakers initially preferred a reform strategy that aimed at governmentwide institutional change. In 1993, Congress adopted the Government Performance and Results Act, which imposed performance reporting requirements on all federal departments and agencies (Senate Committee on Governmental Affairs 1993).[2] The National Performance Review (NPR), a reform initiative begun by the Clinton administration, continued this emphasis on government-wide reform. Its September 1993 report proposed sweeping changes to laws governing personnel, procurement and budgeting within the executive branch of government (Gore 1993).

By 1995, NPR staff gave the agency concept renewed scrutiny. Many of NPR's 1993 recommendations for reform of general management laws were not adopted by Congress. More limited reform initiatives also encountered roadblocks. In 1996, Congress rejected an administration bill that would have given agencies authority to experiment with innovative personnel systems. At the same time, the Office of Management and Budget found few volunteers for "flexibility pilot projects" that had been authorized under GPRA: managers said that the promised flexibilities were outweighed by paperwork requirements. Modest efforts by NPR to establish "reinvention labs" within federal departments were also stymied by resistance from senior staff within departments and central management agencies (General Accounting Office 1996).

The agency concept gained attention as an alternative, and possibly more effective, strategy for achieving substantial reform of management systems. A leading advisor to NPR, David Osborne, also reported that the British agencies were reducing operating costs by an average of 5 percent per year (Osborne 1996). The promise of large efficiency gains appealed to reformers within the Clinton administration, which had emphasized its desire to achieve fiscal discipline without cutting government services.

The agency concept gained popularity for another reason. After the November 1994 elections, a Republican majority took control of the House of Representatives and began advocating more radical action to restructure the executive branch, including extensive privatization of federal functions and the wholesale dismantling of departments, such as the Department of Commerce. The agency concept proved useful as a method of deflecting calls for these more extreme reforms. Several of the functions that were eventually nominated by NPR as candidates for "agency" status were components of the besieged Commerce Department, or had been the object of privatization proposals.

NPR's adaption of the British model was unveiled in March 1996. Under the NPR plan, many service delivery functions within the federal government would be reorganized as "performance-based organizations," or PBOs. As in Britain, the PBO model had two key elements. First, PBOs would be freed from many of the laws, regulations, and policies that normally constrain managers within government. Vice-President Al Gore explained:

> [F]or these PBOs, we're going to toss out the restrictive rules that keep them from doing business like a business. All the red tape, personnel rules that keep managers from using people effectively, the budget restrictions that make planning or allocating resources almost impossible.
>
> (National Performance Review 1996c: 7)

Second, new incentives would be created for PBOs to improve performance. PBO executives would be hired on short-term contracts, with pay and tenure contingent on their success in meeting annual performance targets.

By Fall 1996, nine organizations, accounting for about 2 percent of the federal civilian workforce had been identified as PBO candidates (Table 7.1).[3] However, advocates of the plan suggested that it could be applied more widely. A senior OMB official said that "significant areas of the federal government" would benefit from the application of the concept (Koskinen 1996). David Osborne suggested that three-quarters of the federal bureaucracy could be transformed into PBOs by 2004 (Osborne 1997: 97–8). During the 1996 election campaign, President Clinton suggested that hundreds of PBOs might be established within the federal government (Clinton 1996).

NPR and its allies made bold promises about the savings that would be realized through the PBO plan, based mainly on their understanding of British experience. NPR suggested that the plan would attain operating cost reductions of 5 percent a year, while maintaining or improving service (National Performance Review 1996c; National Performance Review 1996a). A senior advisor to Vice-President Gore claimed that the Next Steps initiative had caused a one-third reduction in the size of the British civil service (Executive Office of the President 1996). Osborne suggested that the PBO plan could yield twenty-five billion dollars in savings by 2004 (Osborne 1997: 98–9 and 105).

Resistance to implementation

From a distance, the challenges which the British government had confronted in implementing Next Steps may have been obscured. Britain's executive agencies did not "toss out restrictive rules," as the Vice President implied. On the contrary, attempts to deregulate Next Steps agencies were often met with resistance from central agencies, parent departments, and legislators.[4] American reformers encountered similar difficulties as they attempted to win new freedoms for PBO candidates.

PBO proponents had calculated that Congressional subcommittees responsible for oversight of specific agencies might become effective advocates for legislation to give those agencies relief from general management laws. The premise appeared, at first glance, to be a reasonable one. In August 1995, the House and Senate aviation subcommittees had obtained passage of provisions that exempted the Federal Aviation Administration from most federal personnel and acquisition laws.[5] At the same time, the House subcommittee on intellectual property had proposed legislation that would give the Patent and Trademark Office – soon to be one of NPR's PBO candidates – significant new exemptions from personnel and procurement laws.[6]

However, these subcommittee initiatives were resisted by other elements within Congress. The Senate Governmental Affairs committee, which held responsibility for oversight of general management laws, reacted angrily to the FAA exemptions, arguing that the agency's real problem was "incompetent management" (Roth 1995). Committee members later told administration officials that they would also oppose attempts to obtain similar flexibilities for other PBO candidates. Meanwhile, the proposal to exempt the Patent and Trademark Office from personnel laws was strongly opposed by PTO's unions, who noted that bills such as this were likely to undermine the Clinton administration's attempt to improve labor-management relations within the federal government (National Treasury Employees Union 1996). The subcommittee then revised its bill to include a substantial concession to the unions, allowing them to negotiate over pay and other forms of compensation.[7] This provoked the ire of Congressional Republicans who opposed stronger bargaining rights for public sector unions, as well as that of the Senate Government Affairs Committee, which continued to protest the weakening of general management laws.

Even within the Executive Branch, there was conflict over the PBO plan. Central management agencies questioned the need for legislative action, suggesting that many of the desired flexibilities could be attained under existing law. After the 1996 announcement of the PBO initiative, NPR worked with the Office of Federal Procurement Policy (OFPP) and the Office of Personnel Management (OPM) to develop guidelines for future PBO legislation. These negotiations significantly curtailed the breadth of the initiative. OFPP's guidelines stipulated that PBOs would be "required to abide by all applicable federal procurement laws and regulations" (Office of Federal Procurement Policy 1996). Similarly, OPM's guidelines emphasized the need to retain "government-wide approaches" to personnel management and preserve its own oversight role. OPM also warned that PBOs might not be permitted to use flexibilities obtained through legislative amendment without approval from OPM and affected unions (National Performance Review 1997).

Other central management agencies were similarly ambivalent about the PBO plan. The General Services Administration blocked an attempt by a major PBO candidate, the Patent and Trademark Office, to escape its monopoly over the provision of real property services to federal agencies. Similarly, the Department of Justice blocked the Patent and Trademark Office's attempt to avoid its control over the provision of some legal services within the federal government, while the Treasury Department obstructed the Office's attempt to acquire an unlimited borrowing authority.

Parent departments also proved reluctant to give flexibilities to PBO candidates. One candidate unsuccessfully pursued a legislative amendment that would allow it to refuse support services provided by its parent department. This was a legislative solution to a purely administrative problem, but the PBO candidate argued that the provision was essential to give it leverage in its negotiations with departmental executives. The Clinton administration's bill to reorganize the St. Lawrence Seaway Development Corporation as a PBO included a similar provision (Department of Transportation 1997). Many of the most onerous restrictions on the Corporation were said to be imposed by the parent department, rather than central agencies or Congress (General Accounting Office 1997). The largest PBO candidate, the Defense Commissary Agency (DeCA), also faced difficulties with its parent department. Departmental rules required DeCA to purchase a range of services from other units within the Department of Defense. DeCA lobbied for the right to purchase services from other suppliers, arguing that this freedom would improve quality and substantially reduce its running costs (Whittaker 1996). However, DeCA was a major customer for internal suppliers, who argued that the loss of revenue would compromise the readiness of critical administrative systems (Friel 1996).

Constitutional constraints

Resistance to new flexibilities was a familiar problem, arising in every jurisdiction where the agency concept was applied. However, the PBO plan also encountered problems rooted in the distinct constitutional features of the American system of government.

A critical element of the PBO plan was a proposal to change the rules that governed how PBO heads – known as Chief Operating Officers (COOs) – were selected and compensated, and also the relationship between PBOs and their parent departments. COOs were to be hired through a competition that included candidates from inside and outside the public service, and employed on a contract prohibiting dismissal except for failure to achieve annually-negotiated performance targets (National Performance Review 1996c). These new arrangements were essentially the same as those used to govern the British Next Steps agencies. However, they seemed less workable within the U.S. government.

Under the Next Steps initiative, annual performance targets for executive agencies are agreed upon by each agency executive and a minister who is ultimately accountable to Parliament for the activity of that agency. The process of negotiating and enforcing these agreements is simplified by the relative weakness of Parliament. There is little danger that Parliament will intervene in negotiations over annual targets, or use its power to divert executives from agreed-upon goals. The situation is obviously quite different in the United States, where Congress has more influence in shaping the priorities of departments and agencies. The presence of an influential third party – Congress – threatened to complicate negotiations over the content of annual performance agreements.

Congress quickly signaled its ambivalence about NPR's proposal to establish performance agreements between COOs and executive departments. A provision to negotiate annual performance agreements had been included in the Clinton Administration's 1995 bill to reorganize the Patent and Trademark Office as a PBO, but was deleted by Congress. The provision was only reinstated after the Administration indicated that the President would veto the bill without it. Undeterred, a Senate committee later struck out a similar provision in legislation to establish the U.S. Mint as a PBO.

NPR attempted to allay Congressional concerns about the erosion of its influence by restricting the range of potential PBO candidates. NPR insisted that candidates "have a clear mission with broad-based support from its key 'stakeholders' – both internal and external to the agency – regarding its mission" (National Performance Review 1996c: 19). In practice, the PBO project would be limited to the "paper factories" within the federal civil service – units that performed highly routinized, and largely non-controversial, work.[8] This was a significant limitation on the potential scope of the PBO plan.

Nor was this the only limit imposed in response to constitutional difficulties. The success of the performance agreement system also depended on the ability of the parent department and central management agencies to make commitments about budgets for the period covered by an agreement. (If a PBO agreed to achieve improvements in service quality, and then found that its budget had been cut mid-way through the term of the agreement, it could argue that it could no longer be held responsible for achieving the original targets.) Governments in Westminster systems are usually better positioned to make such commitments. The situation is quite different in the United States. Intense policy disagreements between the Clinton administration and Republican-controlled Congresses meant that appropriation bills were often delayed for months after the beginning of the new fiscal year. The problems that would confront an appropriation-funded PBO during a budgetary deadlock are obvious: the PBO would argue that the performance agreement negotiated at the start of the fiscal year was vitiated by cuts imposed in continuing resolutions.

NPR anticipated this difficulty by insisting that PBO candidates have "funding predictability" (National Performance Review 1996b). In practice, this meant that PBO candidates would typically be organizations that imposed user fees, held those fees in revolving funds, and drew on those funds without the need for an annual appropriation. All of NPR's early PBO candidates were to be funded in this way. By contrast, only twelve of the 110 Next Steps agencies operating in 1995 financed themselves through a revolving fund (Cabinet Office 1996). The need for "funding predictability" became a second significant restriction on the potential scope of the PBO plan. (Comparable comments are made about the agency model in Tanzania and Jamaica in Chapters 12 and 16 in this volume.)

Constitutional problems threatened the PBO plan in a third way. The PBO plan assumed that it will be possible to hire COOs on fixed-term contracts that were terminable only if the executive failed badly in his or her attempt to achieve performance targets. The threat of dismissal for non-performance was expected to sharpen the executive's focus on targets. However, the arrangement would also provide protection for the COO, by precluding dismissal on any basis other than failure to achieve stipulated targets.[9] The COO would then be freed from the obligation to make investments in areas not identified as priorities in his or her performance agreement.

NPR's first legislative proposals would have entrenched this arrangement by authorizing fixed-term contracts between COOs and departmental Secretaries.[10] However, Justice Department officials questioned the constitutionality of this approach. The general rule established by the Supreme Court is that Congress may not limit the ability of the President to remove appointees, unless those appointees exercise quasi-legislative or quasi-judicial functions that require some independence from the administration. In early 1997, NPR adopted new language that required a contract between the COO and Secretary but gave the President an unfettered discretion to remove the COO.

This new provision undermined the idea that COOs would be hired on the basis of a performance-based contract. Executives who had been wrongly dismissed would have had no recourse if the removal had been done in the name of the President. Appointing officials would have been free to judge the performance of COOs by any criterion they wished, regardless of whether that criterion had been stipulated in the annual performance agreement. COOs, in turn, would have been encouraged to adopt hedging strategies, investing in areas that they believed might attract the interest of appointing officials in the future. For example, a COO might invest more heavily in internal controls, knowing that allegations of impropriety, however small, may lead to dismissal. The main goal of the contractual arrangement – to sharpen the attention of the COO on performance targets – would have been defeated.

Modest accomplishments

David Osborne had suggested that three-quarters of the federal civil service might be recreated as PBOs, but this was wildly optimistic. The range of financially self-sustaining units engaged in politically benign "factory" work was always substantially smaller. Furthermore, the hurdles created by parent departments and central management agencies were substantial enough to deter many of these units from aggressively pursuing reform. Only a small handful of organizations responded to NPR's call for volunteers for PBO status. A year after Vice President Gore's March 1996 announcement, only three reform bills – for the Patent and Trademark Office, the St. Lawrence Seaway Development Corporation, and the Defense Commissary Agency – had been sent to Congress by the Clinton administration. The delay was largely attributable to difficulties in resolving internal disagreements about the legislative freedoms that ought to be given to PBOs.

Congress also proved recalcitrant. It was not until October 1998 that Congress adopted legislation establishing the first PBO – the Office of Student Financial Assistance, a component of the Department of Education[11] (Table 7.1). The Patent and Trademark Office became the second PBO in November 1999, after more than four years of legislative wrangling.[12] In the last weeks of the Clinton administration a third PBO, the Air Traffic Organization, was created – by an Executive Order of the President, rather than Congressional action.[13]

These three PBOs were denied significant flexibilities. The Office of Student Financial Assistance was permitted to hire twenty-five technical and professional employees without regard to general personnel rules. Otherwise, it remained entirely subject to existing labor law. The agency was given limited freedom to adopt new procurement methods, while remaining subject to existing rules imposing labor standards and civil rights obligations on government contractors. Legislation for the Patent and Trademark Office was similarly restrictive: while modifying arrangements for appointment of topmost officials, it provided no relief from existing civil service law and no new flexibility in procurement procedures. The Executive Order creating the new Air Traffic Organization simply enjoined its new Chief Operating Officer to "optimize use of existing management flexibilities and authorities to improve the efficiency of air traffic services and increase the capacity of the system."[14] In fact, the most important feature of the Order may have been a new restriction: by declaring the work of the Organization to be "inherently governmental," the Order complicated Congressional efforts to privatize ATO's work.

Table 7.1 Candidates for PBO status (USA)

Organization	Parent department	Staff	Date proposed	Date established
Patent and Trademark Office	Commerce	5,237	September 1995	November 1999
National Technical Information Service	Commerce	406	September 1995	Not established
Defense Commissary Agency	Defense	17,612	March 1996	Not established
Animal and Plant Health Inspection Service	Agriculture	5,300	March 1996	Not established
Federal Housing Administration	Housing and Urban Development	4,544	March 1996	Not established
Government National Mortgage Association	Housing and Urban Development	72	March 1996	Not established
Office of Retirement Programs	Office of Personnel Management	921	March 1996	Not established
U.S. Mint	Treasury	2,347	July 1996	Not established
Seafood Inspection Program	Commerce	200	September 1996	Not established
Air Traffic Organization	Transportation		December 1997	December 2000
Office of Student Financial Assistance	Education		April 1998	October 1998

Overestimating gains

The overall failure of the PBO plan meant that observers were never able to determine whether optimistic promises about the importance of the reform would be fulfilled in practice. In fact, proponents of the PBO plan had greatly exaggerated the gains made under the Next Steps initiative.

One error made by PBO proponents was the failure to disentangle the impact of Next Steps from that of other reform efforts, such as the Citizens' Charter Initiative, under which agencies were directed to publicize service standards and provide remedies for poor service, or the Competing for Quality Initiative, under which agencies were strongly encouraged to expand contracting-out.

Broader claims about efficiency gains were also misguided. The data on British efficiency gains reported by American reformers were not, in fact, measures of *actual* year-to-year reductions in operating costs for Next Steps agencies. Instead, they were measures of the extent to which operating costs have been reduced from the amount *planned* for that year. Statistics based on actual year-to-year changes in operating costs for all Next Steps agencies told a different story. Total operating costs for Next Steps agencies had actually shown consistent, annual increases, even after adjustment for inflation (Roberts 1997: 468).

In short, it was never reasonable to expect that the PBO plan would have achieved the fiscal objective of dramatically reducing the cost of government operations. On the contrary, the PBO plan might have increased operating costs in some sectors. Some PBO candidates, such as the Patent and Trademark Office, had lobbied for legislative amendments that would consolidate their control over user fees collected by the organization, and exempt them from overall caps on discretionary spending. The Office argued that increased spending would allow them to address staff shortages and high staff turnover. In fact, PBO legislation for the Patent and Trademark Office and the Office of Student Financial Assistance contained directions that neither organization should be subject to constraints on the number or classification of employees which they are allowed to hire.

Shift in strategy

The PBO plan effectively ended with the Clinton administration. In its early months the new Bush administration made clear its desire to pursue a strategy of government-wide, rather than agency-specific, reform. In November 2001, the Bush administration proposed a broad set of changes to personnel, budgeting and procurement laws.[15] The administration also proposed the adoption of a new law, the *Freedom to Manage Act* of 2001,[16] that would establish a procedure under which Congress would be required to give quick consideration to presidential requests for reform of government-wide management laws. Analogous to "fast-track" rules sometimes used in Congressional ratification of trade agreements, the law is intended to ensure that new reform initiatives do not meet the same fate as that of the early Clinton administration proposals.

The agency concept in Canada

The evolution of the agency concept in Canada had two distinct phases: an early but limited attempt to create Special Operating Agencies (SOAs) in the late 1980s, followed by the creation of a few large Legislated Service

Agencies (LSAs) in the late 1990s. The SOA initiative was limited to a small range of activities because of a lack of strong political and bureaucratic leadership. A change in fiscal and constitutional conditions gave stronger impetus to the LSA initiative; nevertheless, it remained an opportunistic response to immediate problems rather than a systematic effort at government reform. A range of new administrative and service flexibilities were created for these agencies, but they remained firmly under the umbrella of ministerial accountability as traditionally understood in the Westminster model. The reform response had its origins not in ideology but in fiscal concerns. The accepted scope and role of government remained a strong force in the country, principally the use of "national institutions" to preserve the country from fragmentation.

Special Operating Agencies (SOAs)

The SOA concept, introduced to Canada in the late 1980s and early 1990s, was inspired by Britain's Next Steps initiative. The plan was championed by bureaucrats in central agencies, such as Treasury Board Secretariat, and taken up by a few deputy ministers who saw an opportunity to improve the efficiency of their operations. While ministers permitted experimentation with the model, it was never high on the political agenda. The Mulroney government remained preoccupied with the negotiation of constitutional reforms aimed at addressing regional alienation, as well as new trade agreements with the United States, rather than management reform.

Treasury Board Secretariat stipulated that SOAs should be "operational organizations within existing departmental structures which deliver services, as distinct from providing policy advice to ministers" (Treasury Board Secretariat 1992: 2). They were designed to give these units special flexibilities to more easily carry out their unique roles. Because there was often a commercial element to their work (that is, the sale of a specific good or service and the absence of strong regulatory functions) they were often permitted limited commercial freedoms and the power to retain revenue. It was felt that this would be an incentive to maximize the commercial potential of the organization or, at least, reduce the draw on the Consolidated Revenue Fund.

While SOAs were given few new flexibilities, all were required to continue working within existing personnel legislation. Roughly half of SOAs established revolving funds, while half did not. However, all remained within parent departments under a deputy minister and therefore within the departmental structure of accountability. All SOA heads were career public servants, appointed under conventional public service rules and bound by the traditional conventions of public service.

While the central agency responsible for the SOA initiative, Treasury Board Secretariat, created a policy framework, it was permissive, not directive (Treasury Board Secretariat 1996). The framework deals with the methodologies, especially associated with staff and delegations, should a department wish to pursue this course. The Secretariat did make a limited attempt to encourage broader adoption of the SOA model as part of a reorganization of the federal Department of Public Works and Government Services in 1993, but this proved largely unsuccessful (Roberts 1996).

Restrictions on the SOA model made it unattractive to managers within the federal government, and few were established. Presently, there are nineteen SOAs within the federal government, ranging from the Passport Office to prison industries (Table 7.2). As the Auditor General of Canada has noted: "Notwithstanding these special operating agencies that exist today, the experiment never really took off. Only about five thousand government employees were affected" (Auditor General of Canada 2001).

Legislated Service Agencies

Later in the decade, the agency concept emerged in a new form within the Canadian government. This second phase was driven by a combination

Table 7.2 Special operating agencies and legislated service agencies in the Canadian public service

Name	Year established	Personnel	Budget (2001) ($)
Special Operating Agencies (SOAs)			
Consulting and Audit Canada	1990	420	67MM
Translation Bureau	1995	120	107MM
Passport Office	1990	550	38MM
Training and Development Canada	1990	150	15MM
CORCAN	1992	360	47MM
Canadian Intellectual Property Office	1992	450	40MM
Measurement Canada	1996	380	20MM
Superintendent of Bankruptcy	1997	250	12MM
Technology Partnerships Canada	1996	50	250MM
Canadian Heritage Information Network	1992	34	2MM
Canadian Conservation Institute	1992	78	6MM
Canadian Para-Mutuel Agency	1992	78	15MM
Indian Oil and Gas Canada	1993	67	6MM
Physical Resources Bureau	1993	124	70MM
Canada Investment and Savings	1995	18	130MM
Occupation Health and Safety Agency	1996	210	30MM
Canadian Forces Housing Agency	1995	N/A	115MM
Defense Research and Development Canada	2000	1,050	217MM
Legislated Service Agencies			
Canadian Customs and Revenue Agency	1999	48,000	3,330MM
Canadian Food Inspection Agency	1997	5,026	235MM
Parks Canada Agency	1998	5,278	345MM

of fiscal and political considerations and led to more substantial institutional changes. By the mid-1990s, political, bureaucratic and media leaders recognized that the "deficit situation was extremely grave, and that it could not be addressed through incremental measures" (Pal 1999: 8). The Wall Street Journal worried in January 1995 that Canada might "hit the debt wall and have to call in the International Monetary Fund" (Savoie 1999: 177).

In his 1995 Budget, Finance Minister Paul Martin set the stage for a series of deficit-fighting budgets, promising "a new vision of the role of government in the economy. In many cases that means smaller government. In all cases it means smarter government" (Martin 1995). This budget announced the creation of the Program Review, an internal government process led by the President of Treasury Board, the Cabinet Minister responsible for central government management and financial control. Gilles Paquet suggests that the Program Review "triggered profound rethinking of the governance process" (Paquet 1999). This process created the analytical foundation for the creation of new agencies. The Program Review process converted the targeted reductions given to departments into requirements to find different ways to deliver services or organize themselves.

Departments, principally Ministers and their Deputies, were to bring forward recommendations for change. This reflected the degree of consensus between the politicians and senior bureaucrats that had evolved on the need for drastic action to address the fiscal crisis. Aucoin observes: "Canadian ministers (and their partisan-political advisors) did not perceive the federal public service bureaucracy to be a major obstacle that had to be overcome in order to pursue their public policy agenda" (Aucoin 2001).

During the Program Review exercise, some departments put forward proposals to create new special agencies – by restructuring entire departments or entities within a single department, or combining functions lodged in a number of departments. The first announcements of these agencies were in the 1996 budget statement, in which the Minister of Finance announced the creation of three new "service agencies" (Martin 1996): an integrated food inspection agency; a national revenue agency; and a national parks agency.

The Treasury Board Secretariat described the new organizations as Legislated Service Agencies (LSAs). The terminology served to distinguish LSAs from SOAs, which were administrative bodies created by the Treasury Board rather than Parliament. The Secretariat explained:

A service agency is a mission-driven, client-oriented organization established under constituent legislation to manage the delivery of services with the federal government. The legislation sets out the framework under which the agency will operate including its

mandate, governance regime, powers and authorities, and accountability requirements.

Service Agencies remain organizations within the federal government and are under the direction of a minister who is accountable for
the agency to parliament. The employees remain public servants
under the *Public Service Staff Relations Act.*

Service Agencies demonstrate commitment to enduring Public
Service values and over-riding government commitments such as Official Languages, federal identity, individual, privacy rights and access
to information.

A key consideration for service agencies is their ability to provide
more responsive and streamlined operations and to partner with the
provinces to provide better services to citizens in an efficient manner.

(Treasury Board Secretariat 2001)

The description reflected the government's conflicting objectives: its
desire to experiment with new delivery mechanisms and its concern about
preserving control by central government.

The Canadian Food Inspection Agency

In late 1997, the Canadian Food Inspection Agency (CFIA) merged the
food inspection responsibilities of three government departments. It
became a "separate employer," with responsibility for its own collective
bargaining, classification standards and personnel policies. It was also
granted certain latitude to manage its own finances, human resources and
contracting. In return, CFIA was expected to provide better information
to Parliament, including an annual corporate plan including objectives
and performance expectations, and an annual report on actual achievements. In addition, CFIA was required to structure its finances on an
accrual basis so that it could report in a more business-like manner.

Canada Customs and Revenue Agency

The second – and by far the largest – agency was the Canada Customs and
Revenue Agency (CCRA). In this instance, an entire department moved to
agency status. The principal theme in the government's public communications about the creation of CCRA has been improvement of service to
the public.[17] The agency was to have sufficient flexibility on the administrative side to refocus its orientation toward service. In addition, it could
enter into partnerships with provinces to integrate tax activities, thereby
reducing the tax-processing burden.

Over 45,000 federal employees moved outside the umbrella of the
Public Service Employment Act to become part of the "separate employer"
regime. CCRA was given human resource and financial authorities similar

to those already received by CFIA. The CCRA has built a new human resources regime, begun its own collective bargaining and established a classification and pay system. These have differed from the core public service, but in degrees. The Agency still must seek a bargaining mandate from Treasury Board on economic elements to the collective agreement.

Like the CFIA and Parks Canada, reporting to Parliament was specified and, relative to departments, increased. The CCRA was required to formulate an annual Corporate Business Plan and provide performance reports as well. The law also directed that the CCRA will act in accordance with its plan, a measure of legislated accountability not found in departmental legislation generally.

CCRA's governance structure is designed to ensure that Westminster conventions remain intact. The Commissioner of CCRA – the title given to the chief executive officer – retains the employment status of Deputy Minister. (The same is true of the President of CFIA.) The Commissioner remains accountable to the Minister of National Revenue, the same reporting relationship that a Deputy Minister has to a Minister. The Minister retains decision-making authority for the new agency and is accountable to Parliament for the agency's conduct. A Board of Management representing non-governmental stakeholders has a limited role in advising the Minister and guiding planning within the CCRA.[18]

Parks Canada

The creation of Parks Canada represents yet another variation on the theme. In this instance, a part of an existing department, Heritage Canada, was made into an agency, but remained within the overall portfolio responsibilities of the same Minister. The new Parks Canada Agency (PCA) received financial and human resource flexibilities similar to those granted to CFIA and CCRA. However, reporting requirements are more extensive. Additional obligations include the production of management plans for parks and heritage areas; reports every five years on the effectiveness of the human resource regime; and a biennial report on the state of protected heritage areas.[19] As with the other agencies, governance arrangements for PCA were cautiously drafted. PCA's legislation adds a distinctive obligation to undertake public consultations on the future of the parks system.

What has been accomplished?

Perkins and Shepherd have recently characterized the creation of agencies such as LSAs as efforts at "administrative decentralization" (Perkins and Shepherd 2001). They suggest that the changes, while constituting some innovation in the centralized departmental structure, remain within the broader umbrella of government control, ensuring that the new organizations retain the same accountabilities. As Perkins and Shepherd note: "It was thought that they are able to be more adaptable than regular government departments, which are perceived to be inflexible and governed by process-driven rules" (Perkins and Shepherd 2001). The creation of new agencies is a recent phenomenon in the Canadian context. As such, it is difficult to assess the impact and relative success of these measures. However, preliminary conclusions can be reached.

Few savings realized

A thesis of this chapter is that fiscal concerns, rather than ideological zeal, shaped the development of new agencies. The budget statements of 1995 and 1996 suggested that LSAs would reduce the cost of service delivery; and in one case – that of CFIA – costs savings were promised.[20] Such savings were not realized. On the contrary, the budgets of all three agencies are now larger than before their creation. It would seem that this was not caused by the transition to agency status, but rather to program growth and successful efforts by the agencies to rectify outstanding underfunding issues.

Limited integration

A constitutional element unique to Canada was the provision that the new agencies might be able to integrate services with the provinces to offer more "national" services. In all cases, there was duplication in tax collection, food inspection and park services. The theoretical notion was that duplication and overlap across governments could also be eliminated. This goal took on special importance in the months following the 1995 Quebec referendum on separation. The establishment of more independent LSAs became a first step to building "common national institutions." Canada's Minister of Intergovernmental Affairs, Stephane Dion, cited the LSA initiative as part of the federal government's program to build "harmonious federalism" and promote "economic union" (Dion 1996a; Dion 1996b). However, the reality of Canadian federal-provincial relations soon got in the way of this goal. There was very little take-up by provinces to amalgamate tax services. While some co-operative discussions were taking place on food inspection with Alberta, little more has occurred.

Stronger expectations of accountability

The increased reporting requirements for the new agencies have already been discussed. The expectation is that these would improve parliamentary oversight and transparency. To date, the most widely articulated concerns about the quality of these new reports are those of the Auditor General of Canada. His 2001 report raised concern that the government's experiments had put parliamentary oversight and the public interest at risk (Auditor General of Canada 2001). With specific reference to the Canadian Food Inspection Agency, the Auditor General noted that, as a result of its creation, it had expanded authorities, but also increased reporting burdens. He criticized the quality of the performance information provided by CFIA in its first three years of existence, noting that it "is not providing a clear and complete picture of its performance to allow Parliament and others to judge how well it has carried out its role." Perkins and Shepherd agree that the government's reforms "are challenging the traditional concept and practice of accountability – that is, that public servants are accountable, up the line, through the bureaucracy, to their deputy, the minister, cabinet, the Prime Minister, and Parliament" (Perkins and Shepherd 2001).

The challenge for CFIA and other agencies is that there is an increased expectation about their reporting capabilities as part of "the bargain" and those expectations, regardless of how challenging they are, must be met. It might also be noted that the Auditor General has also praised the Food Agency for its management of the transition to agency status.

Ministerial accountability

The new LSAs are within the ambit of traditional notions of ministerial accountability and the present norms of parliamentary reporting that apply to core departments. Ministerial accountability can best be described as generally undefined in law, but in practice involves a direct relationship of reporting and seeking direction by public servants from their Minister on matters of policy and overall direction.

If one examines the various laws governing Canadian departments in the core and these new agencies, an argument could be made that, in theory, the new legislation for the LSAs describes in much finer detail what ministerial accountability means than existing law. For instance, the legislation governing the Royal Canadian Mounted Police states simply that the Commissioner, "under the direction of the Minister" shall carry out his various duties.[21] No more guidance is provided about the relationship between the Minister and the head of Canada's federal police force. Contrast this with the legislation governing the CCRA, with respect to the responsibilities of the Commissioner to the Minister. Section 38 of the Act explicitly requires the Commissioner to "keep the Minister informed of any matter that could affect public policy or that could materially affect public finance, and any other matter that the Minister considers necessary." The Commissioner must also "assist and advise the Minister" in carrying out his or her duties.

A reading of the legislation for all the new LSAs would suggest that efforts were made to create the strong connection between agency and Minister. Such a modest step toward better defining ministerial accountability shows the concern that the federal government continues to have to ensure unbroken lines of ministerial accountability.

Sandboxes of experimentation?

It is too early to assess how the agencies have faired with their new authorities. However, they have used these authorities to set up their own human resource systems. Both CCRA and CFIA have completed rounds of collective bargaining. Once again, the connection to the central agencies was not fully dropped. As both of these agencies draw from appropriated public funds, they are not permitted to set any salary scale without reference to sources of funds. As such, while they bargain, they must receive a bargaining mandate from the Treasury Board to set dollar limits on what they can, in fact, bargain. Hence, while they have flexibility with respect to such issues as working conditions and hours of work, salary scales are limited by available funding as determined by the core central agency. Given that none of these agencies has been put on a fully self-funded basis, such discipline is consistent with parliamentary democracy.

While all agencies have moved to create their own human resource systems, they have moved in parallel to the government as a whole. For instance, as the core departments create a new classification structure, some of the agencies have adopted elements of it. They continue to be preoccupied by the capacity of staff to move easily within the larger public service and, as such, do not want to be too different.

On the other hand, agencies have experimented with new tools that provide core departments with practical experience in innovation. For instance, the CCRA is planning to broaden the definition of its management cadre. Such an experiment in one organization can offer practical experience to others.

Making departments more like agencies

The question could be asked, why these organizations, and why not others? This reflects the pragmatic and incremental character of the Canadian experience. The Program Review process was also, in essence, bottom-up in that Ministers were expected to bring forward proposals to address the budgetary cuts that they had already received. Some departments seized the opportunity – described by one deputy minister as "creative opportunism" (Prince 2000) – to make needed changes in service delivery; some worked within the existing structure. Hence, the 'why' is best answered with an understanding of the nature of the process (incremental, upward flowing) and the impact that personality and history can have on it.

Another reason that some departments did not pursue agency status is that, in parallel to the creation of these agencies, the Treasury Board and, to a lesser extent, the Public Service Commission, were also pursuing increasing delegations to departments, regardless of their status. Once again, these tended to be business-case driven and specific. In their planning processes, departments were encouraged to address shortfalls in delegations and authorities as well as funds. Increasingly, efforts to retain funds from various sorts of revenues met with success with the Board. This encouraged local-level entrepreneurialism within departmental structures. The core itself started to "loosen up." This resembles the direction of the Bush administration to pursue across-the-board reform.

On the human resources side, departments continued to chafe under an excessive process burden, one that the Auditor General himself focussed on in the last report of his term. Even here, the Government announced that it was, after decades of refusal, prepared to reassess its public service legislation to reduce the process orientation. The Government's proposals were incorporated into Bill C-25, the Public Service Modernization Act, which was passed by the House of Commons in 2003. The incentive to go their own way was reduced by these changes for many departments.

Conclusion

In both the United States and Canada, the initial enthusiasm of some reformers for the agency concept was soon tempered by significant challenges in implementation. Fiscal and political considerations unique to each country shaped – and constrained – the development of the agency concept in profound ways. American and Canadian reform efforts were not systematic, intellectually coherent, or backed by strong support among political executives. Nor did the agency concept become the foundation for a broad reform project, as it had in New Zealand or the United Kingdom. The application of the concept often depended on the initiative of entrepreneurs within the bureaucracy who adapted the idea to resolve immediate policy predicaments.

When the agency concept was embedded in actual reforms, these proved to be incremental in character. Concerns about the potential erosion of accountability or control – expressed by parent departments, central agencies or legislators – often meant that new agencies were given few new flexibilities. Nor were governance structures, and traditional accountability structures, radically changed. Just as there was no radical change in organizational structure, there was no radical change in organizational performance. Where established, agencies did not generate dramatic improvements in efficiency or service quality. More often, they served as demonstration sites for modest innovations in managerial practice.

By 2001, the agency concept had ceased to hold a prominent place in the rhetoric of reform in the United States and Canada. Both countries appear to have reached a point of stasis in which they have a small array of agencies, but do not intend to pursue the creation of any more as a matter of strategic direction. Additional prospective candidates for agency status had been deterred by the obvious difficulties in attaining significant changes in central controls or accountability structures. Many reformers had also begun to revisit the possibilities for reform of government-wide management laws, aiming to improve conditions for all federal departments and agencies at one stroke. In a sense, the pendulum had swung back to where it had been one or two decades before. Such reforms, if successful, would make all departments more like agencies. The outstanding question, both in Canada and the United States, is whether such across-the-board initiatives, tried many times in the past, will actually succeed this time around.

Notes

1 The phrase is Francesca Gains': see Chapter 3 in this volume.
2 *Government Performance and Results Act*, P.L. 103–62.
3 Two other organizations were later added to the list of PBO candidates.
4 For contemporaneous comments on challenges of deregulation within Next Steps agencies, see: (Trosa 1994; Barberis 1995; Campbell 1995: 496–8; Greenaway 1995; Talbot 1996).
5 *Department of Transportation and Related Agencies Appropriations Act*, 1996, P.L. 104–50, sections 347 and 348.
6 *Patent and Trademark Office Corporation Act*, H.R. 1659, 104th Cong., 1st sess.
7 *Patent and Trademark Office Government Corporation Act* of *1996*, H.R. 3460 (as reported by subcommittee), section 113. 104th Cong., 2d sess.
8 For references to "factory" operations that could be converted to PBO status, see: (Sanders and Thompson 1997; Subcommittee on postsecondary education 1997).
9 This principle may have been established in Britain as a result of the controversy surrounding the firing of the head of Her Majesty's Prison Service in October 1995. The fired executive sued the government for wrongful dismissal, arguing that he had achieved all of the targets specified in his performance agreement. In March 1996, the government agreed to pay damages to the executive.
10 The administration's 1995 bill to reorganize the Patent and Trademark Office, H.R. 2533, provided for PTO's executive to "serve on the basis of a six-year contract with the Secretary [of Commerce], so long as performance, as set forth in the annual agreement, is satisfactory" (H.R. 2533, section 103). The same language was used by the House appropriations subcommittee to define the status of the director of the proposed Mint PBO (H.R. 3756 (as reported to the House), section 527).
11 Provisions establishing the Office of Student Financial Assistance Programs as a performance-based organization were contained in the Higher Education Amendments of 1998, P.L. 105–244.
12 American Inventors Protection Act of 1999, P.L. 106–13.
13 Executive Order 13180, December 7, 2000.
14 Executive Order 13180, section 2(a). Contrast the Executive Order with the recommendations of the National Civil Aviation Review Commission, which in 1997 recommended a new PBO with significant flexibilities in key areas (National Civil Aviation Review Commission 1997).

15 *Managerial Flexibility Act* of *2001*, S. 1612, 107th Cong., 1st sess.
16 S. 1603, 107th Cong., 1st sess.
17 As the Minister of National Revenue wrote in the most recent Corporate Business Plan of CCRA: "The Canada Customs and Revenue Agency was created to find better ways to serve Canadians" (Canada Customs and Revenue Agency 2001).
18 *Canada Customs and Revenue Agency Act*, Statutes of Canada 1999, *c.*17, section 38.
19 *Parks Canada Agency Act*, Statutes of Canada 1998, *c.*31, sections 31–5.
20 President Ron Doering, testifying before a Parliamentary Committee, quoted in (Prince).
21 *Royal Canadian Mounted Police Act*, Revised Statutes of Canada 1985, *c.*R-10, section 5.

Bibliography

Aucoin, P. (2001) *Comparative Perspectives on Canadian Public Service Reform in the 1990s*, Ottawa: Office of the Auditor General of Canada.
Auditor General of Canada (2001) *Reflections on a Decade of Serving Parliament* (February), Ottawa: Office of the Auditor General.
Barberis, P. (1995) "Next Steps: consequences for the core and central departments," in O'Toole, B.J. and Jordan, G. (eds) *Next Steps: Improving Management in Government?*, Aldershot, UK: Dartmouth Press, pp. 99–117.
Boston, J. (1996) *Public Management: the New Zealand Model*, Auckland; New York: Oxford University Press.
Cabinet Office (1996) "Next Steps Review 1995," February, Cmnd. 3164. London: Her Majesty's Stationery Office.
Campbell, C. (1995) "Does reinvention need reinvention? Lessons from truncated managerialism in Britain," *Governance* 8, 4 (October), 479–504.
Canada Customs and Revenue Agency (2001) *Summary of the Corporate Business Plan, 2001–2004*, Ottawa: Canada Customs and Revenue Agency.
Clinton, W. (1996) *Remarks by the President to the People of the Portland Area* (September 20), Washington, DC: Government Printing Office.
Department of Transportation (1997) *Proposed Legislation to Establish the St. Lawrence Seaway Development Corporation as a Performance-based Organization* (May), Washington, DC: Department of Transportation.
Dion, S. (1996a) *Notes for an Address on the Economy and National Unity*, Ottawa: Privy Council Office.
Dion, S. (1996b) *Notes for an Address to the Liberal Party of Canada (B.C.)* (March 2), Ottawa: Privy Council Office.
Eisner, M.A. (1994) "Discovering patterns in regulatory history: continuity, change, and regulatory regimes," *Journal of Policy History* 6, 2, 157–87.
Executive Office of the President (1996) *Press Briefing by Mike McCurry and Dr. Elaine Kamarck* (September 20), Washington, DC: Executive Office of the President.
Friel, B. (1996) "Making performance count," *Government Executive* (October): Web edition.
General Accounting Office (1995) *Managing for Results: Experiences Abroad Suggest Insights for Federal Management Reforms*, May, GGD-95-120, Washington, DC: General Accounting Office.
General Accounting Office (1996) *Management Reform: Status of Agency Reinvention Lab Efforts*, GAO/GGD-96-69, Washington, DC: General Accounting Office.

General Accounting Office (1997) *Performance-Based Organizations: Issues for the St. Lawrence Seaway Development Corporation Proposal*, GAO/GGD-97-74, Washington, DC: General Accounting Office.

Gore, A. (1993) *Creating a Government that Works Better and Costs Less*, New York: Times Books.

Greenaway, J. (1995) "Having the bun and the halfpenny: can old public service ethics survive in the new Whitehall?," *Public Administration* 73 (Autumn), 357–74.

Hodgetts, J.E. (1973) *The Canadian Public Service*, Toronto: University of Toronto Press.

Koskinen, J. (1996) *Electronic mail*, correspondence with author, May 24.

Martin, P. (1995) *Budget Speech*, (February 27), Ottawa: Department of Finance. February 27, 1995.

Martin, P. (1996) *Budget in Brief*, (March 6), Ottawa: Department of Finance.

National Civil Aviation Review Commission (1997) *Avoiding Aviation Gridlock and Reducing the Accident Rate: A Consensus for Change*, (December), Washington, DC: Federal Aviation Administration.

National Performance Review (1996a) *Background Information: Clinton-Gore Administration Creating Agencies for the 21st Century*, Washington, DC: National Performance Review.

National Performance Review (1996b) *Memorandum. Creating Performance-Based Organizations*, (October 2), Washington, DC: National Performance Review.

National Performance Review (1996c) *Reinvention's Next Steps: Governing in a Balanced Budget World. Speech by Vice President Al Gore and Supporting Background Papers*, (March 4), Washington, DC: National Performance Review.

National Performance Review (1997) *Performance-Based Organizations: A Conversion Guide*, (April), Washington, DC: National Performance Review.

National Treasury Employees Union (1996) *News Release: Union Voices Opposition to Legislative Proposals that Would Undermine Employment Rights of Federal Workers*, (March 8), Washington, DC: NTEU.

O'Toole, B.J. and Jordan, A.G. (1995) *Next Steps: Improving Management in Government?* Aldershot, England; Brookfield, Vt.: Dartmouth.

Office of Federal Procurement Policy (1996) *Draft Acquisition Reform Template*, (April 15), Washington, DC: Office of Federal Procurement Policy.

Organization for Economic Cooperation and Development (1995) *Governance in Transition*, Paris: Organization for Economic Cooperation and Development.

Osborne, D. (1996) "Bureaucracy unbound," *Washington Post*, (October 13), Washington, DC.

Osborne, D. (1997) "Reform and invest: reinvention's next steps," in Marshall, W. (ed.) *Building the Bridge: Ten Big Ideas to Transform America*, Lanham, MD: Rowman and Littlefield, pp. 93–109.

Pal, L. (1999) "Shape shifting: Canadian governance toward the 21st century," in Pal, L. (ed.) *How Ottawa Spends, 1999–2000*, Don Mills, Ontario: Oxford University Press, pp. 1–35.

Paquet, G. (1999) "Tectonic changes in Canadian governance," in Pal, L. (ed.) *How Ottawa Spends, 1999–2000*, Ottawa: Oxford University Press, pp. 75–111.

Perkins, A. and Shepherd, R. (2001) "Managing in the new public service: some implications for how we are governed," in Pal, L. (ed.) *How Ottawa Spends, 2001–2002*, Ottawa: Oxford University Press.

Prince, M.J. (2000) "Banishing bureaucracy or hatching a hybrid? The Canadian

Food Inspection Agency and the politics of reinventing government," *Governance* 13, 2 (April), 215–38.

Roberts, A. (1996) "Public works and government services: beautiful theory meets ugly reality," in Swimmer, G. (ed.) *How Ottawa Spends, 1996–97*, Ottawa: Carleton University Press, pp. 171–204.

Roberts, A. (1997) "Performance-based organizations: assessing the Gore plan," *Public Administration Review* 57, 6, 465–78.

Roth, W. (1995) *Remarks on Amendment 2340*, Congressional Record, 104th Cong., 1st sess. August 10.

Sanders, R.P. and Thompson, J. (1997) "To boldly go . . . ," *Government Executive* 45.

Savoie, D. (1999) *Governing from the Centre*, Toronto: University of Toronto Press.

Senate Committee on Governmental Affairs (1993) *Report on the Government Performance and Results Act*, Washington, DC: S. Rep., pp. 103–58.

Subcommittee on postsecondary education (1997) *Hearing on H.R. 6, the Higher Education Amendments of 1998*, July 29, Serial no. 105–16, Washington: House of Representatives, Committee on Education and the Workforce.

Talbot, C. (1996) *Ministers and Agencies: Control, Performance and Accountability*, London, England: Chartered Institute of Public Finance and Accountability.

Treasury Board Secretariat (1992) *Special Operating Agencies: Performance*, Ottawa: Treasury Board Secretariat, Program Branch.

Treasury Board Secretariat (1996) *Framework for Alternative Program Delivery*, Ottawa: Treasury Board Secretariat.

Treasury Board Secretariat (2001) *Legislated Service Agencies*, Ottawa: Treasury Board Secretariat.

Trosa, S. (1994) *Next Steps: Moving On*, London: Office of Public Service and Science.

Whittaker, J. (1996) "Talking with Major General Beale," *Military Grocer* (October) 16–18, 66.

Part III

Autonomization in continental Europe and Japan

8   Quangos in Dutch government

Sandra Van Thiel

In the 1980s and 1990s, administrative reform swept through most western states. National, regional and local governments alike changed their organizational structure, introduced private sector management ideas and techniques, contracted out tasks, privatized state-owned companies, or put policy implementation at arm's length (OECD 1997; Pollitt and Bouckaert 2000). The Netherlands was no different in this respect.

This chapter deals with the establishment of so-called quasi-autonomous non-governmental organizations (quangos) (Barker 1982). There is little agreement on the definition of quangos. In fact, it could be argued that there is a continuum of quasi-autonomous organizations, ranging from contract agencies (see several chapters in this volume), to public bodies, voluntary organizations and government owned enterprises (cf. Greve, Flinders and Van Thiel 1999).

In the Netherlands, the creation of quangos is called 'autonomization' (in Dutch: *verzelfstandiging*). There are two types of autonomization, leading to different types of organizations (cf. Verhaak 1997). Internal autonomization renders managerial freedom to units within the governmental organization. These units still fall, however, under full ministerial responsibility. The Dutch contract agencies (*agentschappen*, see Smullen, Chapter 9, in this volume) result from internal autonomization at national level. At local level, an example of internal autonomization is the introduction of contract management. External autonomization refers to the establishment of organizations charged with policy implementation as a main task, paid for by government, but operating at a distance from that government without an immediate hierarchical relationship (Van Thiel 2001a: 5). Examples vary from the Non-Departmental Public Bodies in the United Kingdom to the Crown entities in New Zealand. In the Netherlands, at national level public bodies known as ZBOs (*zelfstandige bestuursorganen*) are found. At local level, municipalities may establish so-called functional committees or establish limited companies. Further examples will be given below.[1]

The aim of this chapter is twofold. First, I will describe some characteristics of quangos in Dutch government, at national and local (i.e. municipal) level. These data show that their number has increased strongly since the 1980s. Second, this chapter offers a theoretical explanation for the proliferation of quangos in Dutch government. The first part of this theoretical explanation has been tested before (see Van Thiel 2001a). Here I will summarize the main conclusions from that test and propose new theoretical predictions for further study.

Quangos at national level

At national level the two most important types of quangos are contract agencies and ZBOs. Because the first type is dealt with extensively elsewhere (cf. Smullen in Chapter 5 of this volume), I will focus here on ZBOs.

Estimates on the number of quangos vary along with the definition one uses. For example, in the UK Hall and Weir (1996) counted over 1,800 quangos at national level, whereas official counts only listed about 300 quangos (only executive non-departmental bodies). In the Netherlands, a similar controversy is taking place about the definition of ZBOs. In 1993, the Netherlands Court of Audit (NCA) counted 545 ZBOs (Algemene Rekenkamer 1995). Departments spent approximately 18 percent of the annual state budget on these quangos in that year. And about 130,000 people were employed by ZBOs then, just a little more than in the national administration at that time.

In 2000, the number of ZBOs has dropped to 431 due to policy changes and mergers, but mainly because of definitional issues (Van Thiel and Van Buuren 2001). In fact, the rate of establishment of this type of quango has gone up; approximately 50 percent of all ZBOs in 2000 have been erected since 1993. Alongside ZBOs, a new category of public bodies has now been identified (RWTs: *rechtspersonen met een wettelijke taak*) listing over 3,200 organizations, including a large number of (former) ZBOs (Algemene Rekenkamer 2001). The distinction between RWTs and ZBOs is not very clear, even to experienced researchers in the field.

The debate on different categories of quangos makes it difficult to get an accurate estimate. Most of the examples and facts below are based on the NCA study of 1993 and my own count in 2000.

Motives

ZBOs are not new to the Dutch government. However, in the 1980s their number increased strongly as they were re-discovered as instruments of reform. Quangos are expected to be more efficient at policy implementation than traditional government bureaucracy. Hence, this is the most important motive for politicians to establish them (see Table 8.1). That is, if a motive is mentioned, for in more than half of the decisions that is not the case.

Other motives relate to the expected de-politicized nature of policy implementation by quangos and a desired reduction of the distance

Table 8.1 Motives of Dutch politicians to establish quangos at national level ($N = 545$)

Motive	Number[a]
To increase efficiency	18%
Closer to the citizens	15%
Self-regulation by social groups	13%
Execution by experts	12%
Other motives[b]	12%
No motive mentioned	53%

Source: Algemene Rekenkamer, 1995 (own calculations).

Notes
a More than one motive can be mentioned.
b Other motives are, for example: no state interference is desired; continuation of a histori-cally grown situation; affirmation of independency of executive agents.

between policy implementation on the one hand and society and citizens on the other hand. Finally, in some cases the establishment of a quango is the end result of a historical process. It is important to realize that ZBOs can be created either by hiving off a division of a ministry, or by hiving in a private organization into the public sector.

Types of quangos, tasks and policy sectors

Quangos are charged with different tasks. Table 8.2 shows that the most common tasks are: quasi-judicature (cf. tribunals), paying benefits (e.g.

Table 8.2 Tasks of quangos at national level in 1993 and 2000

Task	Number of quangos	
	1993	*2000*
Supervision	72 (13%)	20 (5%)
Paying benefits	94 (17%)	103 (24%)
Judging quality	101 (19%)	48 (11%)
Licensing	18 (3%)	15 (3%)
Making regulation	46 (8%)	4 (1%)
Registration	48 (9%)	49 (11%)
Collecting fees	4 (1%)	2 (1%)
Quasi-judicature	118 (22%)	125 (29%)
Advise, co-ordinate, etc.	37 (7%)	19 (4%)
Research	7 (1%)	9 (2%)
Other	− (0%)	37 (9%)
Total	545	431

Sources: Algemene Rekenkamer, 1995; Van Thiel and Van Buuren, 2001.

Table 8.3 Number of quangos at national level per policy sector in 1993 and 2000

Policy sector	Number of ZBOs	
	1993	*2000*
Cabinet of the Prime Minister	0 (0%)	0 (0%)
Foreign Affairs	1 (0%)	1 (0%)
Home Office	6 (1%)	33 (8%)
Education, Culture and Science[a]	65 (12%)	16 (4%)
Justice	85 (16%)	38 (9%)
Finances	7 (1%)	5 (1%)
Defense	1 (0%)	1 (0%)
Housing, Planning and Environment	68 (12%)	85 (20%)
Traffic and Waterways	24 (4%)	55 (13%)
Economics	49 (9%)	42 (10%)
Agriculture, Nature and Fishing	75 (14%)	37 (8%)
Social Affairs and Employment	92 (17%)	17 (4%)
Welfare, Health and Sport[a]	72 (13%)	101 (23%)
Total	545	431

Sources: Algemene Rekenkamer, 1995; Van Thiel and Van Buuren, 2001.

Note

a Between 1993 and 2000, Culture moved from Welfare to Education, and Sport went to Welfare.

unemployment), judging quality (e.g. meat inspection), registration (e.g. of professional groups like architects) and supervision (i.e. regulators).

Examples of ZBOs are the regulator for the telecommunications OPTA, the Netherlands Central Bank, the Chambers of Commerce, Police Authorities, the Bureau for Registration of Architects and the Councils for Legal Aid. ZBOs can be found in all policy sectors, but mostly in the fields of Social Affairs and Employment, Welfare Health and Culture, Agriculture, and Justice (see Table 8.3).

Results

Information on the performance of quangos is scarce. Case study based evidence suggests that there is neither immediate nor overall improvement of performance in terms of (cost)-efficiency and effectiveness (Ter Bogt 1997, 1999; Van Berkum and Van Dijkem 1997; Van Thiel 2001a). In other areas, for example, the quality of products or customer service, improvements have been obtained though. The official evaluations of the establishment of six ZBOs show that the expected efficiency gains are usually not obtained, but stress that these quangos have acquired a new, more business-like style and 'market awareness' (Homburg and Van Thiel 2002). For example, they are more innovative and market oriented.

Therefore, these reports conclude that the establishment of the quangos in question was successful and should not be reversed.

Conclusions

The use of ZBOs at national level has proliferated in the Netherlands since the 1980s. The publication of the NCA report in 1995 led to a hot debate on the (lack of) accountability of these bodies. As a result, new legislation has been developed to restrain the use of quangos (Van Thiel 2001b). A preference for less extreme types of quangos became evident, as the number of contract agencies increased from 1994 onwards. The absolute number of ZBOs dropped as a result of the aforementioned definition debate and the rise of a new category, the RWTs. However, the evidence shows that the rate of establishment of ZBOs has not dropped at all but has in fact increased – despite a lack of evidence on their performance. This raises the question whether quango proliferation is a well-informed choice, or rather an autonomous trend. We will return to this question after discussing the establishment of quangos at local level.

Local quangos

There seems to be a general awareness among practitioners and academics that there are many quangos at local level, but the estimates are not always clear (see, e.g. Hall and Weir 1996, on the UK; Greve 1999, on Denmark; and Wistrich 1999, on New Zealand). For the Netherlands, various cases have been described, but there is as yet no systematically collected information on the number, types and size of local quangos. Below I will present the results of a meta-analysis of available case studies of local quangos in the Netherlands.[2]

Motives

Dutch local government has a strong tradition and position within the national state system. Municipalities have autonomous tasks, which they can fund from local taxes or fees and other revenues. Next to these, they execute tasks that have been delegated to them – and are paid for – by the central government. Dutch municipalities thus have numerous tasks, ranging from refuse collection and road maintenance, to public education, health care, cultural activities, and social welfare benefits. To give some indication of the size of local governments: there are 538 municipalities (in 2000), with 186,387 civil servants (in 1993) spending DFL 72.3 million (in 1997; Derksen 1998: 10).

The establishment of quangos at local level was part of the managerial reforms undertaken by Dutch municipalities from the 1980s onwards. Table 8.4 shows that the most important motives – if mentioned – for the

Table 8.4 Motives for the establishment of local quangos (*N*= 233)

Motive	Mentioned in percentage of cases[1]
Stick to core business	26.7
Increase efficiency	21.0
Reduce costs of implementation	20.6
Separation of policy and administration	14.2
Work like a business	13.7
Improve quality of implementation	13.0
Reorganization of entire organization	7.7
Advantages of scale	6.0
Other (e.g. changes in legislation)	6.9
No motive found	41.6

Note
a In a number of cases more than one motive was given.

creation of quangos at local level were to separate policy and administration so that politicians, policy makers and policy implementors could stick to their core business. Other motives are to improve the efficiency of policy implementation, to reduce costs and enhance the quality of customer service. In sum, quangos are expected to reduce the workload of local administrators and politicians, and to increase the efficiency of service provision.

Types of quangos, tasks and policy sectors

At local level (cf. Verhaak 1997) three types of internal autonomization can be distinguished: self-management, contract-management and the so-called Policy and Management Instruments project (PMI; Van Helden 1998).[3] Internal autonomization gives freedom to manage to unit managers. The agreements on managerial freedoms are often laid down in a contract. These contracts specify tasks, budgets and sometimes also results (output) or targets that have to be met. Self-management and contract-management were combined in the early 1990s in the so-called PMI operation. Local governments adopted a range of instruments in an effort to improve the efficiency of the local administration procedures. Unfortunately, a lack of 'managerial attitude' in local governments undermined a successful and comprehensive implementation of PMI (Van Helden 1998).

External autonomization involves charging a separate organization, at arm's length of the local administration, with policy implementation. These new organizations can be established by hiving off a division of local government, or by hiving in an existing private organization. Dutch municipalities can use different types of organizations. Based on public

Table 8.5 The use of autonomization, and other forms of service provision by Dutch municipalities 1994-9 (N = 181)

	1994	1995	1996	1997	1998	1999
Internal autonomization	1	2	–	–	–	–
External autonomization	3	10	24	30	7	5
Public Private Partnership	–	–	–	1	–	–
Privatization	–	5	15	7	2	–
Competitive tendering	–	–	3	–	–	–
Load shedding	3	3	4	3	2	–
Unknown	1	12	27	8	2	1
Total	8	32	73	49	13	6

law, municipalities can appoint so-called functional committees (e.g. school boards). Or they can decide to co-operate with other local governments. Finally, they can create local agencies (in Dutch: *tak van dienst*).[4] Based on private law, municipalities can establish (limited) companies, associations and foundations for policy implementation or charge existing organizations with that task.

Next to internal and external autonomization, municipalities can also use privatization, competitive tendering and public private partnerships (PPP) to put service provision at arm's length. These modes of operation will not be discussed here any further. Table 8.5 shows the number of cases of internal and external autonomization, and other modes of service provision that were found in Dutch local government between 1994 and 1999.[5] Recently, Dutch municipalities have shown a strong preference for external autonomization, in particular, the use of private companies and foundations.

Local governments are most prone to use quasi-autonomous bodies in the fields of refuse collection, culture, health, utilities, sports and recreation (see Table 8.6). In the fields of education and social welfare services, municipalities are much more reluctant to establish quangos, e.g. in the case of the Social Benefits Office.[6]

Results

The evidence on the performance of local quangos is highly contradictory and inconclusive (cf. Ter Bogt 1997). Most of the reviewed studies (86 percent) do not mention anything about the results, or blame the lack of (information on) results on a number of problems.[7] The problems that are reported most often are: a lack of (organizational and personal) skills to change, high transition costs, continuing interference of politicians with daily activities, and problems with the development of performance indicators. Also, a number of unintended social consequences are

Table 8.6 The use of quasi-autonomous organizations per policy sector by Dutch municipalities (*N*=115)

	Autonomization		Other modes of provision				Total
	Internal	External	Priv	Tenderi	PPP	Other	
Administration	6	–	–	–	–	–	6
Culture	2	18	5	–	–	–	25
Education	1	9	–	2	–	–	12
Finances	1	–	1	–	–	1	3
Health	–	6	3	–	–	4	13
Housing	–	4	3	–	–	2	9
Facilities	–	2	1	–	–	–	3
Refuse	1	23	1	1	–	–	26
Roads	1	1	–	–	2	1	5
Planning	–	–	–	–	–	1	1
Sports	1	12	6	1	–	5	25
Traffic	–	3	–	1	–	–	4
Utilities	–	3	8	–	–	2	13
Welfare	2	3	–	–	–	–	5
Total	15	84	28	5	2	16	150

reported, such as an increase of fees for services and a lack of public accountability for local quangos (cf. Hall and Weir [1996] on the UK).

Conclusions

It is estimated that about 50 percent of Dutch municipalities use quasi-autonomous organizations for the execution of about 50 percent of their tasks (Moret, Ernst and Young 1997). PMI is even adopted by 70 percent of all municipalities (Van Helden 1998). Quangos can be said to have spread throughout local government. Size and political climate do not seem to matter very much in this respect. Quangos are charged mainly with policy implementation and service provision. The development of policies and the political decision making process remain exclusive tasks of the local administration. Some tasks are put at arm's length more often than others. For example, the social benefits office is seldom put at arm's length, whereas in most cities refuse collection is charged to inter-communal co-operation or private contractors. There are, however, hardly any clear patterns regarding which types of quangos are used for particular tasks or in particular policy sectors. The diversity in quango use, combined with a serious lack of motives and evidence on the performance of quangos suggests that municipalities do not apply quango principles in a rational manner, nor learn from each others' experience (Loeff Claeys Verbeke 1994: 30–2). How can the increase in the use of quangos be explained then?

Possible explanations

There is no formal theory yet that explains the increase in the use of quangos. The practitioner theory, i.e. the assumptions underlying politicians' choice to establish quangos is not considered a formal theory here.[8] Instead, a new theoretical explanation is offered below of why politicians would prefer to use quangos rather than government bureaucracy for the implementation of policies.

The model presented here was constructed by deduction, rather than by induction on the basis of empirical information. To carry out such an approach, I have used formal theories on the behaviour of politicians; in this case rational choice sociology (Coleman 1990) and public choice theory (Downs 1965; Mueller 1989; Dunleavy 1991). These theories were combined with elements from neo-institutional economics, in particular principal agent theory (e.g. Pratt and Zeckhauser 1991). Using these elements, a formal model was developed to predict under which conditions politicians will establish quangos for the purpose of carrying out public tasks (for more details, see Van Thiel 2001a).

A rational actor model such as presented here contains numerous simplifying assumptions. It needs further elaboration to become a more complex and realistic model. Therefore, it should be seen as a first step toward finding an explanation of quango proliferation. This first step has been tested statistically already and some results will be discussed below. I will then continue with a number of possible theoretical elaborations on the existing model – which have not been tested yet.

A rational actor perspective

Based on public choice theory, it is assumed that politicians strive to be re-elected. The use of quangos is expected to contribute to this goal because quangos can be charged with the implementation of policies that are favourable to voters. The advantages of using quangos rather than government bureaucracy are twofold. First, members of interest groups can be appointed as quango board members, which ensures the support of those groups of voters to the politicians (patronage). Government bureaucracies are expected to be impartial and hence offer less (formal) opportunities to include interest groups into the organizational structure. Second, because quangos operate at arm's length the responsibility of politicians for quango performance is limited. In case of ill performance, there is less risk that a politician will be held accountable and may lose electoral support. However, there is also a possible backlash to the use of quangos. In the case of ill performance, there are fewer possibilities for intervention because of the larger distance between the parent department and quangos. Or intervention will lead to high (monitoring) costs, threatening the possibility of achieving efficiency gains.

Politicians will have to weigh these possible benefits and risks when choosing an executive agent. Here they can choose either a quango or government bureaucracy. Which choice they make depends on the situation at hand. In such a constraint-driven approach the impact of a number of conditions has to be evaluated.

Contrary to common sense, political and economic conditions are expected *not* to be of influence on politicians' choice for quangos. Political ideology is not expected to be decisive because the aforementioned advantages of the use of quangos are valid to *all* politicians. Economic conditions are also not expected to be decisive. Quangos can be used to reduce fiscal pressure because they are expected to render efficiency gains. On the other hand, prosperity leads to an expansion of the tasks of western welfare states and hence the number of executive agents. So, in both cases the number of quangos goes up; there is no difference in the total effect.

Characteristics that *are* expected to influence the decision concern the degree of corporatism in the policy sector in question, whether elections are being held, and the type of task that is charged to the quango (collective good, specific investments). Elections and corporatism increase the competition for votes between politicians and are therefore expected to contribute to more quangos being established. The reduced responsibility for quangos leads to less political risks in election times and thus to higher chances of being re-elected. In corporatist policy areas the benefits of patronage will be higher. Therefore, it is expected that in these areas more quangos will be established to maximize electoral support. Both conditions will thus contribute to more quangos being established.

With regard to the tasks of quangos, two conditions are discerned that will lead to fewer quangos being established. First, it is predicted that politicians will not charge quangos with the provision of collective goods. The interest of voters in such goods is high. Therefore, the risk of losing control is too high. Politicians are expected to leave these types of tasks to government bureaucracy. The same holds for tasks that require highly specific investments. Low re-deployability and high sunk costs, which are associated with this type of task, will force politicians to keep execution at close range (cf. Williamson 1989: 150–1; Ter Bogt 1994: 215).

These six predictions have been tested (see Van Thiel 2001a: 107–11).[9] Most conditions had no effect on politicians' choice, except for tasks requiring specific investments, although not for all cases. In sum, however, one can conclude that the explanatory model of the rational actor perspective is still somewhat weak. Therefore, the model was expanded.

Imitation

Until now it was assumed that politicians are aware of all the advantages, disadvantages and consequences of their choices. Or in other words, that they have full information. However, this does not seem realistic. It is much more reasonable to assume that politicians' rationality is bounded (Simon 1957). This would imply that they cannot be certain about the effects of their choice. To reduce uncertainty, individuals will seek information. Here two possible strategies are proposed. First, politicians can imitate what others have done already. They simply repeat other people's or their own decision. Second, politicians can monitor the performance of previously established quangos to acquire information. However, monitoring requires investments (monitoring costs). It is therefore predicted that politicians will impose monitoring only if the costs are low or outweigh the disadvantages of quango use.

These two additional predictions were tested also. Imitation indeed proved to be a major cause of the increase in the number of quangos, at least at national level (see Van Thiel 2001a: 120–8, for a full discussion of the other results). This raises two new questions; how and why does imitation occur? To answer these questions we need to expand the theoretical model above. Two strands of theory that deal with the adoption of innovations offer interesting propositions on imitation.

Explaining imitation

Innovation Diffusion Theory (IDT) was developed primarily by Rogers (1995) to explain the adoption of new technologies by individuals. Here, I will expand its validity to the adoption and consequent spread of quangos by governments.[10]

According to IDT, the adoption of innovations can be divided into five stages. The boundaries between these stages are not always strict or clear. The first stage is labelled the 'knowledge' stage. Potential adopters (e.g. municipalities) become aware of the existence of the innovation (quangos). This can happen quite passively ('they just happen to come across the idea') or because they are actively seeking information for example to solve a particular problem or because they have a need for change. The motives for quango adoption (see Tables 8.1 and 8.4) show that quangos are used to solve a number of organizational and economical problems. Moreover, they fitted the new philosophy of New Public Management that was popular in the 1980s. IDT is a functionalist theory, i.e. the instrumental value of an innovation is expected to be decisive to its adoption. Technical features, such as types of quango, and the expected (dis)-advantages will be important. Based on the information governments acquire on quangos, they will form an opinion on the idea ('persuasion' stage) and balance the potential advantages and disadvantages of applying it to the administrative organization. The opinions of others, in particular, opinion leaders, key persons within the organization and the propagators of the innovation, influence the degree to which they will be persuaded to actually use quangos, or not. The knowledge and persuasion stages are partly overlapping and hence difficult to separate analytically.

Once it has been decided to use quangos, the adopting government will have to deal with all the associated practical problems in the 'implementation' stage; what kind of quango will be used, in which policy field, for which task, et cetera. To persist in the decision to use quangos, it will seek confirmation and reinforcement ('evaluation' stage). If this last stage is passed successfully, quangos will become an accepted and legitimate way of working within the public domain.

Rogers' model of innovation diffusion can be used to describe *how* quangos have spread through Dutch government in the 1980s and 1990s. It cannot, however, explain why this occurred or which government organizations were early or late adopters. Nor can it explain why politicians choose to create quangos, even though there is hardly any evidence that they are indeed more efficient than government bureaucracy. And finally, IDT cannot explain the large diversity in the application of the quango model found at local level. This contradicts Rogers' model, which assumes that governments will adopt the same type of quango for the same task because that is the 'best' way.

For such idiosyncrasies we need another kind of theory, one that explains the cognitive mechanisms underlying the adoption of innovations. DiMaggio and Powell's idea of isomorphism (1983; see also Powell and DiMaggio 1991) offers powerful ideas. They argue that in order to survive, organizations will adopt the same structures and ways of working. This similarity between organizations in the same field can be the result of competition or the strive for economic efficiency ('competitive isomorphism'). DiMaggio and Powell were, however, particularly interested in the homogeneity that stems from a quest for legitimacy of one organization with other organizations in its environment. Such 'institutional isomorphism' occurs through three mechanisms: coercive, mimetic and normative isomorphism. DiMaggio and Powell stress that the three mechanisms are not necessarily empirically distinguishable. They may be separate processes, but they can occur at the same time and their effects may not always be clearly identifiable.[11]

Coercive isomorphism is strongly related to the concept of resource dependency; powerful others, such as the EU to the Dutch national government or the national government to municipalities, demand the use of quasi-autonomous bodies (Mizruchi and Fein 1999: 657). As the lower level government is dependent on the higher one, it has no choice but to adhere to its demands. Coercion can result from legal prescription but also from active financial support, rewarding those organizations that adopt the quango model. For example, the PMI-operation in Dutch municipalities was subsidized by the Home Office (Van Helden 1998). Coercive isomorphism shows that the aforementioned persuasion stage does not always imply a voluntary choice to adopt.

Mimetic isomorphism is a response to uncertainty. "In situations in which a clear course of action is unavailable, organizational leaders may decide that the best response is to mimic a peer that they perceive to be successful" (Mizruchi and Fein 1999: 657). Uncertainty is indicated by a lack of legitimacy. In the 1980s governments throughout the western world were faced with a decline in citizen trust and rising expectations with respect to the quality of public services (Pollitt and Bouckaert 2000: ch. 2). Administrative reform is generally seen as a response to both developments. For example, quangos were expected to reduce the distance between citizens and the government, thereby inducing a higher quality of customer service, which would eventually restore citizen trust. Mimetic isomorphism can be seen as one of the ways in which governments come across the idea of quangos in the knowledge stage (see above). However, that does not explain where the idea of quangos came from.

Following DiMaggio and Powell, peer networks could be an important source of information. The dissemination of ideas on quangos through networks could reveal patterns in their diffusion. For example, governments can imitate each other, across boundaries or between layers. Intermediary platforms such as the OECD, the European Union, or the associations of Dutch local governments (VNG) could be important conveyors of novel ideas. The spread of ideas on quangos could be traced back to networks, especially networks with a high degree of participation and ties. Important variables in the study of such networks are therefore the degree of participation, the number of actors (and their origin), the number of ties ('density'), the internal flow of information and the permeability of the network boundaries.

The spread of ideas through networks is strongly related to DiMaggio and Powell's third and last mechanism. Normative isomorphism is the result of professionalization. The training, or socialization, of public managers could, for example, include a favorable opinion toward quangos as a 'modern' form of public management. Or, governments may attract a new type of public manager who is more informed about the New Public Management paradigm. Consequently, quangos will become a more popular mode of operation. Interactions between members of professions are a second source for normative isomorphism, for example between politicians or public managers and consultants. In the Netherlands, about 52 percent of the municipalities have hired a consultant when establishing quangos (Schotman *et al.* 2000). In terms of the aforementioned persuasion stage (Rogers 1995), these consultants could be called opinion leaders or propagators.

In sum, institutional isomorphism can help to explain why quangos have proliferated in Dutch local government. Coercive isomorphism could have played a role; powerful others force, either directly or implicitly, governments to implement particular types of quangos. Mimetic isomorphism could have occurred in response to a loss of legitimacy. The spread of NPM through government networks made the concept of quangos available. And as more and more governments adopted it, quangos became an accepted mode of operation (normative isomorphism). In the evaluation stage, they will be convinced that they have made the right choice. Such 'symbolic' purposes of creating quangos also explain how it is possible that they continue to create quangos without clear evidence on the consequences, i.e. quango performance. Apparently, innovation adoption can serve more than merely instrumental or functional purposes. Using the idea of institutional isomorphism, we can expand the assumptions of Rogers' model.

Moreover, it also becomes clear why quango proliferation can lead to such a large variety. The choice to create a quango will be influenced by the type of isomorphism at work and hence the source of information. The network in which governments participate, the type of managers it employs,[12] the consultant it hires, can all influence the choice to adopt a particular type of quango. The variation in such variables will thus affect both the proliferation of quangos, and the variety in practice. These new predictions will be tested in ongoing research.

Notes

1 Next to the national and municipal level, there is a third tier of government in the Netherlands: the provincial level. Unfortunately, there is hardly any (systematically collected) information on quangos at the provincial level.
2 In total 135 articles, books and master theses of Public Administration graduate students were reviewed as well as six volumes of a journal on privatisation, revealing 233 cases of the establishment of quasi-autonomous organizations in 155 Dutch municipalities. See for a full overview Van Thiel (2001c).
3 This type of autonomization is comparable to the use of contract agencies by national governments (cf. Pollitt *et al.* 2001). However, contrary to the national level, internal autonomization in Dutch municipalities does not lead to the establishment of separate units within the administration. Existing units are given more managerial freedom ('a mandate') but keep their (hierarchical) position in the organization. At local level, the establishment of agencies would appear to bear more similarities with the process of external autonomization.
4 Local agencies operate at arm's length of the government, which means that the accountability of local politicians is limited. Their legal basis is in public law. Examples observed in Dutch local governments are, among others, utility companies, hospitals and theatres. Local agencies should not be confused with the agencies at national level. Perhaps they can be compared more to public bodies at the national level such as the Dutch ZBOs or the British Non-Departmental Bodies (cf. Greve *et al.* 1999; Van Thiel 2001a).
5 Unfortunately, only 181 of the 233 case descriptions contained an accurate characterization of the type of autonomization that occurred.
6 For the Dutch case, this is contrary to findings at national level where implementation of social benefits policies is (almost always) charged to quangos.
7 Note that not all reviewed studies aimed to describe performance, which could explain the lack of information on this topic in part. However, the lack of evidence on performance results is quite systematic, both at local and national level (cf. Van Thiel 2001a).
8 In fact, it could be argued that the fact that most quangos do not obtain their

expected efficiency gains refutes the practitioner theory, i.e. the sum of the motives mentioned in tables 1 and 4.

9 Data were used on ZBOs, which had been collected by the NCA (Algemene Rekenkamer 1995) and from other secondary sources (see Van Thiel 2001a, for a full account). In total, 392 decisions were taken between 1950 and 1993 involving the establishment of a quango. The data were analyzed by a Poisson regression analysis using a time-lag (Long 1997: ch.8; Agresti 1996: 80–93).

10 My main interest here is in the process of adoption in general, not in the adoption of one type of quango, nor how any individual government uses a particular type in practice. It should be recognized, however, that the type of established organization or degree of autonomy might influence the actual process of its adoption and diffusion.

11 A review by Mizruchi and Fein (1999) showed that in 26 selected North-American studies the researchers claimed to be using only one type of isomorphism – mimetic – but, in fact, described phenomena that could be attributed to normative and coercive isomorphism as well.

12 An interesting question in this respect is what benefits public managers have to gain from the decision to put policy implementation at arm's length.

Bibliography

Agresti, A. (1996) *An Introduction to Categorical Data Analysis.* Wiley Series in Probability and Statistics, New York: John Wiley & Sons, Inc.

Algemene R. (1995) *Verslag 1994. Deel 3: Zelfstandige bestuursorganen en ministeriële verantwoordelijkheid*, Tweede Kamer, vergaderjaar 1994–1995, 24 130, nr. 3.

Algemene R. (2001) *Verantwoording en toezicht bij rechtspersonen met een wettelijke taak*, Tweede Kamer, vergaderjaar 2000–2001, 27 656, nr. 1–2.

Barker, A. (ed.) (1982) *Quangos in Britain*, London: Macmillan Press Ltd.

Coleman, J.S. (1990) *Foundations of Social Theory*, Cambridge MA: The Belknap Press of Harvard University Press.

Daemen, H. and Schaap, L. (2000) *Citizen and City: Developments in Fifteen Local Democracies in Europe*, Delft: Eburon.

Derksen, W. (1998) *Lokaal Bestuur*, Den Haag: Elsevier Uitgeverij.

DiMaggio, P.J. and Powell, W.W. (1983) "The iron cage revisited: institutional isomorphism and collective rationality in organizational fields," *American Sociological Review* 48, 147–60.

Downs, A. (1965) "Non-market decision making: a theory of bureaucracy," *American Economic Review* 54, 439–46.

Dunleavy, P. (1991) *Democracy, Bureaucracy and Public Choice: Economic Explanations in Social Science*, New York: Harvester Wheatsheaf.

Moret, Ernst and Young (1997) *Trends in uitbesteding*, Utrecht: Moret, Ernst & Young.

Greve, C. (1999) "Quangos in Denmark and Scandinavia: trends, problems and perspectives," in Flinders, M.V. and Smith, M.J. (eds) *Quangos, Accountability and Reform: The Politics of Quasi-government*, London: Macmillan Press, pp. 83–108.

Greve, C., Flinders, M.V. and Van Thiel, S. (1999) "Quangos: what's in a name? Defining quangos from a comparative perspective," *Governance* 12, 1, 129–46.

Hall, W. and Weir, S. (1996) *The Untouchables: Power and Accountability in the Quango State.* The Democratic Audit of the United Kingdom, London: Charter 88 Trust.

Homburg, V.M.F. and Van Thiel, S. (2002) "Lessen en inzichten voor zbo-beleid," *Openbaar Bestuur* 12, 2, 21–4.

Loeff C.V. (1994) *Nederland Privatiseert*, Den Haag: Sdu.

Long, J.S. (1997) *Regression Models for Categorical and Limited Dependent Variables*. Advanced Quantitative Techniques in the Social Sciences, Thousand Oakes: SAGE Publications.

Mizruchi, M.S. and Fein, L.C. (1999) "The social construction of organizational knowledge: a study of the uses of coercive, mimetic and normative isomorphism," *Administrative Science Quarterly* 44, 653–83.

Mueller, D.C. (1989) *Public Choice II*, Cambridge: Cambridge University Press.

OECD (1997) *Managing Across Levels of Government*, Paris: OECD.

Pollitt, C. and Bouckaert, G. (2000) *Public Management Reform*, Oxford: Oxford University Press.

Pollitt, C., Bathgate, K., Caulfield, J., Smullen, A. and Talbot, C. (2001, forthcoming) "Agency fever? Analysis of an international policy fashion," *Journal of Comparative Policy Analysis* 3, 3.

Powell, W.W. and DiMaggio, P.J. (eds) (1991) *The New Institutionalism in Organizational Analysis*, Chicago: The University of Chicago Press.

Pratt, J.W. and Zeckhauser, R.J. (1991) *Principals and Agents*, Boston, Massachusetts: Harvard Business School Press.

Rogers, E.M. (1995) *Diffusion of Innovations*, 4th edn, New York: The Free Press.

Scharpf, F.W. (1997) *Games Real Actors Play: Actor-centered Institutionalism in Policy Research*. Theoretical lenses on public policy, USA/United Kingdom: Westview Press.

Schotman, W.L.M., Van der Sluis, W., Driessen, H.H. and Bos, S.B.P. (2000) *Verzelfstandiging op lokaal niveau: de 100 meest gestelde vragen*, Alphen aan den Rijn: Samsom.

Simon, H. (1957) *Models of Man: Social and Rational*, New York: John Wiley.

Ter Bogt, H.J. (1994) "Verzelfstandiging van overheidsorganisaties, bezien vanuit de neo-institutionele economie," *Beleidswetenschap* 8, 205–39.

Ter Bogt, H.J. (1997) *Neo-institutionele economie, management control en verzelfstandiging van overheidsorganisaties*, Capelle a/d IJssel: Labyrint Publication.

Ter Bogt, H.J. (1999) "Financial and economic management in autonomised Dutch public organizations," *Financial Accountability and Management* 15, 3, 329–50.

Van Berkum, J. and Van Dijkem, K. (1997) *Verzelfstandiging van rijkstaken in Nederland: de eerste schreden van Drie zelfstandige Bestuursorganen*, Zoetermeer: Omslag Groep.

Van Helden, G.J. (1998) "A review of the policy and management instruments project for municipalities in the Netherlands," *Financial Accountability and Management* 14, 2, 85–104.

Van Thiel, S. (2001a) *Quangos: Trends, Causes and Consequences*, Aldershot: Ashgate Publishing Company.

Van Thiel, S. (2001b) "Kaderwet zelfstandige bestuursorganen: uniformiteit of verscheidenheid?," *Bestuurswetenschappen* 55, 2, 189–93.

Van Thiel, S. (2001c) *Lokale verzelfstandiging: vormen, motieven en resultaten van verzelfstandiging door gemeenten*, Rotterdam: intern rapport.

Van Thiel, S. and Van Buuren, M.W. (2001) "Ontwikkeling van het aantal zelfstandige bestuursorganen tussen 1993 en 2000: zijn zbo's 'uit' de mode?," *Bestuurswetenschappen* 55, 5, 386–404.

Verhaak, F. (1997) "Shifting frames of reference in Dutch autonomization reforms," in Kickert, W.J.M. (ed.) *Public Management and Administrative Reform in Western Europe*, Cheltenham: Edward Elgar, pp. 157–76.

Williamson, O.E. (1989) "Transaction cost economics," in Schmalensee, R. and Willig, R.D. (eds) *Handbook of Industrial Organization*. Volume I, Elsevier Science Publishers B.V., pp. 136–81.

Wistrich, E. (1999) "Quangos in New-Zealand," in Flinders, M.V. and Smith, M.J. (eds) *Quangos, Accountability and Reform: The Politics of Quasi-government*, London: Macmillan Press, pp. 84–93.

9 Lost in translation?

Shifting interpretations of the concept of 'agency': the Dutch case

Amanda Smullen

Introduction

This chapter describes the evolution of the Dutch program of agencification. These experiences are presented as local translations of international trends in public sector reform. In addition, the idea of translation is applied not only to the exchange between international and national portrayals of the agency idea, but also to the exchange between national and organizational representations of agencies. A content analysis of four Dutch agency annual reports is conducted to illustrate the convergence and divergence of meaning and activities associated with the agency idea. It is argued that while the international language surrounding agencies has been adopted at a number of government levels, this adoption has been selective and translated in ways quite specific to national and organizational contexts. Contrary to global accounts of convergence in public sector arrangements, the conclusion of this analysis indicates considerable variation in applications of agency reform, even within the same national context.

In the first section of this chapter, agencies as an international category are discussed and specific ideas associated with the agency label are identified. These ideas are portrayed as global phenomena upon which there appears to be much agreement. Moreover, the correlation between these ideas and the doctrine of New Public Management (NPM) is high. Two theories are proposed that may explain this international convergence, NPM theory and new institutionalism's theory of isomorphism. While NPM is described as a totalizing discourse that proposes uniform conformance to international talk, the theory of isomorphism is shown to be capable of much greater nuance and subtlety. This nuance is promoted by the combination of Latour's concept of translation with the theory of isomorphism. In the second section of this chapter, a general description of the formal implementation of Dutch agencies is presented. It is argued that while adopting the international language surrounding the agency idea, Dutch policy makers, had, at least from the outset translated these ideas to a quite specific set of financial definitions. Employing Latour's terms, this is recognized as a translation from the international story to a meaning that correlates with what is perceived as satisfying local interests and levels of acceptability. Finally, the third section of this chapter presents the findings from an analysis of four Dutch agency annual reports. These findings illustrate the scope that the agency idea offers for a whole range of meanings and thus practices. It reveals that the agency story is malleable to a whole range of translations in different organizational and national cultures.

Agency – one label many ideas and practices

The last two decades would suggest that a new international reform category has emerged, the agency. Although not always consistent with local titles, the agency label has been associated with public sector arrangements observed in countries as diverse as England (O'Toole and Jordan 1995), Sweden (Fortin 1996; Fudge and Gustaffson 1989), Japan (James 2001), the Netherlands (Ter Bogt 1999; Van der Knaap *et al.* 1997), Latvia (Pollitt *et al.* 2001) and Australia (Armstrong 1998) – to name just a few examples. In contrast to previous periods, this diffusion of agencies seems to represent far more than simply the application of a rather non-specific English word to public sector reform. On the contrary, the agency label has come to embrace a range of specific ideas and values about public sector solutions.

Without delving into the details of agency practice, it does not take long for an observer to realize that this recent agency identity is somehow correlated with efficiency, results-orientation, output, autonomy and responsiveness. This characterization may be illustrated by recent references in OECD reports, which note the 'greater use of agencies or their equivalents ... (for) purposes that include better service, greater efficiency, a focus on results, as well as clearer accountability relationships between the institution and government' (OECD 1997a: 19). Or the 'widespread practice of granting greater autonomy to devolved organizations' to promote 'performance management' (OECD 1995: 8). Some descriptions seem to imply these kinds of arrangements even have something to do with 'AGENCY,' in the empowering sense of the word adopted by sociologists, and are (therefore) certainly far removed from images of slow moving bureaucracies (Osborne and Gaebler 1992). This is because 'agency' in sociological terms describes the ability of individuals to create the world around them independently of structural constraints. Although the author concedes the analogy is not quite right when applied to agency as an organization, as opposed to the agency of an individual, the symbolic baggage of the term in the context of bureaucratic reform is ironic.

Furthermore, one notes not only mere descriptions of the agency landscape, but also some important signposts that act as agency landmarks. Contracts, business plans, performance indicators and accrual accounting systems, as many government documents and OECD reports will verify, supplement this vision of the 'common knowledge' surrounding agencies (see for example; OECD 1997a, OECD 1997b, OECD 1995; Ministerie van Financién 1991). Because of the way these texts appear to conform to a fairly consistent story about results and performance, one can be forgiven for concluding that agencies, and all their accessories, represent a universal way to organize the public sector, with undisputed benefits. At least, this appears to be the discourse that the OECD has been able to 'package' and make available to reformers in a number of countries (Sahlin-Anderson 2001) – despite the origins of this agency talk in the English language.

A more critical assessment of these texts, however, and a bit of digging around about agency practice would raise a number of questions about this representation of agencies. Agency stories may well consistently speak of results, steering, and performance, but the agency identity is hardly a consistent whole and even agency accessories like contracts or performance measurement are subject to significant variation in practice (Greve 2000). Contrary to what often seems like a simple arrangement, Pollitt *et al.* (2001) have noted that when examined more closely 'agencification' actually represents a very complex bundle of ideas. Shifting from the rhetoric surrounding the agency identity, they have provided a more sober account of ideas associated with agencies and suggest there are 'many ways the agency bottle may be filled.' Some insight into the realm of possibilities is illustrated in Figure 9.1 below by a presentation of Pollitt *et al.*'s Agency Ideas Schema. Pollitt *et al.* (2001) suggest that the dimensions of structural disaggregation and performance contracting represent the essentials of the agency identity, although even these may be actualized in different ways or proceed from different points of departure. It becomes apparent that the agency label and ideas like results or performance may be associated with a whole range of practices.

Figure 9.1 Agency Ideas Schema.

1.	Structural Disaggregation	2.	Performance "Contracting"
1.1	Task Specification	2.1	Achievement Performance
1.2	Task Specialization	2.2	Performance Reporting
1.3	Unit Accountability	2.2.1	Performance Accountability
1.3.1	Chief Officer Accountability	2.2.1.1	Performance Audit
1.4	Managerial Autonomy	2.3	Performance Improvement
1.4.1	Financial Flexibility	2.3.1	Improved Economy
1.4.2	Personnel Flexibility	2.3.2	Improved Efficiency
1.4.3	Organizational Flexibility	2.3.3	Improved Effectiveness
		2.3.3.1	Improved Outputs
		2.3.3.2	Improved Quality of Service
		2.3.3.3	Improved Outcomes
		2.4	Performance Budgeting
		2.4.1	Improved Policy Making
		2.5	Performance Management
		2.5.1	Improved Strategic Management

Accounting for convergence and divergence

Popular and academic theory offer two different accounts that attempt to explain recent agency growth and apparent similarities across national borders. In the first instance, it is claimed that globalization has made entrepreneurial government inevitable (Osborne and Gaebler 1992) and reform practices like agencies are illustrative of the New Public Management (NPM) that is sweeping the world. Since the artifacts associated with agencies above are symmetrical to many of the characteristics attributed to NPM, this explanation appears to hold some currency. Hood (1996) describes NPM as a doctrine composed of a number of prescriptions and these correspond neatly with the international agreement about agency identity. These prescriptions include greater autonomy, a focus upon outputs, transparency of financial resources and allocation, and the introduction of explicit performance standards. In the scenario provided by NPM, the international talk and titles associated with agencies is presumed to be illustrative of actual and consistent practice.

However, there are some problems with the globalization thesis generally (Weiss 1998; Hirst and Thompson 1996) and, for the purposes of this chapter, with NPM more particularly (Pollitt and Bouckaert 2000). First, the prescriptive stance of some NPM proponents often makes it difficult to separate their prescriptions from what they claim to observe. The language of NPM is businesslike and thus all that its proponents perceive is fitted into business categories and a business narrative more generally (Clarke and Newman 1997). As Pollitt (2001) has noted the problem of categorization is also evident in PUMA publications, where tables are presented denoting an asterisk to those countries that have adopted a reform. The appearance of convergence may be supported, also in the case of agencies, even though 'it is hard to know exactly . . . whether one asterisk is equal to another, or whether the adoption is a brief flirtation or a deep, meaningful relationship' (Pollitt 2000b: 5). This is an important point because a number of scholars have refuted the totalizing arguments implicit in NPM discourse. They claim there are important distinctions in the extent to which NPM ideas have been incorporated into the public sector reform agendas of different countries (Premfors 1998; Kickert 1997; Pollitt and Bouckaert 2000; Hood 1996; Greve *et al.* 1999). This point may also be extended to the experience and practice of agencies in different contexts. Furthermore, critics have questioned the positive impact and actual evidence of reforms like agencies upon efficiency, quality and accountability (Van Thiel 2000; Ter Bogt 1999; Pollitt 2000b).

An alternative scenario is offered by new institutionalism's theory of isomorphism. This theory is explicitly concerned with the phenomena of homogeneity in organizational fields, where an organizational field is defined as, 'those organizations that, in the aggregate constitute a recognized area of institutional life: key suppliers, resource and product consumers, regulatory agencies and other organizations that produce similar services or products' (DiMaggio and Powell 1983: 148). The theory of isomorphism suggests that the overwhelming similarities that may be observed across (formal) organizations can be explained by the desire of organizations to maintain legitimacy within their environment (DiMaggio and Powell 1983). Contrary to NPM explanations, isomorphism questions instrumental motivations like efficiency as being the stimulus for such reforms as agencies. Rather it proposes that organizations react to and enact prevailing social standards and ideas about what constitutes good practice. In this way the organization can give, at least in presentation, the impression that perceived external standards are being satisfied and that cultural alignment exists. It is significant that Dimaggio and Powell suggest that organizations may conform to these standards even when they do not satisfy other rationales like efficiency or sound business strategy (DiMaggio and Powell 1983; see also Buchko 1994).

The theory of isomorphism has been criticized for its apparent depiction of organizations 'as passive entities which simply react and adapt to the latest trends' (Sahlin-Andersson 1996: 69, see also Oliver 1991; DiMaggio 1988). It is argued that passive acquiescence to organizational fields is only one of a number of responses that organizations may undertake to deal with external pressures (Oliver 1991). Furthermore, it is noted that much of the empirical research identifying the phenomena of isomorphism has been conducted in a quantitative tradition that merely scans the upper layers of organizations searching for patterns across properties like titles, jargon, technical systems or structures (see Fliegstein 1985; Tolbert and Zucker 1983). It is evident that the theoretical criteria of isomorphism are satisfied without investigating the substance or content of these practices, because even the symbolic counts. Indeed, symbolism is the central focus of the theory (Scott 1995). This observation has led to a useful clarification of isomorphism by Sahlin-Andersson who writes, 'What spreads are not experiences or practices per se, but standardized models and presentation of such practices' (Sahlin-Andersson 1996: 78). She incorporates Latour's notion of translation, or rather editing, into the theory of isomorphism, opening up the conceptual space for the rewriting of stories as they spread (Sahlin-Andersson 1996; Latour 1987).

For Latour, translation describes the travel of ideas that are reshaped, reinvented and modified every time they are picked up by individuals and organizational members (Latour 1996; Boons and Strannegård 2000). Unlike diffusion, where the transmission of an initial idea undergoes only minor change, Latour argues that translation may push ideas further through time and space, enabling interpretations where the initial idea 'may barely count' (Latour 1996). Translation occurs because followers in a particular local context interpret (successful) experiences presented by others according to their own perceived specific problems and interests (Sahlin-Andersson 1996; Sevon 1996). To this extent, 'the initial source of knowledge is enriched with new ways of interpreting their experience' (Sahlin-Andersson 1996: 82), but it is also continually transformed across time and space by the alternative summations that different translators make about an initial idea.

As a linguistic metaphor, the concept of translation seems an appropriate addition to the theory of isomorphism and its emphasis upon symbolism. It also introduces a new dimension to observations of convergence in the agency story and associated agency talk and titles, since it suggests that different meanings may be attributed to these in different cultural contexts. This is eloquently explained by Sevon, who writes, 'the translation model can help us to reconcile the fact that a text is at the same time object-like and yet it can be read in differing ways' (Sevon 1996: 23). Similarly, agencies as a reform category associated with general ideas like results, performance and efficiency may also be subject to numerous interpretations and applications. This is despite, the predominance of English as the language in which public sector ideas are exchanged (which then must be literally translated back and forth between international forums and the national arrangement) and the Anglo-American visions about the public sector that are more generally predominant in NPM.

Agencies: the Dutch translation

An analysis of Dutch government texts and formal implementation requirements provides an insight into how agencies have been understood and practiced in the Netherlands. Contrary to the context-free descriptions of NPM, Dutch agency constructions suggest that convergence across the symbolic realm of talk is associated with quite specific meanings unique to formal agency practice in the Netherlands. In this section the concept of translation is used to describe how Dutch central authorities have selected and actualized agency ideas.

The word agency, or in Dutch *agentschappen*,[1] entered the Dutch reform vocabulary in 1991 when a government report, *The Further Cultivation of Management*, was published (Ministerie van Financién 1991). This report explicitly borrowed from ideas about agencies in the international community. Agency reforms in other countries were recognized and the Dutch agency initiative was described as following in the footsteps of the UK's Next Steps program (Ministerie van Financién 1991; Verhaak 1997). Furthermore, the language of the report conformed to a familiar international narrative about agency reform. Terms like 'results orientated management,' 'steering on the head-lines,' and 'performance' were recurrently adopted throughout the report to explain the changes that agency reform was intended to realize. A quick tally of the short summary at the beginning of The Further Cultivation of Management shows that these words were used respectively at least 8, 10 and 6 times (Ministerie van Financién 1991). Furthermore, 'autonomization,' a particularly Dutch addition to this vocabulary was also employed to describe becoming an agency.

This portrayal of agencies and expectations about agency effects, like improved efficiency, extended beyond the initial accounts of Dutch agencies, and was also appropriated by Ministers embracing agency reform within their own departments. This is illustrated in Table 9.1, which presents the motives that ministers identified when informing the Dutch parliament of their intention to create an agency. It is evident that the language of NPM has informed the way agencies are described in the Netherlands and has promoted assumed facts about the beneficial impact of agencies. Aside from the motives referring to quangos, which will be discussed below, these characterizations of Dutch agencies suggest that there exists a lot of homogeneity with international descriptions of the agency identity.

However, in the terms set by Dutch government texts like the *Further Cultivation of Management* and the formal definition of Dutch agencies that was applicable until 2000, one is also able to identify some very specific translations that have been associated with this agency talk. Agencies in the Netherlands were from the outset formally defined through the inclusion of the agency title into the Dutch Government Accounting Act (Brief van de Minister Financien 1993). This gave Dutch agencies the formal definition and actual content of an organization within the public sector permitted to use an accrual accounting system. In this respect, the results orientation of Dutch agencies obtained a primarily financial character and

Table 9.1 Motives for creating agencies in the Netherlands ($N=64$)

Motivations identified	Percentage of total reasons identified
Efficiency	23.4
Effectiveness	7.8
Quango inappropriate	12.5
Flexibility	12.5
Insight into costs	17.2
Clarify products	1.6
Improve quality	3.1
Separate policy and implementation	7.8
Able to specialize	1.6
Develop independent identity	1.6
Work for results	1.6
Possible future quango	3.1
Capital intensive task	3.1
Can work for third parties	3.1
Total	100

Sources: The information statutes that are presented to parliament by ministers intending to create an agency. See 'Instelling brief' in reference list.

was used to refer to a shift from focussing upon expenditure in the cash-based accounting system to focussing upon costs in an accrual accounting system (Ministerie van Financién 1991; Brief van de Minister van Financien 1996). It may be suggested that this translation, while satisfying some of the international expectations about the agency label, was also acceptable because it corresponded to discussions about reforming the Dutch Accounting Act that had been in progress since the late 70s (Boorsma and Mol 1997; Sorber 1996).

The Dutch Government Accounting Act was also the specific source for other kinds of translations from international talk to the local Dutch context. In initial accounts of agency reform, this Act was described as providing the means for 'steering at the head-lines' (Ministerie van Financién 1991: iv). Unlike Osborne and Gaebler's vision of setting outcome and output targets for delivery organizations, this application of steering referred to formal criteria within the Dutch Accounting Act that gave the Ministry of Finance the role of assessing which organizations could be granted agency status. From 1991–2000, the criteria required prospective agencies to:

- Identify measurable products and services.
- Obtain an approved accounting declaration.
- Present real possibilities for efficiency gains.

Although ideas about making agreements, calculating cost prices and creating performance targets were presented in the *Further Cultivation of Management*, these were ideas about performance conceived of entirely in financial terms and were left outside formal legal or financial requirements (see Ministerie van Financién 1991). Furthermore, in the case of agreements, implementation was left largely to the discretion of ministries. An overview of the kind and extent of steering through performance measurement is presented in Table 9.2. This table shows the measures that were actually identified at the time of agency creation. It should be noted that because the actual yearly agreements made between agencies and ministries are not, in most cases, made available to the general public, it is difficult to assess to what extent these measures have been used across time to make evaluations about agency performance or to direct future work practices.

Since 1998 changes to the Dutch Accounting Act have made the performance information requirements of Dutch agencies more explicit. They must now develop a performance measurement framework, including cost prices, prior to becoming an agency (Ministerie van Financién 1998; Brief van de Minister Financien 2000). The publication of this information is still subject to some differentiation. The agreements that have been made with the agencies created since 1998 are only partially presented to Parliament at the time of their creation. Cost prices are not

Table 9.2 Performance measures identified at the time of creating Dutch agencies
          (*N*= 23)

Performance measures	Percentage agencies uses measure at time of creation	Percentage that plan to use performance measures[a]
Inputs	100	
Cost price	45	45
Output	63.6	13.6
Efficiency	0	13.6
Quality	40	18
Outcome	0	9
Targets set	4.5	0

Sources: The Information statutes that are presented to parliament by ministers intending to create an agency. See 'Instelling brief' in reference list.

Note
a In this case the performance measure has been proposed for the organization but no indication is given of how it will be measured.

presented, for example, although the performance indicators that are to be collected are identified. Also only some agencies present their cost prices in the annual budget.

Alternatively, structural disaggregation in the Netherlands has entailed the identification of agency products and the extension of managerial discretion over the allocation of apparatus costs in the agency budget. This has made it possible for agency managers to employ contract staff, although the majority of agency employees continue to be civil servants and employed under the conditions negotiated with public sector unions.[2] Also agency managers are not free to negotiate their own accommodation and continue to be required to use other government services for this purpose.

Autonomization has also remained a purely financial condition, although concerns identified within public sector organizations would suggest much broader connotations. An evaluation in 1998 found that a number of public sector organizations believed to satisfy the criteria for agency status were inhibited by the agency title itself (Ministerie van Financién 1998). Both ministries and delivery services had respectively expressed concerns about the impact of the agency title upon public perceptions of their accountability and work ethos (Ministerie van Financién 1998; Zaat 1998). This is because appearing to be too businesslike can also damage public beliefs about the trustworthiness and reliability of government organizations. In January 2000 a rather pragmatic but startling solution was implemented. The agency title has been removed from the Dutch Accounting Act and no longer exclusively refers to an organization within the public sector permitted to use an accrual accounting system (Zevende wijzing van de Comptabilitietswet

2000). This has created a situation whereby public sector organizations permitted to use an accrual accounting system can choose whether or not they will also adopt the agency title. According to what had previously been established Dutch agency practice until this change, an agency in the Netherlands can now be by name and content, or merely by content and not by name.

The idea of 'autonomy,' as expressed in descriptions of agencies and it would seem the agency title itself, seems to have become less popular as agency reform has proceeded. Findings by both the National Audit Office and a Parliamentary Commission, plus an associated commitment by the current government to the primacy of politics, may be argued to have presented significant difficulties in some aspects of agency translation. First, findings in 1995 that Dutch quangos were poorly monitored and presented a threat to ministerial accountability encouraged a preference for Dutch agencies[3] (Algemene Rekenkamer 1995). Contrary to agency talk, which had emphasized autonomy and flexibility in general, this preference developed because agencies had less formal autonomy than quangos and were thus deemed a lesser threat to accountability (see also motivations in Table 9.1). Second, a further commission argued that commercial activities by public sector organizations disrupted the market and had negative side effects for the private sector (Commissie Cohen 1997). This has led to the prohibition of commercial activities for a number of public sector organizations including Dutch agencies. Despite these events, which suggest that Dutch agencies have quite limited autonomy and must conform to a very specific idea of public sector organizations, agency title and talk – as confirmed by recent changes to the Dutch Accounting Act – continues to associate autonomy with businesslike activities within the public sector.

Although Dutch authorities have presented agency reform in a way that is consistent with international descriptions of the agency identity (and thus informed by NPM), it is also evident that these international ideas have been translated in ways quite specific to the Netherlands. Agencies in the Netherlands have been largely a financial construction that have only recently and slowly embraced broader conceptions of performance and results. This conservative translation of agency ideas has also been subject to difficulties, as meanings associated with agency appear to be deemed unacceptable by various national actors within and outside the public sector. Significantly, it would appear that the businesslike identity that has been associated with Dutch agencies – predominantly through the medium of talk and not practice – has presented barriers to the continued spread of the agency title.

Translations from the national to the organizational

The portrayal of Dutch agencies by central policy makers in the Ministry of Finance has also been differentially edited at the organizational level.

An overview of a selection of Dutch agency annual reports from 1998 illustrates that even national ideas about agencies are vulnerable to translation at lower levels. Reports published by the Immigration Service (IND), the Meteorological Institute (KNMI), Botanical diagnosis bureau (PZD) and Senter, an organization responsible for granting and processing of subsidies to industry, reveal a range of agency personalities. In this section, the results of a content analysis conducted on these reports is presented. This selection is insightful because it includes agencies from different ministries that conduct different kinds of tasks and have different levels of financial dependency upon their ministry. In this latter respect, only the IND obtains all of its financial receipts from its mother department, while the other organizations all receive significant (in excess of 20 percent) contributions from other sources. The annual reports have been assessed for two different kinds of information; first, in what way does the organization present itself as an agency, and second, to what extent does this coincide with national and international portrayals of agencies. The method used to answer these questions was to conduct a content analysis of all documents, looking for the key words associated with agency ideas. These words were 'agency,' 'results,' 'efficiency,' 'quality,' 'product' and 'client.' And then, to identify how these words were included in the text and how this compared with the texts in the other annual books. Finally, the extent and kind of performance information that was provided within each annual report was recorded and compared. The kind of 'results' they represented were observed with particular interest.

It is perhaps important to make some distinctions about the context in which these reports have been produced and some general comments on the style in which the organizations are presented. The annual report published by Senter was an accountability requirement placed upon the organization at the time of its creation. For Senter, however, this was not a new arrangement because the organization was publishing an annual report prior to becoming an agency. Alternatively, KNMI and PZD publish an annual report even though this is not a part of the formal accountability arrangements with which they must comply. In the case of IND, the annual report has become part of the formal accountability arrangements of the organization, although this was not the case when the organization became an agency.

In a ratio of pictures to words, the annual reports of KNMI and IND could be described as picture-heavy with graphics constituting, in both instances, approximately one third of the entire report. These graphics include respectively full or half page photos of meteorological phenomena (e.g. impact of natural disasters, the ocean, the earth) and close ups of personnel (who are also interviewed). The report of Senter is rated somewhere in the middle, although it is also the longest report with some pictures and many words, while the report of PZD contains almost no graphics at all. Furthermore, although both the reports of Senter and

KNMI are printed on glossy paper, the reports of PZD and IND are printed on matte (and in the former case recyclable) paper.

A number of observations can be made about the different ways that ideas about the agency construction have been employed in the annual reports. KNMI mentioned its agency identity only once while IND mentioned it more often but only in the final section of the report. This is in contrast to Senter, which was the only organization to use 'the agency' in place of its own name and which did so repeatedly throughout the report. The results of the content analysis are presented in Table 9.3 below.

In accordance with the vision of the Ministry of Finance, both the IND and Senter explicitly identified their agency status when presenting their financial figures; however, for the IND this presentation was about accounting for expenditure while for Senter it was to illustrate efforts in obtaining a positive business result. Both KNMI and PZD also identified a financial result or 'win,' although they did not explain this with reference to their agency status. When PZD did identify its agency status it was to promote transparency and also a business culture, although there was little elaboration about how this would happen. For Senter, being an agency was not just about financial issues, but also about being able to actively promote their clientele, knowing their clients, expanding their advisory functions and cooperating with other organizations. These ideas were identified in the Senter report at least three times.

In some instances, the concept of results was also extended to work activities as opposed to the balance on the accrual accounting system and, in the case of Senter, future plans to attempt to measure the attainment of policy objectives were identified – but not measured. IND associated their results with the number of decisions taken, although at no point was this result associated with ideas like accuracy or speed. A reorganization in IND was also described, which had been introduced according to the logic of 'results accountability,' this entailed each unit being responsible for the processing of a complete product. Apart from their financial result, the PZD called reliable diagnoses their results, and they measured these.

Further terms that were subject to some variation were 'quality' and 'client.' For IND, the term 'quality' was associated with the training and competency of staff, who must enter into a learning contract. In contrast, the PZD used quality to refer to the accuracy of their diagnoses and the average time it took to make these. For Senter, quality was primarily associated with increasing client satisfaction, which was measured (or in some cases to be measured) by indicators of client satisfaction, reputation, access and predictability.

Finally, the performance indicators collected by each organization are presented below in Table 9.4.

All organizations presented information about the balance on their budget and their inputs (mainly information about personnel numbers).

Table 9.3 Use and meanings associated with agency talk in Dutch annual reports

Terms	IND	KNMI	PZD	Senter
Agency	Financial idea	Financial idea Not commercial	Financial idea Developing a business culture	Financial idea Active promotion of clientele numbers
Results	Accounting for how finance used Number decisions Result responsibility: unit specialization in entire process of product	Financial win	Financial results Reliable diagnosis	Business result
Quality	Competent employees Number of complaints	Accuracy of warning systems	Accuracy diagnosis Average time of diagnosis	Client satisfaction
Efficiency	Improved by reorganization/ specialization Not defined	Not defined or mentioned	Not defined but is the focus for the following year	Lower operational costs Reducing personnel costs Increasing clientele
Product	Decision making Interviews Inquiries taken	Scientific research Advice Forecasting	Inspections Diagnosis Policy evaluation	Different projects and subsidy programs
Client	Not mentioned Identified asylum seekers	Not mentioned Not identified	Not mentioned Not identified	Owner Principal Business and knowledge institutes

Table 9.4 Performance indicators presented in Dutch annual reports

Performance data	IND	KNMI	PZD	SENTER
Balance accruals	X	X	X	X
Cost price	X		X	X
Inputs	X	X	X	X
Efficiency				X
Output	X		X	X
Quality outcomes	X		X	X

KNMI was the only organization not to present at least one unit cost of their 'products' while Senter was the only organization that presented measures about efficiency.

In sum, the way these organizations have presented themselves as agencies can be distinguished from each other and from the financial preoccupations of the Ministry of Finance. Although the financial aspects of the agency identity are mentioned in all cases, and measured in most cases, this is presented in different ways by the different organizations. For IND it was about accountable reporting of expenditure, while for Senter and KNMI it was about a 'business result' or 'win.' Furthermore, Table 9.3 illustrates that for KNMI, PZD and Senter, being an agency also represents other ideas like not being commercial or promoting a new clientele. This can be seen as evidence of translation.

KNMI appears to have adopted agency talk the least, which may be partly explained by the audience for which its report has been published. Since accountability arrangements do not require KNMI to publish an annual report, perhaps its choice to do so is related to a desire to publish ideas of a more technical or expert nature to a scientific audience. Perhaps, for KNMI, identifying itself as a scientific organization takes precedence over being a 'businesslike' organization. Alternatively, the agency idea may be merely conceived of by KNMI in the limited terms that it is here represented. Like KNMI, PZD is also an expert organization that is not obliged to publish an annual report. However, it has more frequently adopted agency talk to describe its work. It is interesting to note that neither expert organization has identified a particular client or clients. The IND has also adopted the terms here assessed on numerous occasions except for 'client.' Translation of client may have proved difficult in this case because of the politically sensitive issues surrounding asylum seekers. Finally, in the case of Senter, each agency term was adopted in a way consistent with business activities.

Conclusion

This chapter has been concerned to illustrate the multiple understandings and meanings of 'agency.' In doing so, it argues that while NPM may have informed the categories and labels associated with the agency identity, their meaning and content are subject to wide variation across national and organizational cultures. This can give the impression of a great deal of conformity across national and international borders, while still offering a great deal of discretion in the way organizational work is understood and conducted. The Dutch agency experience, for example, has been able to satisfy themes of results orientation and steering in international circles, while maintaining a quite limited and specific experience of these ideas by policy makers in the Netherlands. Alternatively, this national story has also been subject to translations at the organizational level, so that only appropriate aspects of the agency idea are selected and given meaning. This scope for a wide range of meanings of agency is often ignored by some accounts of convergence, which seem to assume just one translation. At the same time, it is evident that agency ideas or talk cannot just take on any meaning, or that actors have complete discretion over how meanings are translated. This is evident in the case of Dutch agencies, where the connotations of the term 'agency' in the Netherlands impeded the adoption of an accrual accounting system and could not successfully be translated in a way that conformed to the image of some public sector organizations. Instead, changes to the Dutch Accounting Act enabled organizations to adopt the accrual accounting system without the title agency, even though it was those accounting reforms that had constituted Dutch agency reform in the first place.

Notes

1   There are currently 23 agencies in the Netherlands.
2   Agency employees are included for example as Ministry employees in the total figures of each ministry presented in appendix 1 of the Departmental Budget. See also Ambtenarenwet.
3   In the Netherlands quangos are often described as externally autonomized while agencies are described as internally autonomized. This distinction represents differences in their formal autonomy or arms-length distance.

Bibliography

Algemene Rekenkamer (1995) *Verlag 1994. Deel 3: Zelfstandige bestuursorganen en ministeriële verantwoordelijkheid*, Tweede Kamer, vergarderjaar 1994–1995, 24 130, nr. 3. Den Haag: Sdu.
Ambteranrenwet, [on-line]. www.minbzk.nl.
Aucoin, P. (1990) 'Administrative reform in public management: paradigms, principles, paradoxes and pendulums,' *Governance* 3, 2, 115–37.

Armstrong, A. (1998) 'A comparative analysis: new public management – the way ahead?,' *Australian Journal of Public Administration* 57, 2, 12–24.

Boon, F. and Strannegård, L. (2000) 'Organizations coping with their natural environment,' *Studies of Management and Organization* 30, 3, 7–17.

Boorsma, P. and Mol, N. (1997) 'The Dutch public financial revolution,' in Kickert, W. (ed.) *Public Policy and Administrative Sciences in the Netherlands*, London: Prentice Hall/Harvester Wheatsheaf, pp. 217–29.

Brief van de Minister van Financien (1993) Tweede Kamer, vergarderjaar 1993–1994, 23 796, nr. 1.

Brief van de Minister van Financien (1996) Tweede Kamer, vergarderjaar 1996–1997, 25 257, nr. 1.

Brief van de Minister van Financien (2001) *Wijzinging enkele artikelen van de comptabiliteitswet onder andere de verdere invoering van het batenlaasten stelsel: Gewijzigd voorstel van wet*, Tweede Kamer, vergarderjaar 2000–2001, 26 974, nr. 146.

Buchko, A. (1994) 'Barriers to strategic transformation: interorganizational networks and institutional forces,' in Schrivastava, P. and Dutton, J. (eds) *Advances in Strategic Management*, Greenwich: JAI Press, pp. 81–106.

Clarke, J. and Newman, J. (1997) *The Managerial State*, London: Sage.

Commissie Cohen (1997) *Eindrapport Werkgroep Markt en Overheid*, Den Haag, Ministerie van Economische Zaken, Commissie Marktwerking Deregulering en Wetgevingskwaliteit.

Czarniawska, B. and Sevon, G. (eds) (1996) *Translating Organizational Change*, Berlin: De Gruyter.

DiMaggio, P. and Powell, W. (1983) 'The iron cage revisited: institutional isomorphism and collective rationality in organisational fields,' *American Sociological Review* 48, 147–60.

DiMaggio, P. (1988) 'Interest and agency in institutional theory,' in Zucker, L. (ed.) *Institutional Patterns and Organizations: Culture and Environment*, Cambridge, MA: Ballinger, pp. 3–21.

Fliegstein, N. (1985) 'The spread of the multidivisional from among large forms, 1919–1979,' *American Sociological Review* 50, 355–91.

Fortin, Y. (1996) 'Autonomy, responsibility and control,' *Performance Management in Government*, France: OECD.

Fudge, C. and Gustafsson, L. (1989) 'Administrative reform and public management in Sweden and the United Kingdom,' *Public Money and Management* (Summer), 29–34.

Gains, F. (2000) *Understanding Department – Next Step Agency Relationships*, unpublished doctoral dissertation, University of Sheffield, Sheffield.

Greve, C. (2000) 'Exploring as reinvented institutions in the Danish public sector,' *Public Administration* 78, 1, 153–64.

Greve, C., Flinders, M. and Van Thiel, S. (1999) 'Quangos – what's in a name? Defining quangos from a comparative perspective,' *Governance* 12, 2, 129–46.

Hirst, P. and Thompson, G. (1995) 'Globalization and the future of the Nation State,' *Economy and Society* 24, 3, 408–42.

Hood, C. (1991) 'A public management for all seasons,' *Public Administration* 69 (Spring), 3–19.

Hood, C. (1996) 'Exploring variations in public management reform,' in Bekke, H., Perry, J. and Toonen, T. (eds) *Civil Service Systems* Bloomington: Indiana University Press, pp. 268–87.

James, O. (2001) 'Business models and the transfer of businesslike central government agencies,' *Governance* 14, 2, 233–52.

Jaarverslag 1998: Beslist bewogen. Immigratie en Naturalisatiedienst, Ministerie van Justitie.

Jaarverslag 1998: In dialoog met de samenleving. Dienst Justitiele Inrichtingen, Ministerie van Justitie.

Jaarverslag 1998: In het teken van de regen. Koninklijk Nederlands Meteorologisch Instituut (KNMI).

Jaarverslag 1998, Senter.

Jaarverslag 1998, Plantenziektenkundige Dienst.

Kickert, W. (ed.) (1997) *Public Management and Administrative Reform in Western Europe,* Cheltenham: Edward Elgar.

Kickert, W. (1998) *Aansturing van verzelfstandigde overheidsdiensten,* Alphen aan den Rijn: Samson.

Knaap, P. and Sylvester, J. (1999) 'Toezicht op en het financieel beheer van verzlefstandigde organisaties in Nederland,' *Tijdschrift Privatisering* jaargang 7, 1, 12–16.

Krippendorf, K. (1980) *Content Analysis: An Introduction to Its Methodology,* London: Sage Publications.

Latour, B. (1987) *Science in Action,* Cambridge, Massachusetts: Harvard University Press.

Latour, B. (1996) *Arasmis or the Love of Technology,* Cambridge: Harvard University Press.

Ministerie van Financién. (1991) *Verder Bouwen aan Beheer* [The Further Cultivation of Management], s'-Gravenhage.

Ministerie van Financién. (1998) *Verder met resultaat: het agentschapsmodel 1991–1997.* [Further with results: The agency model 1991–1997], Den Haag.

Oakes, L., Townley, B. and Cooper, D. (1998) 'Business planning as pedagogy: language and control in a changing institutional field,' *Administrative Science Quarterly* 43, 257–92.

OECD (1995) *Governance in Transition: Public Management Reforms in OECD Countries,* Paris: PUMA/OECD.

OECD (1997a) *Issues and Development in Public Management: Survey 1996–1997,* Paris: PUMA/OECD.

OECD (1997b) *In Search of Results: Performance Management Practices,* Paris: PUMA/OECD.

Oliver, C. (1991). 'Strategic responses to institutional processes,' *Academy of Management Review* 16, 1, 145–79.

Osborne, D. and Gaebler, T. (1992) *Reinventing Government,* Reading, Addison-Wesley Publishing Company.

O'Toole, B. and Jordan, G. (1995) *The Next Steps: Improving Management in Government,* Aldershot: Dartmouth Publishing Company Limited.

Pollitt, C. and Bouckaert, G. (2000) *Public Management Reform: A Comparative Analysis,* New York: Oxford University Press.

Pollitt, C. (2000a) *Institutional Amnesia: A Paradox of the Information Age? Prometheus* 18, 1, 5–16.

Pollitt, C. (2000b) 'Is the emperor in his underwear?,' *Public Management* 12, 2, 189–99.

Pollitt, C. (2001) 'Convergence: the useful myth?,' *Public Administration* 79, 4, 933–47.

Pollitt, C., Bathgate, K., Caulfield, J., Smullen, A. and Talbot, C. (2001) 'Agency fever? Analysis of an international policy fashion,' *Journal of Comparative Policy Analysis: Research and Practice* 3, 271–90.

Power, M. (1997) *The Audit Society*, Oxford: Oxford University Press.

Premfors, R. (1998) 'Reshaping the democratic state: Swedish experiences in a comparative perspective,' *Public Administration* 76 (Spring), 141–59.

Sahlin-Andersson, K. (1996) 'Imitating by editing success: the construction of organizational fields,' in Czarniawksa, B. and Sevon, G. (eds) *Translating Organizational Change*, Berlin: De Gruyter, pp. 69–91.

Sahlin-Andersson, K. (2001) 'National, international and transnational constructions of new public management,' in Christensen, T. and Laergraid, P. (eds) *New Public Management: The Transformation of Ideas and Practice*, Hampshire: Ashgate, pp. 42–72.

Scott, W. (1995) *Institutions and Organisations*, Thousand Oaks: Sage.

Sevon, G. (1996) 'Organizational imitation in identity transformation,' in Czarniawksa, B. and Sevon, G. (eds) *Translating Organizational Change*, Berlin: De Gruyter, pp. 49–66.

Smullen, A., Van Thiel, S. and Pollitt, C. (2001) 'Agentschappen en de verzelfstandigingsparad ox,' in *Beleid en Maatschappij* 28, 4, 190–200.

Sorber, A. (1996) 'Developing and using performance measurement: the Netherlands experience,' in *Performance Management in Government*, Paris: OECD/PUMA, pp. 93–109.

Talbot, C. (1996) *Ministers and Agencies*, London: The Chartered Institute of Public Finance and Accountability.

Talbot, C., Pollitt, C., Bathgate, K., Caulfied, J. and Smullen, A. (2000) *The Idea of Agency*, American Political Studies Association Conference, Washington, America.

Ter Bogt, H. (1999) 'Financial and economic management in autonomized Dutch public organizations,' *Financial Accountability and Management* 15, 3: 299–351.

Ter Bogt, H. (1999) 'Verzelfstandiging van overheidorganizaties,' [Autonomization of government organizations]. *Bestuurskunde* 8, 1, 205–39.

Tolbert, P. and Zucker, L. (1983) 'Institutional sources of change in the formal structure of organizations: the diffusion of civil service reforms,' *Administrative Science Quarterly* 28, 22–39.

Turner, R.H. (1990) 'A comparative content analysis of biographies,' in Oyen, E. (ed.) *Comparative Methodology: Theory and Practice in International Social Research*, London: Sage, pp. 134–50.

Van der Knaap *et al.* (1999) 'Aansturen op resultaat,' in *Openbare Uitgaven* 4, 184–94.

Van Thiel, S. (2000) Quangocratization: Trends, Causes and Consequences, Doctoral dissertation, University of Utrecht, Utrecht.

Van Thiel, S., Leeuw, F. and Flap, H. (1998) 'Quangocratisering in Nederland?,' *Beleid and Maatschappij* 3, 143–51.

Verhaak, F. (1997) 'Shifting frames of reference in Dutch autonomisation reforms,' in Kickert, W. (ed.) *Public Management and Administrative Reform in Western Europe*, Cheltenham: Edward Elgar, pp. 157–76.

Weiss, L. (1998) *The Myth of the Powerless State*, Cambridge: Polity Press.

Weiss, L. (2000) *The Myth of the Powerless State*, Cambridge: Polity Press.

Wilson, J. (1989) *Bureaucracy: What Government Agencies Do and Why They Do It*, New York: Basic Books.

Zevende wijzing van de Comptabiliteitswet (2000) Tweede Kamer, vergarderjaar 1999–2000.

Zaat, F. (1998) 'Agentschappen: what's in a name?,' *Management en Bestuur* 20–2.

10 Central agencies in Sweden

A report from Utopia

Jon Pierre

Much of the recent restructuring of government in Western Europe has been aimed at separating policy and operations. The preferred strategy to accomplish this goal has been the creation of agencies, operating at arms-length distance from policy makers, and making these agencies the key operative structure of central government. As other chapters in this volume substantiate, the agency concept has quickly gained massive popularity, not least because they are seen as the epitome of the autonomous operative arm of government (see also Pollitt *et al.* 2001). The Swedish system of government probably became somewhat of a role model in this type of administrative reform. Having had agencies in place for centuries, Sweden provided a natural point of departure for an investigation of what could be gained from creating agencies and the institutional and political consequences of such structures on government more broadly. It should therefore be a sobering thought to the advocates of agencification to learn that the past 15 or so years has seen a recurrent debate in Sweden on whether this institutional arrangement is conducive to the role of government in contemporary governance (see Pierre 1995).

The subtitle to this chapter is, needless to say, written in jest. There is, however, a message hidden in it; the institutional logic of the Swedish agency system differs in some ways from that of the agencification we have witnessed in many other countries. Since much of current administrative reform in Sweden remains firmly rooted in a legalistic *Rechtsstaat* thinking – something which has been typical to the Swedish public service for a very long period – Sweden hardly qualifies as a utopia for New Public Management-style administrative change.

It should also be borne in mind that the division between departments and agencies was designed long before Constitutional architects were thinking about concepts such as policy and operations, let alone management. In Sweden, the objective of the system was not to enhance efficiency or give the managers a better chance to manage. Rather, this particular model of government was created in order to constrain the powers of the top executive branch of government – the King – to use the public administration to harass individual citizens. These measures were introduced

after a long period of autocratic Monarchy and was part of a larger political project aiming at liberalizing government and freedom of speech in
the country. Thus, while there could be said to be some degree of similarity in reform objectives – weakening the institutional linkage between the
senior levels of the executive branch and the agencies – the institutional
logic sustaining the reforms differs hugely. Therefore, an important question to address in this chapter is whether, and to what extent, the Swedish
agencies today capitalize on their autonomy vis-à-vis policy makers and
pursue organizational strategies inspired by the New Public Management
vernacular of administrative reform (Bouckaert and Pollitt 2000).

A final word of caution relates to institutionalization and institutional
change. The agency system in Sweden is a text-book case of the process
through which an institutional arrangement, designed to enhance some
objectives, over time acquires slightly different objectives, values, routines,
and meanings, which eventually come to enjoy support and legitimacy.
The notion of agencies as autonomous structures vis-à-vis the political echelons of government is steeped in the Swedish political culture, as the
recurrent debates on the "politicization" of the civil service substantiates
(Pierre 1995, 2002). Such "politicization" manifests itself primarily in
appointing former politicians as Director Generals of the agencies. Such
appointments, critics would argue, are a way for the incumbent party to
ensure loyalty and smooth policy implementation. The typical line of
defense is that former politicians have a great deal of political knowledge
and expertise, which will be of tremendous use to the agency. In any
event, the debates are proof of the strong belief in autonomous agencies.

Institutional stability and change

A significant element of the New Public Management's critique of traditional systems of service delivery argues that the public sector is rigid and
inept at change. This argument is then employed to call for greater
organizational flexibility in the public sector (Peters 2001). This argument
is in some ways valid and in other ways not. It is true that most contemporary systems of government have previously displayed a considerable lack of
flexibility, not least with regard to the long institutional tradition of
having identical structures in charge of both policy and operations.
However, as the case of Sweden suggests, a stability in the overall model of
public sector organization may well mask substantive dynamics under-
neath the surface.

Thus, while the separation between departments and agencies has been
intact for centuries, there have been substantive organizational dynamics on
both sides of the divide. The number of departments can be, and have
been, altered along with the preferences of the incoming Prime Minister
after general elections. The agency system, too, has displayed considerable
change. During the postwar period (1945–95), a number of agencies have

increased from 146 to 205. During this time several agencies have also been abolished. Thus, new agencies have been created either from existing agencies that were merged into new ones, or through other reforms of organizational change (Premfors 1999). Either way, the Swedish agency system dispels the myth of the inflexible public organization rather effectively.

The number of both departments and agencies can be changed any time at the discretion of the Prime Minister, or, in the case of agencies, the Minister in charge of a particular policy sector. While there has been rather significant organizational change at the agency level, most of that dynamic has served to change the agency structure within different policy sectors along with changes in public policy. For instance, when primary and secondary schools were transferred from the state to local authorities, there was a subsequent change in the agencies in that policy sector. Thus, the agency system as a whole has not been very much reduced in terms of organizational strength and policy expertise.

There is also some degree of correspondence between organizational change at the level of the departments and the level of the agencies. The 1990s saw organizational mergers at both levels in several policy sectors. When departments are merged, the driving idea is to create institutional possibilities to integrate related policy problems into one policy. A case in point is the merger in 1998 of the departments of interior affairs, communications, labor market affairs and economic development into a "super-department" created to boost economic development. In this case, however, such a merger took place at the agency level in the early 1990s when three agencies (those devoted to energy, technological research and economic development) were merged into one agency. Institutional arrangements, where several departments communicate policies to one and the same agency, are likely to cause confusion and incoherence at the level of the agency. Thus, in order to make the system as a whole coherent, there should be some degree of institutional correspondence between departments and agencies.

To sum this up, there is more organizational dynamic in the Swedish system of government than the rather stale model of departments and agencies might suggest. While it is true that the policy challenges confronting contemporary policy makers are vastly different compared to when the system was first designed, it must also be noted that the system is frequently redesigned in terms of the number of departments and agencies and the jurisdiction of different governmental structures. If anything, there is probably some truth in the critique which is sometimes voiced that there have been too many institutional changes over the past decade.

Political steering or administrative autonomy?

One of the most frequently debated issues related to the Swedish agencies is the degree of their autonomy vis-à-vis the departments (Jacobsson

1984). We have already mentioned the recurrent debate on the "politic-ization" of the agencies, a debate which probably many observers from other national contexts may find slightly awkward. On the one hand, agencies are the executive arm of government and the key institutional vehicle for the implementation of public policy. On the other hand, however, departments and Ministers are prevented in the Constitution from giving agencies detailed instructions on their decisions and actions pertaining to specific issues and matters. To be sure, Cabinet members giving an agency instructions on how to deal with specific cases are guilty of "ministerial steering" (*ministerstyre*) and may be reprimanded by the Parliament for abusing his/her position. Instead, government and Parlia-ment have to rely on non-targeted and rather subtle methods of steering the agencies, as we will see below.

The Swedish constitutional arrangement thus honors the notion of a non-political, meritocratic public administration. The Swedish system of government also subscribes to the idea of a distinct, institutional separa-tion of policy and administration (or operation, in contemporary adminis-trative reform jargon). The institutional arrangement emphasizes administrative loyalty to the government of the day, combined with a strong legalistic culture espousing equality before the law, legal security and a professional, meritocratic public administration.

All of this having been said, however, the fact that the agencies are pro-tected from direct political pressures does not mean that they are com-pletely autonomous vis-à-vis the government. There is a clear hierarchical relationship between departments and agencies; the Constitution states that agencies are subordinate to the government (*"lyder under regeringen"*). One could of course argue that any other arrangement would not be very conceivable, but given the aura of autonomy that surrounds the Swedish agencies both in the international debate and, quite frequently, also in Sweden, this observation should be stressed.

The more precise institutional nature of this subordination is obviously critical to an understanding of how the system works. On closer inspection we find that the government (i.e. the departments) has three different ways of steering the agencies. First of all, the government appoints the Director Generals of the agencies. We have already discussed the politic-ally sensitive nature of these appointments; governments appointing Director Generals who are sympathetic to the government's policies (or, as is sometimes the case, former members of Parliament or deputy minis-ters) are frequently criticized for using their power to appoint Directors to steer the agencies in different ways. There are two important circum-stances which we need to be aware of in order to understand this, perhaps slightly awkward, institutional arrangement. One such circumstance is accountability. Members of government – or government *tout court* – can not be held to account for agencies' decisions and actions. Therefore, the argument goes, government should not seek to inappropriately influence the agencies. This also suggests, however, that Director Generals have an institutional reason for not taking cues from government, since at the end of the day it is the agency leadership which is held to account and thus will want to have the final say on issues.

Furthermore, we need to understand how agencies are governed and managed. During the past century or so, the intra-organizational decision making of the agencies has been dominated by a strong representation for organized interests. The agency boards have to a dominating degree comprised so-called "laymen." These "laymen" typically represent organized interests, other agencies, and the Associations of regional and local governments, to name some of the most common sources of representation (Rothstein and Bergstrom 1999). Thus, agencies have been part and parcel of the corporatist model of policy making which is typical of the Swedish political system. Agency leadership is to a very large extent embedded in a web of interests, something which probably makes the selection of Director General a less significant matter compared to many other countries.

The second source of government control over the agencies relates to their power to put proposals to Parliament pertaining to the overall regulatory framework of the public administration. This is obviously an extremely indirect way of guiding the agencies, partly because these regulatory frameworks are not revised very often and partly because they do not give any specific cues as to how the agencies are to conduct themselves on any more specific issues. That having been said, this type of steering is important with regard to issues such as transparency and the relationship between the public sector and the surrounding society more generally.

Finally, government and Parliament can give agencies advice and direction by targeting financial resources to specific programs. This is probably the most important avenue for political input, but even so it remains a type of steering which is quite subtle compared to those available to governments in many other national contexts. Typically, this model of steering occurs as departments annually communicate letters to the agencies with budgetary allocation (*regleringsbrev*). These letters define the main activities of the agencies, and, therefore, should be a useful means for the departments to provide guidelines for the agencies (see more below).

There are a couple of reasons why this steering technique is not always very effective. First of all, agencies in Sweden have some budgetary discretion, which allows them to allocate funds for projects that are deemed important, regardless of financial input from Parliament. Second, agencies can mobilize resources for programs and projects – frequently from departments – outside the budget process. The most generous budgetary discretion has historically speaking been enjoyed by agencies that, to a larger or smaller extent, are financed by user fees. This was for a long period the case for agencies engaged in the provision of services in the telecommunication and railway sectors. These agencies were converted to enterprises (with significant state ownership) more than a decade ago. However, all agencies have more financial autonomy vis-à-vis Parliament today, compared to 10–15 years ago, something which suggests that targeting financial resources for specific programs, although important, is not a steering technique which, in and of itself, dictates agency compliance. The letters presenting the agencies' budgets, finally, frequently fail to steer the agencies. Given the overall autonomy of the agencies, the departments sometimes lack a complete view of what the agencies do. Also, as we will discuss later in this chapter, agencies have developed into much bigger institutions than the departments and it therefore becomes difficult for the departments to match the expertise controlled by the agencies.

What is the conclusion from all this? Although they are subordinate to government, the Constitutional framework with regard to agencies prevents government and Parliament from directing them in any greater detail on specific issues. Agencies, however, together with local authorities, remain the key implementing structures of public policy and execute programs laid down by Parliament. They do so under significant autonomy; steering channels are for the most part subtle and indirect. So how can the departments ensure that agencies do what departments want them to do? What makes the system work as well as it does? How, to borrow a popular phrase, is the system of government "joined up"?

"Joining up" the institutional system

In order to understand what keeps this rather disparate system together – i.e. how policy is coordinated, vertically and horizontally – we need to look beyond the Constitutional map of Swedish government. It is a historical irony to realize that what has kept the system going has perhaps not been so much the Constitutional arrangements proper, but rather the different patterns of inter-institutional communication and exchange that have evolved, many of which are fairly inconsistent with the basic norms sustaining the formal institutional arrangement. Thus it is fair to speak of a "Constitutional drift" in Sweden; the institutional arrangements have developed over time in ways which do not always reflect the general ideas in the Constitution. Given the fact that this system has been in place for centuries, that is perhaps not terribly surprising. A similar "Constitutional drift" can also be seen in other areas of the Swedish system of government; before the last revision of the Constitution, which was completed in 1974, Sweden was governed in accordance with the 1809 Constitution, which originally did not recognize some of the very basic elements of democracy that have been integral to Swedish democracy over the past hundred years or so.

There are two overarching sets of explanations to how the Swedish institutional system is de facto integrated. One cluster of explanations refers to the elaborate – and frequently highly institutionalized – informal contacts between departments and agencies. The other explanation is perhaps somewhat more daunting. It argues that policy coordination between department and agencies might not just be the result of successful steering by the former of the latter but by policy initiatives emerging from within the agencies. Let us take a closer look at these two mechanisms or processes of policy coordination.

Informal contacts and networks

A key feature of the current modus operandi of department-agency exchange are the networks between departments and agencies. It was earlier mentioned that Ministers are prevented in the Constitution from giving agencies detailed instruction on how to resolve particular issues. But both departments and agencies have strong institutional interests in maintaining some means, formal or informal, of communication with each other. For the departments, it is invaluable to be able to give agencies informal advice on how a particular program is to be implemented. Also, through these types of contacts, departments can tap into the expertise which the agencies harbor. From the agencies' point of view, on the other hand, maintaining a dialogue with the departments is extremely important because it provides them with input on policies they are later to execute.

The significance of these informal networks can probably not be overstated. The networks appear to exist primarily at the middle-level of departments and agencies and have proven surprisingly stable over time in terms of contact frequency (see Pierre 1995). This type of informal contact could be said to be among the key mechanisms for ensuring policy coordination; it is here that policy meets operations and it is here that some of the most important exchanges on policy design and implementation take place.

An important opportunity for these contacts is the Royal Commission. Such Commissions are usually appointed to prepare legislation on all political issues of any economic, political, or institutional significance. The Commissions are appointed by a Minister and operate under the auspices of a department. The composition of the Commissions varies owing to the nature of the issue to be deliberated – e.g. to what extent it affects organized interests or subnational authorities, to what extent it is an issue where there is disagreement among the political parties or more of a technical matter, and so on – but agencies are considered important sources of input at this early stage of the policy process. Furthermore, Commission proposals are routinely circulated among all potentially affected interests inviting their comments – this is the so-called *remiss* procedure – and obviously this stage in the policy process presents valuable opportunities for agencies to influence policies they are later to implement as they are being formed. By the same token, Commissions offer departments a chance to discuss policy design with agencies to get a feel for what would work and what would not.

What all this means is that once policies are adopted and communicated to the agencies for implementation, they are usually quite well-known documents at the receiving end. These policies and programs frequently reflect the agencies preferences in terms of policy design. Better still from the agencies' points of view, they may be policies initiated by the agencies themselves, as we will discuss in the next section of the chapter. The important observation here is that agencies have a multitude of avenues for influence on the early stages of the policy process and that a good part of policy coordination takes place already at these stages. As we will discuss in the concluding section of the chapter, one could make the argument that had it not been for these and other coordinating instruments between agencies and departments (which do not correspond terribly well with the original ideas in the Constitution), the system would probably not have been as effective as it is.

As should be obvious by now, the separation of policy and operations heralded by the Constitution does not seem to be a very accurate description of how these matters interact in the real world. We should also acknowledge that the notion of departments and Parliament directing or steering the agencies is the Constitutional perspective on institutional relations, which might not necessarily be the way the system works in the real world. Let us now look closer at this aspect of department–agency relationships.

Agencies as sources of policy

In the original design of the institutional system in Sweden, agencies should not be significantly larger than the departments. It was also argued that departments, not agencies, should harbor the thrust of policy expertise and that the key roles of departments were policy initiation and deliberation, long-term policy planning and similar traditional roles of core government institutions (Ruin 1991). Agencies, on the other hand, were supposed to keep a rather small staff and concentrate on policy implementation. This institutional arrangement has drifted considerably. Today, agencies are significantly bigger than departments in terms of staff (Vedung 1992). Furthermore, they have, over time, built up considerable policy expertise. Here lies an important explanation to why the annual *reg-leringsbrev* – the communications from the departments with the agencies budgets – rarely help steer the agencies. Departments' staff frequently lack the necessary detailed overview of what agencies do, or the expertise to properly assess their activities.

These problems became even more evident during the 1990s in a related context. Around 1990, the departments launched "management by objective" (*målstyrning*) or "management by result" (*resultatstyrning*) as the key models for steering the agencies. Drawing on the institutional separation between policy and operations, the basic idea was that departments should define goals and results for the agencies and then leave it to the agencies to devise the best strategy to attain those objectives. A nice plan in theory – and to some extent also in reality – it became increasingly clear during the 1990s that management by objectives was not a very efficient strategy for guiding the agencies. First of all, as is the general problem in this relationship, agencies control more of the detailed know-how than the departments and know what works and what does not. As a result, departments frequently formulated objectives in concert with the agencies themselves, or, to quote the *on dit* among agency staff on these issues, it was seldom not the agencies themselves that tended to design the objectives which they were to pursue. Second, the system lacked a corrective mechanism; there was little that the departments could do to correct agencies which did not pursue the agreed objectives. Thus, although several Governmental Bills on the national budget during the 1990s lamented the poor extent to which agencies pursued the stated objectives, there was very little that the system had to offer in terms of ameliorating the situation. The result of all this has been that a new steering model called *verksamhetsstyrning* (steering of activities) has evolved during the past couple of years. This model draws heavily on performance indicators as a base for reviewing the agencies. At the time of writing (February 2002), the model is just being launched on a large scale.

The institutional drift has several significant consequences for the agencies as well as for the system at large. One important result of these gradual changes is that policy capacity to some extent has shifted from the departments to the agencies. The agencies' staff are bigger and enjoy less turnover compared to the departments' staff. Several agencies have taken a higher policy profile during the 1990s and launched policy proposals. Agencies in sectors like environmental policy (*Naturvårdsverket*), labor market affairs (*AMS*), and economic development (*NUTEK*) have either put forward extensive policy proposals or – by virtue of their institutional autonomy – formulated programs to guide their actions.

These developments have political explanations as well as institutional ones. The 1990s have witnessed extensive cutbacks in the public sector in Sweden. More importantly, there has been a subtle but rather consistent change in policy style, from a pro-active, interventionist style toward an "enabling" policy style. This more reactive if not passive role of the state in different policy sectors has left the agencies searching for a new role; what is, after all, a policy-implementing institution without policies to implement? Equally important, agencies and their staff have a firm commitment to what they believe to be core policy objectives in their respective sectors and that commitment is not necessarily reassessed just because the departments wish to adopt a more subtle policy style. Thus, in the economic development sector, for instance, the policy shift toward an "enabling" policy objective in the early 1990s left NUTEK and other agencies in this sector looking for a role and objectives to pursue. Against the backdrop of the policy "vacuum" that the policy change entailed, NUTEK initiated an internal process of defining a "program" – i.e. a policy – for economic development which they brought to the Department of Trade and Industry as a basis for a discussion on future policies of economic development.

A similar pattern, albeit with slight variations, can be seen in several other policy sectors. AMS, the key agency in the labor market affairs sector, has for a long period been regarded as an extraordinarily autonomous agency, which de facto defines many of its own objectives and extracts financial resources from the government to pursue those goals.

Thus, an important indirect result of the cutbacks and the reassessed policy style of the government has been that agencies have become more involved in the production, explication, and reproduction of the norms and values sustaining their institutional role (see Rothstein 1996, 1998). This is not to say that this role was not important previously, but it is clear that the harsher political climate during the past 10–15 years has helped to emphasize the normative role of the agencies. Defending their legitimacy and *raison d'etre* has become important for other reasons, too. Previously, agencies have played an important role in evaluating subnational authorities and controlling the use of state subsidies. With the decentralization that swept across most policy sectors during the 1980s and 1990s and the replacement of several smaller grants to "lump grants" to regional and local authorities, agencies found themselves in a position where their institutional role had to be redefined to some extent. All of these developments have triggered a process of institutional reaffirmation among many agencies and, as a result, today we frequently see agencies taking a rather high political profile.

Concluding comments

The design of the Swedish system of government could be seen as a Constitutional framework for a strong state with checks and balances to safeguard against abuse of political power. The Swedish political culture has, historically speaking, been a distinctly state-centric and collectivistic culture. By emphasizing administrative autonomy, the Constitution has in some ways created an institutional system which includes the positive aspects of a strong state – a high degree of institutional capacity, legal security and administrative professionalism – while at the same time safeguarding against the negative aspects of a strong state such as clientilism, parochial political pressures or abuse of political power.

Ironically, in some ways, it could be argued that one of the key reasons why the institutional structure of the Swedish government has remained intact for such an extended period is that informal mechanisms of policy advice and coordination have emerged and become fairly institutionalized, and these mechanisms have proven critical to the efficiency of the system. Thus, what some overseas observers see as attractive about the Swedish system of government – the separation of policy and operations – is an institutional arrangement which, in fact, has to a significant extent been sustained and kept operational by organizational strategies, which are inconsistent with the original design of the system. Put slightly differently, it could be argued that the informal contacts between departments and agencies have proven critical to the efficiency of this institutional arrangement.

This is of course not to say that the process of other countries imitating the Swedish agency system is regression to the past. The rationale for creating an institutional division between policy and operations should, however, be assessed within each national context and not be incorporated simply because it has become somewhat of a fad in the Western world. The case of Sweden might serve as a useful benchmark, as long as the significance of history in these respects is not forgotten.

Bibliography

Bouckaert, G. and Pollitt, C. (2000) *Public Management Reform*, Oxford: Oxford University Press.

Jacobsson, B. (1984) *Hur styrs Förvaltningen: Myt och Verklighet kring Departementens Styrning av Ämbetsverken* [How is the Public Administration Controlled: The Myth and Reality of Departments' Steering of the Agencies], Lund: Studentlitteratur.

Johansson, J. (1992) *Det Statliga Kommittéväsendet* [The Royal Commission System], Stockholm: Department of Political Science, University of Stockholm.

Peters, B.G. (2001) *The Future of Governing: Four Emerging Models*, 2nd edn, Lawrence, KS: University of Kansas Press.

Pierre, J. (1995) "Governing the welfare state: public administration, the state and society in Sweden," in Pierre, J. (ed.) *Bureaucracy in the Modern State: An Introduction to Comparative Public Administration*, Cheltenham: Edward Elgar, pp. 140–60.

Pierre, J. (2002) "Politicization of the Swedish civil service: a necessary evil – or just evil?," in Peters, B.G. and Pierre, J. (eds) *Politicization of the Civil Service in Comparative Perspective*.

Pollitt, C. *et al.* (2001) "Agency fever?: Analysis of international policy fashion," *Journal of Comparative Policy Analysis: Research and Practice* 3, 271–90.

Premfors, R. (1998) "Reshaping the democratic state: Swedish experiences in a comparative perspective," *Public Administration* 76, 141–59.

Premfors, R. (1999) "Organisationsförändringar och förvaltningspolitik – Sverige," in Laegreid, P. and Pedersen, O.K. (eds) *Fra Opbygning till ombygning i staten: Organisationsforandringer i tre nordiske lande*, Köpenhamn: Jurist- og Ökonomforbundets Forlag, pp. 145–68.

Rothstein, B. (1996) *The Social Democratic State: The Swedish Model and the Bureaucratic Problem of Social Reforms*, Pittsburgh, PA: University of Pittsburgh Press.

Rothstein, B. (1998) *Just Institutions Matter: The Moral and Political Logic of the Universal Welfare State*, Cambridge, MA: Cambridge University Press.

Rothstein, B. and Bergstrom, J. (1999) *Korporatismens fall och den svenska modellens kris*, Stockholm: SNS.

Ruin, O. (1991) "The duality of the Swedish central administration: ministries and central agencies," in Farazmand, A. (ed.) *Handbook of Comparative and Development Public Administration*, New York and Basel: Marcel Dekker, Inc., pp. 67–80.

Vedung, E. (1992) "Five observations on evaluation in Sweden," in Mayne, J. *et al.* (eds) *Advancing Public Policy Evaluation: Learning from International Experiences*, Amsterdam: Elsevier Science Publishers, pp. 71–84.

11 Agencification in Japan

Renaming or revolution?

Kiyoshi Yamamoto

The Japanese system of government: the political system

The constitution designates the Parliament (Diet) as 'the highest organ of state power,' and the 'sole law-making organ of the state' (article 41). It is a bicameral system, with a House of Representatives (lower house) and a somewhat less influential House of Councillors (upper house). The Parliament selects the Prime Minister, and the cabinet is collectively answerable to it, rather in the British fashion.

However, the dominant actor in the Japanese system is the cabinet rather than the Parliament. The cabinet is supposed to exercise control and supervision over the various administrative branches of government, to prepare the budget, conduct affairs of state, manage foreign affairs and (with the Diet's approval) conclude treaties. Again like the British system, the majority of bills passed by the legislature are sponsored by the cabinet. The cabinet also appoints the chief justice and other judges of the Supreme Court (constitution, article 79). The Emperor, who before the war was actively the head of state, is now only a symbolic figurehead.

The postwar constitution accords extensive authority to local governments. Known as the 'President system' or the 'Chief system,' it gives residents the rights to elect local assemblies and directly elect the chief officer. Governors are also directly elected (having been appointed by central government, pre-war). In practice, however, central government is able to exert considerable control over local authorities through the financial support system. Japan is classified as a unitary state (Reed 1986).

Policymaking

Policymaking is dominated by a central grouping of the majority party, the bureaucracy and industrial interests. Since 1955 the majority party (with a single short exception between October 1993 and June 1994) has been the Liberal Democratic Party (LDP). It ensures the continuance of the central policymaking triad. This picture of centralism should be qualified by recognition of considerable fragmentation into specific issue areas.

There are alliances between the LDP, the *zoku giin* – politicians specializing in certain policy areas – and the senior bureaucrats in the relevant ministries. These networks could be thought of almost as sub governments (Hayao 1993).

The bureaucracy has a strong influence on policymaking. It has several major strengths. First, the senior bureaucracy is prestigious – the top stream tends to attract the brightest and best graduates from elite universities, especially the University of Tokyo. They build up formidable policy-relevant knowledge. Second, unlike, say US politicians, the Japanese politicians usually have few policy staff – so they are more reliant on their civil servants. Third, bureaucrats have life-long tenure, and tend to stay in 'their' ministry for the whole of their career. By contrast, ministers are often in post for quite short periods, since, even if the ruling party remains constant, the Prime Minister frequently shuffles and reshuffles his cabinet.

The route to agencification

Origins

Following Kingdon (1984) we may consider agencification as a policy change that took advantage of the existence of a 'policy window.' In Kingdon's model policy change comes about when three separate streams come together. First, there is a politics stream, which encompasses the current political balance and the state of public opinion. Second, there is the problem stream, which consists of perceived problems with particular attributes. Third, there is a stream of solutions, waiting to attach themselves to problems (the policy stream).

The salient event in the politics stream was the recovery of the LDP during the mid-1990s, resulting in its return to power in June 1994. This coincided with a loss of public esteem for the administrative apparatus, and much criticism of the bureaucracy. In 1994 the LDP had regained power in coalition with the Japan Socialist Party (JSP) and a new party, named Sakigake. The Prime Minister was JSP chairman, Murayama, though he was succeeded by the LDP leader, Hashimoto in January 1996. During 1995 the administration ran into a series of problems with bureaucratic scandals and mismanagement. For example, the Ministry of Finance (MoF) injected a huge amount of public money to underpin bad loans made by private finance companies in the housing sector (*jusen*). This was poorly judged in itself, but additionally the executives of a number of the companies that were 'bailed out' in this way turned out to be individuals who had recently retired from the MoF itself (the Japanese phrase for this practice of lucrative retirement to the private sector can be translated as 'descent from heaven'). Or again, it became known that the Ministry of Health and Welfare (MHW) had for years failed to take action against the use of non heat-treated blood derivatives, despite foreseeing the possibility of HIV infection to patients who received such products. In October 1996 public prosecutors arrested a senior MHW bureaucrat who had engaged in the trade in these derivatives.

Second, in the 1990s Japan faced a flood rather than a trickle of problems. The 1970s and 1980s had been the time of 'Japan as No. 1.' But in the 1990s the 'bubble economy' collapsed and central government moved into a large financial deficit. The ration of government bonds to GDP had been 28.4 percent in 1980 but by 1995 had reached 44.9 percent. In addition, government was beginning to face the (expensive) problems of a rapidly ageing population. In 1995 the over 65s represented 28.4 percent of the total population, but by 2050 this figure was expected to reach 32.3 percent. The consequences for social welfare expenditure were considerable.

Third, administrative reform offered itself as one of the solutions to the perceived malaise of government. In January 1996 Prime Minister Hashimoto announced that he intended to introduce a programme of public sector improvements. During the October 1996 general election campaign the LDP committed itself to the creation of a more efficient administrative system. One component of this was to be the separation of program implementation from policymaking. The campaign pledge was cast in the following terms:

> The enlargement of central government is partly caused by a mixed system of policymaking and execution functions. We therefore envisage dividing these two functions into two organizational parts. The first part will be a set of implementing organizations, created through agencification. This will leave, as the second part, ministries as the policymaking organizations. Agencies will have substantial autonomy in personnel matters, day to day operations and so on, within the framework and budget set by the minister. In addition the agency heads will be responsible to the minister for general operations, and strictly accountable for budgeting and accounting to the Diet and the Board of Audit.

It is evident that this conceptualization echoes that of the UK Next Steps agency program. While, during the election campaign, all Japanese political parties promised to reorganize central government and streamline public services, only the LDP committed themselves to this specific model of agencification.

The election result produced gains for the LDP and losses for the JSP and Sakigake. Hashimoto was able to form a second administration (7/10/96 to 30/7/98) this time formed only of his own party members. The policy window for agencification was thus open. Just two weeks after forming his administration, Hashimoto established an Administrative

Reform Council, under his own chairmanship (21/11/96). This was unusual. Previous councils tended to have been chaired by businessmen, and to have had an obviously advisory function. However, in this case the PM himself took the chair, and the Minister of State for the Management and Co-ordination Agency was vice-chair. Furthermore, senior civil servants – who would normally have been prominent among the membership – were excluded. Thus the PM put himself in a position where he could act – in Kingdon's terms – as a policy entrepreneur for public sector reform.

Hashimoto had considerable previous experience of administrative reform. Between 1981 and 1983 he had been the President of the Research Council for Administration and Finance in the LDP. During that time he had visited the UK and studied, *inter alia*, the Rayner efficiency scrutiny process. In the Japanese system the LDP Research Councils had played a central role in policymaking, being closely consulted by the cabinet before final decisions were taken. An experienced politician, Hashimoto's main interests lay with reform methods rather than the enunciation of a particular reform ideology.

Reasons

The basic concept and design of agencification was discussed and settled in the Administrative Reform Council. Its final report was published in December 1997 (Administrative Reform Council 1997) and cited three reasons for the program:

- downsizing and outsourcing
- improving service efficiency and quality
- enhancing transparency.

The first of these three aims was fundamental. Professor Fujita, a member of the Council, later indicated that the primary objective was downsizing, to be achieved through the separation of implementation from policymaking (Fujita 1999). 'Vertical downsizing' was supported by a principle of delegation 'from the public to the private sector' and 'from the central governments to the local governments' (final report).

The second – improving the efficiency and quality of services – might seem to be the foundation of a genuine reform of public management, but, as professor Fujita's paper submitted to the Council meeting on 21/8/97 indicated, it was assumed that these benefits would follow from the separation of policymaking from implementation. In other words, the different organizations would become more efficient and would raise quality simply by being able to concentrate on their own function – a division of labor. Fujita argued that the inflexibilities of policymaking were caused by interests capturing the process, while those in implementation occurred because the legal/financial system had little regard for efficient implementation.

Third, transparency was supposed to be enhanced by the creation of agencies that were separate from central government. Each agency would have its own judicial personality and would publish its own reports and accounts. In the past, although some types of public service had operated special accounts, which used a type of corporate accounting, these nevertheless gave financial performance data which related to the totality, including policymaking functions.

The establishment of legally separate agencies should also be seen in the context of the proposed restructuring of the ministries. The Administrative Council was recommending a reduction of the number of ministries from 23 to 13. Thus, without agencification there would have been a real risk of creating ministries so big that they were beyond the effective span of control of a minister.

There were further, political reasons for agencification, beyond what was formally mentioned in the Council's report. One of these had to do with the number of civil servants. Technically, the staff of agencies would fall outside the civil service, thus enabling the Hashimoto government to claim that it was reducing the size of the central bureaucracy.

Additionally, there was an issue of nomenclature. The *dokuritsu-gyosei-hojin* (Independent Administrative Institutions – IAIs) were expected to appeal to the public as a very visible new form of organization. It is worth noting, however, that the emphasis here was on organizational reform rather than management reform.

Support for agencification

There were three main groups of supporters. The first were politicians, particularly those involved in the Management and Co-ordination Agency (MCA). Given its remit to promote restructuring, the MCA was a strong supporter. MCA belonged to the Prime Minister's Office and was headed by the Minister of State in charge of administrative reform. It argued that agencification would indeed improve public accountability (through management by objectives) and reduce public expenditure (by increasing efficiency).

The second group came from the world of business. Universities and national institutes were among the leading candidates for agencification, and the business world believed that this would assist the development of joint academic/business research programs. The reason was that, so long as they remained civil servants, the staff of these academic institutions were highly restricted in the for-profit work they could undertake. The National Civil Servants Law obliged them to concentrate on their public work.

The third supportive group was the accountancy profession. Like many countries, Japan had previously formed its central government accounts on a cash basis. However, it was assumed that the new agencies would adopt a corporate (accruals) system of accounting. Such a shift to a business form of accounting was likely to create a new market for members of the accounting profession to offer advice, accounting and auditing services.

Opponents

There were two main groups of opponents to agencification. One comprised the ministries themselves, and their supporting bands of politicians (*zoku*). The second was the civil service union, allied with the opposition parties, especially the Social Democratic Party (SDP) and the Japanese Communist Party (JCP).

At the beginning, all the ministries (other than the MCA) were opposed. They feared that policymaking itself would be damaged if implementation was separated. Feedback from implementation to policymaking would become more problematic. Also, it was argued that management by objectives would tend to overemphasize short-term results and narrow efficiency considerations, because effectiveness and longer-term impacts are more difficult to quantify. Finally, it was said that hiving off the agencies would make international exchanges and joint programs more difficult to achieve. Behind these arguments lay a fundamental fear that ministries might lose full control of implementation – that agencies would be given too much autonomy. Senior bureaucrats have an important administrative tool in the shape of resource allocation at project level. They can exert real influence here, within the broader framework determined by politicians or the Diet. Connected to this the politicians known as *zoku-giin* feared the disturbance of their existing patterns of influence, whereby they supported particular ministries in budget or legislative matters in return for administrative decisions favorable to their electorates. If autonomous agencies were responsible for implementation it might well be more difficult for these politicians to exert their usual influence over the details of program execution. One further anxiety was that the traditional pattern of personnel management would be upset. Hitherto, implementation work provided a career ladder for fast stream civil servants and enabled ministries to select individuals demonstrating suitable capabilities to work in policymaking roles. This would henceforth be a separate system.

The second group of opponents – the civil service union and the opposition parties – shared some of these fears, but were concerned about other possible impacts as well. The union was naturally concerned that loss of civil service status for agency staff would mean loss of life-long employment security. Opposition parties were also worried in case the senior executive positions in agencies would be filled by the 'descent from heaven' – i.e. by senior civil servants from the parent ministries, resulting in agencies that were like subordinate companies to the ministries. This would undermine the thrust for agency autonomy, and it would reduce the number of senior posts in agencies available to talented members of agency staff. On the other hand, opposition parties were also concerned about there being too much autonomy. Parliamentary control might be eroded. Agencies would receive a block grant and enjoy considerable freedom to allocate it. The Diet would be required only to approve the grant, not the total expenditures or revenues.

In the event, the scope of agencification was significantly limited by the exclusion of activities where state authority was used to constrain the behaviors of citizens. This compromise left advisory, educational and research functions as the chief candidates for agency status. Thus, although their were some protests from museum staff and scientific researchers, opposition was muted (Yamamoto 1999). The majority of implementation functions, therefore, remained inside the ministries, staffed by civil servants.

Japanese agencies in practice: the general framework

Governance and performance management

IAIs are independent organizations which provide public services. They are legally separate from central government ministries. They own the assets necessary for the discharge of their functions. They operate under a law of General Rules for IAIs. Under this statute the competent minister sets 3–5 year objectives, comprising decisions concerning the budget, the financial plan, efficiency improvements and service quality. The IAI then drafts a medium-term operational plan, which is designed to achieve the objectives it has been set, and submits this plan to the minister for approval. This plan also covers facilities, equipment and human resources. Once approved, the IAI operates within this plan, submitting more detailed annual plans. Within the terms of these plans, the IAI has discretion to manage.

In 2001 a new Ministry of Public Management, Home Affairs, Posts and Telecommunications was created by a merger of three previously separate ministries. This new ministry shares the task of periodically evaluating each IAI with an Evaluation Committee, which is supposed to be established within each 'parent' ministry. Each year these Evaluation Committees monitor the performance of the IAIs. They may recommend changes in the IAI's operations. There is also a Committee for the Evaluation of Policies and IAIs, which receives the results of these evaluations (see Figure 11.1). This Committee may make recommendations to the responsible minister, including the possible privatization or abolition of the IAI in question. Members of both committees are appointed by the relevant

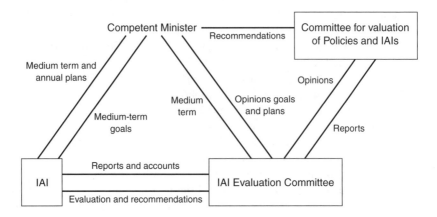

Figure 11.1 Operational framework for IAIs.

minister, together with the Minister of Public Management, Home Affairs, Posts and Telecommunications. They include academics and other experts in the fields of management and accounting, but none of them are civil servants of the relevant ministries.

Financial management

The relevant legislation prescribes that the government may allocate a part or the total financial resources deemed necessary for each IAI, but until now the full amount has always been given. Each IAI receives two types of funding – a grant to cover operating costs, plus capital expenditure. Operating costs are estimated as expected operating costs minus any revenues. In contrast to the line item input budgeting system in the ministries, IAIs enjoy full discretion in their use of the operating grant. They may carry forward unspent balances to the following financial year. Freedom with capital spending is, however, more constrained. Capital monies cannot be used for current expenditure and, if cost savings are made, they may not be retained. On the other hand, IAIs may borrow money directly from the private sector if the minister approves it.

IAIs use business-style accruals accounting and double-entry bookkeeping. However, there are some important differences with commercial corporate (GAAP) accounting. First, it is assumed that the IAI's net operating surplus will be zero – if it works in accordance with its medium-term plan. The funding principle is that the grant is equal to the net operating deficit. Second, the depreciation of fixed assets are excluded from the profit and loss statement, but the cost of depreciation is deducted from the balance sheet capital reserve. IAIs are not fully accountable for capital expenditures and investments where these are the responsibility of the relevant ministers.

If an IAI has capital in excess of 10 billion yen then its accounts (including its performance report) must be examined by an auditor or certified public accountant. This requirement is in addition to the requirement for internal audit and continuing access enjoyed by the national Board of Audit.

Personnel management

IAI chief executives are selected by ministers. The appointees are supposed either to have high knowledge and experience of the particular field of the IAI in question, and/or to have relevant management knowledge. Executive members of the IAI are appointed, in turn, by the Chief Executive, while inspectors are appointed by the minister. Chief executives are appointed on term contracts, and their salaries contain a performance-related component. In practice, although it would have been possible to hold open competitions, most chief executives came from the parent ministries, and were usually the heads of the former functional divisions (e.g. the head of museum division became chief executive of a museum IAI).

IAI employees have one of two statuses. The first group have the status of civil servants, being classified as belonging to the group Specified Independent Administrative Institutions (SIAIs). In practice, a large part of the staff have this status, partly because of a compromise with the trade unions. Crucially, though (at least for presentational purposes) SIAI staff are not included in the official total of Personnel of Administrative Organs (i.e. they are not counted as part of the central civil service). The second group do not have civil service status. Both groups are appointed by chief executives, not by ministers. A performance-related pay system is applied to both groups. Thus chief executives do have some flexibility in personnel management, and at the time of writing the Koizumi administration is envisaging transferring the status of many agency staff to non-civil service status. Thus, for example, in 2002 it was decided that university staff would be transferred to non civil service status from FY 2004.

The present shape and possible future development of the Japanese agency system

The scope of agencification

As indicated earlier, all functions involving the exercise of compulsory authority over citizens were excluded from the agencification process. Mainly because of this, the proportion of civil servants that moved over to

Table 11.1 The size and scope of IAIs (as at 1/3/02)

Type	No. of IAIs	% of IAIs	No. of staff	No. of IAIs	% of IAIs
R&D	32	56.1	1–99	18	31.6
Cultural and training	16	28.1	100–199	18	31.6
Examination	4	7.0	200–499	15	26.3
Operations	4	7.0	500–999	4	7.0
Other	1	1.8	1000+	2	3.5
Total	57	100		57	100

IAIs was modest – about 2.2 percent in 2001. Most IAIs are concerned with R&D, cultural functions and training and education (see Table 11.1).

Strengths of IAIs

IAIs are legally independent of central government – statutory corporations (unlike, say, the UK Next Steps agencies). Operational autonomy, within ministerially-determined strategic goals should, in theory, lead, via flexible management, to greater efficiency and higher service quality.

IAIs, each with its own report and accounts, should advance the cause of transparency and accountability. Each should be more exposed than when it was 'dissolved' in a larger, multi-functional ministry. Even in the Special Accounts of central government, accruals accounts and the addition of performance information was a rarity. So IAIs marked a step forward in this respect. Furthermore, IAIs with substantial capital are subject to external audit by professional accountants, whereas central government accounts are examined by the National Board of Audit alone.

The exclusion of IAI staff from total national civil service numbers was also an advantage. The introduction of regular performance appraisals for all staff and the non-civil service status of some staff gave chief executives more personnel discretion than in the ministries. Given that, overall, personnel costs account for roughly 60 percent of operating costs across the IAI sector, this is a potentially important element of flexibility.

Fourth, the system of annual and medium-term evaluations described earlier means that it is possible to 'make managers manage.' This should counterbalance the operational freedoms given to IAIs.

Fifth, there are certain advantages to single-function status. There is perhaps less need for management to be constantly concerned with co-ordination with other functions – as often occurs in multi-functional ministries. And having a single function should make performance measurement more straightforward.

Finally, IAIs provide a vehicle for introducing private sector business methods to the public sector. Accruals accounting and management by objectives are two of these. Also, there is the provision for regular evaluation (see fourth advantage, above). While the 2001 Evaluation Law for Administrative Organs also makes central government subject to performance measurement, the evaluations in that case are determined by the ministers looking at their own ministries, and sometimes are constrained by the lack of clear targets. IAIs, by contrast, should have clearer targets and should be evaluated through an external process.

Weaknesses

Alongside the potential strengths, one may discern a number of weaknesses in the Japanese model of agencification. First, despite the potential increase in transparency, the statutory independence of IAIs could reduce parliamentary control of public services. Budgetary control by the Diet becomes one of net operating cost control, so comprehensive control of revenues and expenditures is ended. Chief executives of IAIs are accountable to the relevant minister on operational matters, but not directly to the Parliament. They are not 'accounting officers' in the sense which obtains in the UK Next Steps agencies.

Second, in practice, many of the outputs of IAIs are not quantified. In fact, at the time of writing, of 2,081 medium-term objectives only 277 (13 percent) are quantified and measured.

Third, the potential for the introduction of business methods is not necessarily fully taken up. According to a survey by an accounting firm, only 6 out of 46 IAIs acknowledged the usefulness of accruals accounts (Asahi Audit Corporation 2002). This apparent passivity may well stem from a lack of knowledge and skills about business management techniques.

To this list of weaknesses we should add three which stem from 'slippage' between the original conceptualization and the actual implementation. The first of these relates to the flexibility of operational management. In practice, the idea of medium-term budgeting is undercut by the Ministry of Finance's insistence on an annual review of requests for funding. This, in turn, is partly because the Fiscal Law prescribes that the grant has to be approved by the Diet every year. The operational discretion of IAI chief executives is also severely circumscribed by the fact that most of the staff have civil service status, and this means that their wage levels have to remain in line with central government personnel.

A second example of 'slippage' is the fact that only 7 of the 57 chief executives actually came from a non-government background. Forty-two of the appointments were from the ministries and the remaining 8 were retired senior civil servants. All 7 of the non-government chief executives are scholars of one kind or another, so the influx of business knowledge and skills at this level has been minimal.

The third piece of 'slippage' relates to management systems and organizational culture. The shift from a focus on inputs and processes toward outputs and outcomes appears to have been slow. Despite the structural change, most IAIs have continued with the same management control systems as previously. For example, purchasing procedures have changed very little. A bureaucratic culture still predominates and is slow to change.

Concluding remarks

Thus far, agencification in Japan has been mainly structural, and systems change has lagged behind. This contrasts with, for example, the UK's approach, which might be characterized as one in which the first emphasis was on systems change, with structural issues following (Yamamoto 2000). It is, however, still early days with the Japanese reforms, and therefore a comparison of the outcomes of agencification in the two countries would be premature.

Bibliography

Administrative Reform Council (1997) *Final Report*, Tokyo (in Japanese).

Asahi Audit Corporation (2002) *Adoption of Corporate Accounting in IAIs*, Tokyo (in Japanese).

Fujita, T. (1999) 'National Universities and Independent Administrative Institutions,' *JURIST*, No. 1156, pp. 109–22 (in Japanese).

Hayao, K. (1993) *The Japanese Prime Minister and Public Policy*, Pittsburgh and London: University of Pittsburgh Press.

Kingdon, J.W. (1984) *Agendas, Alternatives, and Public Policies*, Boston: Little Brown.

Reed, S.R. (1986) *Japanese Prefectures and Policymaking*, Pittsburgh: University of Pittsburgh Press.

Vogel, E.F. (1979) *Japan as No. 1: Lessons from America*, Cambridge: Harvard University Press.

Yamamoto. K. (1999) 'Agencification of national museums in Japan,' paper prepared for the CIMA Conference of New Public Sector Seminar on Third Way, Edinburgh, 23–24th September.

Yamamoto. K. (2000) 'Budgeting, accounting and evaluation for semi-autonomous public organizations: the case of Japanese central government,' paper prepared for the International Conference on Accounting, Auditing and Management in Public Sector Reform, Zaragoza, 7–9th September.

Part IV

Autonomization in the developing and transitional countries

12 New public management in a developing country

Creating executive agencies in Tanzania

Janice Caulfield

Introduction

In 1996 Tanzania was one of a number of developing countries to adopt the agency form of organisation as a part of its public sector reform programme, and legislation establishing 'executive agencies' was passed in 1997. The Executive Agency Programme was assisted by the British Government's Department for International Development (DfID) as a major part of its aid package for civil service reform in Tanzania. The question raised in this chapter is, 'Can new public management inspired reforms, in this case the creation of semi-autonomous agencies, assist a developing country in meeting its goals?' The chapter draws extensively on the findings (and subsequent report) of evaluative research undertaken in Tanzania in September 2000 and May 2001 on behalf of DfID (Caulfield and Talbot 2002).

Agencies, as they have been defined in this volume, can best be described as a tool for 'unbundling the bureaucracy' and creating more flexible, performance-oriented public organisations. These steps are deemed necessary for a wide range of political, policy and administrative reasons. The purposes of this chapter are, first, to describe the experience of establishing executive agencies in Tanzania. Second, to make some assessment of the benefits or otherwise, of importing new public management style solutions into developing country contexts with a very different set of circumstances to those of the developed world. Some have argued that NPM-type reforms are inappropriate in developing countries because of low governance capacity and corruption, while others have argued it all depends on localised contingency factors, rather than general national characteristics (Schick 1998; Polidano 1999).

The first part of the chapter identifies the characteristic features of a New Public Management-style agency. This is followed by a brief introduction to state and politics in Tanzania, and the prevailing economic conditions which led to donor assisted restructuring of its public sector. In the second part of the chapter, the executive agency programme, and processes of implementation, are described. The UK's 'Next Steps' agencies, upon which the Tanzanian programme was modelled, provide a comparative reference point. In the third and final part of the chapter, seven of the new agencies are evaluated against three key variables of agency: finance, autonomy and performance. Not surprisingly for a developing country perhaps, problems encountered by the agencies are found to result from wider, administrative system failures. However, issues of governance, including political commitment, are found to be the more serious threat to Tanzania's decentralisation reform initiative. While it is still early days, some assessment of longer-term prospects of the agencies is offered.

Characteristics of the NPM agency

Agencies as a particular form of public organisation have been an important instrument in the modernisation objectives of governments in many countries in both the developed and developing worlds. Their appeal follows a widespread shift to business-like forms of managing public sectors in the pursuit of improved efficiency and effectiveness in regulation and service delivery. Agencies, particularly the NPM variety which have been unbundled from traditional bureaucratic departments (but without statutory independence) perform task-specific functions of government as entities separate from their parent ministries. The Agency form has four notable characteristics as follows:

- Decentralised management (including some financial autonomy)
- Task specialisation
- Outputs focussed
- Performance contracting

These characteristics reflect the different rationales and stakeholder interests of public sector reform. Decentralised management implies a change in the character of political supervision and accountability. The assumption is that quality management will be increased by distancing activities from central and often politicised departments. The creation of agencies with clearly specified tasks will, it is assumed, increase transparency and better link goals and means in achieving policy objectives. The adoption of an 'outputs focussed' approach to public policy and service delivery establishes the user rather than the provider as the main beneficiary of public expenditure. In the ideal model, agencies allow for managerial autonomy by decentralising decision-making in all areas of the business (including financial and human resource management) to a 'chief executive', who is typically employed on a performance contract basis. Performance 'contracting' is cascaded through the whole organisation where not only the chief but all levels of the hierarchically organised workforce engage in a principal/agent type relationship, working to performance agreements. It is the performance contract relationship which provides the critical link between the semi-autonomous agency and the parent ministry or minister. Ideally, each of the above features of agency is mutually supportive, allowing for a more focussed and transparent public sector.

These characteristics of the NPM agency also point to areas of tension for governments. For example, a structurally disaggregated public sector raises the issue of accountability to Parliament and the public. If the work of government is to be put at a political distance, who is to be held responsible and accountable for the decisions, actions and quality of services of the agency? In a Parliamentary style democracy it is the political office of Minister that ultimately carries responsibility, regardless of the organisational form used to implement government policy. Second, a focus on outputs/outcomes (rather than inputs) demands analytical and methodological sophistication of the organisation in establishing appropriate systems of performance measurement (targets, indicators, etc.) customer surveys, feed-back loops and system linkages, all of which require resources of skill, time and money. Moreover, performance contracting itself carries many transaction costs, which may result in the efficiency gains of task specific agencies being eroded. Third, managerial (and financial) autonomy is itself a questionable ideal in the public sector, especially in policy sensitive areas or functional areas dependent on government budgetary allocations.

Agencies in North America, Europe and Australasia have wrestled with these tensions (often after the event), the solution to which has required a rethinking and sometimes a reorganisation of agencies; the Benefits Agency and the Prison Service in the UK being prime examples (Talbot 1996; James 2001). In countries of the developing world, these tensions have not been well understood, partly through lack of knowledge about the theoretical bases of the idea of agency. The agency concept has frequently been imported uncritically, often facilitated by private sector management consultants who themselves do not comprehend the political dynamics of public service provision which give rise to inherent tensions.

State and politics in Tanzania

Tanzania's post-colonial, single-party and heavily Presidential government has left a legacy that is important for understanding roles and relationships which govern the public service, including its executive agencies. These relationships are elaborated later in the chapter, but here it is worth placing the reforms in context with a brief sketch of Tanzania's political and economic history.

From 1965, shortly after Tanganyika's union with Zanzibar to become the United Republic of Tanzania, until 1992, the new Republic remained a one-party state. The Charma Cha Mapinduzi (CCM) political party was 'the final authority in respect of all matters, an authority reinforced in 1977 by the country's new constitution' (Mukandala and Shelukindo

1994). Policy decisions ranged from the party chairman (also president of the Republic) through to the Central Committee, the National Executive Committee (NEC), and the party general conference held every five years. Alongside the authority of the party, the formal structure of government was headed by the President 'in whom all executive powers relating to the union are vested' (The Constitution of 1977 Section 34, cited in Mukandala and Shellukindo 1994). A cabinet, appointed in consultation with the prime minister of his choice, assisted the president. While the party secretariat could make policy submissions to the NEC, many key decisions have been made on submission of the President himself. Tanzania's first president, Julius Nyerere, was instrumental in the Arusha Declaration of 1967, which established state-owned enterprises – the 'parastatals' – and the agrarian reforms of the early 1970s. Under this one-party state, the Parliament remained a sideshow with a predominance of members being appointed rather than elected.

The effect of this heavily centralised political system on the structure and processes of the public service remains to this day even though multi-party politics was, under liberalisation pressures, legally guaranteed in 1992. Although the governmental system appears Westminster-like in relation to the formal role of Ministers and the civil service, it is in fact not the case. A long-standing mutual distrust between ministers and senior public servants continues, exacerbated in recent times by the donor community, which finds it easier negotiating with fellow technocrats in the bureaucracy than with politicians (Mukandala and Shellukindo 1994). The Chief Secretary (the most senior civil servant) is a powerful figure. He reports directly to the President, and departmental Permanent Secretaries see their primary reporting relationship to be to the Chief Secretary rather than to their Minister.

After a period of sustained growth post-independence, the Tanzanian economy went into severe decline in the late 1970s and 1980s, which resulted in its ranking as the fourteenth poorest country in the world climbing to the second poorest by 1990 (Messkoub n.d.). A number of factors contributed to this decline, among them the oil price shocks of the 1970s, a fall in manufacturing output, the war with Uganda and break-up of the East African community, and severe droughts. Deteriorating terms of trade resulted in macroeconomic problems such as inflation and balance of payments deficits (Messkoub n.d.). So began a period of structural adjustment and economic recovery policies and programmes supported by the International Monetary Fund (IMF) and World Bank, a not unfamiliar story in sub-Saharan Africa.

Reforming the public sector

During the prosperous decades, growth in the civil service had continued to the point where the cost of public sector employment was no longer tenable. In 1989 a World Bank review of public expenditure found that between 1970 and 1984, public service employment had expanded at close to twice the rate of government revenues. Seventy-two per cent of all formal employment in Tanzania was within the public sector (McCourt and Sola 1999). As the economy failed to deliver expected dividends, public finances were squeezed and real pay levels worsened. Inevitable abuses of public office took hold and many qualified professional and managerial staff sought careers elsewhere (Teskey and Hooper 1999). In an attempt to rebuild much needed capacity and resources, the Government of Tanzania (GOT) launched the Civil Service Reform Programme in 1991 with the objective of achieving a 'smaller, affordable, well-compensated, efficient and effectively performing civil service' (GOT 2000). Dismantling or privatising the parastatals, which had in many cases become grossly inefficient and corrupted, was an important part of the reform programme. Another was the creation of 'executive agencies'.

The prevailing view in Tanzania in the mid-1990s was that many functions of the government, though 'non-core', could and should remain in the public sector. The GOT was concerned not to replicate past mistakes by giving too much autonomy to devolved departments, but it was equally concerned not to privatise what it saw as essentially public services. The executive agency was seen as an organisational solution, which would keep public services within government, while promising efficiency and effectiveness improvements by allowing greater autonomy and flexibility to operational managers.

The role of donors was paramount to the wider public sector reform programme with the World Bank and nine individual donor countries involved in funding its various aspects. Among them the IMF set conditions for reform in its credit programmes, especially for a reduction in public employment levels. Over the period from 1992 to 2000 employment in the public service fell 27 per cent from a high of 355,000 to 260,000 personnel (GOT and the World Bank 2001: Vol. II). The process of 'agencification' in Tanzania has contributed significantly to that decline. A trade-off for those remaining within the public sector has been a very significant improvement in their pay, although by 1996 real wages and salaries had only just exceeded their 1980 levels (World Bank 1997). Nonetheless, civil service pay has continued to improve, especially at the upper echelons. In most countries, it is the political-administrative elites that seek to influence the reform processes (Haggard and Kaufman 1992). In Tanzania pressure for the creation of agencies has come primarily from senior permanent officials who saw the prospects of real pay increases (Therkildsen 2000).

Implementing the Executive Agency Programme

In September 1997 the Civil Service Department (CSD) issued a 'policy framework' for the Executive Agency Programme. The model adopted was broadly based on the UK's 'Next Steps' agencies, and was embraced by the GOT after a hesitant start in the early 1990s to give autonomy to some government departments through individual statute.[1] Even though executive agencies in the United Kingdom have no special statute (rather they are creations of executive order), the Tanzanian government decided to introduce umbrella legislation. *The Executive Agencies Act 1997* was a single enabling Act to codify the generic characteristics and status of agencies. It was envisaged that 'framework documents' would set the agency-specific terms and conditions. The programme began in an ambitious way, but the considerable resources required in time and effort have resulted in a slower phasing in than originally planned. At the time of writing, nine agencies had been established, with another eight departments preparing for launch. The current target is for 46 agencies to be established by 2004.

The process of identifying candidates for agency status followed operational and efficiency reviews of eighteen Ministries. Initially, departments so identified were in areas seen to have potential for operating on a cost-recovery basis. Other considerations included whether a department's functions were 'executive' rather than policy, and whether the reform of the department (and thus the way it performed) would have a significant impact on the country. This was defined in terms of contributing to the economic growth of the country by reducing the total cost of the Public Service, and improving service delivery (GOT 1997). The commercial or, at least, 'self sufficiency' goal has proved to be the most elusive for reasons explained later in the chapter. Before an evaluation can be made, the formal processes and structures of executive agencies must be considered.

The programme is managed by the CSD, which is located in the President's Office, giving it considerable leverage in directing the programme. The process of implementation begins with the Ministry responsible for a selected candidate appointing a technical taskforce to work with the Executive Agency Project team within the CSD. Requirements for establishment include:

- the appointment of a Ministerial Advisory Board (MAB);
- a framework document (setting out aims, roles and objectives, authority and performance standards);
- appointment of a Chief Executive (through open competition);
- a Performance Agreement (between the principal and the agent).

A set of 'Rules and Regulations', which are subsidiary to the Act, provide a governing framework for advisory boards, personnel management, conciliation, arbitration and finance, and procurement and stores. Its features include:

- authority of the Chief Executive to appoint, remunerate and discipline staff;
- performance appraisal and evaluation of staff;
- code of ethics;
- Service Level Agreements (protected by conciliation and arbitration);
- Chief Executive as Accounting Officer;
- commercial operations;
- business and strategic plans;
- annual reporting;
- annual audit.

The 'outputs' orientation of agencies is evident in their mandate to:

- provide its services to its customers and the public in the most efficient and effective manner;
- ensure that its operations are designed for the provision of the best service to its customers and to maintain a high degree of responsiveness to their needs (*The Executive Agencies Act, 1997*, 4(2)).

The policy expectation is that agencies will 'conform to modern management practices' by developing business and strategic plans and 'key performance targets' (GOT 1997). The 'how to' of performance measurement, however, is left largely to the agencies to work out for themselves. This was found to be a serious failing of the guidance documents, especially as reporting on 'continuous improvement' is a mandated responsibility.

In almost all respects, the content of the Act and subsidiary legislation in Tanzania mirrors the formal processes of 'Next Steps' agencies in the United Kingdom. One important exception (others are noted below) is that UK agencies are not expected to operate on a cost-recovery basis. In the UK, there is a separate classification for commercial, stand-alone agencies, which are called 'trading funds'.

Roles and relationships

Fundamental to the success of agencies wherever they occur is effective regulation. A first step to achieving this is the specification of roles, responsibilities and relationships between principal and agent. In Tanzania, these are prescribed in the Act but in such a way that reinforces a highly centralised, but politically marginalised system. In setting roles and responsibilities, the Act pays particular attention to the Permanent Secretary (PS) of the parent ministry, the agency Chief Executive (CE) and the Chief Secretary (as head of the Civil Service). Although the Minister is responsible for agency establishment, it is the Chief Secretary that must approve the Agency's official mandate – the Framework Document. The

Permanent Secretary is assigned the role of 'strategic manager' of the agency, and the Chief Executive is held responsible for its day-to-day operations and management of funds, property, business and personnel. The formal relationship between the PS and the CE is consolidated by the Performance Agreement concluded between them. Save for an annual reporting responsibility, Chief Executives answer to their Permanent Secretaries and not, as is the case with most UK agencies, to their Ministers.

The Minister's formal responsibilities include establishment, finance and reporting. It is his/her duty to appoint a Ministerial Advisory Board but, unlike in the UK where the Minister formally chairs the Board, in Tanzania it is the Permanent Secretary who has the official role. The Minister appoints the Chief Executive, but it is the Permanent Secretary, as Chair of the Advisory Board, who is most influential in deciding the appointment. In matters of finance, it is the Minister who must determine (in consultation with the Finance Minister) what monies shall remain the property of the agency, and the amount of revenue to be credited to the Exchequer account. All other financial responsibilities are those of the CE, the PS and the Finance Department; in Tanzania it is not unusual for chief executives to go directly to the Finance Ministry to negotiate on their budgetary allocations. Finally, the Minister has a responsibility to report to Parliament on the Agency's operations. Nothing in the legislation establishes a relationship between the Minister and either the Permanent Secretary or Chief Executive. In formal communications with the Minister, the CE is required only to present to him/her a copy of the Agency's annual report.

A consequence of the Minister's low profile, both in the Act and in practice, has been a general lack of political support (and in some cases open hostility) for the programme. It is, in a sense, a manifestation of deeper concerns that the political elite in Tanzania has with the public sector reform programme generally, given its prime objective to reduce the size of the public sector. When one considers the very large proportion of the country's working population employed by the state, and the substantial downsizing that has resulted from the reforms already, it is not surprising that Ministers feel threatened by a change in the status quo. It is, after all, their constituents who have lost jobs. The only two cabinet members who have shown any real enthusiasm and leadership for the reforms are the President of the Republic and the current Minister for Establishment.

The agencies and their clients

In two field visits, in September 2000 and May 2001, interviews were conducted with the chief executives of seven of Tanzania's nine executive agencies.[2] These agencies and their parent ministries are:

- National Bureau of Statistics (NBS) *Planning Commission*
- Government Chemical Laboratory (GCL) *Ministry of Health*
- Tanzania Civil Aviation Authority (TCAA) *Ministry of Communication and Transport*
- Business Registration and Licensing Authority (BRELA) *Ministry of Industries and Commerce*
- Drilling and Dam Construction Agency (DDCA) *Ministry of Water*
- Tanzania Meteorological Agency (Meteorology) *Ministry of Communications and Transport*
- Tanzania National Roads Agency (Tanroads) *Ministry of Works*

Three of the above agencies – the GCL, TCAA and NBS – were among the first four launched and have been operational for three years. DDCA, Meteorology and BRELA were launched in late 1999 and Tanroads in mid-2000.

All the agencies are service providers but two – BRELA and the TCAA – also perform a regulatory function. As task-specific agencies they each have a different group of clients, some private but many from within government itself. The National Bureau of Statistics, Meteorology and the GCL's major client groups are government departments. The main clientele of BRELA and the TCAA come from the private sector. The DDCA has as its major client local government authorities, but it also has a number of private sector clients. The DDCA works in a competitive environment, particularly in drilling where several private operators exist. To a lesser extent, the GCL operates under similar competitive conditions. Tanroads is an infrastructure provider whose main client is a special purpose authority, the Road Fund Board, through which it derives its revenue via dedicated funding from road tolls, licences, etc. The Board also sets the performance targets for Tanroads, so that while the parent Ministry of Works retains (in principle at least) a 'strategic management responsibility', it is the Board that is the purchaser. In this respect, Tanroads is unique among the agencies and offers an alternative, and possibly more robust model.

How do Tanzania's executive agencies 'measure up'?

The analysis that follows is organised around three key variables of agency identified at the outset, these being finance, autonomy and performance.

Finance

The policy objective of commercialisation for Tanzania's executive agencies, in particular its emphasis on cost recovery, has had mixed results. We found only two agencies – the Tanzania Civil Aviation Authority and the Business Registration and Licencing Agency – that have been able to operate successfully as commercial enterprises and achieve full cost recovery, although both still depend on government for new capitalisation funds. Changing attitudes to the delivery of previously 'free' public services to a 'user pays' basis has been a challenge for most of the agencies. Small businesses and most of the public sector itself have had great difficulty coming to terms with the new marketisation principles. Ability to recover costs, therefore, varies according to who an agency's clients are, and this in turn depends on what service the agency provides. Commercial success for an executive agency in Tanzania thus depends first and foremost on:

a   its core business (agency function), and
b   its major client group (as paying customers).

The TCAA's main client group comes from the aviation industry, for the most part private organisations that understand commercial principles of exchange and pay their bills. Similarly, BRELA's clients are drawn from private sector organisations, international and local businesses.

Agencies that have as their main clients other departments, have had much less success in operating on a commercial basis because parent ministries, in particular, fail to see why they should pay for services provided by their former departments. An example is the Government Chemist Laboratory whose clients include its parent, the Health Ministry, and departments in other Ministries such as the Police Department, which relies on forensic services provided by the Agency. External public sector clients such as the Police Department, appear more willing to accept the relationship as a commercial one, but are typically reluctant or unable to pay their debts because of their own uncertain budgetary climate. Agencies in a similar position to the GCL are Meteorology and the National Bureau of Statistics. Even the TCAA has had to contend with similar problems from the national, state-owned airline. Resistance to the new 'user pays' environment has also come from smaller, private sector clients in the community. The Meteorological Agency, for example, receives many complaints from farmers and related groups over increased charges, even though the government continues to subsidise the agency's operations.

Public sector reform in Tanzania takes place in an environment of weak fiscal control. The release of budgeted funds to Ministries is problematic. A public expenditure review conducted by the Government of Tanzania and World Bank highlighted the lack of predictability of budget releases as one of the main problems afflicting financial administration (January 2001). Month-to-month releases are highly variable and do not reflect the needs of the recipients – extreme cases such as the Ministry of Water received more than its total annual budget in one month. Deviations between annual budgeted and actual figures for Ministries has varied as much as up to 40 per cent in the last two years, but some estimates put this figure even higher (Therkildsen 2000). This unpredictability of resource flows from the Treasury to spending units impacts on both allocative and operational efficiency.

For agencies dependent on government subventions through their parent Ministries, there is a flow-on effect. In one case, an agency's budget was coming to it from the parent ministry in monthly instalments and sometimes not at all, which seriously undermined its ability to plan, threatening its operations. The National Bureau of Statistics is in a slightly better position than other, government-dependent agencies because it has a separate vote from Parliament. In an effort to secure a guaranteed level of funding from the government the NBS recently engaged in a costing exercise, putting a monetary value on its 'core' statistics. A successful bid in this direction was seen by the agency as 'the acid test' of its viability as a commercial operation. As part of its bid to Treasury, Meteorology has also undertaken a similar exercise. In the *Rules and Regulations* governing executive agencies, service level agreements were envisaged as the means by which agencies could enter into contracts and conduct commercial transactions with their clients, including their Ministries. Because of their own budgetary uncertainties, however, client Ministries are reluctant to formalise such agreements. At the time of our investigations, the NBS was the only agency to have concluded an SLA, in this case with an external Ministry, which was made possible only because of donor (i.e. dedicated) funding.

The precarious financial situation of most agencies has been felt in staffing terms. In two cases, senior management positions remained unfilled (a Business Director in one case and HR manager in another), even though selections had been made twelve months previously. The appointees were from outside the Civil Service, and their appointments depended on the Agency generating sufficient funds from own-source revenues to pay their salaries. In addition to their own work, professional staff from within the Agencies were forced to carry the administrative and accounting responsibilities thus generated. Indeed, it is the professional group within all agencies that is most seriously over-worked and relatively under-paid.

Adoption of accrual accounting systems by agencies has, for some, compounded the funding problems. Two agencies told us that their parent Ministry lacked the capacity to understand properly the accruals accounts being prepared by them. Most Ministries operate on traditional cash accounting systems, although they are gradually moving to performance budgeting, but from what we learnt, still have a long way to go.[3] To meet reporting requirements, one agency follows two accounting systems, placing a considerable burden on its sole accountant.

Autonomy

The idea of 'letting the managers manage' free from bureaucratic and political constraints, is believed to improve the efficiency and effectiveness of executive agencies. This means having the freedom to manage their budgets, make their own decisions, operate on commercial accounting principles and reinvest their surpluses. Governments are, however, ultimately accountable to the public for the quality of services provided by public agencies. Thus, it is essential that the freedom of agencies remains a qualified freedom. Getting the right balance between autonomy and accountability is fundamental in agency-type reforms. Performance contracting and performance monitoring and reporting provide the tools for achieving both objectives.

While the *Executive Agencies Act* of 1997 incorporates the principles, concepts and techniques of 'arms-length' government, what we found in practice was a different understanding to the one described above. Tanzania's executive agencies are treated in a far more autonomous way than either the textbooks or, indeed, the legislation prescribes. For example, performance contracting requires that the 'principal' should set the targets for what performance they expect to receive in relation to the 'agent'. This is done for all UK agencies; their Key Performance Indicators are referred to as 'Ministers' or 'Secretary of States' targets. While most agencies in the UK do play a much more active role in developing KPIs, they are still 'the Ministers'.

In Tanzania, most agencies have been left to develop their own operational targets, without necessarily even getting formal approval from the 'principal' about what they should be. Moreover, Permanent Secretaries appear to be unsure about their role as 'strategic managers', preferring instead to leave everything to the Agencies. Some agency chiefs themselves appear unable (or perhaps unwilling) to accept the concept of semi-autonomy, harking after a more independent status such as the Tanzanian Revenue Authority, which is a statutory body. Others feel let down by their parent Ministry's almost total lack of interest in their performance reporting and feel reports are largely ignored or merely 'tabled'. No parent ministry that we visited had a performance-monitoring regime in place. The only real interest in monitoring was in those Ministries that saw it as a means to extract a surplus from their agencies. Monitoring is left largely to the advisory boards, which receive half-yearly reports from the agencies. As a consequence of the general disinterest, there has been no pressure on agencies to produce annual reports, and those that had done so, or were in the process of drafting reports were, on their own initiative, responding to the requirements of the Act.

A weak national auditing environment compounds the problem of performance monitoring in Tanzania. The Act requires that agencies conduct an annual, external audit of their budgets, but they are free to choose their auditors. In the Tanzanian context this is a necessary flexibility because the Auditor General's office has, in some cases, a backlog of as much as five years on the audit of departmental accounts. One agency had employed the services of the Tanzania Audit Corporation, while others, unable to afford private auditors, had left the reporting process unattended.

Performance measurement

Within Tanzania's executive agencies there is an impressive eloquence among senior staff about performance management, and there is a real commitment by managers to creating a performance culture within their organisations. Similarly, senior managers well understand that promotions and pay increases depend on improved performance. As one senior staff said, 'in the Ministries we didn't care, but now our jobs depend on it'. Performance measurement development, however, tends to be focussed on internal (i.e. staff) performance rather than measuring output performance, even though an agency's 'real' performance is perceived by agency managements to be improved client service.

All staff (except the Chief Executive) are technically on secondment from their parent Ministries for the first year, during which time they must apply for their jobs in the agency. In the interim term, the parent Ministry meets staff costs. Downsizing has been a characteristic, indeed objective of the Public Service Reform programme, and the process of 'agencification' has left most agencies with a substantially reduced personnel compared to that which they previously had as departments. Agency staff know that if they wish to stay with the agency then they must perform. Promotions are based on performance, as are other pay incentives. In at least one agency, job evaluations had been completed for the whole organisation; others were in the process of doing the same. Contracting-out to former professional staff who are no longer employed by the agency has become a practice used by some agencies such as the NBS and Tanroads.

In most agencies the staffs are extremely busy. Managing time is difficult for staff: there is a tension between the need for strategic and business planning and the day-to-day demands of routine work. None of this is unique to developing countries. In Tanzania, however, the problem of staff time is compounded by the need to train staff as part of multi-skilling and/or new ways of working, for example, in information technologies. Training staff depletes the manpower available for daily operational duties, which is a dilemma for most agencies. The demands of developing a performance management system have fallen most heavily on the middle level professionals without, as yet, comparable reward.

Whilst agencies in general understand the need to focus on outputs and service delivery, creating effective measures is not an easy task, and many agencies are struggling. Most of the agencies had not developed performance measurements or benchmarks for evaluating outputs. The NBS was in the process of developing some sophisticated measures, and others were developing inventories (Tanroads) and benchmarks (DDCA). All of the agencies had engaged in a self-assessment exercise using the EFQM (Business Excellence) Model which allows them to compare their year-on-year organisational development, but this in no way constitutes a reliable or objective way of measuring actual agency output. BRELA was the only agency that had attempted to evaluate its performance by seeking feedback from clients through questionnaire, while other agencies were found to rely on informal feedback from their clients.

Performance reporting, as already stated, is particularly weak. This is due in part to bottlenecks in the central department of Controller and Auditor General and due to the failure of Ministries to develop perform-ance monitoring systems. The Act requires each agency to produce, within two months of the end of the financial year, an annual report containing evidence of the agency's performance against key targets, a report on its operations, copy of the annual Performance Agreement and 'such other information as the Permanent Secretary may require' (1997: 42(1)). This follows very closely the UK reporting model. At the time of our investiga-tions only one agency had produced an annual report that included audited accounts, when in fact at least four agencies and probably more should have reported. Moreover, the report that we cited contained scant performance data and no copy of the agency's performance agreement. This raises the issue of performance auditing (as distinct from financial auditing). The National Audit Office in the UK, for example, audits not only finances but also operational performance of executive agencies, and these are public documents. In Tanzania, this seems very unlikely to happen in the current circumstances of an undeveloped and/or weak performance monitoring and financial audit regime in parent and central ministries.

Summary and conclusions

The problem for reformist governments that adopt decentralisation pol-icies in pursuit of efficiency and effectiveness improvements in their public services, is how to keep decentralised agencies accountable. This has been solved (at least theoretically) by the use of contract. Principal-agent concepts and performance measurement techniques are its tools. The executive agency model, which combines managerial autonomy with government control, was seen by the Government of Tanzania to provide a solution to the crisis of over-loaded bureaucracy, and was politically more acceptable than either privatisation or corporatisation options.

Tanzania's Executive Agency Programme has much to commend it. Under the guidance of the Civil Service Department, its early develop-ment has been methodical and rigorous. There is no doubt that its legislative mandate, despite shortcomings within the Act, has assisted the establishment process. But the sophistication with which Tanzania's Executive Agency Programme was established, drawing as it did on a wealth of information and experience with executive agencies in the UK, has not been matched by the same level of sophistication in its implementation. This is not to say that the GOT's goal of creating a more efficient public sector through the creation of executive agencies has not been achieved. On the contrary, agency staff are enthusiastic, hard working and generally committed to the reform process, in part, because they see the potential (if not immediate) benefits to themselves. The government has certainly succeeded in its goal to reduce the size of the public sector, and the Executive Agency Programme has been one means to this end.

In terms of effectiveness improvements, there is little evidence to suggest this goal has or is likely to be achieved, although it should be borne in mind that agencies are still in their infancy. Capacity issues are a problem for Tanzania's executive agencies, but this is a problem generated more by the 'self sufficiency' expectations of the Government, rather than any inherent knowledge or skills deficit with agency staff. Most agencies operate on a vastly reduced personnel, and for those agencies unable to afford to appoint new staff, performance management responsibilities have fallen heaviest on the cadre of professional staff. Resources of time and money, therefore, are a major problem. The financial constraints on agencies, especially those agencies that are dependent on government subventions, and whose main clients are government departments, seriously undermine their potential to operate as commercial entities. These constraints threaten the hope that executive agencies will be 'islands of excellence' in a sea of bureaucratic incompetence and inefficiency.

The optimistic expectation that internal markets will work has been an unrealistic one. Agencies responsible for providing a public good and who are wholly dependent on public sector clients, are seriously challenged. Acknowledging these systemic problems is important, especially if the Government seeks to transform other social service departments, for example, in the areas of education and health, to agency status. If agencies are to secure financial stability, government subventions may need to be introduced on a permanent basis (ideally linked to performance improvements), rather than be seen as a stopgap measure. Strengthening the service-level agreement device, through guidelines or legislation to encourage its use, would also improve agencies' financial planning and operational capacity. Without budgetary stability and predictability, strategic planning and performance management cannot be implemented in any effective way. Moreover, failure in these areas undermines agency accountability.

The second issue for agencies is inadequate parenting. Permanent secretaries have failed to grasp the important 'strategic management' role that they must play, especially and most importantly their role in performance monitoring. This is in part a capacity issue, in part a political one. All of Tanzania's executive agencies carry out specialised functions and are staffed by professionals transferred from the parent ministries. A loss of professional capacity from the parent ministries themselves makes the task of monitoring performance of the agencies difficult. This is not a problem unique to a developing country, but, in Tanzania, it is compounded by the absence of a performance regime and culture within the ministries. The inevitable clash between the two organisations, one dynamic and enterprising, the other conservative and rule bound, has a real impact on communications between them, and is manifest in, for example, accounting system differences. With World Bank support, the GOT has recently embarked on a large-scale programme of performance improvement systems for its line ministries. In the longer term, this should improve the relationship between ministries and their agencies.

Perhaps the biggest difficulty for Tanzania's executive agencies is the wider political culture that experiences power as very much centralised on the President, where direct relations with the President and the Chief Secretary are what really counts. In this environment, the concept of ministerial responsibility remains undeveloped and the governance of executive agencies remains weak. Permanent secretaries, whose only real interest in their agencies is as a source of additional revenue have, for the most part, abandoned them. Ministers, who fear a further lessening of an already weak grasp on their Ministries, resent them. Changing political culture is more difficult, but governance issues should at least be given a higher priority by donor countries when planning their aid programmes.

Finally, does the experience of executive agencies in Tanzania help us to say anything conclusive about the question posed at the beginning of this chapter? That is, how useful are NPM-style solutions to problems of public administration in developing country contexts? First, we need to recognise that NPM reforms in the developed world have not been without their problems, some of which are similar to those experienced in Tanzania. Second, we cannot argue that NPM is inappropriate for developing countries without considering the alternatives. As Polidano (1999) has argued, the issue should be settled on the basis of the outcomes of the reforms, not on any a priori arguments about developing country characteristics. In the case of Tanzania's executive agencies, there are mixed results that suggest contingency factors do play an important role.

While a good deal of progress has been made by the newly created agencies towards establishing results oriented management systems and practices, the agencies cannot achieve their goals (or indeed the goals of the public sector reform programme) in isolation. Without appropriate performance measures, adequate systems of accountability, and wider system reform, it is unlikely they will be able to fulfil the purpose for which they are intended: the delivery of better public services at less cost to the taxpayer.

Notes

1 The Tanzanian Revenue Authority and the Medical Stores Department are two recent examples of statutory authorities in Tanzania.
2 Interviews were also conducted with senior officials in the Civil Service Department, the Department of Finance, and with permanent secretaries in several parent ministries.
3 A pilot trial of seven Ministries began in 1998 and was later extended. A review of the programme however, suggests a widespread failure to meet the requirements for performance budgeting.

Bibliography

Caulfield, J. and Talbot, C. (2000) ' "Eyes on hands off": executive agencies in Tanzania', in Talbot, C. and Caulfield, J. (eds) *Hand Agencies in Soft States: A Study of Agency Creation Programmes in Jamaica, Latvia and Tanzania*, Pontypridd: University of Glamorgan.

Fraser, A. (1991) *Making the Most of Next Steps: The Management of Ministers' Departments and their Executive Agencies*, London, HMSO.

Government of Tanzania and the World Bank (2001) *Public Expenditure Review FY00, Volume I: Main Report*, Dar es Salaam: World Bank.

Government of Tanzania and the World Bank (2001) *Public Expenditure Review FY00, Volume II: Consolidating the Medium Term Expenditure Framework*, Dar es Salaam: World Bank.

Government of the United Republic of Tanzania (2000) *Public Service Reform Programme (2000–2011)*, Dar es Salaam: President's Office.

Government of the United Republic of Tanzania (1999) *Public Service Management and Employment Policy*, Dar es Salaam: President's Office, Civil Service Department.

Government of the United Republic of Tanzania (1997) *The Executive Agencies Project: Policy Framework and Programme Implementation*, Dar es Salaam: President's Office, Civil Service Department.

Haggard S, and Kaufman, R. (1992) *The Politics of Economic Adjustments*, Princeton, NJ: Princeton University Press.

Henderson, ?. and Dwivedi, O.P. (1999) *Bureaucracy and the Alternatives in World Perspective*, Basingstoke: Macmillan.

Hubbar, M., Delay, S. and Devas, N. (1999) 'Complex management contracts: the case of customs administration in Mozambique', *Public Administration and Development* 19, 153–63.

James, O. (2001) 'Agencies and "joined-up government" in the UK', Paper presented to *The 5th IRSPM Conference*, 9–11 April, Barcelona.

Kaul, M. (1996) 'Civil service reforms: learning from Commonwealth experiences', *Public Administration and Development* 16, 131–50.

Kaul, M. (1997) 'The new public administration: management innovations in government', *Public Administration and Development* 17, 13–26.

Larbi, G.A. (1998) 'Institutional constraints and capacity issues in decentralizing management in public services: the case of health in Ghana', *Journal of International Development* 10, 377–86.

Maliyamkono, T.L. (1997). *Tanzania on the Move*, Dar es Salaam: TEMA Publishers Company Ltd.

Messkoub, M. (n.d.) 'The social impact of adjustment in Tanzania in the 1980s: economic crisis and household survival strategies', School of Business and Economic Studies, University of Leeds (www.brad.ac.uk/research/ijas/tazadj2.htm).

McCourt, W. and Sola, N. (1999) 'Using training to promote civil service reform: a Tanzanian local government case study', *Public Administration and Development* 19, 63–75.

Mukandala, R.S. and Shellukindo, W. (1994) 'Tanzania: moving beyond the one-party state', in Picard, L.A. and Garrity, M. (eds) *Policy Reform for Sustainable Development in Africa: An Institutional Imperative*, Colorado: Lyn Rienner.

Polidano, C. (1999) 'The new public management in developing countries', *Public Policy and Management Working Paper* No. 13, November. Institute for Development Policy and Management, University of Manchester.

Pollitt, C., Bathgate, K., Caulfield, J., Smullen, A. and Talbot, C. (2001) 'Agency fever? Analysis of an international policy fashion', *Journal of Comparative Policy Analysis* 3, 3 (November), 271–90.

Schick, A. (1998) 'Why most developing countries should not try New Zealand's reforms', *World Bank Research Observer* 13, 1, 123–31.

Talbot, C. (1996) *Ministers and Agencies: Control, Performance and Accountability*, London: CIPFA.

Talbot, C. (1997) 'UK civil service personnel reforms: devolution, decentralisation and delusion', *Public Policy and Administration* 12, 4.

Teskey, G. and Hooper, R. (1999) 'Tanzania civil service reform programme: case study', Paper given to the joint DAC Informal Network/ACBF Workshop on *Institutional and Capacity Development*, Harare, Zimbabwe.

Therkildsen, O. (2000) 'Public sector reform in a poor, aid-dependent country, Tanzania', *Public Administration and Development* 20, 61–71.

Trosa, S. (1994) *Next Steps: Moving On*, London, Cabinet Office: OPSS.

World Bank (1997) *Tanzania Public Expenditure Review*, Dar es Salaam: World Bank, Resident Mission in Tanzania, Country Department 4.

13 Putting new public management to good use

Autonomous public organizations in Thailand

Bidhya Bowornwathana

Introduction

For Thailand, new public management (NPM) is a foreign science.[1] Its body of knowledge has grown from theoretical works and practical experiences of western countries such as the United Kingdom and New Zealand. Now, since the late 1990s, high public officials of Thailand have decided that NPM provides a promising alternative to reform the traditional Thai bureaucracy.[2] Will embracing NPM be a simple exercise of Thais playing soccer or rugby?

The answer is no. This chapter argues that in order to put NPM to good use, we need to take three precautions. First, beware of NPM fever.[3] Second, choose a particular NPM technique carefully. Third, watch out for the intended and unintended consequences of NPM. The author illustrates his arguments by drawing on Thailand's recent experience with *agencification*, that is, the process of establishing autonomous or independent public organizations.[4]

Beware of NPM fever

To detect whether NPM fever exists in a particular country we have to observe the behaviour and thinking of government officials in charge of administrative reform. The symptoms of NPM fever are not that difficult to detect. The authorities in charge of reform will show unusual enthusiasm about a particular NPM innovation in the same manner that a car-lover longs to own the latest sports model. They will think that at last they have found the ultimate solution for all the chronic bureaucratic maladies. If someone starts casting any doubt about a particular NPM technique, the NPM disciples will become very upset. They will accuse critics of being old-fashioned or *tao lan pee* (a million years old turtle) who does not keep up with the development of new management ideas and innovations. Criticisms are definitely not tolerated.

Foreign western ideas about NPM are praised as magic medicine. There is an intense nervous excitement about learning the new fashions of NPM from abroad. A person who introduces the new NPM fashions first will be admired by the disciples of NPM as being progressive and useful to the reform movement. These doctrinarians of NPM truly believe that their newly acquired NPM techniques are perfect, and that the old ones are completely useless. Not to our surprise, in meetings on administrative reform one can hear discussions using NPM vocabularies such as benchmarking, performance measurement, result-based management, customer-oriented, etc. The more one can use, the more impressive one will look.

Another symptom of NPM fever is that government officials in charge of administrative reform have tendencies to isolate themselves from the rest. They have the illusion that they are superior to others because of their knowledge about the NPM methods. They will praise one another. Meanwhile, deviants are kept from the formal channels of the administrative reform process. Since they feel they know best, citizens are also kept from participating in the making of administrative reform decisions. Citizens are considered to be guinea pigs, not NPM scientists. This top-down management perspective of NPM has resulted in the isolation of reform officials from the rest of the population. They eventually become an inner group that does not understand the outside world. They are, in effect, the neo-Taylorists (Hughes 1998: 74–6).

A core belief among NPM followers is that NPM reform takes a long time to materialize. They argue that the NPM innovations introduced do not produce fast results because in the long run, NPM reform is a major cultural change of the traditional values and behaviour of the bureaucracy. We must be patient and understanding. In carrying out NPM reform, the usual approach is the pilot case study. For example, when we want to change all of the thousands of divisions in the bureaucracy, we start by selecting only 4–6 pilot divisions. Then, one spends three to four years experimenting with the pilot cases. Before it is time to implement the programme nation-wide, participants lose interest, and a new reform project comes along. When being asked why it took so long, the answer given by NPM disciples would be that western countries that were successful in carrying out a NPM reform programme also took a long time: citing cases such as the Next Steps Programme of the United Kingdom as an example.

Not only does NPM reform take a long time, NPM followers argue that for best results it must also be expensive. Government officials in charge of reform must constantly travel overseas in large groups to visit and learn about the NPM reform in western countries such as New Zealand and the United Kingdom. The overseas field trips must involve a large group because all those government agencies concerned with the reform programme must be involved. Moreover, international and domestic consultants with NPM expertise must be hired and paid well because of their unusual management and consultancy skills. The question is: where will the money come from?

For a developing country, the answer is to acquire loans and grants from international funding agencies such as the World Bank (1994, 1997, 1999), the Asian Development Bank (1998, 1999), and the UNDP (1995, 1998). In practice, it is easier to spend money acquired from international loans for governance and NPM reform than to pull resources from the national budget, because the spending of loans usually goes unnoticed by the Thai public. Now, the danger with the NPM fever is that the loans acquired for NPM reform programmes may become a heaven for consultants and government officials whose personal economic interests concur. For Thailand, the World Bank recently approved a $400 million loan to Thailand for the public sector reform programme jointly prepared by World Bank officials and high public officials of Thailand. The $400 million loan is distributed among central agencies: the Office of the Secretariat of the Civil Service Commission, the Budget Bureau, the National Economic and Social Development Board, the Office of the Permanent Secretary to the Prime Minister, the Secretariat Office of the Cabinet, and the Juridical Council. No doubt, officials of those central agencies are pleased and enthusiastic about reform. However, the final question will always remain unanswered: what do citizens get from the money and time spent by government officials and consultants? Why can we not carry out NPM reform without loans from the World Bank?

In conclusion, we have to watch whether there are signs of NPM fever in a country that carries out administrative reform. If there are symptoms of NPM fever, it is likely that the introduction of NPM reform may have been done carelessly. For example, the NPM fever may have blinded us to the questionable assumptions inherited in NPM principles and initiatives (Bowornwathana 2000b). Or, we may be victims of careless consultants and government officials who have economic self-interests and power aggrandizement in mind. Awareness of such negative possibilities strengthens the good application of foreign NPM techniques into a particular country.

For Thailand, there was clear evidence of NPM fever in the case of agencification. Enthusiasm and support for the creation of public organizations that run independently from the cumbersome Thai bureaucracy had existed for several years before the passing of the *Public Organization Act* on February 24, 1999. The conviction was that to make Thai government agencies "independent", or in Thai language *issara,* will enable them to escape from the rigidity of the single-hierarchy model of bureaucracy. *Issara* became the catch-word. In the early 1990s, during the Anand Government, university administrators and some political executives tried in vain to pass a law granting "independence" to state universities. The bill was strongly opposed by university lecturers on the grounds that they would lose their freedom of expression and work if state universities became independent. Nevertheless, the perception of independence or *issara* as the cure of bureaucratic maladies caught on. In short, *issara* is equated as goodness.

During the drafting period of the 1997 Constitution, the idea of arranging government agencies as independent organizations resurfaced with the creation of monitoring agencies or watchdogs such as the Election Commission, the Constitutional Court, the State Audit Commission, the National Counter Corruption Commission, the Administrative Court, the Parliamentary Ombudsman, the National Human Rights Commission, and the Anti-Money Laundering Office. These monitoring organizations are independent organizations: they are not under the control of political executives or any government agencies.

In the late 1990s, the temperature of the *issara* or "to be free" fever rose. Discussions about the creation of new types of organizations that are autonomous from the single-hierarchy bureaucracy intensified. Several bills establishing a new type of independent organization were written during the Chavalit and Banharn Governments. When the Chuan II Government came into power in 1998, draft bills of autonomous public organizations already existed. The bills were reconsidered by members of the Administrative Reform Commission appointed by the government. Finally in February 24, 1999 the *Public Organization Act* of B.E. 2542 was passed. Ironically, the word *issara* was deleted. The Thai official word for autonomous public organizations is *ongkarn mahachon* (translated in Thai as public organizations).

Choose NPM carefully

Choosing a particular NPM technique is not as easy as it may seem. First of all, there are many NPM techniques that we can choose from. Second, a single NPM technique may contain several alternative models. This is clearly evident in the case of agency or autonomous public organizations where western countries have their own versions of agency. Who then can confidently suggest which model Thailand should follow? Third, it is not easy to understand the nature and characteristics of a particular NPM technique. What are its basic assumptions? Why is it working in one country and not in another? What are the specific social-economic, political and cultural contexts that facilitate the successful implementation of a NPM technique in a particular country?

Nevertheless, the problem of right choice of NPM is mitigated by the existence of a global trend in administration reform. Many governments are now reforming their bureaucracies in accordance with the philosophies and principles of governance and the new public management. Because of such similarities, we do not have to start from scratch. For example, if we want to create a better customer-oriented government, we can look at examples of other western countries. We will find that there is an abundant list of NPM initiatives such as citizen's charter, performance pledges, one-stop-service, and performance measurement to choose from.

Another point is that when we borrow a NPM technique from another country, we have to understand how the borrowing took place. What NPM ideas are we borrowing? Where are they from? How did they penetrate the minds and hearts of our high public officials? What are the assumptions behind the selected NPM? What are the various decision-making stages involved in the policy adoption process? Who are the actors and members of numerous committees in the complicated policy-making process? From the beginning to the end, the policy process of deciding on a NPM technique is referred to here as the *reform diffusion* process.

I shall propose a typology for the study of the process of reform diffusion. The typology contains two basic properties or dimensions. First, the replica/hybrid dimension covers the extent that the adopted NPM technique is a replica or a hybrid of western NPM models. Sometimes, the NPM techniques borrowed are not exact replicas of western prototypes. Instead, they are hybrids. Why? It would be quite a surprise for many to learn that in making administrative reform decisions, NPM techniques are sometimes brought in as new exciting magic solutions to old chronic problems of the bureaucracy. Sadly however, the truth is that no one really understood the philosophy, principles, and contexts behind a particular selected NPM technique. Government reformers have learned about them from short, study field-trips abroad and constant suggestions by international funding agencies and hired consultants of the healing power of NPM innovations for bureaucratic maladies.

Why does hybridization occur? First, there are many versions of NPM techniques floating around. For example, at present there are many agency models such as the executive agencies of the United Kingdom, the crown entities of New Zealand, the free agencies of Denmark, the agencies of Sweden, the performance-based organizations of the United States, the special operating agencies in Canada, and the independent administrative institutions of Japan. Which one(s) should we choose? Second, hybridization can also occur simply because of the self-interests of powerful actors in the decision making. They ask the question: how could they alter the reform proposal so that they might benefit from NPM reform? Third, sometimes hybridization occurs because of sheer ignorance. No one has a firm understanding of the western NPM prototypes. No one really knows which NPM technique suits Thailand. Fourth, the decision-making process of the Thai government is very complicated involving several hierarchical committees and members, thereby allowing those involved the opportunity of twisting and altering the original NPM reform proposal several times (Campbell, Bowornwathana, Goetz and Zubek 2000).

The second dimension of the typology is the rational/political. It covers the manner in which decisions about choices of NPM techniques are made. Is it a highly political process or simply a matter of adopting ready-made western NPM models? Very often, the process of reform diffusion in a country such as Thailand is highly political and complicated, shaped by domains and interests of maximizing agencies (Bowornwathana 2001a, 2001b, 2001c, 2000a, 2000b, 1999a, 1998, 1997b, 1996a, 1996b, 1996c, 1996d, 1994). Powerful key stakeholders are political executives and central government bureaucrats, who make reform decisions that favour their own interests and power. Since there are many steps in the decision-making process of the government, stakeholders are able to alter the original reform proposal at various decision stages. Many decision makers at various stages do not have any understanding of the philosophy, methods and techniques of the NPM. They do not know that if they change a particular clause in the bill, the change may completely undermine the principles of the selected NPM tool.

Why does the phenomenon of politicization exist in the making of choices about NPM reform? First, decisions about choices of NPM innovations are usually highly political if the NPM proposals have major implications for the power and authority of high officials involved. For example, the autonomous public organization scheme may take away power of career bureaucrats and at the same time increase the authority of political executives. In such a case, each party may try to alter the NPM proposal to fit its own interests. Therefore, the final shape of the agency model chosen may be drastically changed from the original one through the highly political process of reform diffusion. Second, in some countries such as Thailand, administrative reform is high on the agenda of political executives. The Prime Minister who heads the major political party in the coalition government directly oversees administrative reform work. Signs of reform progress will help boost the image of the government.

Table 13.1 summarizes the properties of NPM fever along the two dimensions of replica/hybrid and rational/political.

From Table 13.1, four alternative models of reform diffusion with opposing features can be derived: the Type I (rational-replica), the Type II (rational-hybrid), the Type III (political-replica) and the Type IV (political-hybrid).

As mentioned earlier, Types I and II are rare cases in which the stakes involved are small. High public officials pay little attention to choosing NPM techniques. However, Type III and IV are more common cases where the stakes are usually high. Political executives and central bureaucrats will try to make sure that the final choice of NPM techniques will be

Table 13.1 Types of reform diffusion processes

		Nature of the adopted model	
		Replica	*Hybrid*
How decisions were made	Rational	I	II
	Political	III	IV

to their advantage. Reform diffusion process of Type IV is the most political, and likely to produce a twisted and compromised hybrid.

The case of agencification in Thailand, unfortunately, fits very well with Type IV category. Decisions about autonomous public organizations are highly political. As a result, the decisions are compromises reached among stakeholders, political executives and senior bureaucrats (Bowornwathana 1996a, 1996c). It also involves a complicated decision-making process among members of the Administrative Reform Commission set up by the Chuan II Government, which supported different versions of agency. Therefore, the final product of the Thai agency model is a hybrid rather than a replica because proponents of competing models bargained and compromised.[5]

According to French-trained members of the Administrative Reform Commission (ARC), the French prototype of agency is a type of organization called in French, *establissement public* (Nitthikraipot 1999, 2000; Sawaengsak 1999). These *establissement public* are autonomous organizations, which provide very specific (usually small scale) public services such as national theatres, specific research centres, national libraries, cultural centres and universities. On the other hand, members of the ARC who are familiar with Anglo-Saxon models of agency, such as executive agencies of the United Kingdom and crown entities of New Zealand, were expecting that the Thai model would follow the executive agency prototype. There are two major differences between the two competing approaches. First, the Anglo-Saxon model suggests that agencies be applied for large-scale, service-providing organizations (not just for specific small-scale services as in the case of the French model). Second, supporters of the Anglo-Saxon model see the creation of agencies as part of a major reform based on the principal-agent model, which separates policy making units from policy implementation units. All implementing units will be moved out from the ministry's hierarchy and become autonomous organizations. At the end, the size of ministries will be greatly reduced. Meanwhile, the French model of agency does not seem to incorporate the goal of downsizing the central government and macro reform of the public sector.

At the end, the French model predominated. The supporters of the French model in and outside the ARC successfully lobbied the political executives to choose their model. However, compromises were made by incorporating principles of NPM from the Anglo-Saxon school such as the hands-on professional management, explicit standards and measures of performance, and greater emphasis on output controls – into the *Public Organization Act*, B.E. 2542. The Thai model of agency is thus a hybrid between the French *establissement public* and the Anglo-Saxon's agency model. As a result, autonomous public organizations in Thailand are more similar to the French *establissement public* than to the British executive agencies. Unlike executive agencies, Thai autonomous public organizations are not part of the central government, employees of autonomous public organizations are not civil servants, and they do not deliver core government services such as tax collection. In fact, the Thai model of autonomous public organizations is similar to the British model of public organizations. The latter provide public services but are not part of the central government. A major difference between the Thai model of autonomous public organizations and the British model of public organizations is that the latter is involved in large-scale public services. Thai autonomous public organizations perform small-scale service delivery. Examples of British public organizations are: the British Council, the BBC, and the Post Office.[6]

It is worth mentioning that the French-trained public law Thais did not know what the Anglo-Saxon model of agency was. Nor did the Thais who admired the British executive agency model know much about French *establissement public*. The final product of the Thai agency model as outlined in the *Public Organization Act* B.E. 2542 is therefore a compromise between the two competing schools of thought. It is a twisted, and perhaps an illogical hybrid. The Thai autonomous public organization model is very French, with touches of the Anglo-Saxon's agency model. Making good use of the agency model in Thailand is restrained by the ignorance of French-trained Thai public lawyers about the Anglo-Saxon model who, especially with the recent institutionalization of a French administrative court system in Thailand, have become a very powerful interest group.

Watch out for reform consequences

The application of NPM reform has both intended and unintended consequences (Bowornwathana 2000b; Hughes 1998). In practice, high public officials who make reform policies do not pay much attention to the issue of reform consequences. They completely disregard uncertain outcomes of NPM reform. They forget to ask two basic questions. First, what are the specific bureaucratic problems that the selected NPM techniques are supposed to solve: inefficiency, red tape, rigidity and lack of flexibility, corruption, non-performance, insensitivity towards the public clients, lack of vision and planning, nepotism and favouritism, accountability, openness and transparency? The point is that perhaps one is not scratching where one itches. Second, what are the unintended consequences of adopting a particular NPM technique? Has the introduction of a foreign NPM innovation into the targeted country caused new problems in the bureaucracy? What are the properties of the new emerging problems: political or non-political, short term or long term, specific or nation-wide and minor or serious?

Table 13.2 illustrates the consequences of NPM reform along two dimensions: first whether the old problems which the adopted NPM

Table 13.2 Typology of reform consequences

		Old problems	
		Solved	*Unsolved*
New problems	Minimized	I	II
	Maximized	III	IV

reform are supposed to tackle are solved or not, and to what extent progress has been made; and second, whether the adopted NPM techniques have minimized or maximized new problems.

From Table 13.2, the concept of reform consequences can be categorized into four types: The Type I (old problems solved, new problems minimized), the Type II (old problems unsolved, new problems minimized), the Type III (old problems solved, new problems maximized) and the Type IV (old problems unsolved, new problems maximized). The worst case scenario is of course Type IV.

The case of autonomous public organizations in Thailand represents the Type IV scenario: old problems are unsolved, serious new problems are surfacing.

In the two years following the passing of the *Public Organization Act* B.E. 2542 in 1999, only nine small autonomous public organizations were created. They are:

- the Office of the Education Reform (created in November 25, 1999)
- the Health Promotion Office (June 30, 2000)
- the Community Organizations Development Institute (July 27, 2000)
- the Mahidol Wittayanusorn School (August 25, 2000)
- the Phan Phaew hospital (September 11, 2000)
- the International Institute for Trade and Development (May 31, 2001)
- the Education Quality Evaluation and Standardization Institution (November 3, 2000)
- the Aerospace Technology and Geographical Information Office (November 2, 2000)
- the Sirinthorn Anthropological Centre (November 15, 2000).

Moreover, other possibilities for the creation of new public organizations being discussed, are: Channel 11 TV Station of the Public Relations Department, Science Services Department, Food and Agricultural Product Radiation Center (a division in the Office of Peaceful Atomic Energy), Special Highway Project (of the Department of Highways), and six hospitals.

The question is, if the autonomous public organizations were such a good idea, how come only nine were created in approximately two years? Furthermore, the establishment of new autonomous public organizations seemed to be slowing down during the end of the Chuan II Government and the beginning of the present Thaksin Government. To understand the reasons, one needs to look at the reform consequences of agency reform in Thailand. Have the problems that agency reform aimed to solve, been solved? What are the unintended consequences of agency reform?

First of all, efficiency claims of the autonomous public organization model of Thailand are based on the principle of management flexibility or hands-on professional management of chief executives to run the public organization. Therefore, central bureaucrats from the old hierarchy should let the new autonomous public organizations go by allowing CEOs to run their organizations freely. However, in reality the central officials in Thailand still treat the autonomous public organizations like any other government organizations by retaining substantial control over the autonomous public organizations. For example, the Civil Service Commission and the Administrative Reform Commission (ARC) are keen to set up a salary ceiling for CEOs and employees of the autonomous public organizations. The Budget Bureau is devising a standardized budget system for Thai autonomous public organizations; and the ARC is working on a performance evaluation system for autonomous public organizations. These new central control mechanisms devised by central agencies are features that will hinder 'the freedom to manage' of autonomous public organizations. The fact is, the new CEOs of autonomous public organizations do not have the autonomy to run their organizations freely.

Second, the CEOs of autonomous public organizations in Thailand are also under the strict control and monitoring of board members, who are appointed by the cabinet. Each autonomous public organization has its own composition of board members. However, there are representatives of the old centralized ministry (such as permanent secretaries and representatives from central agencies) in the boards. This in turn further strengthens the power of the old centralized ministry, whose control autonomous public organizations are supposed to escape from, at least in principle, for management flexibility reasons.

Third, the fact that the cabinet appoints board members, and the responsible minister monitors the autonomous public organization, have left senior bureaucrats, who are used to exercising absolute control of all government agencies, uncomfortable. They feel they are beginning to lose control of the government machine. Their version of the desired agency model is one in which senior bureaucrats retain appointment and monitoring power of autonomous public organizations. Their dissatisfaction will worsen if employees in autonomous public organizations start receiving rewards and salary increments that far surpassed theirs. For example, if board members of an autonomous public organization decided to give a 50 per cent pay increase to the CEO, the senior bureaucrats in the ministry will be bitter. Therefore, senior bureaucrats who sit on the boards of autonomous public organizations will try to prevent huge CEOs' salary increments.

Fourth, NPM fever makes us believe that agencification will definitely transform the organization into a better service provider unit. The excitement and publicity about the successes of the Bhan Phaew Hospital is a case in point. Finally, the spell was broken with news that a villager became blind after receiving treatment from the hospital. There are now doubts about claims of service delivery improvements after organizations are transformed into autonomous public organizations. Several problems are emerging. First, the hospital CEO does not have the kind of management flexibility as professed by the principle of autonomy because board members, who are mostly high government officials, are accustomed to the old centralized ways of administration. Second, hospital staffs are negatively affected by the change of status from government officials to contract employees: they have lost their job security and their morale is worsened. Third, the hospital staffs become more entrepreneurial (business-minded) and profit-oriented, which may affect the poor who have less purchasing power.

Fifth, old problems of the Thai bureaucracy such as the spoils system and nepotism are expected to be marginal after the installation of autonomous public organizations. It was hoped that clear performance measurement and contractual agreements would minimize nepotism and favouritism. However, in practice, the new autonomous public organizations were not free of spoil practices. Internal conflicts also escalated in some autonomous public organizations. Even before the creation of an autonomous public organization, civil servants in the targeted organizations were already in conflict about the benefits and drawbacks of the agency model.

Sixth, some reformers expected that most of the implementing units in ministries would voluntarily rush in to become autonomous public organizations. The Thai bureaucracy will then be drastically transformed with a clear separation of policy and implementing units. In practice, however, such a principal-agent model has never taken off the ground in Thailand. Government officials seem to prefer the status quo with the typical departments, offices, and divisions as the preferred organization structure. There has been no serious downsizing of government structure and manpower in Thailand.

Seventh, the creation of autonomous public organizations in Thailand is leading towards a bigger government, not a smaller one. Such an expansion runs against the principle of governance, which supports the transformation of government organizations into autonomous ones.

So far, new autonomous public organizations are created by upgrading a sub-unit in an organization, or by merging two or more small units belonging to different organizations together. New autonomous public organizations can also be created out of nothing. Thus, the total number of government organizations increases with the creation of new autonomous public organizations. An example of unit-upgrading is the Princess Maha Chakri Sirindhorn Anthropology Centre (SAC), which was previously a unit of Silapakorn University, Ministry of University Affairs.

Examples of mergers are: the Geo-Informatics and Space Technology Development Agency (GISTDA) merges together the division of satellite exploration of natural resources of the National Research Council and the geo-informatics section of the Office of the Permanent Secretary of the Ministry of Science, Technology and Environment; the Education Quality Evaluation and Standardization Institute combines the budget of a national education research and evaluation project of the National Education Commission with a quality assurance project under the Ministry of University Affairs; the Community Organizations Development Institute joins the urban poor development project of the National Housing Authority with the Rural Development Fund Office of the National Social-Economic Development Board.

Out-of-nothing autonomous public organizations include the Education Reform Office, which was mandated by the new *National Education Act* of 1999, and the International Institute for Trade and Development, which was born through an agreement between the Thai Government and the United Nations.

Eighth, the highly centralized nature of autonomous public organizations boards may not be cost-effective in the near future if the number of autonomous public organizations multiplies. Since, autonomous public organizations in Thailand are very small scale units, requirements for high government officials to be appointed as board members is not practical. Imagine a permanent secretary of a ministry having to sit on the boards of one hundred autonomous public organizations. The over-centralized nature of the Thai bureaucracy meant that there were already too many eggs in one basket, why add more? Most of the existing nine autonomous public organizations already require high officials such as permanent secretaries to become board members. For example, the permanent secretary of Science, Technology and Environment Ministry sits in the board of Geo-Informatics and Space Technology Development Agency; the permanent secretary of the Ministry of Education, Religion and Culture is a board member of the Education Quality Evaluation and Standardization Institute, the Health Promotion Office, and also board chair of the International Institute for Trade and Development; the permanent secretary of the Ministry of Public Health is a board member of the Health Promotion Office.

Conclusion

To sum up this chapter, a central hypothesis emerges from discussions of the three precautions in putting NPM to good use. The most dangerous situation which countries carrying out administrative reform must avoid or be very careful of is when there is clear evidence of NPM fever among key reform players; when the reform diffusion process tends to be highly political, and thus produces inconsistent, unsystematic, and irrational NPM hybrids; and when the selected NPM principle or technique is likely to bring in new problems while leaving the old problems unsolved or worsened. On the contrary, the ideal situation is when administrative reform diffusion process is free from NPM fever, non-political, and negative unintended consequences are kept to a minimal.

Thailand's efforts to create autonomous public organizations represent the worst case scenario: strong agency fever, an agency model which is a highly political hybrid, and intended reform consequences unsolved, with new alarming unintended consequences emerging. One must remember that the author is not saying that techniques of the NPM are in themselves faulty. However, the point here is that what matters most is how these NPM reform techniques are diffused in a country such as Thailand – a subject to which all reform students must pay serious attention. Furthermore, the author is not saying that autonomous public organizations are completely useless. In fact, the creation of a new type of organization, such as autonomous public organizations in Thailand, adds a new alternative for organizing the Thai government beyond the existing organization designs of ministerial departments and state enterprises. Design flexibility is thus enhanced. For example, recent proposals by the Thaksin Government to reform the structure of Thai ministries include the creation of several autonomous public organizations under the new ministries.

New public management in Thailand has not yet been put to good use, at least in the case of autonomous public organizations. The argument of this chapter is that in adopting NPM reform we must take three precautions. First, beware of NPM fever. Second, choose a particular NPM technique carefully and be sensitive to the reform diffusion process. Third, watch out for the intended and unintended consequences of NPM. Perhaps other countries that are carrying out administrative reform can gain insights from the Thai experience with NPM and agencification as described in this chapter.

Notes

1 As several leading scholars have pointed out, new public management (NPM) refers to the introduction of private sector management methods to the public sector with doctrines such as hands-on professional management, explicit standards and measures of performance, and closeness to the customer (Hood 1991; Rhodes 1996; Pollit and Bouckaert 2000).

2 In Thailand, the introduction of NPM is a very recent phenomenon of the late 1990s. In fact, the embracing of western NPM ideas began during the Chuan II Government (1997–2000). Several factors contributed to the adoption of NPM. First, there is an urgent need for Thailand to reform its public sector and bureaucracy. The new 1997 Constitution speeded up the democratization process of Thailand by requiring government leaders to reform the bureaucracy. The Asian economic crisis of 1997 also contributed to the need for Thailand to have a more efficient but smaller government. Second, Thailand has for so long opened the door to globalization, which in turn, brought in western ideas and culture. Success reform stories of western countries with NPM also attracted Thai reformers. Third, officials from international funding agencies such as the World Bank, the Asian Development Bank, the International Monetary Fund, and the UNDP also play a pivotal role in pushing for governance and NPM reforms (World Bank 1994, 1997; Asian Development Bank 1999; UNDP 1995, 1998). Fourth, political executives and high government officials are committed to fast reform results. At present, there are several NPM techniques adopted by the Thai government. They are, for example, autonomous public organizations, performance measurement, quality services and efficiency, senior executive services, and contractual relations.

3 The author got the idea of the word "fever" to describe new public management development in Thailand from a draft paper written by Christopher Pollitt, Karen Bathgate, Janice Caulfield, Amanda Smullen and Colin Talbot entitled "Agency Fever: Analysis of International Policy Fashion". (Christopher Pollitt, Karen Bathgate, Janice Caulfield, Amanda Smullen and Colin Talbot 2001).

4 The word agencification has been used by scholars to refer to the process of creating agency or autonomous public organizations in Western countries in accordance with the principal-agent model. See writings by Halligan (1997), and Hogwood, Judge and McVicar (2000).

5 Information used to analyse the decision-making process during the Chuan II Administration on the creation of autonomous public organizations law is based on the author's personal experience as member of the Chuan II Administrative Reform Commission.

6 This point was brought to the attention of the author by international consultants working in Bangkok.

Bibliography

Asian Development Bank (1999) *Governance in Thailand: Challenges, Issues, and Prospects*, Manila: Programs Department (West), Division III and Strategy and Policy Office, Asian Development Bank, April.

Asian Development Bank (1998) *Memorandum of Understanding Between the Fiscal Policy Office of the Ministry of Finance of the Kingdom of Thailand and an Appraisal Mission of the Asian Development Bank on the Proposed Social Sector Program Loan*, January 16.

Bowornwathana, B. (2001a) "The Thai model of rewards for high public office", Paper presented at the Conference on "Rewards at the Top" organized by the Department of Public and Social Administration, City University of Hong Kong, March 24–25. A research project coordinated by G.B. Peters and C. Hood.

Bowornwathana, B. (2001b) "Thailand: bureaucracy under coalition governments", in Burns, J.P. and Bowornwathana, B. (eds) *Civil Service Systems in Asia*, Cheltenham, United Kingdom: Edward Elgar.

Bowornwathana, B. (2001c) "The politics of governance reform in Thailand", in

Farazmand, A. (ed.) *Handbook of Comparative and Development Public Administration*, 2nd edn, New York: Marcel Dekker, pp. 421–43.

Bowornwathana, B. (2000a) "Thailand in 1999: a royal jubilee, economic recovery, and political reform", *Asian Survey* XL, 1 (January/February), 87–98.

Bowornwathana, B. (2000b) "Governance reform in Thailand: questionable assumptions, uncertain outcomes", *Governance: an International Journal of Policy and Administration* 13, 3, 393–408.

Bowornwathana, B. (2000c) *Administrative Reform Abroad: The United States, The United Kingdom, France, New Zealand, Japan, and Sweden*, Research report submitted to the Office of the Administrative Reform Commission, The Royal Thai Government (in Thai).

Bowornwathana, B. (1999a) "Administrative reform and the politician-bureaucrat perspective: vision, processes, and support for reform", in Wong, H.-K. and Chan, H.S. (eds) *Handbook of Comparative Public Administration in the Asia-Pacific Basin*, New York: Marcel Dekker, pp. 69–78.

Bowornwathana, B. (1999b) "Fiscal reform of the Bangkok metropolitan administration: from bureaucracy to governance", in Edralin, J.S. and Mani, D. (eds) *Financing Metropolitan Development: Public-Private Sector Roles*, Research Report Series No. 35. Nagoya, Japan: United Nations Centre for Regional Development, pp. 67–92.

Bowornwathana, B. (1998) "Bangkok metropolitan administration into the twenty-first century: the practice of good local governance", in Edralin, J.S. (ed.) *Metropolitan Governance and Planning in Transition: Asia-Pacific Cases*, Research Report Series No. 31. Nagoya, Japan: United Nations Centre for Regional Development, pp. 147–64.

Bowornwathana, B. (1997a) "Transforming bureaucracies for the 21st century: the new democratic governance paradigm", *Public Administration Quarterly* 21, 3 (Fall), 294–308.

Bowornwathana, B. (1997b) "The governance of the Bangkok metropolitan: the old system, the new city, and future governance", in Edralin, J.S. (ed.) *Local Governance and Local Economic Development: a New Role of Asian Cities*, Research Report Series No. 2, Nagoya, Japan: United Nations Centre for Regional Development, pp. 87–114.

Bowornwathana, B. (1996a) "Thailand: the politics of reform of the secretariat of the prime minister", *Australian Journal of Public Administration* 55, 4 (December), 55–63.

Bowornwathana, B. (1996b) "Democratic reform visions and the reinvention of Thai Public officials", *Asian Review of Public Administration* 8, 1 (January–June), 40–9.

Bowornwathana, B. (1996c) "The phenomenon of new ministries and the politician–bureaucrat perspective", *Asian Review of Public Administration* 8, 2 (July–December), 23–32.

Bowornwathana, B. (1996d) "Political realities of local government reform in Thailand", in Kurosawa, S., Fujiwara, T. and Reforma, M. (eds) *New Trends in Public Administration for the Asia-Pacific Region: Decentralization*, Tokyo: Local Autonomy College, Ministry of Home Affairs.

Bowornwathana, B. (1995) "Responses of public administration system of Thailand to global challenges", in Salleh, S.H. and Carino, L.V. (eds) *Globalisation and the Asian Public Sector*, Kuala Lumpur: The Asian and Pacific Development Center, pp. 356–430.

Bowornwathana, B. (1994) "Administrative reform and regime shifts: reflections on the Thai polity", *Asian Journal of Public Administration*, 16, 2 (December), 152–64.

Burns, J.P. and Bowornwathana, B. (2001) "Asian civil service systems in comparative perspective", in Burns, J.P. and Bowornwathana, B. (eds) *Civil Service Systems in Asia*, Cheltenham, United Kingdom: Edward Elgar, pp. 1–23.

Campbell, C., Bowornwathana, B., Goetz, K.H. and Zubek, R. (2000) "Failure of ministerial responsibility and its consequences for policy competence", Draft paper presented at the first Dusseldorf Seminar on the Center of Government Capacity, Ministerial Reliability and Responsiveness. Jointly sponsored by the University of Dusseldorf, University of Sienna and the World Bank, Dusseldorf, Germany, November 23–26.

Halligan, J. (1997) "Agencification: a review of the models, lessons and issues", Paper prepared for the Institute of Public Administration and Australia Annual Conference Academic and Practioners Day, "Evaluating Public Sector Reform Nationally and Internationally", Canberra, November.

Hogwood, B.W., Judge, D. and McVicar, M. (2000) "Agencies and Accountability", in Rhodes, R.A.W. (ed.) *Transforming British Government, Vol. 1: Changing Institutions*, London: Macmillan Press.

Hood, C. (1998) *The Art of the State: Culture, Rhetoric, and Public Management*, Oxford: Clarendon Press.

Hood, C. (1991) "A public management for all seasons?", *Public Administration* 69, 1, 3–19.

Hughes, O.E. (1998) *Public Management and Administration: An Introduction*, 2nd edn, London: Macmillan Press.

Neher, C.D. and Bowornwathana, B. (1987) "Thai and western studies of politics in Thailand", *Asian Thought and Society*, March.

Nithikraipot, S. (1999) "Thai universities as autonomous public organizations: the case of technology Suranari University", in *Office of the Administrative Reform Commission, Public Organizations: A New Dimension of the Public Sector*, Bangkok: Office of the Administrative Reform Commission (in Thai).

Nithikraipot, S. (2000) *The Possibility of, and Approaches to, the Public Organization Act*, Bangkok: Office of the Administrative Reform Commission (in Thai).

Osborne, D. and Gaebler, T. (1992) *Reinventing Government: How the Entrepreneurial Spirit is Transforming the Public Sector*, Reading, MA: Adison Wesley.

Peters, B.G. and Pierre, J. (2000) "Is there a governance theory?", Paper presented at the International Political Science Association's Conference, Quebec City, Canada, August 1–5. RC 17, Panel 1 "Globalization and the State".

Peters, B.G. (1998) "What works? The antiphons of administrative reform", in Peters, B.G. and Savoie, D. (eds) *Taking Stock: Assessing Public Sector Reform*, Montreal and Kingston: McGill-Queen's University Press and Canadian Centre for Management Development.

Polidano, C, and Hume, D. (1999) "Public management reform in developing countries: issues and outcomes", *Public Management* 1, 1, 121–32.

Pollitt, C., Bathgate, K., Caulfield, J., Smullen, A. and Talbot, C. (2001) "Agency fever? Analysis of international policy fashion", *Journal of Comparative Policy Analysis: Research and Practice* 3, 3, 271–90.

Pollitt, C. and Bouckaert, G. (2000) *Public Management Reform: A Comparative Analysis*, Oxford: Oxford University Press.

Pollitt, C. (2000) "Is the emperor in his underwear? An analysis of the impacts of public management reform", *Public Management* 2, 2, 181–99.

Rhodes, R.A.W. (1996) "The new governance: governing without government", *Political Studies* 44, 4 (September), 652–67.

Royal Thai Government Gazette (1999a) Public Organizations Act of 1999 (in Thai).

Royal Thai Government Gazette (1999b) The Office of Education Reform Decree of 1999 (in Thai).

Royal Thai Government Gazette (2000a) The Health Promotion Office Decree of 2000 (in Thai).

Royal Thai Government Gazette (2000b) The Community Organization Development Institute of 2000 (in Thai).

Royal Thai Government Gazette (2000c) The Mahidol Wittayanusorn School Decree of 2000 (in Thai).

Royal Thai Government Gazette (2000d) The Bhan Phaew Hospital Decree of 2000 (in Thai).

Royal Thai Government Gazette (2000e) The Geo-Informatics and Space Technology Development Agency Decree of 2000 (in Thai).

Royal Thai Government Gazette (2000f) The Education Quality Evaluation and Standardization Institute Decree of 2000 (in Thai).

Royal Thai Government Gazette (2000g) The Sirinthorn Anthropological Center Decree of 2000 (in Thai).

Royal Thai Government Gazette (2001) The International Institute for Trade and Development Decree of 2001 (in Thai).

Sawaengsak, C. (1999) *Public Organizations*, Bangkok: Nititham (in Thai).

Scott, G. (2000) "Autonomous public organizations in Thailand", February 10.

Turner, M. (2001) "Choosing items from the menu: new public management in Southeast Asia", Paper presented at the fifth International Research Symposium on Public Management, University of Barcelona, Spain, 9–11 April.

UNDP (1995) *Public Sector Management, Governance, and Sustainable Human Development*, New York: United Nations Development Program.

UNDP (1998) *Public Sector Management Reform in Asia and the Pacific: Selected Experiences from Seven Countries*, New York: Regional Governance Program for Asia-Pacific, United National Development Program, October.

World Bank (1994) *Governance: the World Bank Experience*, Washington: World Bank.

World Bank (1997) *World Development Report, 1997: The State in a Changing World*, Oxford: Oxford University Press.

World Bank (1999) *Thailand: Public Sector Reform Program Concept Paper*, Washington: World Bank.

14 The design, performance, and sustainability of semi-autonomous revenue authorities in Africa and Latin America

Robert R. Taliercio Jr

Introduction[1]

During the past decade, or so, diverse countries have introduced radical reforms in the way their fiscal bureaucracies conduct one of the most pressing national tasks: the collection of taxes (Jenkins 1994; Taliercio 2000). The reform, an early version of which originated in the developing world in Bolivia and Ghana in the late 1980s, has now been adopted by more than fifteen countries, including Malaysia, New Zealand, Singapore, Ghana, Kenya, Malawi, Rwanda, South Africa, Tanzania, Uganda, Zambia, Bolivia, Guatemala, Guyana, Mexico, Peru, and Venezuela. More precisely, there is a pattern in each of these countries in that the traditional line departments (income tax, value-added tax, and sometimes customs) are being separated from the ministry of finance (MOF) and granted the legal status of semi-autonomous authorities. These semi-autonomous revenue authorities (ARAs) are designed with a number of autonomy-enhancing features, including self-financing mechanisms, boards of directors with high ranking public and private sector representatives, and *sui generis* personnel systems.

The success of the first wave of reforms, in which the ARA model, bolstered by good tax policy reforms, boosted revenues significantly and improved service delivery, has encouraged imitation. The worldwide trend towards semi-autonomous tax authorities has picked up speed recently, as more and more countries adopt this organizational design. In addition, international financial institutions (IFIs) have proposed on an ad hoc basis, though not yet as a matter of formal policy, the adoption of the ARA reform. The future of more autonomous tax administration would appear to be bright.

Moreover, the ARA reform has coincided with the vogue of autonomization of executive agencies in the OECD and other developed countries. Interestingly, the march towards autonomization in the sphere of fiscal administration (not to mention the phenomenon of autonomization in the sphere of monetary policy through independent central banks) in developing countries began a few years before the launch of executive agencies in Europe and the US, though ideas about NPM-type reform were certainly percolating wide and far by the mid-1980s. It does not seem to be the case, however, that the ARA wave of reform was directly inspired by the NPM agenda. To a large extent, I would argue, the ARA model has developed independently of this New Public Management (NPM) vogue (possible explanations are explored in the next section).

There are three central questions which the chapter seeks to tackle: first, what has motivated the wave of ARA reforms in Africa, Asia, and Latin America over the past decade? If the basic assumption has been that ARAs will improve performance, what is the logic that underpins the argument? The chapter will consider the theoretical case for administrative autonomy in the implementation of fiscal policy by marshalling an argument that credibility is central to a well-functioning tax system. In brief, politicians have become motivated to make credible commitments to taxpayers that tax administration will be fairer, more effective, and more competently managed in order to increase revenue collections.

Second, is there a connection between autonomy and performance? That is, have ARAs actually improved performance, and, if so, along what administrative dimensions? Focusing on revenue collection, compliance with the tax code, and taxpayer services, and using quantitative indicators when possible, the chapter will argue that autonomy is associated with higher levels of performance, with the appropriate caveats about the challenge of measuring administrative performance. The chapter also makes the case that higher levels of autonomy are associated with higher levels of performance.

Third, how sustainable are these reforms? At the same time, however, that new ARAs sprout up, their predecessors are coming undone. Semi-autonomous revenue authorities have proved to be less sustainable than their founders intended. In case after case, challenges to the newly minted revenue authorities have succeeded in undermining, and in some cases eliminating, their autonomy. Thus, the ARA model presents something of a puzzle: why is this administrative reform, which is both highly regarded and widely imitated, struggling to survive? The chapter will examine the prospects for sustainability of the existing model of ARA reform, focusing on Latin America and Africa.

The chapter examines a subset of ARAs from both Africa and Asia. Cases were selected based on the importance of the country's economy to the region (Mexico, Venezuela, Kenya, South Africa) as well as the extent and length of reform (Peru, Uganda). Table 14.1 lists the cases and summarizes some basic information about each of them.

Rationale for reform: credibility and tax administration

One major difference between the ARA reforms and other executive agency-type reforms is that the ARA reform has occurred in one sphere

Table 14.1 Selected revenue authorities in Africa and Latin America

	Foundation	Form	Character	Creation	Type of autonomy
Kenya	Kenya Revenue Authority (KRA)	KRA Act (1995)	Corporate body with perpetual succession	Separate legal character	Parliamentary Act	Unspecified
South Africa	South African Revenue Service (SARS)	SARS Act (1997)	Revenue service outside the public service but part of the public administration	Separate legal character	Parliamentary Act	Administrative
Uganda	Uganda Revenue Authority (URA)	URA Act (1991)	Corporate body with perpetual succession	Separate legal character	Parliamentary Act	Unspecified
Mexico	Tax Administration Service (SAT)	SAT Law (1995)	Deconcentrated service	No separate legal character	Legislative Law	Management, budgetary and technical
Venezuela	National Integrated Tax Administration and Customs Service (SENIAT)	SENIAT Decree (1994)	Autonomous service	No separate legal character	Presidential Decree	Functional and financial with its own human resource system
Peru	National Tax Administration Superintendency (SUNAT)	SUNAT Law (1988)	Decentralized Superintendency	Separate legal character	Legislative Law	Functional, economic, technical, financial and administrative

(the fiscal) of the public sector but in many countries, while the executive agency reform has been implemented across the entire public sector but in a small number of countries. The reason for the use of autonomy as a key feature of organizational design in tax administration, I would argue, is that autonomy is meant to respond to a particular problem that exists in the fiscal sphere of public administration: credibility. That is, the ARA reform represents an attempt by politicians to create a credible commitment to taxpayers that tax administration will be more competent, effective, and fair. The factor that enables politicians to make the commitment credible is the level of autonomy of the revenue authority.

The credibility problem in the context of tax administration has not yet been fully appreciated by the literature on credible commitment. Why would politicians need to make a credible commitment to taxpayers? At the theoretical level the credibility problem has to do with time-consistency. Some types of policies are dynamically inconsistent in that those actors affected by the policies realize that politicians have future incentives to deviate from previously announced intentions (Kydland and Prescott 1977; Persson and Tabellini 1994; Root 1989; Weingast 1995; Keefer and Stasavage 2001). Believing that politicians will not make good on their announced intentions in the future, other actors have incentives to adjust their behaviour in ways that make politicians (and possibly themselves) worse off. The time-consistency problem has been identified in many different contexts, including present day macroeconomic policy and royal fiscal policy in France and England (Root 1989, for example).

Assume a two period game with two players: the taxpayer and the politician. In period t the taxpayer sets his/her compliance rate based on his assessment of the current effectiveness, efficiency, and fairness of the tax administration. For example, in making tax payments in period t, the taxpayer makes a subjective assessment of the likelihood of being audited in period $t+1$, and sets his/her compliance rate accordingly. If the taxpayer believes real reform is forthcoming, he/she will increase his/her compliance for fear of being audited. The politician, who would like to maximize the taxpayer's compliance rate, has an interest in reforming the tax bureau. Yet, making such improvements are costly, as they require investments in personnel and equipment. Perhaps more importantly, the politician would incur political costs, as he/she would have to reduce patronage and give up discretionary use of the tax bureau.

If the politician announces in period t that in period $t+1$ the tax agency will be more effective, efficient, and fair, he/she is making a commitment that the taxpayer must assess. If the politician's announcement is credible, the taxpayer will increase his compliance rate in period t and beyond. Once period $t+1$ arrives, however, the politician has different incentives. Given that the taxpayer already increased his compliance, and thus paid more taxes, it is not optimal for the politician to invest in a better tax bureau. Therefore, the politician's announcement is dynamically inconsistent; it is an incredible commitment. Realizing this, the taxpayer has no incentives to increase his/her compliance.

The dynamics of the interaction are such that no matter what the taxpayer does, the politician's dominant strategy is not to "invest" in reform. The taxpayer, realizing that it is always better for the politician to maintain the status quo, is better off by not complying. The problem is further compounded by the relatively shorter time horizon of the politician vis-à-vis the taxpayer. Thus, the equilibrium outcome is neither reform nor compliance.

To solve the time consistency problem, which is essentially one of too much discretion, politicians need to employ a "commitment technology" to convince taxpayers to increase their compliance (Persson and Tabellini 1994). The literature suggests three such technologies: the formation of corporate bodies, the delegation of authority to third parties, and reputation. All three of these purported solutions address the same problem and are not mutually exclusive in practice. In fact, all three may be present in some institutional arrangements.

The corporate bodies solution (Bates 1996; Root 1989) entails creating institutions of "joint decision making", thereby involving stakeholders in the policy making process. Kathryn Firmin-Sellers (1995) argued that the opening of the traditional ruling council to non-chiefs in colonial Ghana represented the creation of a corporate body to solve the credible commitment problem. Weingast (1995) made a similar argument about the strengthening of Parliament in fiscal matters in seventeenth century England. The corporate bodies solution may also be found in cases of ARA reform. In Zambia, for example, the board of directors of the ARA has several members nominated by peak private sector organizations, including the association of chambers of commerce and industry, the bankers' association, the institute of certified accountants, and the law association. Empowering stakeholders to participate in the decision-making process is one way to solve the time consistency problem.

The other possible solution is delegation, which consists of transferring power to third parties who have credible incentives to act in the way that politicians would like to act. Power is thus delegated to bureaucrats or technocrats in order to convince other actors about future policy choices and administrative decisions. For example, the Kenya Revenue Authority (KRA) helped to solve politicians' problems of having to dole out political favours through costly tax exemptions by delegating authority to professional tax bureaucrats in the KRA. Solicitors of political favours would be directed by the minister of finance to the KRA, which would then turn down their exemption requests. On such occasions the minister was reported to have said to his would-be beneficiaries: "My hands are tied."[2]

However, the decision to delegate or create corporate decision-making bodies does not necessarily solve the problem for all time. For solutions to the dynamic inconsistency problem to be credible, and sustainable in the long run, they must be self-enforcing (Weingast 1995; Keefer and Stasavage 2000). Politicians must have continued incentives to support reform, such as higher benefits from support and/or higher costs from withdrawal of support (Bates 1996). Bates argues that these archetypal solutions may create constituencies to maintain the reforms and monitor their implementation, thus increasing the costs to politicians of reneging on the reform.

Note that these archetypal solutions are institutional, that is, they change the rules at a certain point in time. Non-institutional reforms, such as increasing the agency's budget or conducting a meritocratic recruitment drive, would be easily subject to political reversals and would therefore not be credible. Such reforms, though observable by taxpayers, do not establish the institutional context necessary to convince taxpayers to change their behaviour. It is important to recall, however, that even the credibility of institutional reforms such as ARAs or independent central banks may wax and wane over time. Given that these types of agencies are always subject, ultimately, to executive control, changing incentives and political conditions could undermine in the future what was a credible solution in the past. The simple model presented in this section foreshadows problems of long-term sustainability of the ARA reform by pointing out that politicians' incentives may change, in the absence of countervailing forces, when compliance and revenues have increased.

Viewed from this theoretical perspective, I argue that the basic ARA reform is intended to make a credible commitment to taxpayers by delegating power to bureaucrats charged with making the tax agency more competent, effective, and fair. Additionally, in some cases in which the reform establishes a board of directors with private sector participation, the reform creates a "corporate body" in order to share decision-making power with taxpayers. The question then becomes: how are semi-autonomous revenue authorities designed so as to create a credible commitment? The next section takes up the topic of ARA organizational design.

Revenue authority design

Semi-autonomous revenue authorities are defined as tax administrations that have greater than typical autonomy along several organizational design dimensions, including: legal character, corporate governance, financing and budgeting, personnel policy, procurement policy, and accountability relationships. The following section focuses on the most important of these design features, namely, legal character, corporate governance, financing, personnel, and accountability.[3]

Legal foundations

National governments have different legal forms they can use to create more or less autonomous agencies, according to their constitution and legal tradition. The corporate status of an ARA depends fundamentally on whether or not it has its own separate legal character. ARAs generally have their own separate corporate status, with the exception of SENIAT and the SAT. ARAs without their own corporate character have proven to be inherently less autonomous.

The legal framework of the ARA also defines its place in the hierarchy of public administration law. In some cases, ARAs are granted blanket exemptions from public administration law pertaining to staff benefits and procurement, among other things. In the case of Kenya, the KRA is exempt from the State Corporations Act, which means that the tax agency has autonomy on a whole series of administrative issues. In the case of Uganda, however, the URA is not exempt from government-wide regulations.

Corporate governance

ARAs are characterized by two general governance models: a chief executive officer (CEO) model, used only in Latin America, and a board of directors model, used mostly in Africa. There are fewer variations between CEO-based models than board-based models. The main organizational design difference observed within CEO-based models is the appointment of the CEO. Venezuela's SENIAT is managed by a superintendent, who is appointed and removed by the minister of finance. SUNAT's superintendent, on the other hand, is named and removed by the president of the republic. The appointment of the superintendent by the president is a mechanism that has the potential to increase ARA autonomy.

The design of the board of directors is potentially one of the most important organizational features of the ARA. There are four key design issues: (1) the role of the president and minister of finance with respect to board appointments and dismissals, (2) the use of fixed appointments, both ex officio and officio, (3) the role of private sector representatives, and (4) the nature of tenure on the board.

ARAs have approached the issue of board composition quite differently. Some, like Kenya and Mexico, allow the minister a free hand in naming and removing appointees. Others, like Uganda, specify board positions to be filled by individuals in certain positions (for example, a representative from the chambers of commerce and industry, the institute of certified accountants, etc.). Almost all ARAs, however, use some fixed positions to determine board composition, though in many cases these positions are reserved for ex officio government officials.

The use of non-ex officio fixed positions has had two effects in several of the cases. First, it has limited the influence of the minister of finance on the board for the simple reason that he/she is not empowered to appoint the entire board. Second, it has institutionalized the influence of certain interest groups, whether the civil service, government ministries, professional associations, or economic groups. It establishes a centre of power on the board that is more autonomous from the ministry of finance in particular and the government in general. The potential benefits of establishing fixed positions with voting rights are greater autonomy for the ARA and the guarantee that interests affected by the tax agency will have input into how the agency is managed.

The second potential benefit accrues largely to the tax agency's main constituents: taxpayers. In some cases, taxpayer representatives have provided invaluable information to the agency on compliance and corruption costs faced by taxpayers. Taxpayer representatives have also identified critical bottlenecks and problems in tax administration, and have suggested solutions, based on their private sector experience. Private sector representatives on the board have also helped free the tax agency from undue political influences. In some cases, private sector board members have opposed political interference.[4]

The third issue is the nature of tenure on the board. In most countries, tenure is loosely specified. Provisions for appointment and dismissal grant the minister of finance a great deal of discretion. If board members do not have some security of tenure, however, their ability to provide independent guidance might be compromised. In fact, there have been cases in which board members have been fired en masse over disagreements with the government. Security of tenure is thus an indispensable element of board autonomy.

Financing mechanisms and budget formulation

The design of funding mechanisms for ARAs centres on two key issues: (1) whether funding is automatically earmarked for the authority; and (2) whether funds are directly retained. The first issue concerns the percentage-based funding mechanism, in which some fixed or variable percentage of funds is automatically earmarked for the authority. In the simplest case, exemplified by Peru, a fixed 2 per cent of actual collections is earmarked for the authority (according to the SUNAT law). A variant on this basic case employs a dual percentage-based mechanism, in which the base budget is equal to a fixed percentage of revenues and an additional performance-based component is added if collections exceed the estimated target. This variant is exemplified by the Kenyan case, in which the base budget is equal to 1.5 per cent of revenues and the performance component is calculated as 3 per cent of the difference between actual and estimated collections (subject to a total maximum of 2 per cent).

A criticism of any percentage-based funding mechanism is that it subjects the ARA to forces beyond its control, whether positive or negative. Given that tax agency efforts only determine a limited share of revenues collected, the agency could experience shortfalls or windfalls through no fault or merit of its own.

On the other hand, the percentage-based funding mechanism has an additional benefit for the ARA in countries with malfunctioning public expenditure management (PEM) systems: it allows for greater stability in agency funding. Based on its projected collections, the ARA would know exactly how much it would receive. The only uncertainty in its budget would be fluctuations in revenues. An important source of fluctuations – periodic resource allocation by the treasury – would cease to be a problem. The percentage-based funding mechanism would help insulate the ARA from poor PEM. This in turn would help to stabilize revenue collections, which would feed back greater stability into the PEM cycle.

In practice, the financing mechanism has depended greatly on the mechanism providing for the transfer of funds; most ARAs have not consistently received the funds due them. SUNAT is the only ARA in which funds are directly transferred to agency accounts; there is no intermediation by the ministry of finance. This mechanism makes it more probable that SUNAT receives the funds legally assigned. In the case of SENIAT, in which the president determines the precise percentage of financing and the minister of finance transfers the funds, the ARA has never received the level of funding required by law. In Kenya, interestingly, the KRA has not received its full statutory income from the treasury on direct and indirect taxes, though it has received its share of the road maintenance levy, which it retains directly. Clearly, having these mechanisms on the books is no guarantee that they will work in practice.

Personnel systems

The main personnel issue is the extent of the ARA's autonomy to craft a personnel system independent of the civil service. In some cases, namely Kenya and Peru, the ARA is virtually independent of the civil service, at which point the main constraint to reform becomes the agency's budget. In other cases, the authority's personnel system must comply with certain civil service regulations. As discussed above, the goal of an autonomous personnel system is to allow the agency the flexibility necessary to attract and retain the number and quality of professionals necessary to improve performance. The cases suggest that a good deal of autonomy from the civil service is necessary to make this a reality.

SUNAT has a great deal of control over its personnel system as compared with the other ARAs in Latin America. The president granted SUNAT the authority (by issuing a separate decree based on a legislative enabling law) to adopt a non-public sector personnel regime. SUNAT has the authority to appoint and remove its employees without the need to consult with any other public sector entity. SUNAT also has the ability to set its own salary structure, the limitations being its budget and, in some cases, government-wide salary caps.

In the case of the KRA, for example, the CG is authorized to appoint all staff members, except commissioners. The board's staff committee, however, approves all hiring decisions for senior management positions. The staff committee must also approve all disciplinary actions for management positions, based on the KRA's code of conduct, which is the principal instrument guiding staff behaviour and spelling out the procedures for handling disciplinary matters. The terms and conditions of employment, including benefits and salary structures, are also determined by the board's staff committee.

Accountability mechanisms

Formal accountability mechanisms vary significantly from case to case, perhaps because they are part of the system of corporate governance, around which there has been much debate and ambiguity. What is non-controversial is the need to balance autonomy with effective accountability. How exactly that is done, however, is open for discussion, as the cases show. Several of the cases, notably Kenya, offer potential models for other countries to emulate.

Accountability relationships vary considerably in Latin America. Mexico's SAT is the only ARA in Latin America that has a direct accountability link to the legislature. Every trimester the SAT is required to present a report to congress on its performance. In addition, during the first six weeks of the year the president of the SAT is required to send a report (approved by the board) to congress on the programmes to be implemented, the budget, and the previous year's collections. SUNAT has few formal reporting relationships with other government entities, though it falls within the sector of the ministry of finance. SUNAT must report on its budget to the ministry, which also undertakes periodic evaluations of SUNAT.

The Kenyan case is characterized by several overlapping accountability mechanisms. The first line of defence is the traditional internal audit unit, which is charged with performing quarterly audits and presenting the results to the CG. The second accountability link is between the CG and the board. The CG is required to present the quarterly audits to the board, as well as to the Controller and Auditor General (CAG), who forms the third link. In addition, the CAG is charged with auditing the annual accounts of the ARA. The fourth layer of accountability is between the CG and the MOF. The CG must present the authority's financial statements, performance indicators, and annual report both to the board and the MOF. The minister establishes a fifth accountability link with the National Assembly by furnishing it with copies of the KRA's annual report and the CAG's report. Lastly, the KRA must publish its audited accounts in the public record and make them available to the public.

Administrative performance

The ARAs show a mixed performance record, due principally to the problems of sustainability associated with many of the cases examined here
(discussed in the next section). The best performers across a range of
indicators have been Peru, Kenya, and South Africa, though others have
had more limited success in some areas. The preliminary finding of this
research is that performance improved most when autonomy was relatively high and stable (Peru, Kenya, and South Africa). Performance
improved least where autonomy was low (Mexico) and performance
varied, initially improving then levelling off or falling, in cases in which
autonomy was unsustainable (Venezuela and Uganda).

At the same time, a word of caution is in order. It is difficult to measure
with precision the marginal impact of tax administration reform on outcomes like revenue and debt collection, as many exogenous factors exert
causal influence on these and other related outcomes. From economic
growth to the price of oil, to changes in the tax code, to the effectiveness
of the judiciary and police forces, tax administration-related outcomes are
affected by a host of causal factors. Moreover, even if performance
improved, the counterfactual (of no reform or other types of reform)
should be taken into account. Thus, the goal of this section is modest: to
shed some light on the performance of ARAs in the areas of revenue collection, taxpayer registration and audit, and taxpayer services, qualifying
to the extent possible the impact of exogenous factors and counterfactual
considerations.[5]

Interestingly, most ARAs have had success in the most basic of their
tasks: raising revenues. SUNAT increased total tax revenues (excluding
customs revenues) from 8.4 per cent of GDP in 1991 to 12.3 per cent in
1998, during which time tax policy reforms included the rationalization of
the tax structure and the reduction of many tax rates. SENIAT increased
total revenues (excluding customs) from 5.9 per cent of GDP in 1994 to
8.5 per cent in 1998, though the increase is due in part to the introduction of a new sales tax. The URA had one of the most spectacular
increases in revenues (including customs) as a percentage of GDP: from
7.0 per cent in 1991 to 11.9 per cent in 1999. In Kenya total revenues
(including customs) declined from 27 per cent of GDP in 1994 to 21 per
cent in 1999, though the decrease was due largely to significant tax policy
reforms, including the significant reduction of tax rates across the board
(the reduction of the top marginal income tax rate from 40 per cent to 30
per cent, the top import tariff rate from 45 per cent to 25 per cent, and
the standard VAT rate from 28 per cent to 15 per cent). Thus the accomplishment of the KRA was to maintain revenues by increasing administrative efficiency in the context of drastically reduced tax rates. In South
Africa the SARS also helped increase revenues by over 57 per cent from
1995 to 1999 (in nominal terms). Mexico's SAT, which benefited from the

least autonomy, increased revenues only marginally.[6] What the data show is that the introduction of ARAs is associated in most cases with either significant increases in revenue collections, or maintenance of collections in the face of significant tax rate reductions.

On another measure related to collection performance, VAT productivity, which is defined as the percentage share of GDP generated by VAT divided by the VAT rate, shows an association between level of autonomy and performance: Peru is the most productive (0.32) of the Latin American cases, followed by Mexico (0.26).

Another important measure of performance is the ability of the tax agency to keep an up-to-date registry of taxpayers and ensure that they are submitting their tax declarations and making their tax payments according to schedule. The cases show that Peru and South Africa have done well here, and that Kenya has made some strides in the area of taxpayer registration. In Peru, the number of active registered taxpayers increased from 895,000 in 1993 to 1,766,000 in 1999. Moreover, of the large and medium taxpayers, 100 per cent of those registered made declarations and paid by 1997, which is indeed an impressive accomplishment on the part of SUNAT.

In South Africa, SARS has steadily increased the tax base with impressive year-on-year growth. For example, from 2000–1 the percentage of active individual taxpayers grew by 13.9 per cent while the growth of corporate taxpayers reached 16.3 per cent. Note that the growth of corporate taxpayers was due principally to compliance activities by SARS as company registrations did not grow much over the same period. In Kenya, the VAT registry grew by more than 55 per cent from 1996 to 1999 as KRA made a concerted effort to register firms for the VAT (KRA, however, has not been as successful with individual taxpayers).

In terms of the compliance function SUNAT, the KRA, and SARS have made significant progress, while other ARAs have made only minor headway at best. SUNAT's overall audit presence for the period 1997–9 averaged 1.45 per cent, as compared with a pre-reform rate of 0.17 per cent. Additionally, SUNAT's audit rate for its largest taxpayers is nearly 11 per cent, which is quite high by developing-country standards. In Kenya, significant advances were taken when the KRA introduced field audits; prior to the KRA only desk audits were performed. The KRA has also refined its audit selection procedures to rely less on auditor discretion and more on quantitative indicators, such as gross profit ratios. SARS has established a formal audit policy, which it did not have previously, and has reorganized internally to create "compliance centres" that will foster teamwork among auditors and between auditors and collections officials. SARS's tax assessments issued by auditors have also been increasing, jumping 24 per cent from 1999 to 2000 alone.

Several ARAs also made headway in the improvement of taxpayer services, an important yet oft-overlooked function of tax agencies. The KRA introduced a Taxpayers' Charter, which is intended to provide transparent standards of service for taxpayers. The SARS has introduced service desks in all larger customs offices and in some larger revenue offices. In Peru one stop service offices ("Plaza SUNAT") were established in many of the countries largest cities. The cases demonstrate that the more autonomous revenue authorities have been those most concerned with improving taxpayer services.

Behind these gains in performance are internal reforms to management and personnel systems. Both the KRA and SUNAT used their autonomy to make significant advances in the area of personnel management. The KRA increased salaries in real terms, which was a break from the previous salary policy and actually reduced the total number of staff by over 30 per cent over a five-year period. SUNAT, at its founding, gave all employees the option of either submitting to a rigorous evaluation process or accepting voluntary retirement. Of the initial 3,051 workers, 2,034 were separated from the organization, leaving 1,017 (Haltiwanger and Singh 1999: 44). Subsequently, as new staff were hired according to a merit-based recruitment system, the total number of employees grew to 2,297, still well below the original staff complement. Salaries, due to a new personnel scheme, increased dramatically. Whereas on average a tax administration employee earned approximately US$50 per month in early 1991, the average salary for the remaining workers increased roughly twenty times to US$1,000 (Haltiwanger and Singh 1999: 44). These radical personnel reforms would not have been possible without autonomy, yet they are among the most important for the success of the reforms.

Of the other cases, Venezuela was perhaps the most successful in the area of personnel reform. In the initial phase of its reform, SENIAT also used its autonomous personnel regime to recruit managers from the top private sector accounting and law firms, which resulted in a vast improvement of the managerial ability of the organization. Uganda and Mexico, on the other hand, have made the least progress in personnel reform.

Moreover, these gains in performance have not come at great financial cost. As Table 14.2 shows, the more successful and more autonomous ARAs have lower average collection costs than the less successful ones. Kenya and Peru are both at the low end of the set. At the same time ARA collection costs (as an average of these cases) are comparable to or less than those of non-autonomous developing country tax agencies.

Survey data have also shown that corporate taxpayers in Latin America associate higher levels of autonomy with higher levels of performance (Taliercio 2000b). That is, perceptions of higher levels of autonomy are associated with perceptions of better performance along the three key dimensions of administrative capacity in tax administration: competence (delivering high quality services that impose reasonably low compliance costs), effectiveness (the capacity of the tax agency to detect non-compliance), and fairness (the impartial and technical application of tax

Table 14.2 Average collection cost as a percentage of revenues collected

Country	Average collection cost
Peru	1.9% (1996–8)
Mexico	1.7% (1995, 1997–8)
Venezuela	2.0% (1995–8)
Kenya	1.2% (1995–2000)
Uganda	3.6% (1991–2001)
Average	2.1%

Source: Taliercio 2002.

laws to all taxpayers). Moreover, autonomy is shown to be important in its own right, not only as a means to better services, but as an end in itself. These results, along with the objective performance indicators discussed in this section, provide support for the contention that semi-autonomous revenue authorities are mechanisms to promote credible political commitments to reform in developing countries.

Sustainability

One of the conundrums of the ARA reform experience around the world is that even as they are increasingly hailed as model reforms, their sustainability has proved increasingly problematic. The problem has to do with the relationship between the newly autonomized and professionalized ARA and the unreformed, often politicized, public administration that begets it. The cases show that the main challenger to the autonomy of revenue authorities has been the government itself, mostly via the ministry of finance.[7] There appears to be a built-in pattern of conflict in which consistent political predation has eroded ARA autonomy. Given the conflict between the two organizations, and given the vulnerability of the limited autonomy of the ARA vis-à-vis the ministry, the outcome is predictable: semi-autonomy gives way to little or no autonomy.

The reason ARAs have not been sustainable is that the semi-autonomous design establishes a dynamic of conflict and competition between the government, represented by the ministry, and the ARA. In particular, the problems concern accountability and incentives. The finance minister has two problems with the ARA reform: administrative and political. The administrative problem is that he is held accountable for a bureaucracy that he does not fully control. That is, the minister is held accountable for the ARA's performance, yet has little authority over the ARA. Even in cases in which the ARA is rather autonomous, the ARA still falls within the sector of the ministry of finance, which makes the minister responsible to some extent for the ARA. The disjuncture between accountability and authority creates a dilemma for the minister.

The political problem is that the reform sacks the minister of finance with high costs, yet provides little in the way of benefits. From a political perspective the main benefit of reform is greater revenues. Yet it is largely the president, not the minister, who benefits politically from greater expenditures. The main costs of the ARA reform are lost patronage opportunities, less political control of the tax agency, and less influence over tax policy making. The minister is affected by all these costs as the ARA reform removes a large percentage of ministerial employees from his control[8] (which results in a substantially decreased budget), reduces his political control over the tax administration, and reduces his tax policy control by establishing another centre of tax policy expertise. According to this simple cost-benefit analysis, ministers should generally have incentives to oppose the reform (even while presidents support it).

The cases reveal that the conflicts between ARAs and MOFs develop along predictable lines and over similar issues. The principal points of contention between ARAs and ministries in practice have been control over personnel, finances, and tax policy. In case after case, the MOF and ARA have each attempted to wrestle as much control as possible over personnel, finances, and tax policy from the other. Though the story told here suggests that the minister is the culprit, ARAs themselves have added fuel to the fire, especially concerning their tendency to usurp the tax policy-making function.

Contention over ARA finances was perhaps the most common source of conflict. Tussles between ARAs and their parent ministries over funding occurred in Venezuela, Peru, Mexico, Uganda, and Kenya. The result was, more often than not, that ARAs received less than the due statutory funding level. Disagreement over ARA personnel policy, and who would control it, caused strife in Venezuela, Mexico, and Uganda. In Venezuela, an extreme case, SENIAT's human resource management statute was changed by the ministry of finance so that administration of the system was transferred from the superintendent back to the minister. Tax policy making also became a contentious issue, fomenting conflict between ARAs and ministries of finance, especially in Peru, Venezuela, and Mexico. In Mexico, part of the tax policy unit (TPU), which had been transferred to the SAT after the reform, was brought back to the ministry. In Peru, public disagreement over tax policy erupted between SUNAT and the ministry on more than one occasion, and led to a lack of coordination between the agency and the ministry. On several occasions, for example, SUNAT and the ministry presented conflicting testimony to congress on particular tax measures, including tax exemptions and amnesties. Even though SUNAT had played an important role in the design of the VAT and the reform of the income tax in the first years of the Fujimori administration, its policy wings were eventually clipped by the ministry in later years.

This is not to say that ministerial opposition is always generated.

Though this chapter makes the case that the semi-autonomous organizational design builds in conflict between the ARA and the ministry, there may be scenarios in which ministers support the reform. However, even in those scenarios, the semi-autonomous ARA reform leaves the tax administration dependent on the benevolence of the minister of finance, which, the cases show, is not always a prudent decision. Moreover, ARAs are vulnerable to becoming pawns in larger political games (as in the Mexican case).

It is clear that the problem of ARA sustainability revolves around executive branch politics, particularly the relationship between the finance ministry and the tax agency. However, the sustainability of the agency does not depend solely on its relations with the ministry. The cases show that two other actors play important roles: the executive and the private sector. The executive invariably weighs in on the agency-ministry tussle. How the executive intervenes depends on his incentives at the time of the crisis, though in practice his incentives tend to favour the ministry over the agency. As the model in the second section of this chapter suggests, once compliance, and thus revenues, have increased, the executive is tempted to undo the reforms by increasing patronage appointments to the agency and using the agency for political purposes.

There is another potentially important factor that can impact sustainability: support from a powerful constituency. In Peru, large corporate taxpayers preferred SUNAT over the pre-reform agency and publicly expressed their support, even to the extent of explicitly opposing its reintegration with the ministry of finance. This powerful lobby, which expressed its opinions through its peak organizations, warned Fujimori that a return to a corrupt, inefficient, and politicized tax administration would cost him. Private sector support for SUNAT was thus instrumental in protecting the agency's autonomy, though some erosion inevitably took place.

SUNAT attained the support of corporate taxpayers because it was viewed as competent, effective, and fair. SUNAT's reputation for probity and professionalism was forged by the management strategy of its first superintendents. For example, the fact that SUNAT launched campaigns to audit informal vendors and combat contraband as well as to audit highly paid professionals, and the fact that it closed down many firms that evaded taxes, from small informal vendors to firms owned by powerful politicians to state-owned enterprises, earned SUNAT the support, perhaps grudgingly, of the corporate private sector. SUNAT's taxpayer management strategy was proactive, aggressive, and even dramatic. It set the stage for the creation of a constituency that later offered support against the threat of old-style public administration practices.

The KRA also benefited from private sector support, through its board of directors, at a critical juncture. When political interests had a KRA commissioner fired for acting against illegal tax-related activities, the private sector representatives, backed by international organizations, resisted the blatant political interference. After months of a stand-off, and the dismissal of some board members, the commissioner was reinstated. The protection of professionalism exemplified in this case would not have been possible without the organizational autonomy that the KRA possesses.

In sum, the cases show that while new institutions were created, there were still a number of unresolved conflicts simmering below the surface. Some of these conflicts concerned the organizational design, while others concerned issues of strategy and leadership. Once the reform was in place, these conflicts surfaced in the relationship between the ministry of finance and the revenue authority. Given the argument that the minister of finance is confronted with disincentives towards supporting the reform, and given empirical support for the claim that these disincentives matter, reformers must rethink the semi-autonomous revenue authority reform model in terms of sustainability. Focusing on ministerial disincentives provides a way to think about how to build design features into the genetic template of the tax agency so that it can better survive in a hostile political and organizational environment.

Conclusion

This chapter has taken up three critical questions about the introduction, performance, and sustainability of semi-autonomous revenue authorities in Africa and Latin America. It has argued that ARAs are used by politicians to make credible commitments to taxpayers that tax administration will be more fair, competent, and effective. The theoretical literature, as well as survey data from several Latin American countries (Taliercio 2004), support this hypothesis, thus offering an explanation of why the agency model has been adopted in the sphere of tax administration across the developing world.

The chapter has also addressed the link between autonomy and performance, finding that if one compares the pre- and post-reform state of affairs in these cases, the ARA demonstrates improved performance in most of the cases. Moreover, the chapter finds that the more autonomous revenue authorities have been more adept at increasing performance than the less autonomous ones. Thus, autonomy seems to matter, and more autonomy seems to matter more.

This is not to say, however, that autonomy is the only factor that determines ARA performance. It would be foolish not to recognize the importance of professional, capable managers in these success stories. Indeed, autonomy without a professional management team would produce little of value. It is, however, to suggest that autonomy is a necessary ingredient for the rapid and radical improvement of tax administration in developing countries.

Lastly, the chapter has pointed out that in spite of the appeal and success of the ARA model, political pressure has undermined many reforms in both Africa and Latin America. The politics of patronage and corruption have reared their ugly heads and undone some of the progress that had been made. The more autonomous authorities, such as those in Peru and Kenya, were able to resist political pressure more successfully precisely because they had built up external support in the business and international community. This would also suggest that more autonomy is linked to a higher probability of sustaining reform.

Notes

1 The author is grateful to Glenn Jenkinds, Merilee Grindle, and Bob Bates for helpful comments on an earlier version. Any remaining errors or omissions are the author's responsibility. The author also extends his gratitude to the US Department of Education for funding through a Fulbright-Hays DDRA and the David Rockefeller Center for Latin American Studies at Harvard University. The fieldwork for this chapter was carried out in 1998–9 in Latin America and in 2001 in Africa. The views expressed in this chapter are those of the author and do not necessarily represent the views of the World Bank, its Executive Directors, or the countries they represent.
2 Interview, KRA official, 6/21/96, Nairobi, Kenya.
3 For a comprehensive analysis of organizational design issues, see Taliercio (2002).
4 The potential danger of conflict of interest does not yet appear to have emerged as a significant problem in cases of ARAs with private sector participation on their boards.
5 Taliercio (2003) attempts to gauge ARA performance through a microanalytical lens. The chapter is based on fieldwork in which managers were asked specifically how autonomy mattered for their performance. The chapter thus highlights internal reforms and measures that were only possible given autonomy and also explores reforms that are still impossible to launch given the limited (semi-) autonomy that characterizes most revenue authorities.
6 All data from Taliercio (2004) and Taliercio (2003).
7 For comprehensive, detailed analyses of the sustainability problem, see Taliercio (2001 and 2003).
8 In the Mexican case, the ARA hived off about 36,000 of the ministry's 39,000 employees.

Bibliography

Bates, R.H. (1996) "Institutions as investments", Development Discussion Papers, No. 527, Harvard Institute for International Development.
Firmin-Sellers, K. (1995) "The Politics of Property Rights", *American Political Science Review* 89, 4, 867–81.
Haltiwanger J. and Singh, M. (1999) "Cross country evidence on public sector retrenchment", *The World Bank Economic Review* 13, 1, 23–66.
Jenkins, G.P. (1994) "Modernization of tax administrations: revenue boards and privatization as instruments for change", *International Bureau of Fiscal Documentation* 75–81.
Keefer, P. and Stasavage, D. (2000) "Bureaucratic delegation and political institutions: when are independent central banks irrelevant?", World Bank Policy Research Working Paper 2356. Washington, DC: World Bank.

Kydland, F.E. and Prescott, E.C. (1977) "Rules rather than discretion: the inconsistency of optimal plans", in Persson, T. and Tabellini, G. (eds) *Monetary and Fiscal Policy, Volume I: Credible Commitment*, 1994. Cambridge, MA: The MIT Press.

Persson, T. and Tabellini, G. (eds) (1994) *Monetary and Fiscal Policy, Volume I: Credible Commitment*, Cambridge, MA: The MIT Press.

Root, H.J. (1989) "Tying the king's hands: credible commitments and royal fiscal policy during the old regime", *Rationality and Society* 1, 240–58.

Taliercio, R.R. (2000) "Administrative reform as credible commitment: the design, performance, and sustainability of semi-autonomous revenue authorities in Latin America", PhD dissertation, Harvard University.

Taliercio, R.R. (2004) "Administrative reform as credible commitment: the link between revenue authority autonomy and performance in Latin America", forthcoming *World Development*.

Taliercio, R.R. (2001) "Raising revenues and raising hackles: the problem of sustainability of semi-autonomous tax agencies in developing countries", Presented at the 2001 Annual Meeting of the American Political Science Association, Hilton San Francisco and Towers August 30–September 2.

Taliercio, R.R. (2002) "Designing performance: the semi-autonomous revenue model in Africa and Latin America", Ms.

Weingast, B.R. (1995) "The political foundations of limited government: parliament and sovereign debt in 17th and 18th century England", Ms.

15 Castles built on sand?

Agencies in Latvia

Christopher Pollitt

Introduction

This chapter offers a case study of agencification in a 'transitional' state – one of the central and eastern European states which is in transition from a Communist to a liberal democratic regime. Although Latvia itself is a small country, and one with a number of distinctive characteristics, several of the larger features of the Latvian 'story' are echoed in other transitional states. Hopefully, therefore, the analysis here may identify a set of key variables, the importance of which is sustained in other transitional states (and perhaps in some parts of the developing world – see Chapters 11 and 15), not solely in Latvia.

The main 'message' of this analysis will be that the Anglo-American idea of performance-managed agencies can only work when a number of pre-requisite contextual factors are in place. To take just one (obvious) example, agencies can only be steered by their parent ministries if the ministries have the information, the appropriately skilled staff and the authoritative levers with which to steer. Unfortunately, in Latvia, many agencies were created rather fast, and in many cases the pre-requisites were not in place. Castles were built on sand. The Latvian authorities are therefore left with the difficult task of retrospectively reconstructing an appropriate framework within which its existing agencies can operate.

Background: the Latvian political and administrative system

For hundreds of years the territory which is now Latvia was occupied by a variety of imperial and quasi-imperial powers – Prussia/the Teutonic Knights, Sweden and Russia. With the collapse of both Germany and Russia at the end of the First World War, Latvia became independent in 1918. However, the country's democratic institutions failed in 1934, when Karlis Ulmanis established an authoritarian regime. In 1940 the Soviet Union occupied Latvia, and the Communist power continued to rule for the next 50 years.

Independence was regained in 1991. However, in terms of public opinion the new freedom was characterised by an assertion of cultural identity more than any strong popular support for the state. Indeed, the Latvian state tended to be the object of continuing distrust, not least (but not only) because many former *nomenklatura* remained in positions of power. Ownership of economic institutions was more concentrated than in the other Baltic states. Cultural and trade relations with Russia remained important. Political interference and corruption was a feature of early Latvian privatisations. Independent and 'watchdog' institutions were not highly developed. Even the state audit office, although independent, did not have a strong client in the shape of a parliamentary public accounts committee (like many Western-style reforms in Latvia, the creation of a PAC has been proposed but not implemented). Governments changed frequently, but the leading political figures much less so. "Latvia is a small country. Almost everyone knows everyone else. You cannot make rotation. The people are the same." (Interview – see note on Sources and Acknowledgements, at the end of this chapter.)

Formally, Latvia has two levels of government. The democratically elected Parliament (*Saeima*) has 100 members. It uses a system of proportional representation. In the October 1998 elections six parties won seats. The *Saeima* elects the President of the Republic for a four-year term (and can dismiss, on a two thirds majority). The President holds the right of legislative initiative, and can withhold promulgation of new legislation for up to two months. S/he designates the Prime Minister, who, in turn chooses the ministers. There are 12 main ministers (and ministries). According to the constitution, all draft laws must be discussed by the Cabinet of Ministers before they go to Parliament. Recent governments have usually been coalitions of three parties.

There are also a large number (589) of local authorities, some of them very small. Each has a directly elected council. Local and district government is not part of this case study.

Latvia lacks a unified civil service. Staff belong to a particular ministry, and the culture is one of appointment to a specific post rather than to a 'career'. Civil service pay is generally too low to attract and retain able staff. However, the ministries account for only a small proportion of the state public service – around 2,500 people. Almost 50,000 others are employed in a range of public bodies with different legal status (often private law status). These display differing and non-transparent pay and employment statuses, varying budgetary statuses and higher or lower degrees of accountability and responsibility for their actions.

To speak of a 'public sector reform programme' in Latvia is to risk exaggerating or distorting the process which has actually taken place. It is true that there have been many reforms – indeed, the collapse of the Soviet regime necessitated wholesale changes in almost every aspect of government. It is also true that there have been many programmatic documents, such as the 1995 *Concept of Public Administration Reform*, the 1998

Public Administration Development Strategy and the 2000 *BLUEPRINT*. However, these schemes have frequently lacked any detailed basis for implementation.

Many countries experience 'implementation gaps' in public administration reform (Pollitt and Bouckaert 2000). However, Latvia is an acute sufferer. Attention is frequently concentrated on drafting and proclaiming new legislation, with weak follow-through and monitoring. The solution to perceived problems tends to be to draft a fresh law rather than attempt to tighten up on the implementation of the laws which already exist. This form of political and administrative amnesia has been exacerbated by the rapid changes of government which Latvia has tended to experience in recent years.

Agencification in Latvia

Many agencies were created in Latvia during the first decade of independence. Again, however, it would be an exaggeration to describe this as a 'programme', as though it proceeded within a planned overall framework, with clear criteria and timetables. The practice was far more ad hoc. The exact number of agencies is hard to determine, both because of definitional uncertainty and because of the lack of a strong central system for recording and overseeing public sector changes.

Legislative forms

The term 'agency' is itself far from clear. In Latvia it has been used to cover three distinct types of legal entity:

a   subordinate bodies
b   supervised bodies
c   bodies under ministerial management.

The degree of control exercised by the Ministry is highest with type a) and lowest with type c). This chapter is mainly concerned with type c). Little will be said about state enterprises and for-profit companies (although they have plenty of problems of their own). For-profit state enterprises and joint stock companies are excluded from our working definition of agencies. Much of the discussion will focus on the non-profit joint stock company format. At least 19 agencies take the legal form of a 'private', non-profit joint stock company owned by the government. This legal form seems to have been used because it was thought to be the least unsuitable one available. Nevertheless, it has some inherent problems. In particular, the company model is essentially permissive – that is, a company can perform any functions or services other than those expressly prohibited by its statutes. This contrasts with the typical situation in, say, the UK or the

USA, where an agency can only undertake those tasks specifically assigned to it in its founding legislation or framework document.

The creation of new agencies continued well after concerns began to be expressed about various negative features of the proliferation of these bodies. Indeed, it was not until negotiations over a World Bank Structural Adjustment Loan (SAL) were taking place in 2000 that the Latvian government decided to institute an informal moratorium on new agency creation.

Scope

Agencies perform many different kinds of task. They exist in virtually every sector, e.g.

*   Agricultural Market Intervention Agency (non-profit joint stock company, Ministry of Agriculture)
*   New Riga Theatre (non-profit organisation, Ministry of Culture)
*   Car Depot of the Ministry of Defence (non-profit joint stock company, Ministry of Defence)
*   University of Latvia (non-profit state enterprise, Ministry of Education and Science)
*   Spatial Development Planning Centre (non-profit state enterprise, Ministry of Environmental Protection and Regional Development)
*   State Border Construction (non-profit joint stock company, Ministry of the Interior)
*   State Obligatory Health Insurance Agency (VOVAA) (non-profit joint stock company, Ministry of Welfare)
*   State Centre for Tuberculosis and Pulmanological Diseases (non-profit state enterprise, Ministry of Welfare)
*   Latvian State Road Administration (non-profit joint stock company, Ministry of Transport)
*   State Information Network Agency (VITA) (non-profit state joint stock company, Ministry of Transport)
*   Road Traffic Safety Directorate (CSDD) (non-profit joint stock company)
*   Regional Development (non-profit limited company, Ministry of Economy).

Sometimes the activities of the many different state agencies and enterprises may overlap or collide with each other. For example, in the past there has been friction between Lattelekom (the state monopoly telecommunications company) and VITA (the State Information Network Agency)

Framework

It seems unlikely that there was any overall co-ordination or strategy behind the precise legal forms chosen for particular functions. Only now, with a draft law on Public Sector Agencies going through the *Saiema*, is a general framework on the horizon (see later for information about this draft law).

There is fairly widespread agreement about *the reasons for agency creation* during the mid- and late-1990s. "The initial wish was to run away from the old bureaucratic system as quickly as possible" (interview). "In Latvia agencies were established not so much to manage defined sets of resources as to escape bureaucratic control and low salaries" (another interview – in translation). In the early years of independence ideas of what the border between public and private sectors should look like were understandably often vague or uninformed. There was "a lack of understanding of the differences between the public sector and the private sector" (interview). Agencies were seen as a way of introducing private sector-style efficiency and escaping bureaucratic rigidities. Pro-business governments were in power. Freedom from traditional bureaucracy was perhaps given more importance than freedom to carry out specified tasks within a clear policy framework.

The law and its categories

The law and its categories were not geared to the creation of public sector agencies. "There was no legal basis for institutions such as agencies" (interview). As indicated above, many of the new agencies were given the legal form of private sector joint stock companies, wholly owned by the state. This format had the considerable practical advantage of permitting agencies to pay higher salaries than those available in the ministries, so that they could attract staff. [Of course, it also had the disadvantage of making civil service jobs relatively even less attractive to ambitious, well-qualified people.] However, the sometime combination of the joint stock format and non-profit status was an uneasy one (e.g. in relation to the State Obligatory Health Insurance Agency – SOHIA).

There is a second type of legal issue in relation to agencies, and that is the low level of legal advice frequently available to policy divisions in the ministries. Civil service salaries were so low that often the only lawyers who could be recruited by ministries were students working on dissertations (who subsequently left the civil service when they were qualified). A situation in which central government ministries can regularly be legally 'outgunned' by agencies or sectional interest groups is an unhealthy one for good governance.

Accountability and service quality

Issues of accountability and service quality were not usually high on the agenda. Given the widespread perception that the 'dead hand of the ministries' had to be removed, it is not surprising that in many cases little attention seems to have been given to the arrangements for the ministry to hold its agencies to account. It has also to be borne in mind that there is little in the way of activity by civil society associations to hold either ministries or state agencies up for parliamentary or public scrutiny. 'Non-governmental organisations, interest groups and associations can influence the legislative process only through the mass media' (SIGMA 1999: 16). In any case, the associations and institutions of civil society remains weak, compared with the longer-standing liberal democracies of Australasia, Western Europe and North America.

Even basic financial accountability was not strong, partly because the Ministry of Finance was not particularly powerful, and could not direct other ministries to follow a particular set of financial procedures for managing agencies. This led to a number of concerns. First, there was evidence of a rapid growth in the pay and benefits for staff in agencies, outpacing those available to core civil servants. Second, there was also evidence of a growth in administrative costs. Third, there were instances of fraud and corruption, or of the suspicion thereof. Fourth, there was the danger of an uncontrolled build-up of liabilities. Fifth, there were instances of the holding of private bank accounts outside the centralised Treasury system. On the other hand, it should be reported that some critics in the agencies accuse the Ministry of Finance of being narrow mindedly obsessed with financial regularity and procedural correctness, and of failing to understand issues of service quality, performance and the need for flexible, dynamic action. Possibly there was some truth on both sides?

Non-financial performance

For the most part, non-financial performance (quality standards, customer service, accuracy, speed, etc.) was neither quantified nor closely monitored by ministries. This was by no means entirely the ministries' fault – they were poorly staffed, poorly paid and there seems to have been little political understanding of, or pressure for, systematic performance monitoring. This means that, for the most part, there is simply no reliable evidence about productivity or quality gains – or losses – resulting from agencification.

Thus the Anglo-American-Australasian idea of a 'performance framework' for each agency is only beginning to emerge in Latvia. The more traditional attitude was well-encapsulated in one interview:

> Author (to agency manager): "Do you have performance targets?"
> Manager: "Yes and no. It is how I deal with my boss. I see him, I want to do this, and he says yes or no. Sometimes there is a direction from the top."

It must be acknowledged that the variation between agencies in these respects is very great. In the best case quite sophisticated financial and non-financial data was freely available, and there was extensive documentary evidence of quality improvement (e.g. the Road Traffic Safety Directorate – see CSDD 1997; 2000). This, however, was rare.

It is, of course, conceivable that the creation of agencies has indeed led to large gains in efficiency and service quality. No one can know for sure. However, it would be a rash assumption to make, other than in a few exceptional cases where particular circumstances and/or charismatic and skilful leadership has left a clear record of achievement. What is more certain is that the new population of agencies has brought with it a long list of specific problems.

Supervision and guidance

One important issue has been the guidance (or lack of it) given by ministries to agencies. No consistent principles seem to have governed the appointment of the 'proxies' who, theoretically at least, are the guiding, strategic link between ministers and their agencies. In some cases these have been political party friends of the ruling coalition, with few other qualifications for the role. In a number of cases (e.g. the State Information Network Agency; the State Obligatory Health Insurance Agency) the board of proxies mixes the interests of the state as stockholder with the main customers or clients of the agency, thus confusing essentially different roles. Proxies may come and go quickly, as governments change. In these circumstances there is thus little opportunity for the proxies to build up any knowledge of the agency's 'business'. Proxies may sometimes be line civil servants in the supervising ministry (thus helping to ensure a single, co-ordinated relationship between the ministry and the agency) or they may be quite apart from the professional, line relationship, making it easy for divergences to develop between the 'professional' guidance from the relevant ministerial department and the 'political' guidance from proxies.

The overall state of affairs described in the preceding paragraphs has allowed dubious practices and irregularities to flourish. Just a few examples will suffice to illustrate the risks. The State Audit Office criticised the State Roads Administration for restricting tender negotiations for road signs to a single Latvian contractor when substantially cheaper signs were available from Lithuanian contractors. The State Information Network Agency (VITA) was criticised when it was found to have opened an additional account at a private bank through which collected service fees were credited to VITA's account. Its director and board were replaced several times in a few years. There have also been serious problems at the State Real Estate Agency (SREA). Failure to publish agency annual reports and accounts does not seem at all unusual.

It has been extremely difficult for central bodies such as the Treasury, the Ministry of Finance and the State Audit Office to be able to form an overview of the incidence and severity of problems of loss of budgetary control, inefficiency and irregularity across the large population of agencies. Even to collect a complete set of agency reports was an elusive task, since the list of agencies itself required constant updating. Lists of agencies held, respectively, by the State Treasury and the Bureau for Public Administration Reform were substantially different. Quarterly returns from agencies (introduced in 2000) appear to comprise just two columns of figures – budget code appropriations and expenditures. The Treasury is developing criteria to analyse this new data, but their resources are so stretched that this is taking some time.

Current reforms

Since mid-1999, however, significant new legislation has been passed, presented to the Latvian Parliament, or put into the drafting process. Five developments are particularly worthy of mention:

- *Law on Openness of Information, 1999.* This was intended to be an important step towards transparency, and therefore, indirectly, accountability. However, implementation is once more a problem. Enforcement mechanisms are weak, and in any case ministries frequently lack the capacity to respond to requests for information from the public.
- *Amendments to the Law on Budgetary and Financial Management 1999.* The *Saiema* passed amendments which now require all budget-holding institutions to have their accounts with the State Treasury, thus reducing the dangers of agencies holding 'outside' bank accounts.
- *The Law on State Civil Service, 2000.* This has the purpose of establishing 'the legal status for the civil service that is loyal to the government, professional, politically neutral thus ensuring and based on the rule of law, stable, effective and transparent functioning of the public administration' (Article 1). Its provisions cover appointment procedures, basic duties, pay and conditions, performance appraisal, and termination of employment. This act extends civil service provisions to approximately 25,000 of the 45,000 state employees (as compared with roughly 6,000 previously).
- *Administrative Framework Law* (in draft at the time of writing). This is intended to specify the range of organisational forms available for public sector bodies, thus reducing the incidence of variant and sometimes inappropriate legislative forms noted above.
- *Law on Public Sector Agencies* (going through Parliament at the time of writing). This has the purpose of establishing the 'legal status, formation procedure, sources of financing, principles and procedures of

operation, supervision and accounting for the public sector agency...' (translation of draft of article 1). It specifies, *inter alia*, that the minister will, in each case, enter into a 'management contract' with the agency director (article 6). S/he will also 'evaluate the agency performance indicators' and will appoint a top official to oversee the operation of the agency.

Clearly this last law, in particular, if it is both passed and implemented, could go far to address the problems detailed above. However, it should also be noted that, by itself, a law cannot make up for the shortage of resources and skills in the ministries. Neither, in view of past experience, can it be assumed that implementation will be either quick or thorough.

Analysis: castles built on sand?

Clearly, a number of problems manifest themselves in the Latvian story. Moving from the most general towards the more particular, these include:

- Weak development of the institutions of civil society. This is not unusual for ex-Communist states. In this instance, it creates a problem because it means that 'consumerist' and independent, voluntary, non party-political bodies – organisations that would critically engage with ministries and agencies, and hold them up to public and media scrutiny – are only now beginning to emerge.
- The presence of corruption, both 'petty' and at higher political levels. This means that giving public agencies greater freedom also carries substantial risks that that autonomy will be exercised for perverted ends. In Latvia's case both 'state capture' and 'administrative corruption' are widespread, but the former (undemocratic influences over law- and policymaking) appears particularly rife (Anderson 1998; World Bank 2000).
- The absence of a suitable legal form for agencies (and therefore their adoption, in the Latvian case, of a dubiously appropriate joint stock company format, sometimes uncomfortably married with non-profit status).
- The frequent absence of clear policy objectives, meaning that the 'missions' of agencies often remain vague.
- The lack of a clear and comprehensive framework for financial management (permitting a variety of dangerous practices, such as the holding of accounts off-budget and the creation of liabilities without the knowledge of the Ministry of Finance).
- Inadequate capacity for strategic thinking about agencies at the centre of government (tradition of the independence of ministries, resistance to giving authority over other ministries to the ministry of finance, lack of personnel skilled in strategic policymaking and

planning). So agencies were created ad hoc, in many different forms, without any effective central guidance or concept of their place within the overall system of governance.

- Weak links in the chain of external, public accountability (an inadequately resourced state audit office, with no parliamentary public accounts committee to report to). More generally, the concept of bodies which are statutorily independent from the central executive power – and can regulate or criticise the exercise of that power – has yet to achieve wide political acceptance.
- Ministries lack the skills and knowledge to set realistic targets for agencies and to monitor their performance against those targets.
- The ministries' lines of responsibility for agencies are in any case made ambiguous by the presence of other interests as proxies or supervisors of agencies ('other interests' here including party politicians or those with business interests which are connected to the agency's work).
- Agencies themselves lack a proper internal audit function

New laws should certainly help a good deal, but attitudes and expectations do not change on the morning new legislation comes into force. Furthermore, there is a history of weak implementation of reforms. There are powerful actors with strong interests in the continuance of aspects of the *status quo ante*, and while fresh legislation and skills training may strengthen the hand of reformers, perseverance and political courage will be required over a period of time before any sea change in actual practices will become visible.

Finally, it should be noted that a number of the above problem areas are far from unique to Latvia, or even to transitional countries. The existence of policy vacuums or the lack of good performance management skills in ministries (to take only two examples) have been issues in some Western European states also. In Latvia, therefore, one is not looking at a unique or wholly unusual menu of difficulties, but rather at a particularly heavy combination of known elements (for parallels in other countries, see, e.g. Condrey, Purvis and Slava 2001).

There is at least one further problem with the Latvian system of agencies, and that is the brake which its fragmented character places on any attempts to co-ordinate cross-sectoral actions and achieve 'joined-up' government. Senior civil servants are well aware of this problem, but tend to see it as an issue for the future – currently an unrealistic goal given the more basic deficiencies which require urgent attention. "Latvia may come to this problem in due course" (interview – for accounts of similar problems in Lithuania and Slovakia, see Rekerta 2000; Miklos 2000).

Paradoxically, path dependency theory (Pierson 2000) may be of considerable assistance in generating an understanding of the course of events in Latvia (and in other transitional states – see next section). I say 'paradoxically' because it may be thought that a theory which concentrates on explaining why things tend to stay the same would be just about the last candidate for doing the job of unravelling the sweeping changes which have so rapidly come about in countries such as the Baltic States and other ex-Communist countries. Yet, despite this, path dependency may be of use in identifying some of the incentives which have defeated or diverted so many 'NPM'-type reforms in these states. In this case 'the path' was one in which the status of civil servants was low, and their management skills and resources very limited. It was also a path where corruption, both large and small scale had become endemic, partly as a way of 'getting round the system', when the system had been authoritarian and deeply inefficient. This structural and cultural foundation could not be dug up overnight. Many of the incentives which had sustained it remained more or less in place. The building of bright new structures on this soft sand was always likely to lead to cracking, slipping and the occasional collapse, and so it has.

Conclusions and remedies

The first, and most obvious conclusion, is that rapid agencification, in circumstances such as prevailed in Latvia, was highly risky. Too many factors were working against the possibility that agencification would actually lead to improvements in the efficiency, quality or responsiveness of public services. In this particular context, decentralising many functions to autonomous agencies was trying to run before the public service could walk. Arguably, other things should have come first.

The more difficult question, however, is 'What should have come first?'. It would be easy to slip into an idealistic but quite impractical perspective that demands, say, the bringing into existence of a fully-active civil society, bristling with consumer and citizen pressure groups, before any real autonomy is given to public service agencies. But this is a task that will take at least a generation, and this kind of prescription therefore takes little account of the real and pressing problems of governance now, in a less than perfect socio-political context.

A more limited, though still ambitious approach might focus on the need for significant strengthening of the civil service core as a first priority. In other agencification programmes, such as those in New Zealand, the Netherlands or the UK, the essence of the reform has been a kind of 'deal' in which greater managerial freedom was exchanged for new forms of performance-oriented accountability. One central problem with the Latvian case was that the 'deal' was usually one-sided. Freedom was given, but matching new arrangements for accountability and performance orientation were not – initially at least – put in place. A major reason for this imbalance was that the ministries lacked the capacity and the skills to create such frameworks of accountability, or to maintain them. Therefore, one (admittedly hindsighted) strategy for stabilising the position would be to equip the ministries to play a more active role, both strategically and in terms of monitoring of operations.

Specific measures may be divided into those relevant to the initial creation of a new agency, and those relevant to its subsequent 'normal' activities. As a 'parent' to a new agency, a ministry needs to possess certain capacities and to use those capacities to take certain specific actions. The capacities are related to basic features of the civil service and its position in society, such as:

- open and impartial procedures for appointment and promotion of its own staff;
- pay and conditions which enable the ministry to hire and retain staff with the skills and experiences necessary to deal with the staff of their agencies as at least equals.

As for specific actions, the ministry concerned needs to:

- be able to state a clear set of strategic objectives for the agency – a policy framework;
- be able to propose an initial list of performance indicators (both financial and non-financial) which reflect those objectives in operational terms (even if this list is modified with subsequent experience and discussion). Taken together, these indicators constitute an operational framework which complements the policy framework;
- be able to set a budget for the agency;
- be able to draw up a regime of financial reporting, related to the budget;
- be able to ensure the creation of an internal audit within the new agency;
- be able to designate one senior official through whom all reporting from the agency must go.

In the later stages, as an agency develops, the parent ministry can adjust its stance. If the relationship works well, mutual trust will grow between parent and offspring, and certain controls can be progressively relaxed. However, even when an agency is well-established, the parent ministry will need to retain certain powers and competencies. It will need to be able to:

- clearly locate within its own 'organogram' the responsibility for co-ordinating all the ministry's business with the agency in question;
- periodically review the policy framework, and adjust it;
- review, at least annually, the operating framework (financial and non-financial performance indicators) and, in negotiation with the agency, adjust them. The normal assumption would be one of continuous, realistic pressure for performance improvement;

- routinely monitor both financial and non-financial performance, using the indicators agreed in the operational framework;
- report to the legislature, at any time, on its supervision and guidance of the agency;
- activate, if necessary, reserve powers to intervene when an agency appears to be developing major problems, whether these be seriously declining performance, financial mismanagement, activities beyond its legal and policy frameworks, or corruption.

In the Latvian case, very extensive efforts are now having to be made to ameliorate the ambiguities and vulnerabilities built into the system during the early years (see discussion on new legislation, above). It is unfortunate that these energies are therefore not available for moving on to future issues, such as the need to achieve better strategic co-ordination across the large number of separate public sector entities.

Finally, it must be pointed out that the kind of strategy sketched out in the preceding paragraphs is still essentially a 'technocratic fix', with most of the limitations which that implies. Better procedures, better laws, better paid and trained civil servants – all these factors will help build foundations in the sand, foundations from which paths could be laid in a new direction. Taken together they could create a capacity to make policies and manage in a different way. But this capacity is unlikely to be fully taken up and used unless yet deeper political and cultural change also takes place. If politicians are not interested in issues of performance and accountability, then the mere existence of good procedures and well-equipped civil servants will not by themselves produce a dramatic shift towards better governance. *How a political culture can be changed* is a topic not addressed within this chapter. Nor is it a topic upon which the rich countries of Western Europe, North America and Australasia can necessarily feel themselves well-placed to lecture states in other regions.

Sources and acknowledgements

This chapter is based partly on published sources but partly also on material gathered during a consultancy study of Latvia carried out in 2000. In order to respect the sensitivity of some of the material obtained during the consultancy I have anonymised the (few) interview quotations I have used, and I have also removed specific references to internal documentation made available to me in my consultant role.

My deep thanks go to all the Latvian public servants who talked to me. I very much appreciated their attempts to be helpful and candid, not always under easy circumstances. Evidently, many Latvian civil servants are strongly committed to the challenging task of building a fair, efficient and democratically accountable public service. They continue to pursue these goals, despite low pay and a frequent lack of regard by the Latvian general public. It is appropriate that visitors from the more historically fortunate liberal democracies (such as myself) should mix large doses of both admiration and humility with our supposed expertise.

One name I will mention is that of Normunds Malnacs, of the World Bank office in Riga. He was exceptionally helpful in arranging visits and providing background information. I am also grateful to Gunite Bullite for the efficiency of her translations. Neither of these persons is in any way responsible for my interpretations, or for any errors I may have unwittingly committed.

Finally, I would like to express my regret that the software available to me does not include Latvian accents. Some words may therefore be incompletely reproduced.

Bibliography

Anderson, J. (1998) *Corruption in Latvia: Survey Evidence*, Washington, DC: World Bank.

Condrey, S., Purvis, K. and Slava, S. (2001) 'Public management reform under stress: the Ukrainian civil service experience', *Public Management Review* 3, 2 (June), 271–80.

CSDD (Road Traffic Safety Directorate) *1997 Annual Report*, Riga: CSDD.

CSDD (Road Traffic Safety Directorate) (2000) *Kvalitates Standarts*, Riga: CSDD.

Miklos, I. (2000) 'Report recommends restructuring in Slovak public sector', *Public Management Forum*, (SIGMA) VI, 2, 5.

Misa, R. (2000) 'Investment projects of the Latvian State Information Network Agency', *Baltic IT Review* 2, April–June.

PHARE (1999) *An Evaluation of PHARE Public Administration Reform Programmes: Final Report*, Brussels, March.

Pierson, P. (2000) 'Increasing returns, path dependence and the study of politics', *American Political Science Review* 94, 2, 251–67.

Pollitt, C. and Bouckaert, G. (2000) *Public Management Reform: a Comparative Analysis*, Oxford: Oxford University Press.

Rekerta, K. (2000) 'Audit of Lithuania's administration highlights areas for action', *Public Management Forum* (SIGMA), VI, 2, 3–5.

SIGMA (1999) *Public Management Profiles of Central and Eastern European Countries: Latvia*, Paris: PHARE/OECD.

World Bank (2000) *Anticorruption in Transition: a Contribution to the Policy Debate*, Washington, DC: World Bank.

16 A radical departure?

Executive agencies in Jamaica

Colin Talbot

This chapter looks at the growth of an Executive Agencies Programme in the Caribbean island state of Jamaica. It was written on the basis of field work conducted in Jamaica in 2000 and events will undoubtedly have progressed since then. At that stage, only four agencies had been established, but visits and interviews were conducted in all these agencies and various central government bodies and parent departments.

The Cabinet Secretary in Jamaica has argued that:

> the creation of executive agencies has been the 'pièce de résistance' of the reform efforts ... because it represents the most radical departure from the norms of public service organisations while still remaining a 'classical' department of government. (Speech, Canada, undated).

This chapter recounts the initiation of this reform programme and makes some very tentative evaluative analysis of how well it was being implemented and was working.

Background

Jamaica has been a relatively stable parliamentary democracy since independence in 1962. Two political parties have become dominant in the political process – the People's National Party (PNP) and the Jamaica Labor Party (JLP). It is worth quoting from the World Bank's overview of governance issues:

> On governance more broadly, Jamaica appears to fare comparatively well overall, although problems persist in key dimensions. Aspects of (perceived) comparative strength – relative to other LAC and developing countries – include well-established formal traditions of democratic participation and accountability. Jamaica also scores comparatively well in cross-country surveys of perceptions of corruption. Political participation is broadly exercised, as exemplified in

high, if declining, voter turnout (around two-thirds) at elections. Jamaican civil society includes a free and active media, and a rich, often vocal, array of civic, professional and labor groups and other non-governmental organisations. Information about key policy issues typically circulates freely and is widely debated, as evidenced recently in the public commentary on the Government's Memorandum of Economic and Financial Policies (MEFP) for the SMP (World Bank 1999).

Whilst this judgement is generally correct it tends to obscure the period of political turmoil during the 1970s and 1980s as Jamaica underwent 'structural adjustment' programmes. It also underestimates the size and impact of the informal sector on the economics and politics of Jamaica. The World Bank report does, however, go on to mention the rising crime problems, which are acute, especially violent and drug-related crime, and the important negative impact this has on the economy.

In terms of the 'machinery of government', the Jamaican system is closely based on the Westminster model with the government-civil service structures closely resembling those of Britain. Specifically – unlike Tanzania where the role of Ministers is relatively weaker and the Cabinet Secretary/Permanent Secretaries axis much stronger, reflecting their more Presidential system (see Caulfield, Chapter 12, this volume) – the Jamaican minister-departmental structure is much closer to the UK model in its power relationships. In Jamaica, the Minister of a department seems to wield power closer to that of the Whitehall minister and permanent secretaries and the chief secretary relatively less power.

The same World Bank report goes on to analyse the curious phenomena that Jamaica has had virtually 'flat-line' economic performance for 25 years (i.e. no GDP growth) and yet poverty has significantly declined. The report notes that the popular explanation is that there has been a rapid growth in the informal economy and this has reduced poverty, whilst the official economy has stagnated. For example, the traditional 'higglers' – small traders in the informal sector – are said to have transferred their enterprising skills from linking town and country, in the past, to linking town and the (smuggled) import of foreign goods. Some 'higglers' are even said to have incomes now the equivalent of professional and white-collar jobs (Franc 1994).

There were clear signs of impact of this informal economy on the public administration. A small but significant example was the Registrar-General's Department, one of the new Agencies, which managed to significantly increase its income by taking steps that cut out various 'unofficial' channels for obtaining documentation. The new Chief Executive reported that as a result she had received threats to her person sufficiently worrying to have a personal guard for 9 months until the situation cooled down!

The position in Jamaica has been summarized as:

> Like in many other developing countries, corruption in Jamaica has occurred in a variety of forms, including (i) the selling of public services, such as expediting the provision of birth certificates, passports, drivers' licenses, and motor vehicle certificates of fitness; (ii) acceptance of bribes by some government employees, especially in the police force, the judiciary and customs; (iii) the disposal of politically-owned assets, such as land and other scarce benefits to relatives, friends and political supporters; (iv) discrimination in the award of government contracts; (v) nepotism in appointments and promotions within the Civil Service; and (vi) engaging in business activities which represent a conflict of interest (Mills 1997: 25–6).

Some of the measures that have been attempted in Jamaica to combat corruption, albeit with limited success, have included (i) a law requiring disclosure of assets, liabilities and income by senior public officials in an attempt to avoid a conflict of interest; (ii) the establishment of the Office of the Contractor General since 1986, as an impartial institution in monitoring the award of contracts by government agencies; (iii) the Office of the Auditor General together with the Public Accounts Committee which investigate government financial accounts in order to promote financial accountability by government departments; and (iv) the launching of a citizens' charter by the Prime Minister in December 1994, which preaches, among other things, higher standards of conduct among government employees and improvement in the delivery of government services to a well informed public (Government of Jamaica 1995) (Tindigarukayo and Chadwick 1999).

Public sector in Jamaica

The Public Sector in Jamaica supports *c.*100,000 employees – although historically the figure has been as low as 65,000 and as high as around 105,000.

Quoting the World Bank and its assessment of public sector performance in Jamaica:

> in spite of its numerous agencies and employees, the performance of the public sector is inadequate in many critical areas. The general level of efficiency and effectiveness of public entities is very low. The quality of service to the public is poor and characterized by cumbersome procedures, long delays and indifference to public convenience (World Bank 1997).

Generally, the Jamaican public service is seen as typically bureaucratic in the particular way of developing countries bureaucracies – long on detailed regulation, both externally and internally, but short on effective implementation and subject to corruption. Like many developing countries the public sector had grown during the post-war and post-independence period, only to be partially rolled back by (partial) structural adjustments (Franc 1994). Personnel problems appeared acute – with wide wage differentials between public and private sectors, especially at managerial and technical levels. Internal processes are cumbersome and in some cases antiquated, inheriting the worst of colonial administration. Financial control systems were bureaucratic and simultaneously ineffective with resulting widespread waste and mis-spending (Orane 1999).

Some progress has been made in recent years, but "as regards central government, the Administration remains committed to further efficiency ... the improvements and efficiency gains which have already been achieved indicate the full potential in terms of application to the whole service" (MoFP, 2000/01 Budget Presentation).

Public service reforms

The Public Service Modernization Project (PSMP) served to underpin the Government of Jamaica's (GoJ's) efforts to "steer more and row less" (PSMP Project Director, 30/03/99) with the overall goal being enhanced:

- accountability
- transparency
- responsiveness to clients
- service quality.

Creation of Executive Agencies was the cornerstone of this reform effort. Initially, seventeen entities that had been identified for customer service improvement – including possible agency status. Consultation exercises involving these bodies, two ministries, the Trades Unions, stakeholders and the media took place. Six task forces were established covering the areas of: human resources; finance; legal affairs; operations; implementation; and public relations/education. The reports from these task forces provided the basis for the contents of the Public Sector Reform Act, the human resources policies and procedures manuals and the Executive Agency Financial Instructions.

It was acknowledged that the overall programme was influenced by the limited absorptive capacity of the entities involved. As a result, high priority entities that provided a service to a wide cross-section of the public were targeted for initial reform. This strategy was seen as reducing the risks associated with innovation and allowed for the transfer of experiences as a basis for extending the reform process throughout the entire public sector.

In carrying out the reforms concentration focused on two strands:

- entity specific reforms that would modernize the targeted institutions
- systemic reforms that would realize improvements in the general public sector.

The current PSMP differs from previous reform programmes in that "it seeks to convert selected government agencies into decentralized and autonomous, but accountable and transparent 'Executive Agencies' that will operate according to private sector principles" (GOJ, Ministry of Transport and Works, 2000).

The specific objectives of the PSMP include:

- the achievement of major improvements in the quality of service provided by selected public agencies
- assistance for selected ministries to formulate sound sector policies, to effectively monitor and evaluate downstream agencies to ensure achievement of objectives, and to perform corporate management functions efficiently
- to either privatize or contract out services where government has no comparative advantage
- to improve transparency in government procurement and contracting
- to enhance public sector accountability by strengthening both internal and external controls
- to improve the quality of financial and personnel management in the public sector through computerized information systems
- finally, to prepare the next stage of the modernization process which will include extending reforms contained in the PSMP relating to the pilot agencies to the rest of the public sector (Tindigarukayo and Chadwick 1999).

Management of the Executive Agencies Programme

At the outset of the current reform programme the Government of Jamaica (GOJ) reiterated its understanding that the public sector is a key component of social and economic development. As such, the GOJ, with the help of funding from the Japanese government, established in 1994 a Project Management Unit within the Cabinet Office, which itself forms part of the Office of the Prime Minister. The aim of the Project Management Unit was to oversee and develop a 'Public Sector Modernization Project' (PSMP). The mission statement guiding the PSMP is "to create an appropriately staffed, efficient, effective and accountable Public Sector that delivers high-quality service to the people" (PSMP Fact Sheet). The project has three organizational strands:

- first, policy direction is to be provided by the Inter-Ministerial Committee for Administrative Reform (IMCAR), with the chair being the Prime Minister
- a working group of the IMCAR is to provide technical guidance and is to be chaired by the Cabinet Secretary
- the Project Management Unit was to undertake the preparatory work for the project and report directly to the Cabinet Secretary. Additionally, the Unit had responsibility for managing and co-ordinating the implementation of technical and administrative assistance for the project.

During the transition period each Agency was required to produce:

- a modernization plan providing a detailed review of the entity and possible future developmental directions
- a framework Document to establish the rights and obligations of the management of the Agency and the GOJ
- a Medium-Term Financing Plan to provide analysis of projected expenditures covering a five-year period.

The Jamaican model of agencies

As with all administrative change, the exact definition of what constitutes an 'Executive Agency' in the Jamaican context tends to be various and varied. KPMG's team (the main consultants involved) described agencies as public sector bodies which:

i   are customer and performance oriented
ii have enhanced delegated authorities over the management of their resources
iii are part of their parent ministry
iv are staffed by public servants
v   have CEOs employed on short-term performance contracts
vi have clear performance targets recorded in their Framework Documents
vii receive funding from the Ministry of Finance and Planning as part of a Framework Agreement that included the achievement of key performance targets (KPMG 1999: 3).

There had been an intention to enact a special Executive Agencies Bill, which was apparently superseded, by the intention to pass a more general Public Sector Reform Bill. (We are unsure of the status of this legislation at present.) In the absence of specific legislation, a set of 'Financial Instructions to Executive Agencies' were published and amendments made to the Financial Administration and Audit Act and a Delegation

Order drafted, which also took into account the Civil Service Establishment Act.

In the absence of a legal basis for Agencies a formal government definition/description is given in the 'Financial Instructions to Executive Agencies':

2.1.1 Formal definition of Executive Agencies

An Executive Agency is a government entity, which has been formally designated as an Executive Agency in accordance with the provisions of section XX of the Public Sector Reform Act. The process for establishing Executive Agencies is set out in the Public Sector Reform Act.

2.1.2 Description of Executive Agencies

Executive Agencies are government entities which focus primarily on the delivery of services with a results oriented approach to governance. In exchange for delegated managerial autonomy, the Chief Executive Officer of each Executive Agency is held accountable for achieving state results economically, efficiently and effectively.

2.1.3 Activities of Executive Agencies

An Executive Agency is an organization where operational activities can be performed separately from policy activities and where improvements to economy, efficiency, effectiveness and customer service delivery can be achieved by granting greater financial and human resource management responsibilities to a Chief Executive Officer whose actions are governed by a performance contract.

2.1.4 The key principles governing Executive Agencies

The establishment of Executive Agencies is based on three fundamental principles:

- delegated authority, which would incorporate a certain level of autonomy
- accountability
- transparency.

Whilst it is possible to speak of a 'Jamaican' model of Agencies, in fact there are three distinct types of Agency allowed for (see Table 16.1). These are Agencies wholly dependent on state funding (Model 'A' Agencies); agencies partially dependent on state funding, but with substantial income from 'sales' of goods or services (Model 'B'); Agencies wholly independent of state funding that raise more revenue than they spend (Model 'C').

This model of distinct types of Executive Agencies closely resembles the UK approach where Agencies were either 'grossly' funded (i.e. completely

Table 16.1 Comparison of the different Executive Agency financial management models

Features	Model A	Model B	Model C
Will the Executive Agency have to operate within its Frameworks Document and agreed corporate and business plans?	Yes	Yes	Yes
Will the Executive Agency be subject to rigorous and regular performance measurement based on a range of key performance indicators?	Yes	Yes	Yes
Will the Executive Agency remain part of the Consolidated Fund?	Yes	Yes	No
Will expenditure be controlled on a gross basis?	Yes, but levels of income will be considered when setting gross expenditure limits	Partially, expenditure not covered by appropriations in aid will be controlled on a net basis	No
Will appropriations in aid be used?	No	Yes	No
What will Parliament appropriate?	Total gross expenditure	Appropriation in aid plus, if necessary, ordinary appropriation	Subsidy payable to Executive Agency, if any
Will the Executive Agency have budget heads?	Yes, it will have one: Recurrent (including capital A)	Yes it will have one: Recurrent (including capital A)	Yes it will have one: Recurrent (including capital A)
What ability to vire funds will be given to the Executive Agency?	Executive Agency can vire funds from recurrent to recurrent or from capital to	Executive Agency can vire funds from recurrent to recurrent or from capital to	Executive Agency can vire funds from recurrent to recurrent or from capital to

	capital, but not from capital to recurrent or vice versa so long as the total allocation made for the head is not exceeded	capital, but not from capital to recurrent or vice versa so long as the total allocation made for the head is not exceeded	capital, but not from capital to recurrent or vice versa so long as the total allocation made for the head is not exceeded
Will the Executive Agency be encouraged to levy fees and charges?	Yes	Yes	Yes
Should it generally set its fees and charges on a full cost basis?	Yes	Yes	Yes
Can the Executive Agency retain any income (excluding taxes) it generates?	No	Partially	Yes
Can the Executive Agency retain any amount unspent, having achieved its KPIs?	No	Partially	Yes
Will assets be assigned to the Executive Agency?	Yes	Yes	Yes
Will the Executive Agency be able to write off and dispose of assets?	No	Yes	Yes

funded directly by government); 'net' funded (i.e. they can retain revenue to cover direct costs associated with revenue-raising service provision); 'trading funds' (i.e. completely self-funded from revenues). Whilst not exactly identical, the parallels are obvious.

Selecting and establishing Agencies

As in the case of many agencification programmes, the aims of the programme in Jamaica were to reduce central controls by delegating authority to managers within the Agencies or the central civil service departments (those not covered by statute or falling under the Companies Act). The Agencies targeted all had public service delivery goals and, as such, the improvement of quality of service had to be evidenced through the efficient use of resources and staff commitment to enhanced efficiency and management.

The entities targeted were grouped into clusters:

- The first four Agencies created on 1st April 2000 were: the Office of the Registrar of Companies (ORC); the Registrar General's Department (RGD); the Administrator General's Department (AGD); and the Management Institute for National Development (MIND).

The remaining components of the PSMP are:

Cluster I
- The National Environment and Planning Agency
- The National Land Agency
- The National Estate Management Agency
- The Ministry of the Environment

Cluster II
- The Jamaica Promotions Corporation (JAMPRO)
- The Jamaica Information Service (JIS)

Cluster III
- The Ministry of Transport and Works (re-orientation to a policy Ministry)

Cluster IV
- Jamaica Customs (modernization as a revenue agency)
- The Audit Component (improvement of Audit Management in Government)
- Procurement (strengthening of Procurement institutions and processes)
- European Union Component – the Planning Institute of Jamaica

(PIOJ) – (institutional strengthening and transition of commercial mode)
- Works Division of the Ministry of Transport and Works (conversion to National Works Executive Agency).

Throughout the transition to Agency status for the first four entities, the PSMP/PMU worked on the understanding that certain basic considerations had to be addressed for successful transition (the following points cited in PSMP/PMU, 'Minimum Standards for Executive Agency Model', n.d.).

- *Political will to establish agencies* was of primary importance – in particular, the strong political commitment shown by the Prime Minister added credence to the reform process.
- *The legal and administrative framework* underwent analysis to produce a clearly articulated framework for the basis of Agency establishment.
- *Leadership*: the requirements for CEO post-holders were: an appropriate level of training or experience in management, Public Administration or a related social science; a high level of competence and creativity; knowledge of the Public Sector; at least five years' experience at senior management level; the ability to motivate staff and manage change effectively.
- *Performance measurement* and the setting of measurable targets, in consultation with the appropriate minister, were seen as the major means of standard operational practice. In terms of staff, the CEO had delegated authority over human resources and financial management. This meant that establishing greater flexibility over pay enabled the CEO to employ and retain appropriately skilled and qualified staff as deemed necessary by the Agency's operation.

To make this possible the Minister was required to ensure an adequate allocation of resources to enable the Agency to achieve its targets. Equally, the appropriate balance between management and incentives was seen as the basis for success since a lack of managerial independence and rewards would undermine the whole process.

In terms of revenue, "the savings generated from efficient use of resources, increases in user fees, and the retrenchment of staff will form the initial source of funds to provide incentive bonuses to staff once targets have been achieved." It also appears that there was an understanding of the consequences of failing to meet targets, although there still remains little evidence, according to interviews, of any system of sanctions being operative.

- Additionally, *Performance Contracts* were to be developed for each agency with the purpose of clearly delineating the terms and conditions of performance. These contracts are signed by the CEP, stake-holders, the responsible Minister and the Minister of Finance/Finan-cial Secretary.

- *Reformed structures, systems and procedures* were to be in place to efficient use and control of resources. Not only were current operations and business processes to be analysed to secure maximum efficiency, but each Agency was to establish a Human Resources Development Unit to ensure adequate staff development.
- *Financial Management Systems* were to be developed for each agency – including installation of necessary hardware and software and the training of staff to ensure that proper financial accounting proce-dures were observed.
- *Human Resource Management Information System* was to be operational within the Agencies. Within this system the CEO has full authority to fire and hire staff.
- *Training* of staff was a priority. This included developing new approaches to management with the focus being on demand-led training.

It is worth noting that, in parallel with Tanzania, the priority has been given to potential agencies that fall towards the 'Model C' end of the spec-trum – i.e. agencies that have the greatest ability to raise their own rev-enues from fees or services.

Established Agencies

The four established Agencies share certain characteristics, whilst also having some differences. Their similarities include: their relative smallness in relation to the overall public service; their ability to generate income; their relatively clear remit and focus; their 'U-form' internal structures (unitary hierarchy); etc.

Their main differences include: some were already de facto organi-zational structures, whilst others were relatively recently forged into single units; some are purely service delivery whilst others have regulatory func-tions as well; the size of their perceived 'problems' varied enormously with some being relatively successful before Agency status and others under a distinct cloud. (One Agency described itself as the 'gulag' for poor per-formers in the Civil Service.)

These characteristics – especially their relatively small size and ability to generate income – make this 'sample' of Agencies a difficult one for drawing generalizable conclusions about future possibilities for Agencies in Jamaica. They seem, as we will report below, to have been relatively suc-cessful so far (although some of the objective evidence is problematic). Whether this would be true for future Agencies with very different characteristics (e.g. large and resource dependent) is not easy to forecast.

Practice

During 2000, in 2 field visits to Jamaica, extensive interviews were conducted with most of those intimately involved with the agency programme – Agency Managers and staff, departmental managers, central departments and regulatory bodies as well as various external commentators. Evidence from these wide-ranging interviews is collated here in an initial assessment of the Agency Programme in practice, as opposed to the formal programmatic and policy position outlined above. The analysis has been grouped under four headings: leadership, freedom, finance and performance.

Leadership

In 1999 a warning had already been sounded about the Executive Agency programme:

> Given the fact that the 'Executive Agency' approach to Civil Service reform requires ample technical and human resource skills, both of which are scarce in Developing Countries, it is vital that the Jamaican Government seriously assesses and plans how to acquire these requisites before completely embracing the approach. (Tindigarukayo and Chadwick 1999)

In the four Agencies that were already formed at the time this research was conducted, the impression was that – at least at senior management levels – there appeared to be no major problem with 'human resource skills'. All of the four (female) Chief Executives seemed very competent in their posts and were impressive in the leadership they were providing. This does not mean, of course, that there might not be problems further down the road. The cautionary note sounded above also suggested:

> Moreover, the government should develop a policy to pre-empt potential tensions that are likely to develop between highly ranked Civil Servants in central Ministries and heads of large Executive Agencies, where the latter are more likely to be paid more than the former. (Tindigarukayo and Chadwick 1999)

This is clearly a problem which has arisen elsewhere and there were already signs that the self-confident new Chief Executives were having some rather abrasive 'discussions' with their counterparts in the Ministries and especially in Finance.

Freedom

Interviews with the Executive Agencies suggested that, on balance, the granting of autonomy to agencies was working well from their point of view.

They were particularly impressed that the human resources freedoms granted to Agencies, and strongly supported by the Public Service Commission (PSC), seemed to be both real and to have been seriously implemented. The PSC itself seemed to have a strong understanding of the need for a 'light touch' in the regulation of Agencies' personnel practice, whilst maintaining overall standards of probity, equity and merit in personnel policies and practices. Interviews with its officers suggested a sophisticated understanding of these tensions and a rather stronger commitment to the changes than some of those in ministries and Finance who were supposedly driving them. Reforms to the formal role of the PSC were seen as necessary to formalize the new roles and were being developed.

The four Agencies seemed to have well-developed plans and performance targets and whilst there are clearly problematic issues, by and large this seemed to represent successful delegated management in action.

There were, however, according to the Agency senior managers, a number of problematic issues relating to freedom in finance and performance measurement that are mentioned in the relevant sections below.

Finance

In general, the reaction of Agency managers to their new financial freedoms was very positive. The greater freedom to 'vire' funds within budgets; ability to put cash on deposit; greater retention of income; etc. were all cited as positive advantages.

All of the agencies are allowed to retain 50 per cent of extra revenue generated – which in some cases was substantial – the four agencies had already jointly made over J$100m in operational savings in the first half of 1999/2000 (PSMP Project Management Unit 1999). This incentive of retention of extra revenue was mentioned often as a very positive (if somewhat crude) development.

The first problematic issue identified by the agencies was this 50/50 split in increased agency income and/or savings between the Agency itself and the consolidated fund. Agency CEs pointed out that this formula was introduced by the Finance Ministry and did not, in their view, form part of the original Agency Programme. It was a rigid and bureaucratic 'solution' to the problem of how, and how much, agency income should be passed on to Finance. Agency CEs argued, with some justification, that a solution was needed on a case-by-case basis and that any formula ought to relate to overall financial performance, rather than simply be based on income. It should be added that there is a danger that such crude targets can lead to a focus on agencies as income generators rather than service deliverers. In the case of the Office of the Registrar General, for example, this did subsequently seem to lead to a loss of initial gains due to under-investment and a crucial reform in service delivery terms – regional offices – having to be pulled back.

The second complaint related to less formal systems but to more informal practices. Agency CEs claimed that despite their formal freedoms they were still subject to arbitrary budget decisions, informal regulation and 'raids' on agency resources – mainly from the Ministry of Finance. One Agency CE complained that they received "little help from the Ministry of Finance" and promises by the latter were not delivered. Another complained that Finance "don't seem to have even read our Corporate Plan before they imposed arbitrary budget cuts", a comment that was echoed by a third Agency CE, who complained her corporate plan was also ignored. Finally, an Agency CE accused Finance of providing only "peculiar, detailed, nit-picking, comments" on plans and no useful strategic advice and support. The entire group of CEs complained about being grilled on minor budget issues by junior members of Finance staff.

Third, formal monitoring seemed to have increased to levels that appeared excessive. One Agency CE mentioned demands for 2-weekly financial reporting, for example. Another comment from an Agency CE went so far as to say that "Agency autonomy was being systematically eroded by the Ministry of Finance with more and more bureaucracy being imposed". The Ministry's 'Monitoring Unit' for Agencies came in for particular criticism.

Such comments come as little surprise to those who have studied processes of 'autonomization' in other contexts – they closely resemble, for example, similar complaints from Agencies in the UK in the early stages of the 'Next Steps' programme. They may be problems of perception – Agency Chief Executives expecting more autonomy than can reasonably be granted in the public sector. This was certainly partly the case in the UK. On the other hand, it was also true that central organizations (Treasury, Cabinet Office) and parent Ministries took a long time to adjust to taking a more strategic role (Fraser 1991; Trosa 1994; Next Steps Team 1995) and more recent evidence suggests they still have not done so in important respects (Alexander and Agency Policy Review Team 2002). The real issue will probably be whether these problems, whether perceived or real, diminish over time or increase.

An ominous sign in Jamaica may have been the attitude of the Ministry of Finance themselves to this research – whilst every other agency and body cooperated readily with the research, the Finance Ministry simply failed to keep appointments and supplied little other help. The litany of complaints from the agencies – many of which were substantiated by ministry and other officials – were unfortunately not, therefore, explored with the Ministry of Finance. Undoubtedly, they would have a different perspective.

The issue of audit of Agency accounts is covered by the 'Financial Instructions to Executive Agencies' which lays out a well-developed system for internal audit (including an Audit Committee) and for external audit by the Auditor-General. There were no specific issues raised about these financial audit arrangements, although there were some issues about audit of performance information (see below).

Performance

All of the Agencies have developed an extensive (probably sometimes too extensive) performance reporting system and seem to be developing robust systems for reporting externally (including publicly).

Probably most impressive, if relatively small scale, in terms of public communication was the publication of the 'Review of Executive Agencies 2000' by PSMP in 2000. This little pamphlet gave brief but useful reviews of each of the four agencies, together with some remarkably frank 'question and answer' sessions. Whilst a great deal more detail is obviously required to make sober judgements, this initiative is certainly useful in stimulating the interest in public accountability for agencies.

The Agencies themselves have very developed performance reporting systems. There are attempts to make these into 'balanced scorecards' covering a range of important indicators.

A reading of these reports, at present, suggests a number of comments:

First, the Agencies are clearly struggling with developing performance targets and there is a tendency to adopt a 'scatter-gun' approach measuring anything and everything that comes into view. For example, one Agency reported that they had started out with 33 KPIs (which is at the extreme-high end for UK Agencies) but that this had subsequently risen to 61 KPIs. A more sophisticated approach is to have a small set of high-level indicators linked to lower level, more operational, targets that are more for internal and managerial use. There is obviously some learning to be gone through on these issues.

Second, responsibility for setting targets seems not to have been 'settled'. Examples were cited of everything from Agencies effectively setting their own targets, through strong input from parent Ministries, through to strong inputs from Finance and even – in one case – external auditors who were alleged to have invented their own targets for the Agency in question. There seemed to be at least a degree of confusion about the process, roles and responsibilities for setting targets that would appear to need clarifying.

Third, although the theory is that targets should be directed clearly towards outputs (and outcomes?) in practice there is still a tendency to fall back on process targets. This is hardly surprising as it is a common enough phenomenon in the early stages of performance measurement and reporting systems (Talbot 1996). Conversely, where outcome-based targets were selected, one Agency CE complained that these were too 'externally dependent' and unrealistic. While this may or may not be true, a continued dialogue and developing a better consensus between Agency leaderships and others about targets would seem to be developing, if somewhat haphazardly.

Fourth, it is clear that the amount (if not always the quality and focus) of performance reporting is impressive and represents a real effort on the part of Agencies to be held accountable. Besides the PSMP 'Review' of agencies there has been formal reporting to Parliament (for example Ministry Paper 39, tabled by the Prime Minister in April 2000) and this in turn has led to considerable press debate about Agencies (see, for example, *The Jamaica Gleaner*: 11 Feb. 2000; 20 and 26 Mar. 2000; 28 Apr. 2000; 15 May 2000; 10 and 17 June 2000; 8 July 2000; etc.). This is obviously a very healthy degree of transparency and debate which the Agency Programme was, in part, intended to create. This compares pretty favourably with some developed countries where such reforms rarely excite this degree of press interest.

Fifth, the 'Financial Instructions to Executive Agencies' allows for "review of procedures for calculating the value of key performance indic-ators for each Executive Agency" by the Auditor-General. One Agency reported that a recent external audit team had effectively set their own 'targets' for the Agency and then reported against these (rather than the Agency's own targets) to the Public Accounts Committee. We were not able to verify this allegation, but the fact that it was made at all raises issues about the relationship of trust and mutual understanding between Agen-cies and external audit. This may just be an initial 'blip' in the relation-ship and will settle-down but it may also need attention.

Finally, most Agency CEs seemed to believe they had a long way to go in embedding a 'performance culture' in their organizations. Given the early stage of the transformation process, this is hardly surprising. Indeed our impression was that the degree of cultural change achieved was already considerable. The efforts at internal communications – at least if the volume of publications was anything to go by – was an impressive testa-ment to a very real commitment to change.

The actual performance of the first four Agencies seems impressive. Substantial gains in customer service, improved revenue generation, internal process improvements and staff morale all seemed well docu-mented (see the performance reports mentioned above and PSMP Project Management Unit 1999).

Conclusions

The Executive Agencies Programme in Jamaica has – in the context in which it was being carried – apparently made very good progress. Agency performance seems to have improved and despite some difficulties there are improved relationships with Ministries and central departments and some regulators. Relationships with external auditors and the Ministry of Finance seemed more problematic.

The future appears less certain. The context of a 'soft state', widespread corruption and a large informal sector suggests evident dangers in large-scale autonomization (Talbot and Caulfield 2002). These will not inevitably create problems, but they do inescapably pose potential dangers. Even in developed states such reforms can create problems of probity (Public Accounts Committee 1994) and inappropriate political interference in operational management decisions (Talbot 1994). More-over, the creation of 'islands of excellence' may make dramatic improve-ments in their particular niches without necessarily translating into gains in the wider public services.

Bibliography

Alexander, P. and Agency Policy Review Team (2002) Better Government Services – Executive Agencies in the 21st Century (The Agency Policy Review – report and recommendations), London: Cabinet Office.

Franc, E.L. (ed.) (1994) *Consequences of Structural Adjustment*, Kingston: University of the West Indies.

Fraser, A. (1991) *Making the Most of Next Steps: The Management of Ministers' Depart-ments and their Executive Agencies*, London: HMSO.

Government of Jamaica (1995) *Minimum Standards for Executive Agency Model*, a pamphlet produced by the Public Sector Modernization Project, September 20.

KPMG (1999) *Government of Jamaica – Executive Agencies – Guide to Best Practice*, Kingston, Jamaica: KPMG.

Mills, G. (1997) *Westminster Style Democracy: The Jamaican Experience, The Grace Kenney Foundation Lecture 1997*, Kingston, Jamaica: Stephensons' Litto Press.

Ministry of Finance and Planning (2000) Budget Memorandum 2000/2001, MOF website: www.mof.gov.jm/budget_memo/2000.

Ministry of Transport and Works (2000) Modernization Plan, MTW, Kingston, Jamaica (web page: www.mtw.gov.jm/html/ModPlan.htm).

Next Steps Team (1995) *The Strategic Management of Agencies*, London: Cabinet Office (OPS).

Orane (1999) *Report of the Task Force to Reduce Waste in the Public Sector*, Kingston, Government of Jamaica.

PSMP (2000) *Review of Executive Agencies*, Kingston, Jamaica: PSMP.

PSMP Project Management Unit (1999) *Project Biennial Report to the World Bank*, Kingston, Jamaica.

Public Accounts Committee (1994) *Eighth Report: The Proper Conduct of Public Busi-ness (154)*, HMSO.

Talbot, C. (1994). *Reinventing Public Management – A Survey of Public Sector Managers' Reactions to Change*, London: Institute of Management (formerly BIM).

Talbot, C. (1996). *Ministers and Agencies: Control, Performance and Accountability*, London: CIPFA.

Talbot, C. and Caulfield, J. (eds) (2002) *Hard Agencies in Soft States*, Pontypridd: University of Glamorgan.

Tindigarukayo, J. and Chadwick, S. (1999). *Civil Service Reform in Jamaica*, UNDP.

Trosa, S. (1994) *Next Steps: Moving On*, London: Cabinet Office (OPSS).

World Bank (1997) *Jamaica: Public Sector Modernisation Project (Report No PIC774)*, World Bank, Washington, DC.

World Bank (2000) *Jamaica: Country Assistance Strategy (Report No. 21187-JM)*, World Bank, Washington, DC.

Part V

Overview

17 Theoretical overview

Christopher Pollitt

Introduction

The purpose of this chapter is to take stock of current theorizing about agencies, principally as that theorizing has been done within the covers of this book, but also, necessarily, with some references to the wider literature. 'To take stock' is a fairly imprecise (though perhaps for that reason often-used) phrase. Here I will give it the following more specific meanings:

- To review how the contributing authors have used theory – in particular, which theories have they used, and for what purposes?
- To assess the usefulness of these theories for the ends to which they have been put (and occasionally to speculate on other ways in which they might be used).
- To comment on the connections (if any) between academic theories on these matters and 'practitioner theories' – the rationales offered by the ministers and civil servants who have been most responsible for the many acts of agency creation and agency reform which have been described herein.
- To explore the scope for *integrating* different theoretical approaches, or, in some cases, to take note of the *incompatibility* of alternative theories.
- To offer some concluding reflections about possible directions for future research on agencies.

But before starting out on even the first of these steps, some elaborations and qualifications (and a few pre-emptive apologies) are already necessary. First, I want to make clear that the purpose of this exercise is not to pick the 'best' theory, and consign all the others to the rubbish bin. Competition between theories, in order to produce better explanations, is a very fine thing and an essential part of the academic endeavour. As far as agencies are concerned, however, I would suggest that this book shows (if further demonstration were needed) that we are as yet a long way from the happy state of advancement where tightly-ordered theories can be matched against each other in some kind of controlled trial, and a winner duly declared. As Geert Bouckaert and Guy B. Peters showed in Chapter 2, theorizing about agencies is currently quite immature – the phenomena are ill-defined, the data-collection strategies unsystematic, the institutional and cultural assumptions of much of the dominant Anglo-Americo-Australasian literature unduly parochial. Hopefully, this book has itself pushed the boundaries outwards somewhat, but certainly not to the point where 'winners' can be chosen. Rather, we are still hacking through the undergrowth, trying to get a clearer view of the nature of the landscape. That is the spirit in which I will be assessing the usefulness of the various theories which are in play.

Second, the question 'for what purposes' (see above) is a vital one, which will be taken up in greater detail in the next section. A theory that does a good job in answering the question 'Why did the UK launch an agency programme in 1988?' may not work well in answering the question 'Why is the Benefits Agency so different from the Wilton Park Conference Centre?' (both agencies) and probably won't do at all if the question becomes 'What accounts for the respective performances of different agencies in Tanzania?'. In short, different theories are more or less appropriate to different kinds of question, and so discussing one in the absence of the other is usually rather a fruitless exercise.

Finally, I should apologize to my fellow contributors because I have written *my* review of *their* use of theory with only limited consultation. This is one of the privileges but also perils of being 'tail-end Charlie' in an edited collection such as this. The overview is written after the others have finished their contributions. All I can say is that, from the reader's point of view, this may help to guarantee a measure of independent assessment – there has been no 'fudging' in the *collegium* to preserve professional relations! More importantly, however, I would emphasize that what I am trying to do here is not at all to assess the quality of individual chapters, but to assess the usefulness of the theories themselves. In any case, as any academic knows, it is occasionally possible to write a brilliant paper on the back of a weak theory, and the opposite is certainly also true – many awful papers claim to be based on perfectly respectable theories.

Which theories and for what purposes?

Unbundled government offers a veritable zoo of theories. Different authors utilize different theories and combinations of theories with different degrees of explicitness. Some use rational choice theory. Some favour historical institutionalism, or institutional isomorphism, or path dependency or network theory or Kingdon's policy process model, or whatever. Some acknowledge their theoretical allegiance at the outset, others launch forth into a description and analysis of their subject matter with their theoretical tool kit hidden beneath their flowing prose.

One (but not the only) reason for this theoretical pluralism is that different chapters have addressed different key questions. For example, Gains (Chapter 3) seeks to explain the variation in the way that agencies were conceived and set up within the UK Next Steps programme. Johnston and Romzek (Chapter 5) ask what explains the variations in the effectiveness of contract accountability in the social services sector in the USA. Taliercio (Chapter 14) wants to know what has motivated the recent wave of creations of autonomous revenue authorities in the developing world, whether there is a connection between the degree of autonomy and the level of performance of those authorities, and how sustainable such reforms are likely to be. Obviously, these are quite different kinds of questions, set in quite different institutional and cultural contexts.

Table 17.1 attempts to capture something of this variety by showing the main theoretical perspectives deployed in the book, and the types of questions they have been set to answer. Not all chapter authors are mentioned in the Table because not all of them have been explicit in their selection of theories, and, in any case, the purpose here is a broad overview, not a stamp collection of every specimen.

The theories represented in Table 17.1 come from very different parts of the social sciences universe, and themselves rest upon profoundly different assumptions about the nature of human behaviour, judgement and communication. As a preliminary to further discussion, it may be worth here reminding ourselves of what some of the key assumptive differences are.

One might say that there are three broad families of theories present within the list given in Table 17.1. These are as follows:

- 'Traditional', mainstream social science: innovation diffusion theory, some network theory (but see below), contract specification and design, Kingdon's model of the policy process.
- Economistic approaches: rational choice theory.
- Interpretive/constructivist theories: historical institutionalism, institutional isomorphism, some (other) network theory, Latour's translation theory.

The traditional social science model

The traditional social science model concentrates on a clear definition of terms and concepts, and on identifying a set of independent variables which 'explain' most or all of the variance in the dependent variable. The Johnston and Romzek chapter gives a clear account of this method in action. The Peters and Bouckaert chapter (2) is cast within broadly the same mould – they want clear definitions, a random sample of agencies, a coding and measurement of autonomy along several dimensions and a search for patterns between these variables – what varies with what, and

Table 17.1 Theories used in 'unbundling government'

Theory	Questions addressed	Comments and findings
Rational choice theory	1. Why have Dutch politicians made increasing use of quangos (van Thiel) 2. Why have politicians in many countries opted to set up Autonomous Revenue Agencies (ARAs)? (Taliercio)	1. Found to be quite a weak explanation on its own. 2. Found to be quite a strong explanation. Also degree of autonomy explains performance and sustainability.
Innovation diffusion theory	1. How and why have quangos spread in Dutch central and local government? (van Thiel)	1. Some use for explaining *how* (the pattern of spread) of quangos, but not useful for explaining why the form was chosen, or why it varies.
Kingdon's policy process model	1. Why did Japan launch an agencification programme in the late 1990s? (Yamamoto)	1. Kingdon's model well describes how political trends, policy development and particular problems come together in a 'window of opportunity'
Contract specification and design	1. What explains the variations in the effectiveness of contract accountability in US social policy delivery agencies? (Johnston and Romzek)	1. Certain features do appear to support effective accountability. However, the larger picture with respect to contracts is one of 'muddling through'
Network theory	1. Why has the UK government begun to make efforts better to co-ordinate and 'join up' agencies and departments? (James)	1. Network-style interdependencies explain why narrowly conceived performance measures for single agencies can produce negative systemic effects.
Historical institutionalism/path dependency	1. Why do agencies vary so much, even within a single programme? (Gains) 2. How can we best explain the longevity of the Swedish agency system? (Pierre) 3. Why have some Latvian agencies got out	1. Path dependency at departmental levels influenced which functions were agencified, and how the agencies were operated. 2. Informal (but institutionalized) practices

		of control? (Pollitt)	have developed which offset the disadvantages of a strict policy/operations split. 3. Path dependency helps explain weakness of Latvian ministries, lack of accountability and persistence of corruption.
Institutional isomorphism		1. Why have Dutch politicians made increasing use of quangos? (van Thiel) 2. Why has Jamaica launched a programme of agencification? (Talbot)	1. Some evidence for various types of isomorphic copying. 2. Jamaica has been strongly influenced by the UK agency programme (mixture of coercive and mimetic isomorphism)
Latour's translation theory		1. How does the notion of agency seem to change as it crosses national and sectoral boundaries? (Smullen)	1. Latour's model describes well how international representations of the 'agency' form were strongly edited, first, to fit the Dutch national context and then, second, to fit particular departmental interests.

under what conditions? The hope is to find empirical regularities, and then identify the underlying causes of these patterns, so that generalizations – and, ultimately, predictions for other, similar situations – can be made. This kind of theory normally employs a correspondence theory of truth – the basic assumption is that reality is 'out there' and the job of social scientists is to uncover it by patient observation, classification and measurement. The better they do their job, the closer the correspondence will be between the theories and the real world.

The limitations of this approach are reflected in the two following models – the economistic and the interpretive/constructivist. In a sense, both launch themselves on the back of a critique of traditional social science (though a very different one in each case). The economistic model claims to be more elegant and precise – fewer assumptions yielding clearer, more measurable predictions. The economistic model may seem really 'scientific' because it can express so many of its key insights as mathematical formulae. Meanwhile, the interpretive/constructivist model claims to be more sophisticated – to discard the naïve correspondence theory and put our slippery, reflexive mental and rhetorical processes back at the heart of understanding. From this perspective, the 'patterns' which the traditional social scientist claims to find turn out to be no more than artifacts which s/he him/herself put there – not 'real' empirical regularities but merely the output of a particular set of chosen definitions and methods. We can now look at these two alternatives to 'mainstream' social science in slightly more detail.

The economistic model

The economistic model is less inductive, more deductive than traditional social science. It sets up its initial assumptions very explicitly, and formulates hypotheses for testing. Behind rational choice theory stands the model of a rational actor, bent upon maximizing his/her utility (Allison and Zelikow 1999; Douma and Schreuder 1998). Actors have goals, identify alternative choices of action and calculate the consequences of each. In their interactions with other actors (taxpayers with politicians, in the Taliercio chapter) they make strategic moves based on their assumptions about the goals, alternatives, etc. of the other actors. These rather simple assumptions about human motivation are often criticized by other social scientists, but they have at least one great advantage – that they permit and encourage the formulation of hypotheses which predict behaviour under given conditions, and which, in principle, can be tested. This model has proved very popular over the past quarter century, not only in economics (especially the 'New Institutional Economics'), but also in political science and public management (see, e.g. Dunleavy 1991; Peters 1999: Chapter 3).

Considerable differences – and controversies – exist even within the 'rational choice' camp. For example, the economistic model of civil servants as 'budget maximizers', made very popular by Niskanen and others in the early 1970s, is now widely rejected as both too US-specific (Goodin 1982) and far too simple (Dunleavy 1991 – for the original, see Niskanen 1971). Dunleavy puts forward a much more sophisticated model of senior civil servants as 'bureau-shapers', actively seeking organizational re-arrangements which will leave them with more interesting, higher status work, while putting boring routine work and difficult tasks (where the outside world may resist implementation) safely 'at a distance' and in other hands. In short, most civil servants would rather be in the ministerial prisons strategy unit, giving advice, than in the prisons agency trying actually to manage a prison full of dangerous criminals and poorly paid, disaffected staff. It goes without saying that this kind of model has major implications for the study of agencification.

'Externally', criticisms of rational choice theory abound. One rather worrying practical problem for the researcher is the nature of rationality itself. Behaviour is explained in terms of the actor's pursuit of certain goals, within a system of feasible choices and constraints. In analysis, an action is 'explained' by tracing it back to the actor's goals – by showing that, in terms of consequences, it was the logical thing to do at the time. However, since we cannot look directly into the minds of actors (indeed, since many politicians and civil servants are past masters at *concealing* the nature of their true thoughts) we have a problem. At the level of general theory, the problem may not look so bad – actors maximize their utility (or, in bounded rationality versions of the basic model, they satisfice – Allison and Zelikow 1999). But when researching specific and particular problems – the reasons for creating agencies for example – the difficulty is considerable. What were the goals of the politicians involved? Frequently, all we can find is an untidy tangle of official statements and sound bite pronouncements – incomplete, multivalent, sometimes internally contradictory (see van Thiel's section on 'Motives', Chapter 8). And if the researcher goes to interview the aforesaid politicians afterwards, the problem of hindsight bias looms large – the interviewees' knowledge of subsequent events is highly likely to influence them, consciously or otherwise, towards a too-neat, sanitized account of their former reasoning (Fischoff 1975). Furthermore, we have good reasons to suppose that politicians' preference schedules can shift rather rapidly – indeed, it is one of the hallmarks of an acute politician that they 'move with the times'. So their motives for creating agency X in 1999 may not be the same as their motives for splitting it or adding to its responsibilities or otherwise reforming it in 2003. Thus the data requirements for a full rational choice analysis of agency reforms would appear to be rather formidable.

Thus rational choice theories may work best in situations where it is highly plausible to make some fairly straightforward assumptions about the goals and preferences of the main actors – in a competitive market where profit maximization seems paramount, for example, or during a military campaign where the goal of the general is to outwit and defeat his opponent. The reform of public sector organizations seldom provides such a clear-cut situation. More commonly it involves multiple, shifting agendas, and sometimes complex linkages with other issues. Even in these situations, however, individual elements of rational choice theory (such as transaction costs or asset specificity) may still prove useful, despite the fact that other parts of the theory may be discarded.

Interpretive/constructivist theories

These theories step away from the traditional assumption that reality is out there waiting to be uncovered, classified, measured, predicted, etc. Their adherents maintain that most or all social artifacts (definitely including agencies!) are constructed and constantly reconstructed in minds and texts. So there is no such thing as a 'real agency' that can be captured like a butterfly in a net, and then pinned to the board as an ideal specimen. Instead, there are various competing perspectives on what things are, and what they mean, and the best the social scientist can hope to find is a temporary, partial consensus on what constitutes a particular 'agency'. Often, however, the consensus will be weak or non-existent, so that an 'agency' will mean different things to different people in different countries or even that a given agency in a given country at a given time will mean different things to its different stakeholders. The borrowing of terms will go on, as will attempts to copy allegedly successful practices, but each 'translation' will be imperfect, so that certain meanings will be lost and new meanings gained. All sorts of accidents and unexpected conjunctures will affect the course of events (as in the famous 'garbage can' model of organizational decision-making – Cohen, March and Olsen 1972). These fluid processes are by no means necessarily random, however. Translations, borrowings and reform attempts are extensively moulded by the agendas and understandings of the powerful.

Users of the interpretive/constructivist approach are also extremely interested in the spaces which can and do open up between what people say, what they decide to do and what they actually end up doing (or not, as the case may be). Such scholars often point towards startling gaps between rhetoric and practice – as in Nils Brunsson's memorably titled book, *The organization of hypocrisy: talk, decisions and actions in organization* (1989). This kind of perspective would lead the researcher to approach the fine words of ministerial speeches and White Papers with great caution.

In much of the constructivist approach to organizational analysis a different type of logic is held to prevail from the consequentialism on which the economistic paradigm is based. Organizations, according to the influential work of March and Olsen (e.g. March and Olsen 1989), usually work on the basis of a *logic of appropriateness*. That is, the members of an organization 'will think more about whether an action conforms to the norms of the organization than about what the consequences will be...' (Peters 1999: 29).

The weaknesses of this approach are several. At the extreme, this kind of thinking may generate post-modernist denials of any possibility of generalizations or 'meta narratives' (though, as many have noticed, this denial is itself a massive generalization). Since this type of radical 'deconstruction' is not represented among our contributors, I need refer to it no further here, though it does have a presence in organization studies. However, even more 'mainstream' texts within the broadly constructivist paradigm often display certain characteristic limitations. To begin with, they tend to be much less specific than traditional social science about research methods and criteria (there are honourable exceptions to this generalization). 'Interpretation' can easily become an excuse for sliding over difficult methodological issues. There is seldom the same sharp sense of 'warranted' knowledge as one finds in good mainstream social science. One finds excellent and persuasive characterizations of situations, marvellously ingenious textual interpretations, but a less-than-clear account of how these were arrived at, and how alternative interpretations were ruled out. There is frequently heavy emphasis on *how* things happen – or how things are presented – a predominantly processual view of the world. There is less concern – or even a certain reluctance – to address the fundamental task of explaining *why*. Furthermore, like rational choice theories, the practice of a thorough-going social constructivism makes huge information demands on the researcher who is interested in public sector reform. One has to access and understand so many meanings and assumptions, on the part of so many actors, and fit these into a wider knowledge of organizational standard operating procedures and norms of appropriateness. Comparative work is especially challenging, as different cultural assumptions come into play. Some of the most convincing examples of the social constructivist approach are quite small scale – little jewels of description and analysis. An international, or even inter-sectoral comparative study of agencification or contractualization would be challenging indeed.

How successful have these theories been?

The short answer is that different theories have been more or less successful in answering different questions. In an ideal world we would be able to compare the answers which rival theories produced to the *same* question, but, as Table 17.1 indicates, that situation has occurred seldom, if at all, within these covers. [Neither does it occur very often anywhere else.] Van Thiel's chapter is the only one where several theories (rational choice, innovation diffusion theory, institutional isomorphism) are compared. In most of the other chapters the authors introduce just one theory, or model, and see how much it helps with the question(s) they want to pose. Usually their answer is that the theory/model in question *is* useful (James, Johnson and Romzek, Smullen, Taliercio and Yamamoto all seem to fall into this category). Van Thiel's analysis of the spread of quangos in Dutch central and local government is particularly interesting because she begins with rational choice theory and then, when rational choice doesn't seem to work very well, moves on to look at two other theories. She finds that innovation diffusion theory does help to explain the pattern of spread of agencies – *how* the organizational form is propagated, but not *why* that form was chosen in the first place or *why* it varies from one location to another. She then argues that the theory of institutional isomorphism also provides us with an understanding of *why* copying takes place and can even account for local diversity. My own gloss on this most interesting account would be to say that institutional isomorphism *à la* Powell and DiMaggio does indeed offer a set of three mechanisms for the convergence and copying of forms, but it does not really explain why that particular form was the one that was chosen in the first place. Nor am I entirely convinced that it works well in explaining diversity – after all, it is a theory that was built in order to explain precisely the opposite – similarities within an organizational field. I do not wish to be misunderstood here – van Thiel's description of why diversity occurs strikes me as an entirely reasonable one; it is just that I am not sure it can be attributed to Powell and DiMaggio!

I have dwelt on van Thiel's chapter somewhat because it leads me to – or rather back to – a more general point. It is that different theories are constructed to answer different questions. Therefore, there may be some insight to be gained if we reverse the order in Table 17.1, put questions first, and then see what we can say about the usefulness of the various theories for answering those particular types of question.

What questions do we have about agencies and contracts? Very many, obviously. The second column of Table 17.1 gives some indication of the variety. We can boil these down to a smaller number of more protean questions. These would include the following:

- Why was the agency/quango/contractual form chosen?
- Why has it spread so far, so quickly?
- Why does this spread, on closer inspection, appear to yield such diversity?
- Are agencies/contracts more economical/efficient/effective than [some other form of organization or relationship]?
- If they are more economical/efficient/effective, why are they (under what conditions)?
- How much autonomy is enough?

Why agencies/quangos/contracts?

Curiously, this most basic and obvious of questions is one of the least satisfactorily answered. Practitioners may have answers (higher efficiency, better customer focus, etc.) but academics are not so sure. Rational choice theories tend to assume that the popularity of the form must be due to its greater efficiency, but that is highly debatable (see below). Innovation diffusion theory is focused on the pattern and timing of diffusion, less on the underlying reason why, which is taken for granted (van Thiel, Chapter 8). Network theories (James, Chapter 4) may help us understand why and how some of the fragmenting consequences of agency creation can be ameliorated, but are not focussed on the original reasons why agencies were brought into being. Johnston and Romzek (Chapter 5) are less concerned with the issue of why there has been a move to contracting out than with the consequent problems of how to design contracts to achieve certain desired effects. Historical institutionalism/path dependency theory show why agencies are less revolutionary than some of their advocates would have us suppose – how they are 'tamed' within the existing politico-administrative system rather than why they were chosen in the first place (Pollitt, Chapter 15 and, at least implicitly, Caulfield, Chapter 12). Institutional isomorphism shows why particular organizational forms spread and multiply, but not why they were first chosen (van Thiel, Chapter 8). Latour's model of translation was not built to deal with this question – in many respects it is more of a 'how' than a 'why' theory (Smullen, Chapter 9).

Perhaps there isn't a strong reason why the agency/quango form was originally chosen. Perhaps it was a kind of guided accident. 'Guided' because it formed part of a long-term alternation of opposites, a steady swing of fashion between one pole and another. Other theories explain rather well why, once the idea of an autonomized public agency was on the scene, it was copied, edited, translated, disseminated (see next question, below). But why should there be such an oscillation between different organizational forms? There are some quite strong theories why this may happen, although they do not happen to have made an appearance in this volume until now. One exponent of these – Christopher Hood – has developed an anthropological scheme in which dominant ideas in public management alternate between different ideals (Hood and Jackson 1991; Hood 1998). Among doctrines of how to organize, for example, he suggests that the idea of better decisions through specialization (one of the arguments used for agencies and quangos) alternates with the idea of better decisions through consolidation (the idea of joined-up government, discussed by James in Chapter 4) (Hood and Jackson 1991: 114–16). From this theoretical perspective the answer to the question 'Why agencies?' is 'because, after a period of strategic planning and centralized thinking, it was time for doctrines of disaggregation and decentralization to take over –

for a while'. But why should this alternation exist? Hood says 'cultural dynamics work by mutual antagonism among opposites seeking to blame adherents of alternative ways of life for the social ills they are held to create' (Hood 1998: 11).

In short, the grass on the other side is always greener. We choose one particular way of organizing (centralized/decentralized/hierarchical/ egalitarian) and then, as we experience its character, we begin to see the advantages of its opposite. This kind of theory should perhaps be given greater attention in future work on agencies, quangos and contracts.

Why have agencies, quangos and contracts spread so fast and far?

This question has attracted somewhat more attention than the basic question of 'Why agencies?'. Rational choice offers an essentially functionalist explanation – agencies and quangos have multiplied because they are more efficient than whatever forms preceded them (Taliercio, Chapter 14). Institutional isomorphism theory describes three mechanisms which, jointly or severally, encourage a convergence of forms within a particular field. Organizations copy other organizations either because they are told to do so (coercive isomorphism), or because, under uncertainty, they think the best course is to copy high reputation/apparently successful organizations (mimetic isomorphism), or because professional or technical norms have been established which everyone feels obliged to observe (normative isomorphism). Two or more of these three forms may be mixed together in a particular case.

Several of our contributors found evidence to support an 'isomorphic' interpretation. In Yamamoto's chapter on Japan, for example, it becomes clear that senior Japanese policymakers were familiar with the UK Next Steps programme, and regarded it as a success. In Tanzania (Chapter 12) and Jamaica (Chapter 16) the influence of models from the ex-colonial power was clear to see. In the Netherlands, Smullen shows that the original reports promoting agencification also drew on Next Steps. In my own chapter on Latvia I outline how agencies were understood as something modern and 'businesslike', that would stand in contrast to the alleged bureaucratic inertia of ministries.

Why is there so much diversity, within the general trend?

Van Thiel attempts to explain this using institutional isomorphism, arguing that, with many different templates, many different variants are likely to be copied. Smullen turns to Latour's idea of translation. Here translation is a process that goes far beyond simply paraphrasing or reproducing the same entity in a different context. Latour describes a process in which the 'translation', far from being a 'copy' turns out to bear little relation to the core elements in the original. One might argue that this was true of the relationship between Japanese IAIs and UK Next Steps agencies, or, indeed, the even weaker resemblance between Latvian agencies and those of the Netherlands, Sweden or the UK

Are agencies/quangos more economical and/or efficient and/or effective than some specified alternative?

Surprisingly, perhaps, most of the theories listed in Table 17.1 have nothing to say about this issue. Historical institutionalism/path dependency are theories which show why fundamental change is usually constrained. They are not concerned with the '3 "E"s', one way or another. Likewise institutional isomorphism – Powell and DiMaggio offer no hints on how to identify or measure efficiency or effectiveness. They do point out that a reputation for high performance may act as a reason for copying ('if Rank Xerox does benchmarking, then so should we!') but they are not so concerned with how to tell whether that reputation was deserved or not. Kingdon's policy process model certainly does not address efficiency in any direct way – it is focused on chance coincidences of problems and solutions and political capacities. And the idea that Bruno Latour might be interested in measuring efficiency is faintly comic – he has other fish to fry. In short, from the portfolio of theories used by our contributors, only rational choice theory (Chapter 14), network theory (Chapter 4) and contract specification and design (Chapter 5) really trade at all in the currency of efficiency and effectiveness, and even they come at the issue in varying and somewhat oblique ways.

First, rational choice theory. Here efficiency, in the sense of technical, 'X' efficiency (productivity, high input/output ratios) is assumed to be the fuel which powers the drive towards new organizational forms. They are chosen because they lower transaction costs and increase effectiveness. If this is true, then it certainly provides a powerful answer to the question, 'Why agencies?' Unfortunately, however, there is hardly any reliable evidence to support this assumption (it *could* be true, but we just don't know). Neither in the UK nor in the Netherlands, nor apparently in any other country has there been any scientific study that shows that conversion from a division in a ministry to an autonomous agency or quango consistently produces enhancements in efficiency or effectiveness. [Another interesting question, which for reasons of space cannot be pursued here, is 'Agencies compared with what?'. We tend to assume that the correct comparison is a division in a multi-functional ministry, but in practice many new agencies and quangos were, in their previous lives, already rather specialized units, and not necessarily 'ordinary' divisions of ministries at all.] A detailed study of autonomized schools, hospitals and housing agencies in the UK concluded that in no case could the managers of the autonomized organizations systematically compare their post-autonomy performance with the pre-autonomy state (and neither were they particularly interested in doing so – Pollitt, Birchall and Putman 1998). So what we are dealing with is, at best, a plausible working assumption or, at worst, a piece of empty doctrine. If we really want to know whether autonomization – or contractualization – enhances efficiency – then we need some very precise studies. Even in the area of contracting out – where quite a few direct studies of efficiency have been carried out – the picture remains murky, and many of the academic studies contain serious methodological flaws (Boyne 1998).

Second, network theory. This is a rapidly developing field, already sporting many varieties. Much of the literature is rather weak methodologically, and quite a few network theorists seem reluctant or incapable of formulating specific, testable and non-trivial propositions, preferring to stay on the high ground of general descriptions and assertions of the growing importance of networks (Pollitt 2003, Chapter 3). The potential, however, is strong. In the case of UK agencies the argument is that networks offer a way of preserving some of the original efficiency objectives of agencification whilst reducing the fragmentation/hollowing out of the public sector and achieving 'joined-up-ness' (James, this volume, Chapter 4). But we must beware sweeping generalizations – as James points out, there are different types of networks, co-ordinated through different kinds of mechanism, and these are each likely to have different performance characteristics (both in terms of advantages and weaknesses). For social security (a function with highly specific characteristics) James favours the solution of a regulated network, guided by some strategic performance targets which will encourage different agencies and authorities to work together instead of each ploughing its own furrow. This type of analysis is persuasive, and has the merit that it does compare a number of different approaches to solving a particular co-ordination problem. In its present form, however, it is still suggestive rather than systematic. There is a long way to go before one could pronounce, on the basis of empirical analysis, that one particular formation (a set of X ministries and agencies performing functions p, q, r organized as a network of type A) was more efficient or effective than set X organized in a different way – perhaps as a quasi-market of type B or a fragmented hierarchy of type C.

Third, contract specification. The main thrust of the Johnston and Romzek chapter (5) is that careful designing of contracts can lead to certain desired outputs (in this particular case, transparency and accountability). The theory is that the presence of certain independent variables (e.g. clear specification of responsibilities, ease of performance data collection) will indeed promote the looked-for results (accountability as the dependent variable). However, it is also clear from the analysis that much depends on the specific characteristics of individual functions (foster care, in-home care for the elderly) and on the capacities of the various organizations involved. In other words, the contract designer needs to understand the capacities and interrelationships of the organizations involved in a given function – just writing a clear contract is not enough. Some of these issues also emerge, perhaps in a more oblique way, in McGuire's analysis of performance measurement in Australia (Chapter 6). In general it might be said that, like network theory, this is a promising beginning, but that we need both a more comprehensive classification of types of instrument (contracts/networks) and a matching classification of types of context. There are signs that this work is underway – see, for example, Lane's theoretical treatment of the use of contracts in the public sector (Lane 2000).

What conditions influence the economy/efficiency/effectiveness of agencies/quangos/contracts?

Many of the remarks about the preceding question may be equally applied to this one, i.e. most of the theories used in this book are not particularly concerned with this issue. The three obvious exceptions are rational choice theory, network theory and the type of mainstream 'What makes contracts work?' social science carried out by Johnston and Romzek. In this regard, rational choice theory is a rich source. Principal agent theory, in particular, spells out a number of conditions which should obtain if a principal (the ministry) is to be able to monitor an agent (the agency or quango) (Doumer and Schreuder 1998). What is more, this body of thought has had some direct influence on reform – at least in a few countries (e.g. Boston *et al.* 1996). Network theory is not normally quite so prescriptive. Nevertheless, some network theorists suggest general principles which they believe help to promote the effective functioning of networks. For example, a strong distinction is drawn between *network (re)structuring* and *network management*, with the suggestion that governments may often be well-advised to attend to the former task, while leaving management to some more 'neutral', trusted party (Kickert, Klijn and Kopenjaan 1997). Note, however, that an effective network is not necessarily at all the same thing as an effective agency or even an effective policy or programme. Much agency theorizing is principally directed at procedural goals – how to get the network working well as a network – rather than at substantive goals such as reducing poverty or crime or improving public health. One might say that the chapter on Swedish agencies – although it never mentions network theory *per se* – strongly implies that it is only the existence of strong informal networks which allows a system of agencies and ministries to continue to function reasonably smoothly, despite the fact that it has drifted far away from the 'original design'. Finally, we can mention contract design theory, where it seems (Chapter 6) that clarity of task specifications, clarity of roles and agreement on measurable outcomes are significant influences on contract effectiveness.

Interestingly enough, however, there are a number of other clues to agency performance lying around in the various chapters, but nowhere are they brought together and articulated into an explicit model or theory. Thus, for example, Yamamoto (Chapter 11), Caulfield (Chapter 12), Bowornwathana (Chapter 13) and Pollitt (Chapter 15) all suggest that the absence of certain basic conditions in the administrative context will reduce or prevent the efficiency gains which were supposed to accompany agencification. McGuire (Chapter 6) suggests that, according to the Australian experience, a mixture of contractualization and performance measurement is much more likely to bear fruit in some functional sectors than in others. These are all perfectly plausible interpretations, but they have not yet been strongly connected to theory.

To interrogate these 'clues' a little further, Caulfield (Chapter 12) notes that budgetary instability undermines attempts to make performance measurement for agencies important. In the same chapter she also comments on the difficulty parent ministries have in steering agencies if the agencies know that political power largely resides elsewhere (in the President's Office or some other central department). This last point is not confined to developing countries such as Tanzania. In the US one of the factors limiting the ability of the President and his secretaries of state to steer federal agencies is the network of political allegiances which some agencies maintain with the very powerful US legislature. Or again, in my chapter on Latvia, I point out that steering and performance management is extremely difficult if ministers lack popular authority, and if personnel rules mean that agencies can hire experts who will consistently outgun the understaffed, underqualified ministries. Finally, we can note (McGuire, Chapter 6) that it is easier to measure and steer standardized processes such as social security or licensing than unstandardized processes where professional discretion plays a large part (such as schools or hospitals or social services – see also Pollitt, 2003, Chapter 7). Additionally, the political salience of the activity is likely to influence the degree of 'steering' which ministers wish to undertake (for a tragi-comedy on this subject, you should read the story of the dismissed Director General of the UK Prison Service – Lewis, 1997). The point here is that at least some of the raw materials for a middle-range theory, which distinguishes between the varying 'steerability' and 'measurability' of different agencies and quangos, are already present in our material. Such a theory would be both contingent and complex – not as 'catchy' as institutional isomorphism or even rational choice. It would be 'traditional social science', with all the advantages and limitations that that entails. But it would be a very useful addition to our armoury of ideas about agencies and quangos, and it does not seem to be too far out of reach.

How much autonomy is enough?

This question seems to lurk beneath a number of the chapters. It is, of course, a normative question, and therefore cannot hope to find a single, scientific answer. Much will depend on personal values and cultural norms, and these are likely to be different in, say, a centralized, adversarial political system that stresses individual ministerial responsibility (UK, New Zealand) than in a decentralized, more collectivist system such as Sweden's (Pierre, Chapter 10) or a highly centralized Presidential system like Tanzania (Caulfield, Chapter 12). Gains and James note that the amount of autonomy previously given to Next Steps agencies was considered too much by the New Labour administration which came to power in 1997. Ministers wanted more control and more 'joining up'. In Japan, however, Yamamoto is concerned that the new agencies will not enjoy *sufficient* autonomy. In particular, they will still be caught within the 'iron cage' of civil service personnel rules, and will be run (mainly) by the same types of people who have for so long operated the rather conservative Japanese bureaucratic system. In my chapter on Latvia, however, I see the opposite problem – agencies have been created without the rules or the capacities for the parent ministries to hold them to account. The kind of institutionalized vigilance fundamental to liberal democratic regimes in Western Europe and North America is only weakly developed. The possibilities for agency capture, for corruption or just for downright inefficiency seem, to my English eyes, too great.

Most academic theories don't help too much with this question. Rational choice does offer useful ideas by which principals can monitor agents, but treats the issue of 'How much?' in a somewhat abstract, de-contextualized way (whereas the normative nature of the 'How much' question demands a contextualized, culturally appropriate answer). A traditional social science approach might be helpful in a broad way, in that it would seek to identify the key relationships within each political system and ascertain how each contributed to/departed from the normative standards for accountability. The Johnston and Romzek chapter offers an example of how this might be approached, in the context of designing contracts. That is certainly relevant, but it doesn't answer the underlying question of 'How much?' Rather it assumes that we already know what the answer to 'How much?' should be, and then explores what features contribute to the achievement of that standard. The theory of institutional isomorphism just does not deal with this issue at all, and neither does Latour's model of translation.

One possible answer to the 'How much autonomy' question can be found in the anthropological ideas of Hood, already referred to above. As explained, these ideas contain the idea of alternation between incompatible sets of values (centralized, decentralized, etc.). Perhaps the issue of agency autonomy could be thought of within the same framework? That would be to say that there is no right answer. Rather, there are different poles (high freedom/tight control) each of which has its own characteristic strengths and weaknesses. After a period of time sufficient for the weaknesses to become apparent (corruption or inegalitarian treatment in the high freedom case, bureaucratic inertia and lack of customer responsiveness in the tight control case) the political mood swings to the other side, and reforms are put in train. The last two decades in the UK could be said to follow this pattern – the 1988 Next Steps report claims that civil service managers need more freedom, then more than 100 agencies are set up, then, after ten years, the New Labour government decides that the agency system is too fragmented, and that ministers cannot steer it well enough, so agencies begin to be pulled back in towards the centre (Office of Public Services Reform 2002). Of course things never return to exactly the same place, so this is not a pendulum that swings in a stable environment. It is more like a pendulum that is swinging on a moving vehicle, as the political, technological and social landscape constantly shifts beneath the wheels.

Academic theories and 'practitioner theories'

Towards the end of 2001 an article containing the following extract appeared in a respectable and well-informed British newspaper. It was written on the eve of an EU heads of state summit meeting in Brussels, and concerned a broad agenda of issues, including the creation of some new EU agencies. The article explained that heads of state were linking the agency issue to the issue of who should chair a 'Convention' which would review the future shape of EU institutions. And so:

> Finland, for example, is not pushing Mr Ahtisaari [A former President, and otherwise a good candidate for chairing the Convention] because it is keen for Helsinki to be the home for the new European food agency.
>
> Some believe that France will withdraw its interest only if the food agency is given to Lille. But Spain is also competing for this prize, with Barcelona in the running, while Italy wants the agency – which will eventually have 300 staff – to be in Parma.
>
> Other nations are queuing for a share in the spoils, which include a transport safety agency, for which both France and Portugal are competing. The UK wants an EU police college, to be at Bramshill, Hampshire, but Spain also wants to host it.
>
> One diplomat said: 'The Belgians are offering to house as many as 10 EU agencies in order to give something to practically everybody.' Romano Prodi, President of the European Commission, said 'Horse-trading on agencies is part of the everlasting, unchanging rules of politics.'
>
> (Grice and Castle 2001: 16)

Nothing much about institutional isomorphism, or efficiency maximization here, one might say. [Incidentally, in the event, nobody got the food agency, because the Italian Prime Minister absolutely refused to accept the previous informal understanding that the Finns would house it. So, while Mr Berlusconi was making disparaging remarks about the relative merits of Finnish and Italian food – as though that had something to do with the issue at hand – the summit took one of its characteristic decisions – it postponed the decision.]

Of course, the fact that there was horse trading over what agencies there should be and where they should be sited does not entirely rule out other, more rationalistic influences. Considerations of efficiency and effectiveness could have operated at an earlier stage in the policy process, to get the whole idea of agencies onto the agenda and to point towards those functions that would be most suitable for agencification. But even with a sympathetic gloss, this peak moment in the trajectory towards agency creation does seem to have been characterized by motives that had little to do with agencies and their well-functioning *per se*. It serves to remind us that politicians seldom design organizations with only principles of organizational design in mind. Rather they are addicted to 'linkage' – an organizational reform will be linked with as many other fashionable norms and popular values as possible, and it will also frequently be adapted to pander to national or regional or local interests (especially concerning interests of siting and employment). Finding a politician who is single-mindedly implementing the principles of rational choice theory, or any other kind of theory, is a rarity. Even in the New Zealand reforms of the 1980s and early 1990s, already fabled as an example of unusually pure and decisive 'rational choice' thinking, the researcher soon encounters compromises, exceptions, opportunism (Boston *et al.* 1996).

Nevertheless, politicians and their advisers are certainly influenced by the climate of opinion on issues of governance and organizational design, and academics and consultants can and do make significant inputs to this swirling mixture of ideas and fashions. There is some relationship between academic theories and political ideas, even if it is not a simple, direct or overpoweringly strong one. The New Zealand reforms *were* influenced by rational choice theory, even if that was only one of the ingredients in the Antipodean stew. The Latvians *did* get the idea that 'agencies' were 'modern' and 'western', even if they also saw them as a way of escaping communist-style central bureaucracy (Chapter 15). The enthusiasm of international financial institutions for autonomous revenue authorities *does* owe something to the presence in those institutions of experts trained in rational choice-style economics (Chapter 14).

What is even more prominent at the political level, however, is the process of isomorphic copying. The UK 'Next Steps' model was 'translated' not only for Dutch readers (Chapter 9) but also edited to the tastes of the Japanese (Chapter 11), the Jamaicans (Chapter 16) and the

Tanzanians (Chapter 12). In Thailand the 'UK model' competed and eventually combined (however uneasily) with a French model (Chapter 13). Even the US – in the form of PBOs – briefly flirted with the UK model (Chapter 7). This kind of international borrowing is not the product of politicians embracing some particular academic theory, but rather a passing on of reputations and stories of new practices between practitioners. It does illustrate, however, how, once a particular academic idea is adopted in one jurisdiction (however imperfectly) it can be rapidly passed on around the world, so that its precise intellectual heritage soon becomes obscure.

Theoretical integration/let a thousand flowers bloom?

Since the different theories are commonly acknowledged to have different strong and weak points, can we not simply amalgamate them in order to come up with a composite explanation? The short answer is 'no'. As has already been made clear, the different groups of theories are each founded on fundamentally different epistemological assumptions. Furthermore, each theory was developed in an attempt to answer particular kinds of question, and not other questions. So to 'integrate' all these disparate perspectives would be rather like attempting to combine a bicycle, a jumbo jet and a submarine on the grounds that they were all means of transport, so that it should be possible to create a really useful combined vehicle to meet a range of travelling needs.

Not all is lost, however. Specific combinations of theories taken from the same or similar epistemological groups may well be viable and useful. Innovation diffusion theory can be rather neatly combined with certain types of network theory. Historical institutionalism is a broad church which can help to inform more specific theories such as institutional isomorphism or historically-informed studies of networks. And so on. Indeed, some of the chapters appear to make precisely such combinations (although they do not always openly declare them!).

Future research

That there is so obviously plenty of important research left to be done is both stimulating and disappointing. It is stimulating because it leaves plenty of niches for academics to make their mark and taste the fruits of new knowledge. It is disappointing because it means that, within the academic community, we have thus far been quicker to express opinions and offer generalized taxonomies and interpretations than we have been to do the basic research that is necessary (from most, if not all, academic perspectives) to support (or falsify) our hypotheses and characterizations.

What is more disappointing, however, is that governments themselves appear to have been so profoundly uninterested in undertaking the kind of applied research that would test the strength of their own predictions concerning the results of specific types of organizational change. A number of our contributors have remarked upon this in various ways, including Gains (for the UK), van Thiel (for the Netherlands) Boworn-wathana (for Thailand) and Pollitt (for Latvia). This lack, in itself, might be thought to cast doubt on some of the more strictly consequentialist brands of theory – how interested in 'rational choice' can politicians and senior civil servants be, since both alike have done so little to measure and identify what the consequences of their agencifications actually are? On the other hand, this apparent oversight would seem to strengthen both theories of isomorphism (the agency form is copied rather than closely calculated) and more overtly political theories (agencies are adopted because they serve certain vested interests, not because they can be shown to be more efficient or effective).

For academics, the material gathered here signals some rather pressing research needs. I will confine myself to mentioning just three lacunæ, which I believe emerge from the analysis I offered above.

First, we need more studies in which two or more rival theoretical apparatuses are brought to bear on the same issue or question. It is now 30 years since Graham Allison first published his classic *Essence of decision*, but we have enjoyed far too few successors to that still-fresh comparison of three competing (but also to some extent complementary) models (Allison and Zelikow 1999). Van Thiel makes a limited comparison in her chapter on the Netherlands (Chapter 8) but there is great scope for a more vigorous attack on this front.

Second, we need a clearer articulation of middle range theories which will help us to classify and interrelate the kinds of variables which explain variations between superficially similar organizational forms within a single jurisdiction or even within a single programme. Managing a meteorological agency is not the same as managing a social security agency or a prison service. In this volume Gains, Johnston and Romzek, McGuire, van Thiel and Smullen are among those who have begun to tackle this issue. One way of taking the matter further might be to try to identify common factors – such as the standardizability of the activity in question, the observability of its outputs and outcomes, or the degree of its political salience – which help explain why some agencies and quangos are managed differently from others (Pollitt 2003, Chapter 7).

Finally, this is a field which is crying out for real comparative research. I say 'real' because there is already a good deal of pseudo-comparative material – in the publications of the OECD, or in edited collections which set alongside each other accounts from different countries and jurisdictions (e.g. Chandler 2000). That is a useful first step, but only a first step. Much better would be a research project which deliberately and systematically compared an (apparently) similar development in different countries, and then attempted to explain perceived variations between those countries. Graham and Roberts (Chapter 7) and Taliercio (Chapter 14) give us a foretaste of what work of that kind could yield. But even these two examples were not based on intensive fieldwork within all the countries – the kind of empirical enquiry which could hope to identify and explore the key middle level variables referred to in the previous paragraph, and which could also take fuller account of differences in politico-administrative cultures. The problem, of course, is that research of that type is difficult to set up. One would need fluency in several languages, familiarity with different cultural backgrounds, excellent access, a generous travel budget and, most of all, plenty of time. This is challenging, but not impossible. Watch this space.

Bibliography

Allison, G. and Zelikow, P. (1999) *Essence of Decision: Explaining the Cuban Missile Crisis*, 2nd edn, New York: Longman.

Boston, J., Martin, J., Pallot, J. and Walsh, P. (1996) *Public Management: the New Zealand Model*, Auckland: Oxford University Press.

Boyne, G. (1998) 'Bureaucratic theory meets reality: public choice and contracting in local government', *Public Administration Review*, 58, 6 (November/December), 474–84.

Brunsson, N. (1989) *The Organization of Hypocrisy: Talk, Decisions and Actions in Organizations*, Chichester: Wiley.

Chandler, J. (ed.) (2000) *Comparative Public Administration*, London and New York: Routledge.

Cohen, M., March, J. and Olsen, J. (1972) 'A garbage can model of organizational choice', *Administrative Science Quarterly* 17, 1–25.

Douma, S. and Schreuder, H. (1998) *Economic Approaches to Organizations*, 2nd edn, London and New York: Prentice Hall.

Dunleavy, P. (1991) *Democracy, Bureaucracy and Public Choice*, Hemel Hempstead: Harvester Wheatsheaf.

Fischoff, B. (1975) 'Hindsight foresight: the effect of outcome knowledge on judgement under uncertainty', *Journal of Experimental Psychology: Human Perception and Performance* 1, 3, 288–99.

Goodin, R. (1982) 'Rational politicians in Westminster and Whitehall', *Public Administration* 62, 1, 23–41.

Grice, A. and Castle, S. (2001) 'Horse-trading top of the agenda as Brussels summit plots EU future', *Independent*, 14 December: 16.

Hammond, J. (1996) *Human Judgement and Social Policy: Irreducible Uncertainty, Inevitable Error and Unavoidable Injustice*, New York and Oxford: Oxford University Press.

Hood, C. and Jackson, M. (1991) *Administrative Argument*, Aldershot: Dartmouth.

Hood, C. (1998) *The Art of the State: Culture, Rhetoric and Public Management*, Oxford: Oxford University Press.

Kickert, W., Klijn, E.-H. and Kopenjaan, J. (eds) (1997) *Managing Complex Networks: Strategies for the Public Sector*, London: Sage.

Kingdon, J. (1995) *Agendas, Alternatives and Public Policies*, New York: Harper Collins.

Lane, J.-E. (2000) *New Public Management*, London: Routledge.

Lewis, D. (1997) *Hidden Agendas; Politics, Law and Disorder*, London: Hamish Hamilton.

March, J. and Olsen, J. (1989) *Rediscovering Institutions*, New York: Free Press.

Niskanen, W. (1971) *Bureaucracy and Representative Government*, Chicago: Aldine-Atherton.

Office of Public Services Reform (2002) *Better Government Services: Executive Agencies in the 21st Century*, London: Office of Public Service Reform (www.civilservice.gov.uk/agencies).

Peters, B.G. (1999) *Institutional Theory in Political Science: the 'New Institutionalism'*, London and New York: Continuum.

Pollitt, C., Birchall, J. and Putman, K. (1998) *Decentralizing Public Service Management*, Basingstoke: Macmillan.

Pollitt, C. and Bouckaert, G. (2000) *Public Management Reform: A Comparative Analysis*, Oxford: Oxford University Press.

Pollitt, C. (2003) *The Essential Public Manager*, Buckingham: Open University Press/McGraw Hill (in press).

Powell, W. and DiMaggio, P. (eds) *The New Institutionalism in Organizational Analysis*, Chicago: University of Chicago Press.

Index

Page references in *italics* refer to tables.